Praise for Upside Down Mirror

The Upside Down Mirror was a joint binge venture for my husband and me. We went through the whole story together and it was our special treat. We went to bed after having long meaningful discussions based on the events in the story. It mirrored some aspects of our relationship and we were no longer ashamed to bring these shadows to light. I follow Dr. Rebecca Sullivan and joined her AWAKE Academy. She is truly a magical being who has conquered the art of manifestation. Rebecca exposes her mistakes, praises her successes and went through a journey that led to non-judgement and self-love. It was then that everything she desired appeared. I watched her journey unfold firsthand and wow is all I can say. I highly recommend this book to anyone who is human and needs to master self-love!

Lilian Beems
Michigan

This is a head-spinner! Just when I thought I had gotten to the climax of the story, it actually heightened. At first I thought I was reading fiction, but I was blown away when I found out these paranormal incidents actually happened. I felt as though I was in the story as it unfolded. This says a lot about the truth and passion the author put forth. It's like an enlightened version of Orange is the New Black. You have the drama, romance, and suspense, but also deep spiritual lessons. I revisit these quite often. This is more than just a book about relationships, it's about the profound importance of self-love. I highly recommend this to everyone!

Cynthia Burkett
Utah

This book will change your life forever! It talks about subjects that many people choose to ignore. I was done with the whole story in eight hours. This is my third time through because I just keep digesting it and learning more on different levels. It has bought clarity to so much that has unfolded in my life and the mysteries behind it all. Rebecca has given me the courage and strength to move through my toughest days with hope and courage.

Roger Wells
Idaho

UPSIDE DOWN MIRROR

Sullivan

Dear Reader,

As a thank-you for investing your trust and energy into this book, I am gifting each person who purchases this book a library of meditations and healings that will help you on your journey to self-love, twin flame reunion, health, prosperity, and abundance. These powerful practices will help you deepen and enact the Lessons at the end of each chapter, and they're offered exclusively within this book. Find out how to access these meditations and healings at the end of the book (on page 347).

With love,

Rebecca

CONSCIOUS INFINITY PUBLISHING

Copyright © 2025 by Conscious Infinity Publishing

By Rebecca Sullivan

Edited by Robyn Landis

Designed by Jason K. Watkins

PUBLISHER'S NOTE

This is a work of non-fiction. All efforts have been made to confirm the scientific accuracy of the information contained within. Any errors or omissions are accidental and not the intention of the publisher nor the author. To correct errors in this text, contact the publisher, Conscious Infinity Publishing

THE LIBRARY OF CONGRESS HAS CATALOGUED THE SOFTCOVER:

Upside Down Mirror

I. Title: Upside Down Mirror

II. Subtitle: A Mystery, An Awakening, and a Twin-Flame Love Story

Except in the United States of America, this book is sold subject to the condition that it shall not, by way of trade or otherwise, be lent, resold, hired out, or otherwise circulated without the publisher's prior consent in any form of binding or cover other than that in which it is published and without a similar condition including this condition being imposed on the subsequent purchaser. Scanning, uploading and distribution of this book via the Internet or via any other means without the permission of the publisher is illegal and punishable by law. Please purchase only authorized electronic editions. Do not participate in or encourage electronic piracy of copyrighted materials. Your support of the author's rights is appreciated.

Images, if uncredited, are presumed to belong in the public domain. Efforts were made to identify original authors. Images are reproduced for education and commentary purposes. No infringement is intended by the author or publisher. All rights reserved

ISBN # 9798218674045

PUBLISHED IN THE USA

A SPIRITUAL MEMOIR

UPSIDE DOWN MIRROR

A MYSTERY, AN AWAKENING
AND A TWIN-FLAME LOVE STORY

REBECCA SULLIVAN

2025

UPSIDE DOWN MIRROR

As an act of self-love, I dedicate this book first and foremost to myself, because of the courage it takes to step into your power and the strength it takes to live your truth.

THIS BOOK IS BASED ON THE AUTHOR'S recollections of personal events. While the story is based on real events, to protect the privacy of individuals, some names and identifying details have been changed.

The publisher and the author are providing this book and its contents on an "as is" basis and make no representations or warranties of any kind with respect to this book or its contents. The publisher and the author disclaim all such representations and warranties, including but not limited to warranties of healthcare for a particular purpose. Although the publisher and the author have made every effort to ensure that the information in this book was correct at press time, the publisher and the author assume no responsibility for errors, inaccuracies, omissions, or any other inconsistencies herein.

This book is not intended to provide medical advice. This book is not intended to replace treatment from a qualified medical professional. The content of this book is for informational purposes only and is not intended to diagnose, treat, cure, or prevent any condition or disease. This book is not intended as a substitute for consultation with a licensed practitioner. The use of this book implies your acceptance of this disclaimer.

This publication is meant as a source of valuable information and inspiration for the reader; however it is not meant as a substitute for direct expert assistance. If such level of assistance is required, the services of a competent professional should be sought. The publisher and the author make no guarantees concerning the level of success you may experience by following the advice and strategies contained in this book, and results will differ for each individual. ∎

UPSIDE DOWN MIRROR

Acknowledgements

AS EVERYONE WHO HAS EVER WRITTEN A BOOK knows, it takes a village to draw a story out with eloquence and grace, and get a manuscript into the hands of readers. Inevitably you want to end up thanking everyone who is part of your life—because just as with a twin flame journey, the book writing and publishing process is a microcosm of life!

To have lived and then written down this story is a perfect example of everything I reflect about manifestation in this book. I somehow manifested all of the right people—not only in my life generally, but for this process.

First and foremost I want to thank my beautiful family. My gorgeous, bighearted and supportive twin flame husband Sean, is in so many ways at the heart of this book. His patience, persistence, creativity, generosity, and loving friendship have truly completed my life and helped me grow in ways I never would have otherwise.

My wonderful children Caden, Cody, Ariel and Willow, each magical in their own ways. My supportive mother and four sisters Wendy, Crissy, Kami and Heidi. My mother and sisters allowed me the pleasure of growing up and experiencing true unconditional love and play!!

I also give gratitude to all of my students in the AWAKE Academy, who inspire me with the way they engage this powerful spiritual work. AWAKE is my soul tribe and we have experienced true magic and miracles on all levels. AWAKE students have made sharing this work and the plant medicines such a beautiful, heart-opening awakening experience for all of our courageous and Lovely participants as well as for me.

My editor Robyn Landis played an enormous role in organizing, rewriting, editing, and developing the story based on my podcast, drawing out of me the nuances and depth needed to fill in the story, articulating my messages precisely and often seeming to read my mind about what I really wanted to say. Jason Watkins created a perfect cover for the vision of this book.

My soul brother Ryan who helped so much with our lake house and the energy work.

I am grateful to all the wonderful people in Nosara, Costa Rica, who helped us make a new home there.

I thank Mother Gaia and Mother Ayahuasca for all of the nourishment, inspiration, illumination and transformation.

Finally, I thank my guardian parents, who have never steered me wrong. ■

UPSIDE DOWN MIRROR

Chapter One

IN THIS BOOK, I'M UNVEILING THE TRUE STORY of my twin flame journey. I'm divulging the most vulnerable, private aspects of my life in telling this story, and one of my fears has been that the events might seem made-up or exaggerated. I've gotten over that, because everything I say is the truth, and it's within the truth that we find freedom. There's a lot of healing in telling the truth, and when we free ourselves with the truth, we free others. If sharing my story can help even one other person own, understand, or share their own story, it will have been worth it.

Some days when I reflect on my tumultuous, turbulent, yet transformative journey to my beloved twin flame, it seems surreal and bizarre—and yet, it's also outstanding. This is a tale of soulmates, false twin flames, true twin flames, and the purpose behind it all. It's also a "manual" for the keys to getting through such an odyssey. There are many lessons in my story, and my hope is that those on a similar journey can learn from my experience.

I was a therapist, and now I'm an integrative energy practitioner, and many of my own clients have gone through their own twin flame journeys. They contact me in moments of grief, shock, and panic. The twin flame journey is unique and unparalleled—and can be tremendously destabilizing—and those going through the experience often believe that no one can truly understand what they're going through.

I always respond: "Trust me, I understand. I know you think no one else understands such heartbreak, and that this is the end for you. However, I promise you that if you surrender, live from your heart, and take guidance from your own inner mirror, everything will work divinely for you."

I too have descended to places of deep grief, heartbreak, and sorrow. I have played victim, forgotten that I was a survivor, lived outside of my heart space and through my ego. At times, I gave up who I was—who I truly am—to accommodate someone else. I've done many things that I'm not proud of.

But many years into this journey, I now understand that I need to trust—everything. Everything was unfolding around me in exactly the way it was supposed to. Surrender, trust, faith, and living through my heart is what not only saved me, but helped me create a life of love and abundance beyond my wildest dreams.

THINGS ARE NOT WHAT THEY SEEM

Though we tend to believe that what we are experiencing is reality, things are not always what they seem. Dark can appear as Light. Light can appear as Dark. There are false twin flames and true twin flames. It's not easy, especially at first, to discern who is who and what is what.

This story ends with me marrying and thriving with my true twin flame. However, you'll be introduced to more than one man as this story unfolds (I use pseudonyms for both). You won't learn who the true twin flame was till later in the story. As you read this story with all of its twists and turns—and sometimes seemingly outlandish events—I encourage you to practice keeping an open mind, which is ideally what you'll do in your own life as well.

There are many ways that this story could have ended.

MY MAGICAL WEDDING

We were married in Deep Creek Lake, Maryland, where we first met—in the exact spot where I first laid eyes on my beloved. Our wedding date was February 20th, 2020. My amazing, beautiful guardian parents—who divinely guided me through this journey, and who you'll meet on these pages too—told me I had to get married on that date.

As a result, our wedding took place right before Covid-19 turned the world upside down. Of course, I didn't know that was coming at the time. I just knew my guardian parents were adamant that I get married on that date. Now I realize how important it was to get married before all that chaos.

The date was significant in another way. When you add the "twos" of 2-20-2020 together, you get an 8, which is the infinity symbol. This was perfectly appropriate, because this journey has taught me that there's really no such thing as a beginning or an end. We are everything and nothing at the same time. Each breath that we take is a death and a rebirth.

As our wedding wows stated, we had come full circle. We were married in an infinity symbol, outlined on the ground in red and gold roses. My beloved stood in the divine masculine side of the symbol, and I stood in the divine feminine side. One of my best friends was ordained to marry us. (This turned out to be an interesting choice, as I'll elucidate in a later chapter; suffice to say she was dressed in black and represented the shadows we would have to overcome through our union.)

When it was time for us to come together to be pronounced husband and wife, we both stepped into the center, the zero point of our rose-drawn infinity symbol. This represented the divine masculine and the divine feminine coming together in harmony.

As I looked into my beloved's eyes during our wows, it was hard for me to believe that he had forgiven me after everything I had put him through. It was a miracle and a triumph that we had arrived at this exalted moment.

But even as we arrived at this transcendent moment, having navigated an incredible journey, it was far from the end. It was really just the beginning. We had come through a great deal—and yet we had much, much more work to do. We had reached the summit of one great peak, but we would soon find ourselves at the bases of many others.

I was told by my spirit guides that this marriage, among thousands of other marriages in the world, would be part of a movement to elevate marriage to its true purposes. By example, by our modeling and living of our truth, we would uplift and define marriage according to its true potentials, for the fulfilment of its greatest possibilities. Our marriage would help to banish the false, limiting beliefs about marriage as entrapment, the "ball and chain" image, and other negative stories.

Marriage is not a means to an end. Marriage is a beginning. Vulnerable and open, in love, and breathing in life together, we were about to demonstrate this truth.

THE LAST STAND OF THE FALSE TWIN FLAME

(Note: Be prepared for instances of paranormal activity in this story—and again, I encourage you to keep an open mind.)

My false twin flame haunted me right up until the night before my wedding. I had just lay down after a long day of getting ready for the most beautiful day of my life. Every night for weeks up until the wedding I had been reflecting on how lucky I was to be where I am now, after such a long and arduous journey. On this night, I was again contemplating my gratitude.

Then I drifted off to sleep as usual, and began to dream. Suddenly, a familiar energy entered and took over my dream, I was levitated through the room uncontrollably. I was stuck on the ceiling and couldn't get down. A sense of evil pulsated through me. In my dream, I started screaming my ex's name, demanding that he let me down. At first, I thought he was the only one who had the power to get me off the ceiling and save me from the evil.

Then, a very gifted student, a dream traveler from my AWAKE (Academy of Wealth Alchemy and Kinetic Energy) class, appeared in my dream. Rachel was screaming at me to take my own power back. "Rebecca, it's *you*! It's YOU that has your power. Take it back! Do it now!"

I took a deep breath in my dream and I lowered myself from the ceiling—on my own. I remembered my power, and I came floating to the ground.

When I woke up in real life, there was a fire alarm blaring in the room. What a strange and jarring situation! It took me a while to fall back asleep. But I was happy, too, because I knew this had been important symbolically. I had fully regained my own power.

This was important because only a week before my wedding, the false twin flame called me and begged me not to get married. Of course, there was no way at this point that he could have dissuaded me. I knew I was marrying the love of my life. Yet apparently some last vestige of power had to be reclaimed from the false twin flame, and that dream allowed me to do it.

A LESSON FROM THE TWIN FLAME JOURNEY

This is what I believe, and what my journey has taught me:

Humans are here to become enlightened. When we become enlightened, we will have our own heaven on earth. Until then, we are individually and collectively transcending the shadows within us. All of our earthly experiences are a reflection of the journey through which our consciousness is moving. Our ultimate goal in life is to transcend our shadows and expand our awareness through our life experiences. And we create our own experiences.

We do this work on many deep levels. We're dealing not only with the conscious mind, but the subconscious mind, our genetics, collective belief systems, energy fields, and "Us" on a soul level. Part of why we came here is to purge stagnant, stuck, low-frequency energies, so that we can live as angels on earth. We're purging shame, doubt, guilt, fear, abandonment, rejection, and martyring. Not only for ourselves, but for everybody within our genetic lineage and in the collective.

The twin flame journey is one that takes us through this process. In my view, your heart space is the only place where this clearing and transcending can successfully be done. Your heart space is the command center. Your heart space is where your consciousness and awareness can grow, expand, be purified, and emerge as pure love—the most powerful force in the Universe. In this space, there is no duality—no good, no bad. Everything just is.

Our reality is like a movie that has been conjured up by our inner being to show us the very shadows that need to be lifted and cleared. In order to successfully move through the shadows and embody our authentic self, we must come to understand that we are not victims. We must see what's playing out in our reality as ego aspects that need healing. To embrace our authentic selves, we also need to unconditionally love who we are, and accept every bit of our shadows. Finally, we need to be truly in love with whatever we do.

I invite you to take a deep breath and allow your own consciousness and awareness to go into your heart space—as though your eyes, ears, nose and mouth reside in your heart. See, hear, taste and live from this space.

A SOULMATE IS NOT A TWIN FLAME— MY FIRST MARRIAGE

My story goes all the way back to 1997, when I first met my now ex-husband. We had our differences, and I divorced him in 2009, with the gift of three amazing children.

I consider my ex-husband a soulmate. In my opinion, a soulmate is someone who meets you on your journey to assist you with where you are in the process at that time. I believe a soulmate can help you karmically, but it's not an exact mirror image, as a twin flame is. From my experiences with soulmates, you can feel like you're in love with them; you can laugh, cry, grow, learn, enjoy life or hate life with them. But whether it's happy and constructive or painful and destructive, it's nothing like the twin flame.

When I was 10, I had a vision in which I saw myself walking down a road with my twin flame. But I could only see what he looked like from the back. He had dark hair. He was tall. I couldn't see his eyes, but I knew his eyes were brown.

I entered into a marriage with a man named Darrell who had blond hair and blue eyes, knowing that he wasn't the final one. I actually tried to fool myself in my early twenties by dying his hair dark. I remember his friends making comments to him about how I should accept him for who he is. But he was the person I needed at that time in my reality. I wasn't prepared for true love. I was career-oriented and didn't want to spend my time dealing with emotions. I didn't let him in fully. Because of past experiences, I didn't really want to trust someone. I purposely chose someone I didn't fully and deeply trust, so that I could protect myself from the unpredictability and vulnerability of true love. I told myself this was all good because I was raising my children and furthering my career. And we did a good job of raising our children.

Toward the end of the marriage, there was an instant in my life that propelled me full force onto my spiritual path.

I had traveled to North Carolina with one of my good friends to help her move. While there, I was drugged and raped by a man who was staying in the house. I had no memory of what happened, but there were witnesses. It was obviously a very traumatic experience, and too much to detail here, but there was a court case. On a personal level, I wanted to remember what had happened to me, and I wanted to heal. That started my journey into Reiki, hypnotherapy and neurolinguistic programming (NLP). This beginning foray into energy work and alternative modalities opened up doorways to many other healings and synchronicities that would lead me to where I am today.

My husband at the time was far from supportive. This was one of the big incidents that led to our divorce. I'm sure that many people know that their marriages are over even years before the divorce. That was the case for me. When this happens, the grieving is often finished way before the divorce is final. In 2008, when my ex and I finally separated, I was finally ready to embrace true love and allow myself to fall deeply. I felt that it was time. You know when the time is right for you—there's a feeling of excitement, something to look forward to. You're ready to take that journey within.

MANIFESTATION

We manifest all the time—everything is a manifestation, whether we're aware of it or not and whether we like what we've manifested or not. I've always been very fast at manifesting. I've always had to watch what I say or think, because it will quickly present itself in my reality.

Three weeks after my separation I went to Deep Creek Lake, Maryland, to enjoy and celebrate single life with one of my very best friends. I was pretty straightlaced and rather predictable at that time; I was never very wild. So, what I did that night surprised my friend quite a bit. I walked into this tavern and immediately heard the sounds of the cover band playing. People were dancing and laughing and having a blast. I was completely sober; I hadn't had any drinks. And I walked towards the stage to get a look at the band.

I had a paranormal experience when I laid eyes on the bass player. He took my breath away. He was tall and very sexy. He was like my vision—tall, dark hair, and brown eyes. I looked at him, and time froze. I'd never seen him in this lifetime. But I knew him! Even more strangely, I saw wolves on the stage around him.

I looked at my friend and said, "I have to have that guy." She started laughing and said, "What is wrong with you?" I had an overpowering feeling of urgency, even desperation. Like I hadn't seen him for an eternity, and he'd finally arrived. Like I had been waiting for a really, really long time. And now he was right in front of my face, and I was scared to lose him.

But he didn't even know me yet.

I waited for him to stop playing and take a break. I walked up to him at the bar as he was ordering a drink and asked him to play Brown-Eyed Girl. I don't really remember what he said after that. I was taken by his sexy English accent. I really didn't care what he was saying, even though I was listening to him. It was like I wanted him inside of me—that's honestly the way I felt.

He was very sweet and had an innocence about him. I watched him play the entire night and we stared at each other. My friend kept laughing and saying that I was crazy. But I knew I wasn't crazy.

At the end of the night, when he came off the stage, he leaned against a wall as I was talking to somebody else. My eyes locked with his eyes. He nodded his head. Some kind of unseen force pulled me towards him. I literally walked into his arms and we kissed. It was an amazing first kiss—a kiss that made time freeze. I will never forget that kiss.

We actually got kicked out of the bar for making out so much. Of course, my friend was still thinking I'd lost my mind. She chalked it up to my recent divorce. But I knew it was much more than that.

I invited him back to my hotel room. We made love. I felt very comfortable with him. He knew how I liked to be touched, that I liked my neck kissed. Even though he knew nothing about me, he was completely intuitive, and everything was just so natural.

He had to leave in the morning. He lived in Michigan, and I in Maryland—quite a distance. I was nervous, because I'd just had one-night stand and all of my old programs and paradigms about that descended on me. Thoughts about what men think of women who do that on the first night. What had I done? What had gotten into me? What chance did I really have with this guy?

I wanted to say to him, "Please, don't leave me again." I wanted to tell him that I *knew* him. I wanted to tell him that we belonged together. He obviously was not remembering all that I remembered, not having the same experience of familiarity and reunion. He mentioned something about hitting him up on MySpace. My heart sank.

I still remember to this day what his face looked like as he turned away from me and walked away to go back to Michigan. His name was Sean. And I felt like I had lost him forever. I was heartbroken.

I knew I was not insane. I'm very intuitive. I knew what I felt was real. I *remembered* him. And I knew he remembered me on some level—when we made love and kissed and hugged and laughed as though we'd known each other for a very, very long time. But cognitively, he did not "remember" me.

I went home and spent hours making a MySpace page (yes, this was a very long time ago now in the world of social media!) that I hoped would impress him. I really knew nothing about MySpace, but I wanted to keep in contact with him.

After creating what I hoped was a perfect MySpace page, I finally "friended" him and started to communicate back and forth with him. I asked him how he was doing. He responded very quickly that he was spending a lot of time with a woman at work and that he was going to ask her out. This was about a week after we had been together, and after he had told me he didn't have a girlfriend. (It wasn't until much later when I talked to him again that I found out our little meeting had given him the courage to ask this woman out, because I had boosted his self-esteem so much.)

I was crushed, even though I barely knew him. I moved around for days in a fog. Everyone who knew me, who I confided in, thought I was going through something that seemed crazy. They couldn't understand why I was so incredibly sad about a guy I had just met.

I started keeping track of the entertainment venue at Deep Creek Lake, waiting for his band to come play again. When it did, I had decided, I would show up there once again.

Yet throughout the next year I went about my life, otherwise quite happy with the freedom of being single, even though there was a lingering sadness in the background about Sean. I had let it go, mostly, since he had ostensibly begun another relationship. I was enjoying my career, hanging out with my friends, and having a wonderful time with my children.

In time, I began to feel ready to really meet my person, to create the ultimate connection I knew was possible. I decided, "It's time to manifest my twin flame."

Around this time, in perfect timing, I received some meditations from a friend that were about bringing in St Germain and calling in the twin flame.

Water is a conduit for manifesting for me; I tend to get powerful responses from water. So I sat in my hot tub, taking some deep breaths and calling in St. Germain, who is an ascended master known as the keeper of the Violet Flame of Healing. In my meditative trance, the beautiful purple violet flame entered my heart space. I asked for my twin flame to come to me. And in the meditation, he did: I could feel him, I could hear him, I could sense him, I could even smell him. I invited the purple flame to surround me, and I basked in the frequency of having a twin flame.

I then put that manifestation aside and went about my work.

At that time, I owned a mental health and primary care practice. (I was a therapist at the time; I no longer practice and am now an energy healer—a transition also supported by this transformative journey.) Back then, though, I had a busy practice, and I did a lot of hiring. I needed to hire a psychiatrist. The psychiatrist who was leaving referred a colleague of his—a student who needed some moonlighting hours. That's how I met Gabe.

I had a policy of never dating doctors. Most seemed quite narcissistic to me, and I felt like there was really no room for flexibility in an MD's mind. Perhaps I'm stereotyping, and I apologize for that. But that was how I felt at the time.

Though it was a professional meeting, I didn't dress up. I had just gotten out of an infrared sauna, so my face was sweaty. I had no makeup on. But I looked decent enough for an interview. I went to Deep Creek Lake to interview the psychiatrist who was interested in joining my practice.

We met at a quaint little coffee shop. It was one of my favorites—the perfect place for an interview. It was a little crowded inside that day. But I looked up and saw a man who I immediately knew was my interview subject.

There before me was a man who made me smile shyly, even though I hadn't said hi yet. He looked young to be a doctor. He was gorgeous. Tall, dark, handsome, brown eyes. As he shook my hand and met my gaze, there was a glint of humor in his eyes. I could tell he was studying me. It kind of felt like a test.

Immediately, I remembered the way I was dressed, the way I looked. Definitely not how I would have dressed if I was anticipating meeting someone so good-looking. I pushed it from my mind. After all, this was a professional interview.

We set down at a table, looking across at each other. We began with small talk—careers, what the job opportunity consisted of, his intentions with the job. Every time he smiled, there was more in his smile than his words were saying. Suddenly he stopped, looked me straight in the eye—I felt a spark go up my spine—smiled, and said, "Rebecca, you've manifested me here."

I about fell out of my chair. This was a clinical interview. I had given no indications of my spirituality. I was behaving professionally. I stammered, "What are you talking about?" He repeated, "You manifested me here."

I said nervously, "I do many manifestations." I wondered—how did he know? Was he inside my brain, or spying on me in the hot tub?

He continued to smile at me. Then he told me how wanted me to move to California with him, after he had graduated from his residency. Although this was completely outlandish, since I hardly knew him, instead of pointing that out I said, "I have three kids. I can't move to California." He said, "They'll be just fine."

"This is crazy," I remember thinking. My breath was literally taken away. This was within an hour of a clinical interview. Yet this man knew I had done a manifestation, told me he was my manifestation, and talked about my children and I moving to California with him.

After a little more conversation, he suggested that we leave the coffee shop and go out to dinner because we were both getting hungry. He took me to dinner at a beautiful restaurant. I say "he took me to dinner" because at the end of the meal, and the end of the "interview," he paid for dinner. When I told him, "I usually pay for the business dinners, that's what I do for interviews," he said, "Well, it was really me interviewing you." That was a little cocky.

But I was intrigued.

At the end of the night, Gabe took my hands, looked in my eyes, and said, "Call me. Look at my resume and call me." And then he left.

My mind was absolutely racing. Talk about the unexpected happening when you least expect it. This certainly qualified as a paranormal experience.

I got in my car, got ready to drive home (about a 45-minute drive from Deep Creek Lake), turned on the radio...and then I heard it. The band that Sean—my "one-night stand after eternity"—was in would be playing in a month at the The Black Bear in Deep Creek Lake. My heart pounded with excitement. I immediately planned to go back there with my friend.

Yet at the same time, I was now also enjoying my thoughts about Gabe and what had just transpired. As I drove home mulling over the strange experience of my "manifestation," as well as the anticipation of my return to The Black Bear, I had no idea how much my life was about to change.

Chapter Two

AS THE NEXT FEW WEEKS WENT BY, I COULD not help but feel a strange magnetic pull towards Gabe. I had indeed hired him, and we were working together very diligently to set up his moonlighting at my practice, although most of our correspondence at first was through email, texts, or over the phone. I noticed my heart would beat rapidly just answering his calls or checking emails from him.

Here and there, each of us gave subtle cues that we were interested in the other outside of the work context. But for the most part, I felt like we both worked very hard at trying to hide our attraction. I think each of us was waiting for the other to say something first. Also, there was the significant issue of crossing professional boundaries. With him as the lead psychiatrist at a practice I owned, there was a conflict of interest, so that was also on my mind.

There were other distractions as well, despite the bubbling attraction. I was busy with my practice as well as my children and friends. Paradoxical as it might sound, considering I had attractions to two different men simmering—and had taken that moment to try manifesting a twin flame—I also really was happy just being alone at the time. Life was full.

In the background, although I had mostly moved on, I still held a bit of a torch for Sean.

In fact, before I knew it, it was time to go back to Deep Creek Lake and see Sean's band at The Black Bear. Although I believed I had accepted that there was no way forward, part of me must not have let it go—because as the day approached, I felt excited to see what our reunion might hold. What would he think when he saw me? Had he missed me? Might he still feel that strange pull towards me, as I had (and still did) towards him?

Gabe and our smoldering connection fell to the background as the memory of my night with Sean loomed up into my view.

BACK TO THE BLACK BEAR

I traveled to The Black Bear that night in a state of anticipation and apprehension. When I got there, the message was loud and clear—and it hurt. I think if Sean could have wished me away, he would have. He pretty much ignored me. My heart sank, but I had waited for this moment for months and I wasn't going to walk away without trying.

Undaunted, I went up to him at the stage in between sets, looked at him pointedly, and said, "Hi." He looked back at me impassively and only said, "I'm sorry, but my girlfriend's here." Ouch.

Right then, a gentleman came over and asked me to dance. Sean said, "Why don't you go dance with him?" Stung, I said, "I don't want to." He repeated "I have a girlfriend." His coldness was painful, and he turned away.

What made it weirder was his girlfriend ended up coming up and talking to me and my friend. They had started dating right after he and I were together that one night. She wanted to check me out, I guess.

I tried to enjoy the evening anyway, dancing halfheartedly with the friend who had joined me. But I was heartbroken. I felt used, discarded, and unimportant. And I realized that my attraction to him had not faded.

That night when I got home, I was really questioning myself. I hated feeling like a crazy female who freaked out because she was rejected. And I was questioning my intuition. If I felt a connection with someone, usually it was mutual. And it had certainly felt mutual that night Sean and I were together. I couldn't understand it. But I went to bed and, with a heavy heart, accepted that this was fate.

Remarkably, though, my heartbreak did not last long. Gabe was increasingly weaving himself into my life. He asked me out for business dinners quite often, although he usually invited other staff so I was unclear as to whether that was truly business or if he had an underlying interest in me as well. Other signs were there: we were often making eye contact, smiling and touching each other on the arms and shoulders when opportunities arose. When I was around him, I was pulled towards him like a magnet. I found myself thinking about him a lot.

Finally, after many dinners and small business meetings, getting things organized for the practice, he invited me to dinner at Deep Creek Lake—just the two of us. After dinner, we went for a walk at Swallow Falls. The weather was perfect. The sun had just gone down. We hiked over to a rock right in front of the falls, where we could feel the water splashing onto our faces.

Then Gabe asked me if I would meditate with him. That was astounding. I've been always spiritual, and to have a man wanting to meditate with me made me feel comfortable and at home. I said yes. Gabe sat right across from me, with our knees touching, took a deep breath, took my hands, closed his eyes, and started to meditate.

I immediately felt the presence of his energy intertwined with mine. I've always been attuned to energy. I was born psychic. I was surprised to learn that he could do the same thing. I could tell that he had very powerful abilities. I could feel his energy reading me, searching me, curious to understand what was going on with me. His energy was navigating through my body. He was imprinting on me, and it was intoxicating.

I opened my eyes, watched him as he continued meditating, leaned over and kissed him.

He quickly opened his eyes and jokingly protested, "What is this all about?" But then, he pulled me towards him and gave me a very tender kiss. It started out soft, and then became more passionate.

Kissing him lit me on fire. Every single atom of my body lit up. I could have kissed him forever. He was passionate and beyond intuitive. He had the ability to read my mind, body and soul from the start. He was kissing me and touching me in exactly the way I needed. It was almost like he was part of me. He could read what I needed, wanted and desired.

Sean had been very intuitive with me also, but that felt like more of a natural and innocent familiarity. Gabe giving me exactly what I needed felt more calculated to produce an effect in me. His affection, and his kisses, were almost addicting. What I mean by this is that normally, when you kiss somebody, and it's a nice kiss, you feel secure when it's over. Just thinking about it, lingering in the aftermath of the kiss, makes you feel good. But with him, as soon as he was done kissing me, no feeling lingered. There was no aftermath. Nothing to bask in. It was like being cut off cold turkey. In order to feel that excitement, I had to *be in the kiss*, in the embrace, in the touch.

This soon would become quite a problem—as would many other things that began to emerge. But I didn't think too much of it at first.

I didn't realize how abnormal this neediness was. I just chalked it up to missing him because our connection was so strong and so powerful.

Right after that first kiss, by the falls, we took each other's hands and walked back to the car. He looked me in the eyes. It was a mischievous look, like someone who was planning something. He said, "Please, don't tell anybody about this. Don't tell anybody about the kiss." My heart sank. I thought "Great, another guy who just wants to hide the relationship." He squeezed my hand and said, "Don't worry, it's not because I want to hide the relationship." Once again, he was reading my mind.

He explained, "It's because I'm a doctor, and you're the owner of the practice. I don't want people to get the wrong idea about me before I even start. I don't want people to think that I'm trying to get a raise or sleep my way to the top." He said he wanted to be able to make his own first impressions.

I understood and respected that. So for weeks after the first kiss, we kept everything quiet. We didn't do much. We went out to occasional lunches, stole kisses here and there, flirted, talked quite a bit on the phone.

However, certain things were already bothering me. Many women at the practice were hitting on him—and the way he handled it was undesirable. He seemed to like all the attention. He was flirting back and leading them on. He was also letting me know, in indirect ways, how much power he felt he had in this position. Over me, and with people at the practice.

Yet by this time I was already so into him that I rationalized his behaviors. I made up excuses for him. I was uneasy, but I shoved those instincts to the background.

STEPPING IT UP

After about four months, things intensified between us.

He asked me out one night after work. He wanted to take me to dinner. Just the two of us. We left our stuff at the office and went to a Japanese place. The conversation was great. He made me laugh. He was a gentleman. He told me during dinner how much he really liked me, how much he enjoyed talking to me. How he could see me in his life. That he was extremely attracted to me. He also told me that I was a good friend to him. I was charmed. He was saying everything I wanted to hear from a man.

After dinner, we went back to the office. It was quiet. Everybody had left. We walked into my office. We faced each other, looking into each other's eyes. He had absolutely gorgeous brown eyes. Every time Gabe looked at me, his eyes sparkled—like he knew a secret that he was about to tell me. And it felt like the only way I would learn that secret was to connect with him through kisses and caresses.

He was seductive in a way that I'd never encountered in my entire life. Surrendering into his energy felt like a web that I wasn't sure I could get out of. The scariest thing was that I wasn't sure I *wanted* to get out of it. This felt dangerous. I knew I could get lost. But it was also so intoxicating.

In Gabe's web, I wasn't attached to anything. Everything felt like it was up in the air, spinning in some sort of chaos. It was exhilarating and dizzying. My intrigue won out over any fear of danger. I was ready to go full force into whatever I was feeling.

We began kissing and exploring each other's bodies. When I got to his penis, I was shocked by how incredible it was. Large, but not too large, just perfect. Everything about this man was physically perfect. And his seduction was perfect, too. His ability to know what I was thinking, feel what I was feeling, was out of this world.

I put my hands in his wavy, dark hair, covered his full lips with mine, and caressed his gorgeously sculpted body. I was totally lost in him.

This first time we made love, he did not finish. He satisfied me, stopped, and did not pursue his own climax. I had never experienced that before, so I asked him what was wrong. He only said, "Soon you'll see." It was a little unnerving.

The entire experience had a paranormal quality. Towards the end of the lovemaking, right after he told me that he was going to withhold his orgasm, I heard music all around us. Angelic fairy music. We often play music in the office, so I figured that one of the secretaries had left the music on. I asked him if he heard it, and he said, "yes." We got up to walk around the office building (it was about a 2000-square-foot building), looking to find the music that was playing. But there was no music playing. None.

We went back to gather our things, and we both stopped hearing the music, so we forgot about it for a while. But as he was walking me to my car in the parking lot, when we got to the door of my car, we heard the music again! The same angelic music, as though there were speakers in the sky. We were listening to music from a different dimension—a dimension of angels.

I took this as a sign that he was an angel, and that he was bringing forth the music. I thought this must explain why he was psychic, why being with him felt so paranormal, why everything about him was completely magical.

Yet I left him feeling turned upside down. I'd never been with someone who made me feel so good, yet also so needy afterwards—craving more and more and more, like I could hardly wait. Once again, I excused this strange phenomenon. I told myself, "Maybe this is what it feels like to really fall in love, to really connect with somebody."

For the next few days at work after this dalliance in my office, I noticed some changes in him. Suddenly, he wanted to know everything about what I was doing with the business, who I was talking to in reference to the business, who I consulted with to make business decisions. I asked him why all of a sudden he was concerned with these matters. He replied that it was because he was trying to build a future with me, and he wanted to build a foundation where both of us were making the decisions and had a say. He also said he wanted to learn about my life and everything about me. Again I accepted this, though with some unease.

The second time we were together sexually was even more paranormal than the first time. The first time we were together was amazing. But this time *blew me away*. We were at my house a few weeks later. We started to make love. Once again I became totally lost in his kisses. I could kiss this man for hours upon hours. I could make love with him for hours too. His stamina, his strength, his endurance—I'd never experienced anything like it.

When I orgasmed during this second encounter, the orgasm lasted for an hour. I couldn't stop orgasming. I said, "I'm going to have to go to the emergency room, because I can't stop this orgasm." He chuckled knowingly and said, "It'll stop, just give it some time." I asked him where he had learned how to do this. He said, "I never learned how to do this. I thought you knew. Because we just experienced full-blown Tantra."

As it turned out, neither one of us had practiced Tantra, studied Tantra, or knew anything about Tantra. But our energies were communicating together as if we had—very natural and in sync. Our breath took on its own life force. A Tantric orgasm can last for hours at a time, and this was new to me.

After this experience, our sex life progressed quickly and became extremely satisfying, to say the least. We made love using Tantric practices at least three times a day—sometimes for hours. I assigned other people at my practice to take over my work and I would leave for a few hours to go home and have sex.

I would often have full-blown Tantric orgasms, and so would he. After a while, it became a game. He would count how many Tantric orgasms I had. One time after hours of lovemaking, when we got to about 30 orgasms, I remember telling him "I don't know if I can do this anymore." But he would insist that we continue.

If I was caught in his web after the first kiss, it was nothing compared to how entangled I was after the Tantric lovemaking.

At the same time, with me now entrapped and addicted, he suddenly turned completely controlling. He would be seeing patients while I was at work, and when it was time for me to leave—even to go see my kids, like practice basketball with my son—he would say "If you don't stay here with me, I'm leaving." Or he would threaten to break up with me.

The worst part was that I complied. I would give up things that I normally wouldn't give up for anybody. I would just sit there, under his control. In my fixation and my addiction, I somehow believed that this was explained by how connected we were.

Everybody, by that time, knew that we were in a relationship. Many of my friends and family were concerned about how attached I was to him. There were a few people that didn't like him, saying that they could see right through him. However, I was thinking, "There's no way that I'm giving up a relationship where I'm this close to a person."

Every time I would think about being mad at him, or get concerned about his behavior, he would do something amazing. Something that I had always dreamed about a man doing for me. And I would immediately forgive him. This, of course, is classic abusive patterning.

He would take me to lunches, bring books that he knew I would be captivated by—such as books about the paranormal and spiritual worlds that fascinate me—and read them with me and discuss them over lunch. One of these times he invited me to his house, which was about an hour away from my practice and from where I live. He took me for a ride in his truck, and the entire time he simply listened to his favorite meditations with binaural beats. There were times I would go home with him to his house, and he would cook with me, start a fire, and we would just cuddle.

While the reading, talking, meditating, cooking, and cuddling were cozy and made me feel connected and pampered, the sex continued to be elevated to new heights as well. In addition to Tantric touch, we began having energy sex across the room. (When I was about 10 years old I watched the movie *Cocoon*, and when I saw the aliens "doing it" in the pool, I somehow knew that someday I would have that experience too.) He would sit on one side of the room, I would sit on the other. I would orbit my energy into his body and he would orbit his energy into mine, and it was a beautiful, blissful communion.

His psychic connection to me continued to escalate as well, where more and more it really did appear that he was literally in my mind. One time he was at work, and I was at my house, exercising. I heard my cell phone ring, so I ran to the phone and I answered it. I wasn't out of breath when I answered it. But he said, "I called you because I could feel that you were out of breath." Other times he would call me right after I was done laughing, and he would say, "I could feel that you were laughing."

If that wasn't uncanny enough, I became completely convinced when I was driving someplace one time and I wasn't sure where I was going; I was looking at a sign that said, "East or West," and I didn't know which way to go. Out of the blue, he called me and he said, "Go West." Stunned, I said, "How did you know?" He said, "I know you, Rebecca. I know what you're thinking, I know what you're feeling, and I know what you're seeing." As weird as it was, and it might have seemed creepy to some, this made me feel protected. It made me feel safe. It was like he was always around me, even when he wasn't. I could feel him in me.

So with all of this—the moments of solicitousness and sweetness, the sex, and the psychic connection—in spite of the many strange warning signals, I fell in love with this man with all of my heart. I knew he could feel it. I knew he knew it. And I was entrusting him with my life.

But the unnerving, uneasy aspects also began to accelerate.

THE DARK SIDE

One time when he took me to lunch, he looked deep into my eyes. As I said, his brown eyes were normally absolutely amazing, expressive, gleaming. This time, as he gazed at me, his eyes went a little dark and opaque, almost like some of his soul left, and he stood up and said, "You know, I have to take your light. But I don't want to." I was shocked and shaken by this chilling statement. I didn't quite understand what he was saying, but it sounded disturbing and frightening—the dark side of the paranormal that I experienced with him.

He continued, "You're like a delicate white flower, growing. With beautiful light around you, Rebecca." He added, "I'm going to take that light, but I don't want to. I really don't."

I didn't understand this till much later (I'll definitely get to that). But at the time, in my naivete, all I could think was, "I will love him enough that he won't hurt me." And "Once he falls in love with me, he won't want to do this." (Whatever "this" was.) At some level, also, I felt confident in my abilities to "keep my own light." So I looked at him and shot back, "If you don't want to take my light, then don't take it." He paused, then smiled and hugged me. So I felt like it was going to be okay.

But I was also naïve. At this time, I didn't yet fully understand or believe in the extent of paranormal or dark forces that I eventually encountered with him. He's Egyptian, and his family had some customs that seemed strange, so to some degree I attributed all the strangeness to his background. Although it was dark and chilling to hear him say what he did, I convinced myself that maybe the "taking my light" thing was metaphorical in some Egyptian practice.

Another troubling element: we were about four months into dating when he started to bring up the fact that he believed he and I were to have a child together. He claimed that the God-Creator-Source had told him that I was to have his child. He said he could see that in our future.

This was in some ways a wakeup call for me, because when it came to something this monumental, I had to be honest. And if I were honest, I knew this man was way too selfish to be a father. As in love with him as I was, as enthralled and entranced, I had not yet introduced him to my children—which says a lot. My maternal instinct took over, and was the one thing that superseded the obsession that led me to give myself over to him in so many other ways.

It was also a sign that at least at some level, I didn't trust him. I never allowed him in my home or near my home when my children were there. My children had no clue that I was dating this man. I would see Gabe only during the weeks that my children were with my ex-husband, since we had joint custody.

I told Gabe that I didn't want to have a child with him. That fathers have to be selfless and seem like they want to take care of other living beings. I was in love with him, yes, but I did know he was selfish and narcissistic. I told him as much, though not in those exact words. I just absolutely felt from the bottom of my soul that he would not make a good father.

I remember trying to tell him this one day at the office when we were discussing it, and he was listening with impatience, kind of shaking his foot with nervous energy at his desk. I told him "Fathers help with baby care, you don't seem like that, you don't seem to like children." He was silent. I knew him well enough at that point to know he was thinking of ways to get around my arguments, the wheels spinning in his head. He would plan to make me feel safe. He wasn't accepting no for an answer.

The more I resisted it, the more the idea of this child became an obsession with him. He talked about it constantly. He kept saying that it was our destiny to have this child. But on this one point, I didn't let my guard down. I held firm. In fact, his insistence caused me to take the kind of strong stand I was not taking in the business or other areas with him. Rather than acquiesce, I did the opposite: I got on birth control pills. I've never believed in birth control pills. I always felt this hormonal type of medication was very toxic for a woman's body. But he was so adamant about getting me pregnant, and we were so sexually active, there was no way I was taking the chance.

Meanwhile, the business was expanding quite a bit. My patients really had no room in the waiting room. There weren't even enough offices for the practitioners to see patients. I knew I had to make a decision about a larger building.

My plan was to rent a bigger building. But Gabe found a particular building he wanted—a 3600-square-foot building—and he wanted me to *buy* it.

I was extremely hesitant. It was a huge commitment to buy a building. I'm a spiritual person, I loved energy work, and I wasn't even sure I wanted to commit the rest of my life to primary care and mental health practice. I didn't believe in psychotropic or pharmaceutical medications. My passion for integrative energy medicine and spiritual healing was growing and calling to me, and I thought I might take a different path in the future.

Gabe became extremely angry when I explained this. He screamed and yelled at me, and stated that I *was* going to keep the practice, that he was going to be a part of my life through the practice, and that I needed to be responsible and buy a building instead of renting a building.

I wish I had been as firm and unwavering about this as I was about not having his child at this point—but under the spell of enmeshment and neediness in which I allowed this abuse, I reluctantly agreed.

I was very heavyhearted about the decision of buying a building and committing full-time to a mental health practice. I just felt so disheartened with this decision. But I honestly felt like it was the only way to keep this relationship with him. In hindsight, of course, I was seriously compromising myself to placate him, which is a hallmark of an abusive relationship with a narcissist. But I had become caught in his web.

As I mentioned, he had found a building that he was very interested in purchasing. At first, I didn't like the building at all. It was downtown. I didn't like the surroundings. It wasn't peaceful. It was urban. But he was adamant about that building. He insisted, "That's the exact location that we need to be in."

I agreed to go look at the building. My sister (who worked for me) and a few of the administrative staff got together to go look at the building with him one night after work. Once again, something paranormal happened on the way to look at that building. Every single stop light turned green before we got to it, as though it was giving the green light to buying the building. I wasn't the only one in the car who noticed it. Even people who weren't into the paranormal mentioned it. Once again, Gabe smiled that secretive, satisfied smile. Meanwhile, I did take that as a sign that this was the building I was supposed to get.

We walked inside the building. It was huge, like a warehouse that we could turn into office space. He turned to me, hugged me, and said, "We can do this together. I'll do the blueprint engineering of the rooms, and we can hire people to build the offices. I'll help." He said he was very good at construction and engineering. "And it's something that you and I will work together on, Rebecca." For the first time, I was actually excited about the building.

My excitement was short-lived, though. A few nights after the decision to buy the building, he and I were making love and he was telling me everything I wanted to hear once again—about how connected he felt to me, how much a part of his life. I still can't begin to even explain in words how I felt in this man's arms. It was like the whole world could have stopped. It was eerie. It was like nothing else mattered.

He was already making quite a bit of money at my practice; he was a 1099 subcontracted employee. I was responsible for 100% of the business expenses—the overhead, the inventory, anything this business had to pay for or buy was completely my responsibility. And suddenly, during this sweet lovemaking, the sweet talk stopped and he abruptly switched gears. He told me that he deserved *95%* of what he was bringing in.

This would be unheard of for a subcontracted employee who's not paying for any of the overhead or expenses. I looked at him in disbelief. First of all, it was a completely jarring and inappropriate time to bring up business. We were making love! Secondly, it was an outrageous demand.

I sputtered, "That's ridiculous. I would lose money on you. I won't be able to pay for things!" He countered, "I deserve it. I deserve 95% of what I bring in. And if you don't give me 95% of what I bring in, then I may have to consider quitting."

Of course, it's the measure of how entangled and dependent I had become that I even *considered* this aggressive and manipulative demand. But I thought about it. I was reasoning it. I said, "Well, how am I going to be able to afford everything else in that practice if I'm giving you all of that money?" He said, "All of the good fortune that I bring to you will pay for the remainder of the expenses."

This was obviously not a rational or reliable proposal, yet I was torn. I was terribly confused and I didn't know what to do, but unbelievably, I eventually agreed to this horrible proposal. It was extremely difficult to tell my sister, who was the business manager. She literally thought I had gone crazy. And in a sense, she was right. But I did it!

Not surprisingly, this was the beginning of everything crumbling underneath me. Things were about to happen that I could not even imagine possible at this point.

LESSON

Everything internal is reflected in our external world. One of the biggest lessons through this whole experience is how everything that happened to me was ultimately a reflection of how I felt about myself. I allowed myself to be manipulated, misled, misguided, and pushed into decisions against my better judgment based on neediness, a sense of powerlessness, insecurity, and a disconnection from my own power. Keep that in mind throughout this journey with me, and notice if this rings true for you as well. Does any suffering, misalignment, dysfunction, or destruction along your path actually stem from a sense of lack within yourself, and a reaching for validation outside yourself? For love to be authentic, it can never come from lack, dependency, neediness, or compensation for something inside yourself.

Chapter Three

I HAD JUST COMMITTED TO BUYING A BUILDING for my primary care and mental health practice. There was some excitement in our relationship about what this creation would look like. After all, we were taking a building that looked like a warehouse and creating a wellness practice out of it together.

During the weeks before the closing, Gabe and I had some beautiful dates and romantic nights together. I remember one night he had cooked dinner for me, started a fire…it was beautiful! It had been snowing. He put some nice music on, turned off the television and just lay down with me with the lights on and told me he wanted to stare into my eyes. That's what the date consisted of—us staring into each other's eyes, looking at each other, cuddling, listening to the music, and falling asleep in one another's arms.

As we went to bed that night, I remember him kissing me and hugging me. After lying down in the bed, he pulled me on top of him and told me he wanted to fall asleep while breathing my breath. As I was lying on top of him, breathing his breath, once again I felt like the whole world around me could stop and I wouldn't care. It just felt so right, so peaceful.

Sometimes we took showers together. I had a big jacuzzi tub in my master bathroom and I would fill the jacuzzi tub, put bubbles in it and we would take bubble baths together. During those baths, we would talk and he would tell me about various projects he was working on in his residency. Then he would ask me to channel. He would say, "I'm working on this project and I need to find out about…(for example) resveratrol." What were the properties of resveratrol and what would help it cross the blood-brain barrier? I would channel answers and he would look it up later and exclaim, "Oh my gosh, that really works!"

So I was using my psychic abilities with his medical abilities to solve problems within his dissertation that he was working on for school. It was fun. It gave me a window of insight into of how he and I could work together. He was so confident in my abilities and so interested in my psychic awareness that he would ask me random questions and take notes on what I was saying.

In the mornings when we woke up, we would take my dune buggy up into the mountains where I lived. We saw beautiful sunrises. We would pack lunch and just sit there together and eat and kiss—and again, talk about subjects that intrigued us both. From this perspective at least, in spite of the strange and uneasy aspects, the relationship felt healthy. We could communicate, collaborate, and be intimate with one another.

NORMAL..AND PARANORMAL

His paranormal healing abilities, which I had already observed, started to accelerate in noticeable ways within these few weeks before the closing of the building. At one point I had a really bad urinary tract infection. It was probably because of how often we were having sex. He said to me, "I'm going to put this oil on my penis and make love to you, and then you're going to be cured."

I said, "I don't think making love is what I need right now, I'm pretty sure that's why I have the urinary tract infection." He insisted, "No, trust me." I believe it was tea tree oil he put on his penis but it was also his energy, I'm sure of it. When he was inside me I remember feeling like it was like someone doing Reiki inside of me. After our lovemaking, almost immediately, the infection was cured. I was floored. "How did you do that?" I asked. Once again, he just smiled and chuckled and kissed me, like it was going to be his little secret.

A couple of days later I was walking the dogs, and one of my dogs likes to chase cyclists. I was sitting at a picnic table and I had the leash in my hand, not the handle part of the leash but the rope part. A bicyclist rode by and my dog started to run after the bicyclist. The rope burned across all four fingers as it slipped through my hand. It was inflamed and extremely painful, so much so that I was crying. I was putting it under cold water.

Once again, Gabe performed a healing that clearly went beyond the substance he used. He took some sort of cream (something that was already in my house, I can't even remember what kind), rubbed it on my fingers, put his hand over mine, and within minutes it was almost completely healed. Again I asked in amazement, "How do you do that?" Again he just laughed and hugged me, without explaining anything.

I started to feel excited about this potential. I told him, "With you being a doctor and a psychiatrist, and with so many people in the practice, do you know what you could do with these abilities when people come in thinking they need pharmaceutical medications? Do you know how much you could heal them?"

This angel who had just healed me looked me straight in the eyes and said, "I'm not interested in healing anybody else. I'm really just interested in healing myself."

I felt shocked, chilled, extremely let down, and disappointed. I had to wonder again, *who is this man*? He had such immense power and ability, which could do so much good, and yet he didn't seem interested in helping with it or making a contribution—except for himself and sometimes for me. His magic was enchanting, but his intentions about using it (or lack thereof) were disturbing. And if he wasn't interested in healing people, why was he a doctor at all? It didn't make sense.

Also at this time, he was wanting me to activate him by attuning him to Reiki. (When you're a Reiki master, you're able to "attune" Level 1 and Level 2 Reiki practitioners once they're trained so that they can "officially" be Reiki healers. It's a silent ritual that can be done in person or at a distance. The attunement is an energetic rite of passage for all Reiki practitioners and involves attuning the student to specific symbols. You cannot legitimately practice Reiki until you have received the attunement.)

I told him that in order to be attuned, he needed to be in his heart and be prepared to become a vessel for Reiki. Although it's generally a gentle and subtle experience, receiving a Reiki attunement is also a powerful spiritual moment. Your energetic pathways are being opened by a Reiki master, allowing energy to flow freely through your body so you can channel it for your well-being and that of others. You have to be ready, and many Reiki students prepare for hours or days to receive the energy. Afterward, you're advised to let your body settle and process the energy.

As was often the case, he was so demanding and impatient. He was like, "No, I want to do it *now*!" So, against my better judgment once again—and also wondering why this was so important to him when he said he didn't want to heal other people—I gave him the attunement. I wondered how an attunement would affect him, knowing he really wasn't connected to his heart for this process, even though I tried to guide him there.

On the morning of the closing for the building, I felt extremely distraught. I woke up that morning and I felt absolutely clear in every cell of my being: I did *not* want to buy this building. I did not want to commit myself to a medical mental health practice. When I began my practice, it was all about psychotherapy and spirituality and treating clients without medication. Somehow, as the practice had grown, it had evolved into psychiatry, primary care, and the need for pharmaceuticals. It was not going in a direction liked, my heart wasn't in it, and it wasn't reflective of my authentic self. I wanted to steer away from this direction, not commit to it more fully.

So I woke up once again questioning, backtracking. "I don't know if I want to do this," I ventured. Gabe woke up, got dressed, and coldly and resolutely said, "Well, you're doing it." I didn't have much fight in me about it, as bad as it felt. So, resigned, I said, "Okay, let's get ready to go close."

Shockingly, he replied, "I'm not coming, I have something to do." This had been basically his idea, he was pushing me hard into it—and yet he wasn't even going to be there for the closing? I was stunned.

Plus, it happened that the morning of the closing was his birthday, and I had thought we were going to spend the day together after closing. He said, "No, I have things to do. I have people to see. I've got to go." He kissed me on the head and left me to complete the closing by myself.

In spite of my intuition screaming "No!" I went ahead with the closing. I finished the process and the building was mine. At this point we had a lot of work ahead of us, in many different ways: transitioning to practice from one location to another, building rooms, and so on. This was quite expensive and time-consuming, so I definitely needed his support now. It had felt too big for me to begin with, and he had convinced me I had to do it, so I was really counting on his support.

I was wanting mostly emotional support, but something interesting happened then that I probably should have taken note of. I had an office in the new building, as everything else around us was being constructed. He did complete the blueprints, as he has promised. He said his mother was a PhD engineer, and he must have learned from her; he really seemed to be able to do really anything he set his mind to. I had actually gotten a quote for the same blueprints that he had done by himself, and it was a $13,000 quote. He was able to do the blueprints within a day, with the same results. These were things about him that never failed to amaze me.

Anyway, one day he came into my office, took out his checkbook and said, "Okay, how much money do you need?" I looked at him, baffled. I demurred, "Oh, I don't need any money. Why are you asking me that?" He answered, "I'm willing to help now. I'm willing to give and invest in this project."

I obviously should have accepted the help; I was in this overwhelming project almost entirely under pressure from him. But I've always kind of had a rule not to depend on men for money. It's something that my mom literally bashed into my head when I was little. So I waved him off. "No, I'm fine, I don't need your money."

He looked at me and said, "Oh my gosh, when are you going to run out of money? The building, the salaries, me taking 95%...there's no way you can have money left." I looked at him in confusion. It seemed almost like he wanted me to be out of money. Now that I reflect back on it, I think that *is* what he wanted. But right then, I just kind of shrugged and said, "No, I'm good. I don't need your money."

During this time, we were working 14-hour days. He had his work at the university to do, as well as working at (and on) my practice. He was extremely busy, on very few hours of sleep, and we would come home exhausted. The days were going by fast. The work at the practice was stressful, trying to get the building in shape.

Still, even accounting for this, he was increasingly moody and even downright mean to me at times. It seems as though the more I needed his help or support, the more curt he got. He would yell at me, make me feel stupid—even *call* me stupid. Although he had certainly behaved in strange ways that made me uneasy, he had never been like this before. I started to feel like he was belittling me, trying to make me feel that I wasn't worthy. It was becoming overtly abusive.

Still, as soon as I started to feel like that, he would once again take me to a dinner, send me a thoughtful gift, do something that would make me change my mind. He was still capable of wooing me back even after he hurt me or scared me. Again, this is very classic narcissistic abuse.

One very memorable night we were lying in bed and he looked at me and said, "Okay, so we're not going to have a child together because you're on birth control, so what I've decided is one way to be married to you but not be married to you is by doing a business contract." He said he was going to propose a business contract involving stocks, where he would buy stock and invest and he would own a certain amount of the business and I would have to give him returns on all the profits made.

I had never thought about my business that way. It wasn't my thing. But he was adamant. He said, "This is how we will be husband and wife. We will be married through the business." This contract did not sound appealing to me whatsoever, and I should have known by now that when he got one of these ideas about my business he wouldn't let it go, but

I kind of laughed it off and said, "Yeah, whatever." I thought: this isn't something he's really going to go through with.

TELEMEDICINE

Meanwhile, Gabe started to introduce telemedicine in the practice. That's what his forte was at the university where he worked; he was in charge of telemedicine there. In fact, he was obsessed with it. He told me that because he was an hour away and he was really busy, he wanted to start seeing clients via telemedicine, which required us to get getting us contracted and licensed for telemedicine.

This may seem like a random piece of business information, but this telemedicine activity ends up being highly relevant later in the story. My practice was in one of the eleven counties in Maryland where we were eligible to perform telemedicine, but to conduct it, we needed to be appropriately licensed. I knew that, and since it was his area of specialty I let him take care of it and assumed he did it properly. He put the license under my name because it was my business, and I signed the documents he asked me to. I do believe in this case his intent was to set it up properly, but as it turned out later, he didn't finish the licensure process. We were therefore illegally performing telemedicine without proper licensing. My punishment for this lapse was more shocking than you might imagine—but we'll get to that.

SANTA MONICA

Also about this time, right around the holidays, my sisters and I were wanting to go to Santa Monica, California. I taught in Santa Monica periodically, did a lot of energy work there, and I was helping my energy work teacher during this time. My sisters wanted to go to there with me and visit, go to Hollywood, look around, make a vacation of it. So we planned a trip.

Gabe was very unhappy that I was taking this trip with my family. Then he announced that he also had family in California. His brother lived there, and he said that was where his mother was living as well. So suddenly, he was making plans to go to California during the same time to visit his family. This was becoming very typical controlling behavior, and again I was uneasily going along with it.

My sisters and I arrived in California and had a lot of fun together, exploring new places, going to the beaches, having some great sister time together. But in the middle of this wonderful family time, Gabe began to call me constantly, wanting to be on the phone with me and wanting to text. My sisters got the point where they said, "We're going to throw the phone out of the car, because we can't stand the fact that you're constantly on the phone." So I turned the phone off and, before I did, texted him asking for his understanding: "I really do need to pay attention to my family, because we're on this trip together."

Later, when I turned the phone back on, I had a deluge of outraged messages. He was demanding to see me, saying that he was only about 30 minutes away, he was going scuba diving somewhere in the area, and he wanted to take me to dinner.

Again I folded. I told my sisters, "You guys go have fun." They were going to go get tattoos together. I planned to meet Gabe. I told him to meet me in front of the spiritual practice that my teacher had owned on Main Street in Santa Monica.

He parked and walked over to get me. I wanted to go inside and introduce him to my teacher. He got strangely wary. He asked, "She's psychic, right?" I said, "Yes, of course, she's psychic." And he absolutely refused to be introduced to my teacher. My "spidey senses" were going off at this point, thinking "Wow, he's really scared of what this woman would read about him!" I *knew* that, and yet once again, I kind of shoved that under the rug and had dinner with him.

And, of course, afterward we went to a hotel where he made love to me over and over, ensnaring me with his energy again, making sure that I was attached and hooked on him…and then he went on his way.

I continued the trip with my sisters. We continued to have an amazing time together, and then returned to Maryland. Gabe was going to be staying in California two weeks longer to finish his visit with his family.

During the time when he was in California and I was waiting for him to come back, I started having visions of a blond woman in his energy field. I could distinctly feel, see, and experience this woman in his field.

Right around that time, he was also calling and texting me and, with the New Year coming up, saying "You are my New Year's resolution. My goal in life is to create the best life with you romantically, physically, emotionally, financially…" He shared this vision of us creating a Kingdom together. He kept saying that he couldn't stop thinking about me, that I was in his every thought.

So I dismissed my visions of The Blond Woman and convinced myself I was just being paranoid and insecure.

NEW YEAR, BAD NEWS

He came back into the practice after New Year's Day. He was getting comfortable once again, and we were getting back into our old routine.

Then one day he said, "I have to talk to you. It's very important that we talk in my office."

I went into his office and said, "What's up?" He said, "I have my mother moving in with me."

Gabe lived an hour away. I would often go to his house just to hang out with him when he couldn't make it to where I lived. We would spend some weekends there. Now he was telling me that he had to have his mother move in, because she was having a difficult time and wanted to be with one of her sons. She had divorced her husband, Gabe's father, a while back and she was wanting to be with either Gabe or his brother during this hard time in her life.

So he said, "She's moving in with me, and that means that you can't come and visit." I looked at him kind of shocked, thinking, "Why can't I come and visit?" He said, "Well, I haven't told my mother about you. She would be pretty upset because it's against her belief systems that I would be with a woman who already has kids. She sees me marrying someone who doesn't have kids and starting my own family."

I was so hurt. It hit that tender wound of not being worthy, not being good enough. I felt like "used material," a second-hand type of girlfriend. I felt like he was saying I wasn't clean enough. I didn't say too much about that, but I did mention my strange premonitions. I said, "I had this vision of you being with a blond woman. She was in your field." I asked him, "Why am I having that vision? Is there something here that you're not telling me?"

When he didn't answer right away, I added impulsively, "Why don't you take a picture of your mother with your dog on your couch, so that I know you're telling me the truth?" That made him angry. He lashed back, "If you don't trust me, then we can end this relationship right now, because I don't want to be in a relationship with someone who doesn't trust me. I can't believe you're questioning me about my mother living with me."

Once again, I felt bad. I felt like I must be paranoid, and chalked it up to my own insecurity. I dropped the idea of getting a picture of his mother on the couch with his dogs.

Meanwhile, things at the new building were not going well. And Gabe's energy had everything to do with it. Not surprisingly, I was the only one who seemed to see any good in him, or who was willing to tolerate the strange downsides to his energy and behavior.

Within the few months that we had been in this building, one psychologist quit, saying that the energy in the building felt dark and negative. He actually said he felt like he was being suffocated. Then a few other people told me that they also felt like the energy was stagnant there.

I thought, "Okay, this building definitely needs a clearing." I would clear it daily with sage. But it seemed like this dark heavy energy kept coming back. It even felt like there were portals within the land that I couldn't seem to clear or cleanse fast enough. The energy would start to penetrate the building again almost as fast as I could clear it.

Right after Gabe's mother moved in with him, the practice started getting busier and busier. There were now 50 employees serving 4000 patients. It was a lot of people to manage, plus lots of tasks to accomplish still with the new building. This created a lot of stress in our lives, along with all the other moving parts, and it felt hard to bring harmony to everything.

As the stresses and complexities mounted, Gabe really started to lose it. He became extremely angry—even more than he had already shown he could be.

He obviously did not know how to manage people or deal with people. With everything that had been going on, he had become an essential part of the practice for me. I had more or less put him into a management position—mainly because he was my significant other and I wanted him to be a part of the work in that way. My sister had been my right-hand person before Gabe appeared. She and I had done a great job running the practice together. When Gabe came in, he kind of sidelined her role, even disparaged her contributions, pushing me to focus on him as the "right-hand man."

However, his management techniques began to get downright bizarre. One time he thought some of our younger secretaries had done something not quite right, so he told me that he was going to go and throw a chair up against the window right next to her, and scare her to a point where she would listen to everything he said. Of course I was horrified and said, "No, you're absolutely not going to do that! That's extremely unprofessional." I was constantly talking him out of these kinds of irrational, erratic behaviors.

If he didn't get his way, he would throw terrible tantrums that began to get worse and worse. One time he was jumping up and down and screaming like a baby. And then paranoia started to take over. One day he was in my office checking my phone—like every single number I had called. When I caught him, I demanded, "What are you doing?" He said, "I'm checking to make sure you never called your ex-husband from this phone." I said, "Gabe, we're really busy. You need to work. You can't be in here scoping my phone calls." But he kept doing it, obsessed with whether I was calling my ex-husband. (This, as it turned out, would be an ironic projection.)

UPSIDE DOWN MIRROR

The question of me talking to my ex (which shouldn't be an issue anyway since we did share custody of three kids, and we had an amicable though clearly platonic relationship) became an out-of-control manic compulsion for him. He began hunting through my computers, my Facebook, my cell phone, anything and everything of mine that was electronic.

A nurse practitioner was helping me manage an aspect of my business and he demanded her phone, saying that she was conspiring with me to communicate with my ex-husband. It was quite embarrassing. He had cornered in her office and she was giving him her phone while he was looking through it. I felt like, "Wow, I'm losing control. I really don't know what to do at this point."

We were fighting constantly about this. Finally, he started to become physically abusive. He would grab me hard and look at me with such malevolence that it was as if the Devil was coming out of his eyes. I felt like I didn't even know who he was. By the time he would let go of me, there would be bruise marks up and down my arms.

I was beside myself, because obviously I was extremely entangled with this man. I thought I was in love with him, though I now see it was much more toxic than that. At the time, I thought this nearly helpless enmeshment was true love. Whatever it was, I was seeing a side of him that was almost demonic. As each day passed, his eyes seemed to gleam with more rage and hatred.

Just when I felt like things couldn't get any more stressful, my employees started coming to me with complaints about him that just took my breath away. I don't know why I thought his crazy behavior would remain limited to me, but clearly it wasn't, and there was no hiding it or excusing it any longer.

He began telling everybody that the computer screen was talking to him, that there were electromagnetic frequencies coming from it that were telling him what to do. Before any patient came in, he would turn off the lamp and lay it down, so patients would arrive and the lamp would be lying down on the ground, sometimes behind the couch.

During all of this madness, he had the gall to present the contract to me that he had been talking about earlier, where he'd be making an absurd amount of money from this business that I had spent years creating from scratch, when he'd been there less than a year. I looked at the contract and thought, "There is just no way that I'm going to execute this."

But one of the nights that he was at my house he became desperate for me to sign his contract, and once again his intensity was scary. I remember thinking, "This is just written on a piece of paper, he and I are the only ones here, what's it going to hurt if I just sign it? He's going mad.

I don't want him to lose control and give me more bruises if I don't sign this contract." So to placate him, I signed the contract.

GABE HAS TO GO

You would think at this point I would have had enough, seen the light about how classically abusive these patterns were, and extricated him from my life and my work. Apparently, I had quite a few more lessons to learn first.

A few days later he was once again laying the lamps down at the office, talking to everyone about how the computer screens were giving him instructions, and understandably freaking a lot of people out. He also started mumbling to himself all the time as he walked around. He was clearly not well. I thought, "Okay, this is getting out of hand. No one trusts him, he's a medical doctor, he's prescribing medications—I'm absolutely going to have to put a halt to him practicing here."

So we cancelled all of his patients and rescheduled them. I had a meeting with him at home. I was firm: "There's just no way that you can be here right now. You need a break. You're not stable enough."

He left my house furious, after saying things to me that I won't even repeat here. After that, I didn't talk to him for a few days. And I was afraid of him.

My house at the time was 5,600 square feet—a very big house. It had a security system in which if you opened a door, it would tell you what door was being opened. After this experience with Gabe I felt so unsafe, I had a male friend close a section of the garage door so that it couldn't be opened.

But one night a couple of weeks later when my kids weren't there (thankfully), I was sleeping and I heard the garage door open at 2 o'clock in the morning. Somehow, he got in.

I remember sitting straight up in bed, terrified. I had put my Taser gun next to me, because I knew I wasn't safe. By the time I grabbed the Taser gun, Gabe was in my room. I grabbed the gun, turned it on, and shrieked, "This is a Taser gun!" He just laughed at me and ran towards me. I got out of bed and tried to chase him with it. He took it away from me very fast and threw it across the room. And then, he slapped me across the face. It was terrible, and terribly scary. I had *never* been hit before by a man.

Then, while I sobbed in shock, he picked up my cell phone, called my ex-husband, and let him have it about everything that he imagined was happening between us (which was of course all completely false). I just stood there absolutely petrified that he was going to really hurt me.

He started looking through the house for a person, a man he somehow imagined I was concealing. In that process, he put my phone down. While he was searching the walk-in closet, I grabbed my phone back, walked into the bathroom (which in my large house was a good ways from the big closet), and frantically, surreptitiously called one of my sisters.

I asked her to come help me. Thankfully, miraculously, she was there within 10 minutes. When she got inside, she commanded, "Gabe, leave right now!" And he actually left.

SEEKING HELP

The next day, deeply shaken, I knew I needed much bigger help with Gabe. I decided to go in person to the head of the psychiatry department at the university where he was studying for his doctorate. The head psychiatrist was also his supervisor.

I was thankful that I was able to get in immediately to see the supervisor. I told him everything that was happening. I said, "I'm extremely concerned. Please help me. This man is losing it. I'm concerned for his mental health, and for his patients. He's seeing patients at your University as well. And he's physically abusive. He needs help."

I also begged this man, "Please don't tell him I was here. He'll get extremely angry and I don't want him to come try to hurt me again."

The supervisor seemed very nice, looked me in the eyes, and acted like respected me. He seemed to be listening, nodding as I spoke. I felt safe. He agreed he would not tell Gabe. He said, "I will check into it, thank you for telling us, we'll take care of it." He gave me no reason to believe he would do otherwise.

Within 30 minutes after I left, Gabe called me, chuckling, and said, "You think my supervisor wouldn't tell me what you just did? You're crazy. He just thinks you're some crazy woman who's in love with me and is trying to get me in trouble."

It was stunning, a terrible display of misogyny and "good old boy's network." I felt utterly betrayed that a *psychiatrist* would dismiss my experiences and observations, including my very real sense of being in physical danger, and betray my confidentiality. Even if he didn't believe me—which is itself a horrendous thing to do to a woman who is essentially being abused (let alone one who is a fellow mental health practitioner!) — telling Gabe was a total breach of ethics.

But after I took that step, even though Gabe mocked it and the supervisor dismissed it, something must have gotten through, because things seemed to calm down for a bit. Since the University was still allowing him to see patients, Gabe demanded that he get his patients back within our practice as well. While hesitant, I thought "Okay, let's see what he's like when he comes back—if he's able to handle the stress and he's acting rational."

The next few times he was at the office, it appeared that he was more or less back to normal. His eyes had lost that chilling hateful darkness. He started to do a decent job with the patients. He wasn't talking to voices that no one else heard. It seemed as if he was getting his behaviors under control.

So even though the recent experiences had been absolutely horrific, and I should not have forgotten them, I did begin to relax a little bit. We started to pick up our relationship again. He told him how sorry he was, resumed the passionate kisses—and once again, I believed him.

Then one night, about one in the morning, I got a really strong intuitive message to drive to his house. This was highly unusual—I'd never just driven to his house (an hour away) that late at night. But the impulse was strong, and I know I am divinely and intuitively guided, even if I had closed myself off from much of my intuition at this time.

I drove to his house, got there about 2 a.m., knocked on the door, and his dog started barking. Gabe came to the door, looked at me like he was petrified to see my face, and said, "Leave right now or I'm calling the police!" That was when I knew that my intuitive abilities had not failed me. I said, "You go ahead and call the police. What's going on?" I could hear a woman in the background—and it definitely didn't sound like his mother.

For the first time, it was fear I saw in his eyes, not hatred. He said, "Please, please, just meet me a couple blocks down the road and I will explain everything. Just go there now." I was confused and angry and felt foolish for complying, but I went down the road a couple of blocks, waiting for him to come and explain to me what was going on.

He walked down to my car and met me there, and he got in the car. He tried to start kissing me and soothing me and drawing me back into his clutches in the usual way, but I resisted him; I was too distraught and heartsick to be placated any more. And he didn't explain anything then either, just strung me along again. He said, "I will tell you everything that's going on if you come to my house tomorrow."

Stricken, I demanded, "Who are you living with? Who is that? Is that a roommate? Is that your girlfriend? What is going on?" But he wouldn't answer me then. So I agreed that I would come back the next day, and he walked back home. I drove away crying.

I was heartbroken, because I knew deep down that my intuition and visions had been right all along; I had not been merely paranoid or insecure when I'd asked for a photo of his mother on the couch, which he had scorned and deflected with classic abusive gaslighting that made me doubt myself. Now I knew he had been living with this blond woman, whose image I had glimpsed in visions. I just didn't know all the details yet.

Part of me didn't want to know, but the bigger part of me couldn't let it go. As much as I wanted to turn my back on the whole crazy affair at this point, and show some pride, I was too far in and too ensnared to drop it. I had a kind of sick curiosity, like when you can't look away from an accident scene.

It appeared that if I wanted to know the story, I would have to go back, because he wasn't going to tell me there on the street that night. So after I went home, I slept a few fitful hours, got up, showered, and went straight back to his house without stopping to do anything else. When I got to his house, I knocked and he said, "Come in."

I stopped short just inside, because it looked like there had been a hurricane in the house. Holes in the wall, stuff strewn everywhere, broken furniture and glass. There had obviously been a vicious fight. And there he sat on the couch.

I said, "Who was that last night? Was that your girlfriend?" And he said in a defeated voice, "No, not my girlfriend. She's my wife."

I felt like someone had just taken a knife and stabbed me so deep in the heart that I would die instantly. The pain was so great that I was amazed I didn't collapse. I was speechless, paralyzed, and absolutely devastated.

I yelled at him, "I cannot believe you did this to me. I never want to see you again." I turned around and left. And he didn't try to stop me.

LESSON

"WHAT IN ME?"

Any time we're in a relationship and we see dark, ugly, mean or abusive behaviors, or if we feel like "Wow, that person is pure evil," there is something to look at in ourselves. Certainly, that person may in fact be ill, possessed, or malevolent—it's not that what we're seeing is untrue—but we also need to look at how that illness, ugliness, or evil ended up in our field. How or why did we attract such a thing? "What in me is a match for this?" What I've learned to do through this experience is think of myself as a mirror. What about me is calling in such darkness? What in me attracted or manifested it—and moreover, what in me is allowing it, tolerating it, accepting it, not setting appropriate boundaries around it? Where is my sense of self-esteem, self-love, self-preservation? That is what finally saved me through this process. Reflect on this within your own life or your own relationships.

Chapter Four

WHEN I FOUND OUT THAT GABE WAS MARried, I felt shattered, splintered. I was so fragmented that even now, as I tell the story, it's hard for me to remember everything. I believe that as I share my experiences now, I'm reintegrating and actually healing myself.

When someone is traumatized or shocked, the soul can fragment. Pieces of you can splinter off as a way of coping with the trauma. Psychology recognizes this as "dissociation," and many religious and spiritual practices see it as literal fractures in our energy bodies. Either way, soul loss can leave you feeling detached, numb, or seemingly separate from your body.

In soul retrieval, a person is guided by an experienced shaman or other energy practitioner through the process of bringing the lost soul fragments back. Sometimes the pieces will come back by themselves when the time is right, often when the person is in a safe relationship and can be intimate again with themselves and another.

Right after I found out that Gabe was married, Sean started to contact me on Facebook. Now that I look back, I know this was no coincidence. But back then, I thought, "Well, that's coincidental."

He was just asking me how I was, what was going on with my life. I didn't tell him too much. Sean was still with his girlfriend, as far as I knew, because I was communicating with him through Facebook and it seemed as though they were together. But he wanted to let me know that I deserved someone who would treat me well and that he wished me the best of luck. I remember feeling a pang of jealousy, because it looked as though he had been treating his girlfriend so well. And here I was, heartbroken and devastated.

I had loved Gabe with all of my heart. The thought of completely letting him go was unbearable. I was still spellbound, even after finding out he was married. But I really wanted to be able to let go, because some rational part of me (I was a mental health practitioner, after all!) knew this was toxic and downright dangerous. I had decided, "This is enough."

THE WIFE

About a week after I found out, his wife called me. She had found my text messages on his phone, which would obviously have shown there was a lot going on between us. I told her the truth. I said we'd been seeing each other for a year, that I'd had no idea he was married, and that I thought we were planning a future together. I told her how shocked and hurt I was.

At first she accused me of lying, even claiming Gabe had told her a photo of us was Photoshopped, and that the "people who were following him" had created those text messages. I said, "Do you really believe that?" She was silent. Eventually, she had to acknowledge that I was telling the truth. She even admitted that he had done this before. She was still strangely protective of him, though.

We weren't screaming at each other, but it wasn't friendly. I was driving to my son's ninth birthday party at the time—a terrible contrast—and I told her, "You can have him, I don't want him anymore."

She said, "I don't want him either." Right after that, she packed her bags and left him, heading back to California.

GABE LOSES US—AND LOSES IT

Gabe was left confused and fragmented himself. His wife was not talking to him, and I was refusing to be intimate with him either. He was becoming frantic. Yet because of his university supervisor not taking my allegations seriously, he was still allowed to moonlight at my practice, because he had patients. So I was forced to see him in a work capacity. But there was no longer any personal, romantic, or intimate contact.

Everything came to a head about a week and a half after my conversation with his wife when he didn't show up for work and about 30 patients were left sitting in the waiting room. I was furious at his lack of responsibility and accountability. I had to figure out how to get coverage for him, and edify all of the 30 abandoned patients. After I had handled that, I headed to his house to figure out what was going on.

When I got there, I was shocked at what I found. There was aluminum foil covering the windows. He had constructed a makeshift faraday cage to sit in (a faraday cage is an aluminum construct to protect from electromagnetic frequencies, fields, or influences), and his whole house smelled of urine. He came to the door and told me something was trying to attack him with electromagnetic frequencies from the cell phone tower next to his house. Then he glared at me and said, "I know this has something to do with you and your military experiences."

I haven't mentioned this yet, but I was in the Army for over eight years in the Reserves before becoming a therapist. Gabe knew about that experience. After leaving service in 2004, I no longer had any communication with any military authorities whatsoever. But at that moment, Gabe believed I was on a secret mission to destroy him with somebody from high military intelligence or the CIA.

One part of me was thinking cynically, "How convenient that he goes crazy right when he has so much explaining to do with me and his wife." Still, I was trying to talk him down and get his mind in a rational place, so that he could start to move forward with his life and I could figure out what to do with my practice.

I got him dressed and cleaned up, and coaxed him to come out with me a local restaurant. I let him drive, which in hindsight was probably a bad idea, but we made it. I urged him to relax.

The waitress brought him the orange juice he had just ordered. He looked at me and started laughing. He said, "How stupid do you think I am, that I would drink this?" He got up, slammed the orange juice down, walked out, went to a store next door, bought some orange juice, came back to the restaurant and said he was going to drink orange juice that was not poisoned. I sat there the whole time, determined to eat the food we had ordered and not chase him. The waitress looked at us apprehensively but didn't say anything.

Bizarrely, he could still swing between this extreme paranoia to completely relaxed and seemingly normal within seconds. Suddenly he noticed three of his friends sitting across the restaurant and said to me, "Come, I'll introduce you to them." Besides the fact that it was a ridiculous situation because our relationship was in tatters and here I was still trying to coax him down from what appeared to be psychosis, I felt humiliated at the idea of meeting his friends. I was the spurned illicit lover. I said, "No way! I'm not going to be introduced as your girlfriend after what you did— telling me that you were single when you were married. Everybody here must know that you have a wife."

At my refusal to be introduced to his friends, he once again swung back into rage. He looked at me balefully, and walked out of the restaurant.

I followed him outside. We got into the car in silence. We were headed back to his house and suddenly he pulled over to the side of the road, stopped the car and turned to me. He looked straight into my eyes. He took his fingertips and started to trace my eye sockets—first the right and then the left. Then with his fingertip he traced my cheekbones as well. His brown eyes, once filled with charisma and sparkle, were dark and vacant. He seemed to look right through me as he said, "I know that you have microchips in your eye sockets and in your cheekbones. What a beautiful place to put them. I know that they're watching me. I know that they want me. Why don't you just tell them that I'm willing to be on their side and work with them? Tell them to stop torturing me with these electromagnetic frequencies, Rebecca. Why don't you tell them I want to be on their side?"

Of course, I was a mental health professional and had dealt with schizophrenic and bipolar patients with psychotic features. Technically, I recognized this behavior, but I had never dealt with it in the capacity in which I was dealing with it now. Now it was in *my life*. It was in my *love* life. It was happening to someone I dearly cared for, whom I had loved.

When I carefully asked him who "they" is, he said, "I know you think I'm schizophrenic. I know you think I'm bipolar. But there are entities, beings, and they're after me. There are dark forces that want to hurt me."

I got him to calm down as much as possible and he got back on the road, and we drove back to his house.

Shortly after we got back to his house, I discovered that I wasn't the only person around whom he was acting psychotic. There was a knock at the door; three police officers had arrived with paperwork, to emergency petition him into the psychiatric ward *of the very university in which he did psychiatry work!* Ironically, this paperwork had been filed by the same doctor who had refused to believe me when I first told him what was happening.

It turned out that Gabe had been behaving bizarrely at work there too. He was putting people's cell phones in the refrigerator, purportedly to keep people from listening to their conversations, or to protect himself from being followed or attacked. He was walking and talking like a robot, he was often agitated, and he was mumbling to himself. According to these doctors, he was displaying psychotic and schizophrenic features.

So, he was handcuffed and hospitalized against his will.

The next day he asked me to please come and see him and help him. Of course, I went right to his side. There was a panel of high-profile psychiatrists around him. He had pretty much every psychiatrist at the university in that hospital room—the top-tier psychiatrists who teach psychiatrists. They told him that he had to be hospitalized for 30 days in order to (hopefully) stabilize and keep his position at the university and within his residency.

The hospital that they wanted to admit him to was about 50 minutes away. Instead of taking him against his will in an ambulance and handcuffing him once again, they offered him the choice to go home and pack, and—one of the psychiatrists looked at me—"she can even take you to the hospital."

Gabe did a very good job of talking and making us all believe he understood and was on board. Extremely educated people, highly trained to read behaviors, we were all convinced that Gabe was serious about checking himself into the hospital for his own well-being and that of others.

But after Gabe and I returned to his house, he looked at me like I was crazy when I told him to pack his stuff so I could take him to the hospital. He said, "I'm not going." No matter how I urged him, he refused to go.

So…I stayed. My love for him was still so strong that I wanted to make sure he was okay. And I could have reported him, but I was still torn by loyalty.

I turned my phone off because I didn't feel like dealing with any more drama for the night. And we went to bed.

In the middle of the night he started shaking and sweating profusely. He excused himself and went downstairs on the couch. Now I could see that he actually *was* being overtaken by something. It was all happening so fast, it was so hard for me to understand or process. I was caught between the worlds of mental health and spirituality. I actually believed him; I felt that this was not just schizophrenia or bipolar disorder. I did feel that he was being influenced by an outside force. I just had no way at this point of figuring out what was really happening.

I walked downstairs and looked at him shaking on the couch. I asked him if he was okay (silly question, as he obviously wasn't). He told me he'd had to come downstairs because he didn't want to do anything to harm me.

Immediately, I felt a strange sense of well-being. I think I was told by my angels not to worry, that I wasn't going to get hurt. I know that sounds crazy—anyone hearing this would ask why I would stay in a situation like that. However, I just somehow knew I was going to be fine. I felt I was divinely protected.

So I left him on the couch, went back upstairs and went to sleep. Or slept as best as I could, under the conditions.

In the morning, when he woke up, he seemed oddly calm and collected. I knew he had a lot to deal with, because the higher-level psychiatrists at the university and his main job obviously thought he was going insane. I had my own life and business to deal with. I was still heartbroken and betrayed. I knew that the very best thing for me would be to leave him for good.

I had to go to work, so I left his house. At this point, everybody was in agreement that Gabe was not healthy or balanced enough to see patients. I received a letter at my practice from the university revoking his moonlighting privileges, so at least I didn't have to deal with him at work anymore, or clean up his messes there.

I also got a phone call that day from the head psychiatrist at the university. She was extremely concerned and upset with me for endangering myself by staying at his house the previous night. She said that during their assessments, Gabe had expressed that I was the center of his world. He told the psychiatrist that the only time he felt okay, the only time he felt at peace, was when I was near him. He said that when I was in his presence, the demons were unable to get to him. She was worried for my well-being.

Again, I somehow knew I was going to be okay. But convincing her of that was quite difficult, and she had little confidence in my decision-making skills at that point (which wasn't unreasonable under the circumstances). So I had to listen to a long lecture about how I was putting my life in danger, and possibly the lives of my children.

COURT

I imagine that my decision to stay away from him probably had a lot to do with some of the next moves that he made. He was no longer allowed to work for me, and I decided that I could no longer see him. I wanted to try to extricate myself from this situation and heal. My heart went out to him, I had great compassion, but I needed to put my own pieces back together.

This, apparently, spurred him to vindictively torture me. The next thing I knew, I was being served with papers. He was suing me for two million dollars based on the piece of paper I signed that one evening at my house, agreeing to split the business with him through stocks and bonds. I knew that if this were to go to court, it wouldn't ultimately go anywhere based on that scrap of paper.

However, in Maryland, anyone can file a lawsuit for a fee of $140. And if you're a corporation, no matter how frivolous the lawsuit is, you have to defend yourself and be represented by a lawyer. So even though I wouldn't ultimately lose, I did have to mount a defense, and that two-million-dollar lawsuit caused me a lot of problems and cost me a lot of money.

During the two months between the time I left his house and when I was served with the lawsuit, I did not see Gabe at all. Even though my heart felt like it was ripped in half and I missed him every single day, even I had a breaking point. Throughout that two months, he sent me horrible text messages about my involvement in the military and about his being attacked. He called me names that I would never repeat here. He clearly seemed to be losing his mind.

My lawyer was expensive, but I needed him. He told me that it was obvious Gabe wasn't going to win the lawsuit. But the time and money I had to spend on this wasteful exercise were painful. At one point, this attorney pulled no punches when he said, "It's very obvious, Rebecca, that you were thinking with your vagina."

A couple more months passed before the court date arrived, and I continued to feel fragmented, like I was walking around in many little pieces. I lost quite a bit of weight. I was in a daze. But I had to put the practice back together, find a new psychiatrist, and explain to the other staff what had happened. Thankfully, I was immensely supported within my practice by the staff and the management team. But it was still so hard.

The day I went to court for this two-million-dollar lawsuit that Gabe had filed, I was definitely not his biggest fan. But seeing him, once again, I remembered how deeply I had loved him. He was sitting not too far from me. We were waiting for the judge to come in. He looked over at me and said, "Rebecca, take a picture. We're going to use this for our scrapbook," and he chuckled. I thought, "How many levels of evil can exist in one person?" At the same time, I was searching his eyes, trying to find the Gabe that I had originally known. The Gabe I had fallen in love with. The Gabe that haunted my soul every single day.

The judge walked in, looked over the paperwork, gave a deep sigh, talked to Gabe's lawyer for a few minutes, and said, "We're missing some crucial paperwork here. This is going to be postponed for another few months." I breathed a sigh of relief. I practically ran out of the courtroom to my car.

Gabe followed. I could hear him mumbling. I wasn't sure who he was talking to, as usual, but clearly he was still not well. He ran up to me and looked into my eyes and it was almost as though he had the old sparkle back in his eyes. He said, "Hey, Rebecca, we need to talk. I really want to spend some time with you and talk about everything."

If you've ever been in love and you look in that person's eyes and your brain tells you, "Run! Run fast and never look back!" but your heart just aches for his touch…then you know where I was at that moment.

I gave in to that yearning yet again. I said, "Okay, let's talk." He said, "You and I both need to relax a little bit, we need to release, we've been through a lot." And he booked a hotel with a jacuzzi tub.

HOW MUCH WILL I TAKE?

I can hardly believe now that I went for this one more time, but we met there later that night. We made love, and it was a bittersweet connection. Unbelievably, even after everything that had happened, it felt good being in his arms.

But afterward, some kind of self-preservation and shame did kick in. I was disgusted with myself for putting up with all of this; wondering "What is wrong with me? Why does love have to be this hard?" What was I *doing?* I had just crawled back into bed with a mentally ill man who had nearly destroyed my practice and was now suing me for two million dollars!

He was apparently thinking the same thing. We were in the hot tub, right after making love, and he was staring at me. Then he said something I will never forget. It has stuck with me until this day, and it actually eventually helped me to learn to love myself. But it was a huge slap in the face at the time.

He was studying me, and he said, "I'm trying to figure out what your limit is. How much shit will you actually put up with? Is there no end to what I can do to you?" I was speechless that he would actually come right out with that admission of intent. But it was like he was reading my mind, because I had the exact same question. And it finally kind of woke me up.

He was right about that much. He was testing my limits, and I had been allowing him to cross the line further and further. As successful as I was in so many ways, there was clearly some part of me that did not value herself enough to say *enough*. Some part of me that would allow myself to be walked all over—and yes, abused—and keep coming back for more, almost as if I deserved it. Was I ever going to get out of this trap?

HE'S NOT BETTER

I also found out, by spending that night with him, that he still was plagued by the intense paranoia. But I also still felt that it was not just paranoia. I still felt how psychic he was, and that there really were supernatural forces at play that I couldn't even begin to imagine at that time.

His psychic sensitivity made him vulnerable to these entities—perhaps because he *was* unbalanced and ungrounded as a personality, because he didn't have good boundaries or pure intentions.

The next morning at breakfast, and afterward as we went out for a walk, he kept looking over his shoulder, as though someone was following him. He ordered me to follow him as he went into a store and hid behind a clothes rack. I said, "What's going on? Who are you hiding from?" He glared at me and said, "As if you don't know. You know who I'm hiding from."

When we got back to the hotel room, once again he got that evil gleam in his eyes. He demanded, "Give me your phone." He said he was looking for some secret information from the military or other high-profile government agencies.

This time, I wouldn't give him my phone. And so, this time, I ended up with a whole bunch of bruises on my arm.

This time, I was done. I got a restraining order.

The judge granted a six-month restraining order. However, although Gabe could no longer physically come near me, his energy was still all over me. I thought I was going crazy, but his energy felt like it was following me. This became more and more real as I tried to shed the whole experience from my body and spirit. I was also still walking around in a catatonic state, completely fragmented.

SEAN AGAIN

Meanwhile, one day I looked on my Facebook page and saw a message from Sean, telling me that he and his girlfriend had just broken up. I can't fully remember the details, but I do know I ended up making plans with him to go to a masquerade ball in my town. I hadn't seen him for three years at this point. Was this just a coincidence, or the exact synchronicity that I needed?

I tried to get excited about Sean. I remembered—I didn't *feel*, but I remembered—the energy between us that had seemed so electric and profound at one time. Feeling, unfortunately, was still absent from my experience since the brutality of the Gabe experience. I was numb. Also, it was strange, but his penis seemed really small—I didn't recall his penis being that small the first time we were together. (This may sound odd—and, well, small!—but it will be highly relevant later.)

Sean made arrangements to come to town. He even stayed the whole weekend at my house. He took me to the ball. But what I felt when he drove into my driveway and got out of his car was very different than when I had first seen him. I didn't feel that much at all. Physically speaking, I was still aware that he was attractive. I registered that he was a good date, someone you would be proud of taking to the masquerade ball. I just didn't *feel* it. I just felt like there was no one home inside of me.

He kissed me hello, just a peck on the lips. Even the kiss felt different. I tried to fake enthusiasm. I gave him a hug, and we made small talk. We didn't connect very deeply. I was not in any shape really to connect. There was no real kissing. I actually did sleep with him, but I wasn't feeling it. It was mechanical and depressing. He initiated it, and I sort of went along with it in my confused, traumatized, "not in my body" state. I was trying to pretend I was okay and having fun. He might have thought everything was great; we didn't really talk about it.

I did tell him I had been dating and having some trouble, but he didn't know the extent of what I had gone through. He wanted to date me now, finally, so from his point of view, this was a beginning. From my point of view, I wondered if perhaps he was meant to be a friend. The intense intimate attraction I had felt when I first met him just wasn't there. I was mildly attracted to him, in the way you'd be naturally attracted to someone who is physically attractive. It was abstract. But the deeper connection I had once felt for him so fiercely was turned off.

Sean was very supportive in general, a kind and thoughtful person. Still, I didn't disclose any of the events that were going on around me. I didn't want him to think I was crazy. I did ask him about his recently ended relationship, though, during one conversation. He told me that the whole time he was in that relationship, he felt as though he was getting his soul sucked out of his body. He said that if he hadn't left, he would have been soulless. I was so struck by this, because that was exactly how I felt. Soulless.

Meanwhile, even when Sean and I were together, every other thought in my head was about Gabe. Crazy as it sounds, I still missed him. I wondered what he was doing. I was still trying to figure out what went wrong, why these events were happening the way they were.

When it was time for Sean to leave, he gave me a quick peck on the head, hugged me, and drove away. I thought about him for maybe five minutes after he was gone. I just couldn't hold him in my reality at that point. I wondered if the initial flame that had flared so brightly was dead for good—and if I could ever feel myself at home in my body again.

LESSON

WE'RE ATTRACTED TO OUR SHADOWS

We're attracted to our darkest shadows. These are the pieces of us that we try to hide and ignore, the pieces of us that we have not paid attention to or brought into our awareness. These shadows can come alive in people we encounter in our everyday lives. The Twin Flames we attract will reflect our unresolved shadows. When you ignore or hide your shadow, it will find a way to be revealed to you. And when it's revealed, you have such a deep attraction to it, because it's part of you. It's the part of you that you should have learned to love a long time ago. If you had loved it and given it compassion from the beginning, it wouldn't be hurting. My shadow was being reflected back to me through Gabe, and it was obviously pissed for being ignored. And it would go to great lengths to get my attention, as it turned out.

Chapter Five

IT WAS SUCH A DIFFICULT TIME IN 2011. I HAD A restraining order against Gabe. I had just had a confusing encounter with Sean for the first time in three years—intimate in some ways, yet disconnected in others because I was so traumatized and dissociated from my own body and feelings. I was a mess. I was barely eating.

Gabe's energy was all over me, and by that I don't mean, "I couldn't stop thinking about him." His energy was *literally* all over me. As I breathed, I felt like I was breathing in his energy. When I sat down, I felt like I was sitting in his energy. When I slept, I was sleeping in his energy. It was the strangest and most unnerving sensation. Obviously, the restraining order could do nothing about this energy, and I couldn't seem to shake this suffocating, persistent sense of being haunted by him—not even by using my own energy techniques.

I took some time off of work. I really needed it. To get away, I went on a trip to Florida with one of my best friends. Her mom had a house in beautiful Amelia Island. We were on the beach, taking surfing lessons—it was idyllic.

One afternoon we were at the beach, and there was a party there. I thought, "Okay, hopefully this will get my mind off Gabe." All of a sudden, I felt his energy once again. I turned around and there was a huge banner sign across the beach advertising scuba-diving equipment that said, "www.gabe.com." True story! "www" "his name" ".com". Unreal. It was like he was there energetically and saying, "I'm following you wherever you go."

Of course, I thought about him for the rest of the trip, though I tried to have as much fun as possible. I came home a bit more rested, although still feeling hollow and numb, and tried to resume my life and work at my practice.

People in my practice, meanwhile, were complaining about paranormal events there. Some employees felt dark energies or experienced strange events with clients. The office that Gabe had been in was now occupied by his replacement, a psychiatric nurse practitioner. After a few months this nurse practitioner literally started going crazy and doing things that were inappropriate, to the point where I had to let him go. It just seemed as though the energy in this building was very toxic. Now that I look back, I understand better what was going on. The building definitely had portals to dark energy—that's undoubtedly why he chose it. But in the midst of it, I had no clue. It was just scary and confusing.

There were definitely energies around me at that time that seemed to beget horrible luck in my life. One thing after another was going wrong. I just felt sick all of the time. I was full of grief, constantly dreaming of and thinking about Gabe. I was just somehow spellbound by him. It was like I did not feel complete unless he was around. It seemed as if no matter what he did to me, I couldn't let go.

But I *knew* that he was unhealthy. So I refrained from contacting him for the six months, and those six months went by without hearing from him.

THE END OF RESTRAINT

Then the restraining order was up. Right after it ended, I had a dream that he had texted me and he needed my help. I woke up, looked at my phone, and he *had* texted me and wanted help! He said in his text that he had been evicted from his apartment and he had nowhere to go, and he was standing on the side of a road.

In spite of everything, and as hard as I know it must be to conceive of, I was right there. I immediately went and picked him up. When I saw him, I was shocked at his appearance. His skin was all leathery. And he was panicky about it. "Rebecca, I don't know what's going on here, my skin's turning to leather." It was bizarre. I didn't know what to do.

I said, "Do you want to go to the hospital?" He said, "No, this isn't anything medical." He proceeded to tell me that he was being attacked by alien forces and being microchipped. Although now I understand more about those types of things, at the time I just didn't know whether he was crazy or not, or what was going on. Regardless, his skin most certainly did seem to be turning to leather, like a reptile's, and I didn't know what to make of this.

I took him to a hotel and he stayed there for a couple of days. I stayed with him. He was obsessive and terrified, constantly trying to figure out ways to remove these entities that he felt were attached to him. He was washing his skin with bleach, drinking rum to try to drown out their voices…it was intense.

I eventually took him back to my house, because my kids weren't there. But I told him he could only stay a couple of days, because my kids were coming back from their father's house.

While he was at my house, he unplugged everything, even down to the cables outside. It was a big mess. I couldn't figure out how to connect my TV back up for a long time after that. He was once again washing his skin with bleach, walking outside in the woods trying to find portals to go through, trying to get back to his old reality. It was a handful.

EVEN NOW…

I was still dealing with my own attachment—to him. I'll be honest about this, even though I know it may sound crazy—but I still couldn't stop thinking about being intimate with him. It really was a testament to how spellbound I was by his energy (or maybe the energies that had a grip on him) and all the Tantra we had done. Even with all I had been through, and all the chaos he was creating now, his near hysteria about whatever was happening to him…I *wanted* him. I remember even asking him "So, do you think you feel up to being intimate?"

That was definitely not where he was at. He was like, "What? I'm being attacked!" And even as I asked, I was thinking on some level, "Wow, it's crazy that that's all I can think about in a situation like this." But I understand it now. The forces that were working through him were powerful and seductive beyond imagining.

When I was taking care of Gabe, I unconditionally loved him a hundred percent. And I noticed that when I was giving him this unconditional love, no matter what he was going through, he seemed to be able to shift into a different space relatively soon after being around me. Within those few days of staying with me, as I was really caring about him, I noticed that his leathery skin completely healed. It was like he had been turning into a reptile—and with unconditional love, that stopped, and his normal skin returned.

During this time at my house, he told me that during those months that he and I were apart, he meditated constantly to be right near me again. This corroborated how I was feeling about "having his energy all over me." Again, it wasn't so much that I was thinking about him and missing him. It was as if he *actually was right beside me* the entire time. Like he had the ability to just think about me and project his energy. That connection we had was real. And it was extremely hard to disconnect from, no matter what my logical mind said.

GABE GOES WEST

A couple of days later, he told me he was going to drive to Santa Barbara to see his brother. He got in his car and left. I had no idea what was next. I wondered, "Are we going to see each other again?" Is this the end of our relationship?" "Is he okay?" "What's going to happen?" I was scared for his mental health, and tried to keep in touch, but that was all I could do.

On his way to California, he called a lot of people he knew, including his brother and a friend who was a lawyer. He told them that he was being attacked by psychotronics (energy weapons that transmit sounds and thoughts into people's heads and bodies). Many of his family and friends ended up contacting me, terribly concerned about him. We didn't even know if he would successfully reach the West Coast or not.

But he did. He moved into his brother's house, and a couple of months went by. His brother spent a tremendous amount of time and energy trying to get Gabe hospitalized. But Gabe could still fool any psychiatrist. As you recall, he had fooled the top psychiatrist at the university he'd been studying at and working for, and talked his way out of hospitalization there. So there was no way his brother was going to get him hospitalized. Attempt after attempt was unsuccessful.

Around this time Gabe reached out to me, saying that he would respond only to me if we wanted him to get help. If we wanted him to get help, I would have to go there and see him. So, still loving him and connected to him, I went to Santa Barbara.

I picked Gabe up at his brother's and took him to a hotel. I was still very concerned about him. He was still talking about microchips in his teeth. He was looking at people and saying they're not real, that everybody is a minion, everybody's programmed, and dark entities are trying to attach to the world.

His terrified preoccupation had now also extended to, of all things, his penis. He was obsessed about the fact that it had shrunk. And he was having difficulty sustaining an erection. I just figured it was smaller because he was unable to get erect. But he was quite obsessed about it. This would become significant later.

Now that I look back, a lot of his story about being attacked is corroborated by research I've done and things I've learned—even down to the microchips. I now know he wasn't simply losing his mind—although I do think he was unstable and that didn't help.

At the time, though, I still knew little about these sorts of energies, entities, and psychic attacks. I knew about dark energy through my energy healing work, but was out of my depth regarding aliens, entities and the kinds of forces he believed he was reckoning with. I knew there were paranormal elements to what he was going through, but it did also seem as if he were struggling with psychosis.

So I contacted his brother and we made a plan once again to try to get him admitted to a psychiatric hospital. I thought that maybe my testimony and my background could be helpful. We did get him admitted finally, he was there for a day—and talked his way out of it again. He was very angry at me at that point for helping to get him admitted him to the hospital.

His brother suggested that at this point, we just let him go to a homeless shelter—that maybe if he hit rock bottom, he would get help. I felt like, "There is no way I'm going to let him go to a homeless shelter. I'm going to pick him up and I'm going to take care of him, because I love this man."

But his family insisted that first I get away with them for a while and hear them out. Afterward I could go back and decide. His brother and mother had wholeheartedly decided that the only way for Gabe to get back to normal was to be homeless. They absolutely did not want me to save him.

But I was determined and still spellbound and my mind was made up too. Reluctantly, I agreed to go out with them. His brother took me to a lake to go boating. I was very preoccupied, I wasn't having fun, but I was trying to act nice. I knew they were trying to keep me distracted while Gabe was being transferred from the hospital to the homeless shelter, so I wouldn't interfere.

Afterward, unconvinced, I got in my rental car and went back to the city. I now know they were right, but at the time I couldn't see it. Somehow, the timing worked out (or so it seemed) that when I pulled up to the homeless shelter, the bus had just dropped Gabe off. I picked him up.

But I had kids and a whole life to live back in Maryland, so I dropped him off at another hotel (which I paid for) and I told him I'd be back in a few weeks.

And then, something happened that *seemed* as if circumstances were aligning. Of course, now that I look back on it, they were aligning in a way that did not ultimately benefit me.

THE BI-COASTAL "SOLUTION"

My teacher in Santa Monica suddenly contacted me and said, "Rebecca, I really want you to teach here more often." She offered to pay me a fair sum of money for teaching at her practice. It seemed like a golden opportunity, because I would have to get an apartment there. An apartment near the beach in Santa Monica sounded like a dream come true. I thought, "That's what I'll do. I'll get an apartment there, Gabe will live there, and I'll travel back and forth. I'll teach in California, I'll work in Maryland. I'll be able to go home, see my kids, be a good mother, come back, visit Gabe, try to get him healthy…"

When I returned to California three weeks later, I picked up Gabe and, immediately, we went apartment hunting. It took about a week and a half, but I finally manifested a great apartment in Santa Monica. It was right near the beach, beautiful, not too expensive…it was perfect.

For a while, this actually seemed to be working out. I spent time in Santa Monica teaching and working out and doing yoga and seeing Gabe. And Gabe went through quite a transition during this time. He was still talking to himself, but it seemed like whatever energies had been bombarding him were letting up. He wasn't doing much, but he was walking along the beach a lot, starting at the ocean and at trees, communing with nature. I think he was really trying to ground himself.

This new, quiet, mild-mannered man looked at me one day just a few weeks into this new scenario and said, "The most important thing in life is family. All I want to do is have a family. I just want to be with you, Rebecca. It doesn't matter where we are, here or Maryland, I just want to be with you."

During that time, things were completely different with him sexually. He really *was* unable to sustain an erection. And when he did, it wasn't for very long. His penis *had* shrunk. I remember thinking "If I could just put the two together, the old Gabe sexually and this new Gabe emotionally, that would be great!"

The new Gabe was massaging my back, doing my laundry, holding my hand, walking down the pier, kissing me constantly, going shopping for me, wanting to ride tandem bikes together. That was entirely different than the old Gabe. The old Gabe would *never* have done my laundry. I mean, he was *ironing* my laundry! We would watch Netflix together, make dinner, very cozy and warm. In some me ways i felt like he was really into me, and that this *soft* side of him emerged. He loved nature more than ever, and he would stare at the ocean for hours, sitting on the sand.

It was in some ways very romantic—but there was another side to this. He was solicitously tending to all these things, and seemed dedicated to being with me, very much into us spending time together—yet he also seemed very distracted, distant, kind of somewhere else. He was softer, attentive in certain ways, but also not always "all there." Often when I was around him, I felt lonely because of how distracted he seemed. He was deep into his daydream, very present in his own moments, but not totally aware of who was around him.

There were other differences, too. The old Gabe, if we walked past a tree that he didn't know about, or if we talked about a subject he didn't know about, he would immediately research it. He had been an intense go-getter, extremely creative, and loved to figure things out. He *persevered*. That was one of the things I'd really liked about him.

This new Gabe went to the bookstore, bought a book, and could not read it. I noticed it—he would read a couple pages, then he would put it down. His attention span was extremely low. He had little motivation. If I gave him a task to do, he would definitely do it for me. But he would not do much for himself. He didn't do much between my visits, I don't think. I gave him my credit card, kept the fridge full. I think he went for walks, ate, and stared into space.

Still, I was grateful to have this softer side of Gabe. It was confusing, but I was certainly going to take this over the intense, manic, paranoid, and aggressive Gabe.

Back home I was truthful with my children and my family. My kids had never personally met Gabe, but they had known I was dating somebody. They also knew about the restraining order. Now I told them that when I was gone for a couple weeks on the West Coast, I was teaching but also helping this person out.

My kids trusted me. However, my sisters, my mom, and my friends pretty much thought I had lost my mind. They did not know why I was still continuing to help this man. This was understandable given all they had seen Gabe put me through. I knew how it looked.

Meanwhile, Sean was messaging me here and there on Facebook. We had some nice conversations, and he even sent me a gift in the mail, which I really appreciated. I would have moments where I really missed him, and sometimes the thought would come to me: "I should really have *Sean* here in Santa Monica with me. He seems like such a good guy." But then quickly I would go back to thinking about Gabe again.

A BABY AFTER ALL?

Miranda, the teacher I was teaching for in Santa Monica, turned out to be into witchcraft. I was shocked when I learned this, because initially she talked a lot about working the light. But I started to notice as I worked with her more that she'd go to Hollywood and pick up a lot of things that she would say she needed for her craft, and they were odd things—some of it she wouldn't even let me see. So she dabbled in a little bit of the dark stuff as well. I didn't judge it, I was just surprised.

For some reason, she was very interested in my relationship with Gabe. After about six months of my teaching there, she started saying "Hey, do you want me to work on the fact that you two can't have a child together?" I had talked to her quite a bit about my relationship with Gabe.

Gabe had confessed to me soon after the restraining order that, although he'd wanted to get me pregnant early in our relationship, he actually didn't know if he could. He'd been told by doctors that he had some sort of genetic disorder that would make him very likely infertile.

And as I said, our sex life wasn't near what we'd had before. I was basically just taking what I could get. I was dealing with a penis that was about 10 times smaller than it had been, and I'm not exaggerating. He knew it himself. I still wasn't sure what was going on there. But when Miranda offered to help us get pregnant, I was intrigued.

Obviously, I need to explain my new willingness to explore this. As you'll probably recall, early in our relationship I had staunchly refused to have a baby with Gabe, despite his intense pressure bordering on obsession. His motivations were unclear and did not feel wholesome or altruistic or even loving; he did not in any way seem like a father by nature. Plus, I had three great kids, and felt no calling to have more.

But this "new Gabe" kept saying that family was the most important thing for him. Nothing else mattered. He didn't care about being a doctor any more. He just wanted a family. And he was so docile, so gentle at this point, I felt he would never dream of hurting me. And I was still bound and determined to make him happy, to make it work with him.

So now, in a complete turnaround from early on, I said, "Yeah, let's work on this!" And Miranda said, "Okay, for his libido issues you might want to give him some maca, and I'll work on him and you with your belief systems." He even went to her office and she worked on him.

Within a week or two—shockingly, in spite of Gabe's supposed infertility—I was pregnant, at the age of 38.

By this time it was 2013—one year after the restraining order had ended.

Gabe was very happy about the pregnancy. I was actually very happy too. My teacher Miranda was really excited. I went home and told my family. As resistant and boggled as they'd been about my reconnecting with Gabe, my family is very old-fashioned. Once you're pregnant, they will try to accept the man. So they went from absolutely despising him—for good reason—to planning a trip to California right away to meet him and also have a vacation.

So in August 2013 my whole entire family traveled to California. We rented a beautiful house on the beach. Gabe joined us and met everyone. He was fairly awkward. I remember they thought he was strange (and really, he was). But it seemed like everybody got along. He treated me well. He would put his hand on my stomach and say, "I'm so excited to have this little one."

Believe it or not, I didn't really plan for Gabe to move back the East Coast with me. I don't know why I didn't feel that was the thing to do, but during my pregnancy—though it sounds strange—I was still planning to keep him on the West Coast and stay on the East Coast myself.

A DARK ENCOUNTER

When I was only about nine weeks pregnant, and back on the East Coast, I went to a holistic fair in Pennsylvania. This was something I did periodically to offer energy work, psychic readings, and healings. I've always done really well with shielding myself energetically when I do this work, so I don't worry about that.

But when I was at the fair, I was sitting there waiting for clients, and two healers came up to me and urgently warned me not to work on a man who might come over asking me to work on him. They said he had something *extremely* dark attached to him, and it would be dangerous to work on him.

Unfortunately, I didn't take them seriously. I looked at them like they were paranoid. Sure enough, this man came up to me with wide eyes, very scared. He said, "There's something very dark attached to me, and I can't get it off. I'm really scared. Can you please help me?" It seemed like it had just happened to him at the fair. Of course in my compassion, I wanted to help.

So I said, "Okay, sit down." I closed my eyes and I connected, and I remember seeing bat wings with holes. It was very ancient, very dark energy. But I decided it was safe to work on him. I thought, "I can protect myself." I said to him, "Oh yeah, there's definitely dark energy there." I did energy work, I removed the darkness from him, and gratefully he got up and he left.

I had to go to the bathroom. I went, and right than I started bleeding. That's a major sign of a miscarriage. Immediately I went to a hospital nearby. Sure enough, I was miscarrying.

Whatever energy I had removed from that man appeared to have taken away the soul who was planning to come through. The women had tried to warn me. I was stricken.

Little did I know that I would be meeting this energy again in the future.

LESSON

My ability to reflect back on this now is so much different than my ability to see it while it was happening.

When we try to ignore our shadow energy, it comes through and rears its ugly head—sometimes, for some people, in paranormal ways. As much work as I was doing spiritually, both personally and professionally, my shadows were emerging full force. I was working with the light, yet not attending to my own shadows. And by not resolving them in healthy ways, by not being fully aware, those shadows were creating openings and opportunities for the shadow in the universe to come into my life.

We all have our own shadows, our own demons, our own darkness. There are also, I have come to see, dark energies "out there"—reptilian, demonic, alien, or Illuminati. There are many conceptualizations of these energies, beings, or entries—and many different schools of thought about what they are, whether they're real, how they're the same/different/related, and what they're up to.

For me, I saw enough during this experience to know that those entities are real, and they're dangerous. But I also know that our own shadows, our unprocessed material and darkness, can create openings, portals, or weak boundaries where those entitles can penetrate, feed on you, and use you. The dark forces in the universe will find food and shelter in your darkness—your ego, your shadow—if you are unaware, unclear and unresolved.

The parts of you that feel unlovable or think you're not worthy, lack of esteem, lack of self-love and self-compassion—really anything negative, including resentment, jealousy, hatred, judgment or other low-vibration energies—will resonate with and draw in these entities. These are not the beings in the universe that you want to partner with!

The good news is that if we are truly grounded in love, in light, and in the heart, and we completely, unconditionally love ourselves, then those dark entities are unable to come in. We become inaccessible to them. They can't penetrate true light, true love. They come in through our own low-vibration emotions.

(This doesn't mean we never feel fear, grief, anger, frustration,

shame or other supposedly "negative" emotions—this isn't about bypassing healthy expression of the full range of emotions. A healthy human will feel and express all of these, as life inevitably brings loss and challenge. But when we get stuck in those kinds of emotions, when we live there chronically, when we feed them and they don't move through us in a healthy way, we become vulnerable. When we are disconnected from our core goodness and light, we open the door to negative forces as well as harsher lessons.)

When your goal is to have a successful twin flame relationship, and you put that intention out there, "false twin flame" material may confront you, to purge all that is false from you. You and your true twin flame have a humanitarian purpose for the world. If you're not in a space where you unconditionally love yourself, then you're unable to help the rest of the world.

I look back and I understand that this was all part of the process for me, but it was incredibly painful. So it's ideal, even before trying to manifest a twin flame, that you really work on self-love. It all boils down to that.

Chapter Six

MY MISCARRIAGE OF THE PREGNANCY WITH Gabe at the holistic fair—apparently, at the hands of dark energy—was absolutely devastating for me. I'd had a miscarriage in the past, during my first pregnancy, which I had grieved greatly. But for some reason, this was an anguish beyond almost any loss I had experienced. I felt from the depths of my being that this soul was meant to be here. I already missed her dearly. (I knew it was a girl.)

I had dreams—or, rather, nightmares—in which something very dark and headless was chasing me. It seemed utterly, terrifyingly real. At one point, I almost jumped out my bathroom window because I didn't know if I was in a dream. This dark energy that was chasing me wanted something from me, something it thought I had. It wanted *her*, but I didn't understand this until later.

The soul of this baby surrounded me constantly for a very long time after the miscarriage. I felt her. I felt her presence. I knew that she was waiting to come back. I knew that she was meant to come back. However, I had no idea how this would happen. Meantime, I was sleeping a lot, hibernating, just holed up in my grief. I had been through so much, and now this felt like too much.

Seeking to move forward in my healing, I made an appointment with another teacher of mine who I had known for a few years, and from whom I had taken some classes. His name is Richard Bartlett. He was extremely powerful, and I knew him to be always grounded in a very pure and wholesome place. I wanted to work with him to process through the grief of this loss.

Normally, Richard is fairly detached from emotions. He just kind of does his work, very matter-of-fact, without much fanfare or extraneous discussion; he doesn't spend too much time connecting the dots. He doesn't get mixed up in drama. He's very successful at what he does in part for this reason.

However, during our session, he actually seemed to be really connecting with my grief as he was releasing it. He seemed more touched by it than usual. As he was working on me energetically, and I was purging with tears, he said to me, "Rebecca, this soul is meant to be here. It's appearing as though you had an abortion rather than a miscarriage." It was striking that he would interject such a statement, and I felt that what he said was absolutely true.

But who or what had "aborted" this pregnancy? That was something even he could not tell me.

During the days after the miscarriage, I tried to reach out to my other teacher in Santa Monica. I needed to let her know I could not teach right now due to the emotional and physical aftermath of a miscarriage. Her response to the news of my miscarriage (or whatever it was—termination) was shocking and bewildering. Instead of speaking with me, she had a lawyer contact me and attempt to extract money from me—for her supposed loss of income due to my not teaching during that time. She never called to ask if I was okay, or even gave condolences about the loss of the baby.

Of course, the request for money was absurd. I absolutely refused to pay her. At this point, she seemed to turn into a different person. She never wanted to talk to me again—she actually said that. After I had the miscarriage, she wanted nothing to do with me.

Her behavior was utterly confusing to me. She had played a major role in my ability to get pregnant with Gabe. There are still many questions about her involvement and her attitude. Her dabbling in dark magic and her obsessive interest in my pregnancy became very suspect. Why was she so eager for me to be pregnant, and why was I of no interest to her when I no longer was? There are still things I don't understand about all this. How did she even help me get pregnant when Gabe wasn't supposed to be able to? How did the pregnancy end?

A FAMILY AFFAIR

The miscarriage did bring Gabe and I closer together. I had been planning on him living in California up until I had the baby, and even afterwards. We were making plans about me bringing the baby down to visit him regularly. But he was very supportive during and after the miscarriage. After that, we both felt the urge to be together permanently.

We started to entertain, for the first time, the idea of him moving in with me. This was big for me because I had never before contemplated him moving in with my kids. I would have to completely trust someone before I would let them live with my kids. And at that time, I did trust him. He was there for me during the pregnancy, had been very excited about the pregnancy, had expressed his desire to be a family man, and he was saying and doing all the right things. And I missed him tremendously.

So, about six weeks after the miscarriage incident, we started making plans for him to come live with me permanently in Maryland. We booked him a flight and I was all set to pick him up, bring him home and start that new chapter.

But of course, within this story there continued to be confusing, unexpected twists and turns.

About three weeks after the miscarriage, I had a theta healing weekend course that was scheduled to be taught inside my home, and I decided to go ahead with it. (Theta healing is a powerful energy healing technique that clears disease-causing blocks, fears, negative beliefs and traumas; I had been trained in it by one of its founders and now taught it myself.)

Once again, out of the blue, Sean turned up. He was getting my emails because he had subscribed to my email list, and he said, "I'm excited to learn theta healing." I was glad that he was eager to learn it, so I said, "Of course, please attend." I also told him he could stay with me, which I knew was a little crazy and intense given our history and the fact that I had just committed to move in with Gabe. But I also really did feel like we were friends. I felt close to him in a way that didn't feel unhealthy. And besides, I was still quite hollow with grief, and probably not thinking totally clearly.

When Sean got to my house, a couple of days before the actual class, I told him everything that had just happened to me. I thought he needed to understand my involvement with Gabe. I told him about how I'd been pregnant with Gabe's baby, that I had just lost the baby, and how devastated I was. Telling him was actually really cathartic. I cried and cried, and he listened and held me while I cried. And somehow, with him around, I felt the loss of that baby even a hundred times more than I already had.

So it was really beautiful, him supporting me, listening to me, holding me and consoling me. I looked at him at one point and thought, "Gosh, this guy's amazing!" He's absolutely gorgeous, and he was tapping into my needs and wants and desires and fulfilling them. He was easy to be around. I felt like, "Wow, I'm in quite the situation. I have two men who I have overwhelming feelings for. Both are there for me, both are trying to help me through this process..." I really didn't know what to make of it.

Once again, I'm going to be really honest—in the midst of this confusion and vulnerability, during this time of the theta healing course, I was intimate with Sean again. I honestly didn't know if it was because of the devastation I was going through (it's common to impulsively want to make another baby after this loss), or if it was feelings for him—or both.

At one point when we were together, he did not start off wearing a condom, which is unusual for him. Just before he was going to orgasm, he said, "I'm going to have to put a condom on." But the way he said it was more like a question to me, rather than a statement. And for a moment I thought, "Maybe you should tell him not to?" Then, quickly, I was like "No, Rebecca, you're just grieving. Get your head together. Don't do something that you're going to regret." I told him "Yeah, put the condom on."

The next day was the first day of class, and during the class, I used him as a demonstration for a manifestation exercise. After class was over he came up to me, looked me directly in the eyes and he said, "Rebecca, you're so beautiful. You are my manifestation. You're everything I've always wanted in a woman."

I just looked at him, dumbfounded and mute. Here was this man I had been so utterly in love with from the first second I had laid eyes on him, before I had ever met Gabe, at a time when he didn't seem that into me. At *that* time, this was exactly what I would have wanted to hear. Now he was proclaiming his love for me—and I was going to be picking up Gabe at the airport in a few weeks to bring him to live with me. Gabe, who I had come to think was the true love of my life.

It was a lot to process, especially in the aftermath of so much confusion, grief, and pain. I wanted him to feel honored in his feelings, but I also couldn't fully reciprocate. We obviously had a connection. I still felt something for him. But I had a commitment to Gabe. I told him that I had to go and help Gabe in California, and that I wasn't completely done with what I had to do there.

Remarkably, he was very supportive of that. He seemed understanding, and he was really loving and kind.

Interestingly, while Sean was visiting, my children ended up meeting him. They were supposed to be with my ex-husband, their father, since I was teaching and it was his weekend. But one of my sisters had just taken them to play somewhere, and then asked them where they wanted to go next, and they said, "We want to go see Mom!" Not knowing what was going on at my house, she brought them over. And they walked in…and there I was in my bedroom with Sean.

To say this was awkward was putting it mildly. My kids had just met Gabe in California. Sean was being extremely affectionate and loving with me, doting on me, trying to show my children that he's a respectable man with honorable intentions. The kids were understandably puzzled. They looked at me like "What are you doing, Mom? You have a boyfriend."

Helplessly, I said, "I'll explain later. Don't judge me." And they were really cool. They're great kids. But they milked it for all it was worth. They said, "Okay, then let's go out to eat." So we did.

And the thing is, they *completely loved* Sean. They clicked with him right away. He got along with them too. They just did so well together. The kids were actually begging me, "Mom, please make Sean your boyfriend! We really want to see him again. We can tell he really likes you. Is he going to come back?" They said this right in front of him!

What could I say? I just looked at Sean and said, "We'll see." We were all in the driveway when Sean got his stuff together to leave. As I watched him drive away, I thought, "Wow, things are certainly getting complicated now."

GABE MOVES IN

Short after that, as planned, I went and picked up Gabe from the airport. He had his bags, he was excited to see me, and we were about to start our new life together—living together full time, in my home, with my children (who were there half the time).

Gabe took a few days to settle in at home, and then he wanted to start working at my practice again. This was a bit of a delicate matter, because most of the employees already knew him from his time there as a doctor, and remembered all the strange and toxic events that had gone down. But he was no longer working as a doctor. I had him working in billing and doing some administrative work.

As you'll recall, before he went completely crazy and left, he had begun implementing a telemedicine program, since that was something he specialized in at the university and we lived in a rural area where it could be helpful to people. So when he returned, he just took over the billing and administrative oversight of the telemedicine program.

Once people at work saw how much he had truly changed, they accepted him. Again, he really was noticeably different. He was looking at me differently, treating me differently—people were saying "Wow, he's very different, Rebecca! We didn't really believe you, but he *is* different."

Likewise, at home, he was meek, docile and agreeable. He basically did everything my children wanted him to. If they said, "Hey, let's go get milkshakes!" he would take them to get milkshakes. He would never say "no" to them. He never raised his voice to them, or to me.

It seemed like we functioned pretty well as a team now. We both cleaned the house and cooked dinner. We took trips together. We went to Great Wolf Lodge, to amusement parks with the kids. It was exactly what I had wanted, and what he said he wanted—idyllic family life.

But he was still very distracted and distant in that strange way, too. I was pretending not to notice, pretending it was okay. I was thinking, "This is the man I've always wanted, and now I have him." But sometimes, when he looked at me, it was like he was…missing. The smart, creative, dynamic Gabe I had known wasn't there. There was some expression behind his eyes, but it's like it was a different soul. Almost vacant.

This very much presented itself in our sex life, too. Sex was infrequent and fast—and again, his penis really had shrunk. It was *nothing* like it was before. There was no Tantra. I missed that part of our relationship so much. It had been such a vital and profound part of our connection, and had meant so much to me. It had been magic, and I wanted it back. (Now I use Tantra in a healthy way, as it can be wholesome and healing, but I realize now that back then I was addicted to a darker side of it, which can be intoxicating.)

Really, although I kept saying "this was the man I always wanted and now I have him," it like I was dating a different man. I *had* wanted Gabe, yes—but I wanted the old Gabe (without all the craziness, of course). But when the craziness receded, it seemed, so did most of the rest of him.

Still, I thought I was in love with the man. And I still felt like I could help him, maybe even get some of the old Gabe back. So I just kind of went with it.

Sean would reach out here and there during this time. I told him the truth about everything. I told him that Gabe was living with me, and that I was committed to it although there were issues. Sean never gave up, though. He made sure to stay in contact with me—not intrusively, just kindly and thoughtfully.

Things went on like this for a year after Gabe moved in. Working, taking some trips together, having a pretty functional family life. Things were calm and pleasant, if a bit boring in the bedroom and uneasy in the back of my mind regarding his "vacancy."

There was one thing that Gabe was still fired up about, though: he still definitely wanted to get me pregnant. Despite how distant and distracted he was, he was adamant about wanting to have a baby; that was one place where the lights seemed to be on, so to speak.

And we tried. I must have taken about 50 negative pregnancy tests within like a year; it just wasn't happening. To the best of my ability, I tried to replicate what seemingly had allowed me to get pregnant before with him. I did energy work, and we tried the maca once again. It absolutely was not happening.

I'd had three children with my ex-husband, and I planned them to arrive a certain age apart—two and a half years apart for each child. This was easy for me at the time; every woman in my family got pregnant quickly. I knew, somehow, that this was just not in the cards. There was some sort of energy preventing me from getting pregnant with Gabe.

Another aspect of note is that although he was mostly calm, unassuming, and accommodating, Gabe was still talking to himself at times, muttering to himself, and making some strange hand movements. I thought, "Okay, this is him still recovering from an extreme psychotic breakdown." I felt like it was the aftermath of that—and that when he was talking, he was just talking to himself, perhaps a self-soothing behavior. I didn't really think too much of it until later.

THE AYAHUASCA JOURNEY

I've always been someone who gets really strong messages from my guardians or guides, and I usually know when to follow them. In July 2014, after about a year of living with Gabe, I received a very strong message that I needed to attend an ayahuasca ceremony.

Originally, I planned to attend a ceremony in Peru that November. However, I received an even stronger message that I needed to do it sooner than that, that it was important to do the ceremony as soon as possible. So I planned a trip with Gabe to Peru for October.

Gabe was all for it. He agreed to do ayahuasca with me. It would be the first time I'd ever done it. He also said, "Okay, we're going to get spiritually married when we're in Peru. We're going to say our wedding vows." He had wanted to get legally married, but even though I was going along with everything else, including the idea of having a baby with him, something in me stopped short of legally marrying him. It was like I just knew in my soul that was not a good thing to do. But I agreed to the spiritual marriage.

We took the journey to Peru, drove in motorcars to Iquitos in the Amazon rainforest, and prepared to stay for about two weeks.

During the preparation for the ceremony, the shamans interview you. They speak Spanish, so there's a translator. They read your energy and they ask for your intentions.

Well, by this time, it had been well over a year since I'd had the miscarriage. It still haunted me, but was not something I carried with me everywhere I went anymore…or so I thought. Yet immediately, when I was having my assessment with a shaman, the shaman said, "Okay, you're here to work on the abortion you had. To process through the abortion," the translator told me.

I said, "No, I didn't have an abortion. It was a miscarriage!" The shaman replied, in an eerie reiteration of what my teacher Richard Bartlett had said, "Well, it feels like an abortion. The baby was supposed to be here. It was taken." I got chills. And I felt like, "Wow, this is a very important baby! I don't know why the baby's not coming."

Gabe and I performed our spiritual marriage before we did the ayahuasca. And then we experienced the medicine journey. I responded to it mostly positively, although of course it was intense; I found it profound and insight-filled and enlightening and emotionally releasing.

But the ayahuasca affected Gabe harshly. This is not outside the realm of responses to ayahuasca; it affects everyone differently. Some people find it euphoric and illuminating, some people experience anxiety, panic, or terror. And some people experience both. It's not shocking in hindsight that Gabe, with all his demons and mental issues, was super sensitive to it and might have a "bad trip." He was outside screaming and throwing up in the Amazon rainforest. He said it felt like he was being attacked, like someone was torturing him.

As I've said before, whether he'd had psychosis or was possessed or both, Gabe remained one of the most psychic and sensitive people I'd ever met. He probably took half the ayahuasca doses I did, but he was more agonized than anything. He didn't seem to get insight or transformative visions, just anguish. In hindsight, I wonder if the medicine created a new opening for whatever darkness had been tormenting him or working through him.

For me, one of the ceremonies brought a profound vision that I'll never forget. I've explained that I have "guardian parents" who give me messages. They've always been very reliable. They're the ones who gave me the message about doing the ayahuasca. One night, I was is in the maloca (a large circular hut that is the traditional ceremonial space for the journeys), and all of a sudden, they came floating down. I had never seen them physically, I had only heard them before this.

They were tall, white beings with high cheekbones and slanted eyes—the classic characterization of starseed parents. They were the embodiment of the divine masculine and divine feminine, mother and father. They were introducing themselves to me, and I said, "Why don't you come closer?" They said, "If we came any closer to you, you would want to kill yourself, because of the unconditional love that we have for you; you'd want to be with us." They just meant that humans aren't used to feeling that amount of unconditional love. It would blow us away. They had to give me space. They wanted to show me how much love they have for me, but I couldn't allow it fully to come in.

They were there to tell me they loved me, but also to give me a message. They said, "We want you to know that Sean is to be the father of that baby." Gabe was sitting right beside me at the time. I had just spiritually married the man. This was something that my ego did not create out of some desire, because I was in shock and very confused. I got chills all up and down my spine. After they gave me that message, they just left.

There's so much more that happened during that trip. Since then, I've developed a profound love for sacred plant medicine treatment. I teach a course on it. I teach people how to become psychedelic coaches. I've conducted countless ceremonies for others; it has become a core of my work, as you'll read more about later in the book. It's something that has truly changed my life inside and out. I cannot recommend sacred plant medicine enough for the physical, emotional, and spiritual aspects of one's creativity, healing, and transformation.

But for Gabe, the transformation was not so positive. After doing ayahuasca, he seemed irritated. It was as though something began oozing out of him that had been hidden for quite some time. We began to have little fights; that harmony and equilibrium we'd experienced for our first year of living together was disturbed. His placid surface seemed ruffled. I thought "Okay, what's going on here? Why is he starting to act mean and hateful at times?" There was now a part of him emerging that, once again, I did not feel comfortable with.

I again began to question this relationship. Why did I spiritually marry him? What was I thinking? A shaman who did speak English had taken me aside at one point and tried to tell me as nicely as he could that there was something dark still lurking in Gabe. Something that he was trying to bury, something he didn't want me to see. It was unnerving, especially given our history. And now, the medicine journey seemed to have opened the door to that darkness once again.

I came back from this trip thinking "Oh no…What's going to happen now?" I had just gotten the information that Sean was to be the father of this beautiful soul that's supposed to be in my life. And yet, I had just spiritually married Gabe, who I *thought* was the true love of my life (in spite of the unease about the changes in him).

I had a lot of thinking to do. Lots of changes were about ready to happen in my life. I knew this feeling. I took a deep breath, surrendered into my exhale, and opened myself up for what was about to come. It's like when you're on a roller coaster and you know the only thing you can do is surrender, and that's how you're going to make it to the end of the ride. That's how I felt at that time.

LESSON

When you're in the midst of something this convoluted, it's really hard to see what's going on. It's obvious now that there were dark energies, even reptilian entities, at play here. These energies can be hidden beneath layers of false love, entering through the illusion of something good, tricking you.

But these energies—even if they are trying to get to you through your lover—can only enter through your own insecurities, shame, doubt, guilt, fear, worthlessness, hopelessness—the parts of you that are your own shadows. The best thing you can do on a journey like this is to work on yourself constantly. As I keep saying, self-love is everything.

One of the things about self-love has to do with judgement. Don't judge yourself. And don't judge others. As you read my story, there are so many things you could judge me for. "Wow, her kids saw her with a new lover, right after seeing her with her boyfriend." "Why did she keep going back to this obviously extremely messed-up guy?" "Why didn't she go with Sean?" "Why was she staying connected to Sean?"

But judgment upon yourself and/or others will just get you stuck in the ego. It'll keep you frozen, unable to move. Everybody has skeletons in the closet. Shadow work is loving those skeletons. It's when you love the skeletons, truly love you unconditionally, that these dark energies can no longer hurt you or touch you. They can't exist in unconditional love. They can only exist through insecurity, doubt, and judgment.

If you're experiencing anything similar to what I'm describing, do the work to truly love yourself unconditionally. Give unconditional love to the worst things you find about yourself. If you can do this, you will notice miracles happening around you. This is what happened for me when I began to get a grip on what was really going on, and finally do that work. But it took a lot to get there, as you're about to discover.

Chapter Seven

AN AYAHUASCA JOURNEY IS ALWAYS A TURNING point in one's life. Through my journey in Peru, I started to really question the love I had—or didn't have—for myself. This was crucial, because as I've pointed to, the lack of self-love that I hadn't examined and resolved was leaving me dangerously vulnerable to dark energies and entities.

I started to really look at how much I had put up with and allowed and tolerated. Can someone put up with that much if they truly love themselves? If you've ever wanted somebody so much that when you finally "get them" and realize it's not what you thought, but you just keep going because it's what you said you wanted, and you're trying to trick yourself and you keep making excuses for it—that's all a reflection of an internal world that needs a lot of work. Ayahuasca stepped in and helped me start that work. Through the guidance of my guardian parents and the plant medicine, I began to finally, truly wake up.

But there was a lot more awakening to come.

WORKING AND NOT WORKING

Back in the United States after Peru, life went on, but now it was different. Gabe and I started to sleep in different beds. After the trip, it was like he too knew I wasn't going to get pregnant, so he stopped trying. And when he didn't want to get me pregnant, he stopped having sex altogether. So we started sleeping in separate beds; he was all the way downstairs and I was all the way upstairs. When two people are sleeping separately, I think that is the beginning of an end in a relationship.

At this point my mental health practice was going quite well. We had a huge population of patients, including a psychiatric rehabilitation program where we helped children and their families. There was a mental health section, a primary care section, and the telemedicine section. I was the sole owner of this entire organization on paper. But there was obviously no way I could handle all that by myself. I had built this practice, but always with the support of a team. Thankfully, I had a good group of team members, which included some of my family.

Gabe was part of that team again, and I did need his help. I also felt like he needed mine. I felt that if I gave him a role, really let him have some authority again at the clinic, it might empower him and bring back the good parts of his old self. Even though we were basically living as roommates now, in the back of my mind I was still trying to salvage the relationship, thinking that maybe if only I could make him feel as powerful as he once felt, he might "come back" in the way that I once knew him—hopefully, infusing some of that old spark and drive into the gentle soul I had met right after and right before my miscarriage. I was still clinging to hope, vainly wishing for the best of both worlds.

Since he had been a psychiatrist in the past, had experience working in a hospital, and had actually designed and implemented the telemedicine program at the practice initially, it made sense for Gabe to continue working in that area. So I put him in charge of billing for telemedicine as well for as the medical parts of the clinic, plus the implementation and followup for telemedicine. Everything he did for the clinic was under my name, since I was the sole owner.

I was working very hard, and was very successful at what I was doing. We helped a lot of families and kids, people with trauma. But the truth was that I was not happy. I desperately wanted to get out of that field. I didn't want to be in that career any more. I was too much of a spiritual person to be bogged down by all the business and administrative matters, dealing with 100 employees and their problems. I was working 12- to 14-hour days and then coming home and doing my spiritual practice on the side, occasionally going to California or Seattle or somewhere else in the world, treating myself to conferences and trainings.

There was a point back then where I used to say that I lived in heaven and hell. Heaven was when I got to do my spiritual work and hell was going to that practice and dealing with everything else. As far as I could see at the time, there was no way that those two worlds could combine, and there was really no way out of it. My practice was extremely lucrative; I had family members working for me; Gabe was completely dependent on me financially. I just couldn't see a way to transition out of that work without hurting a lot of people: employees, their families, my family, my significant other. So, I just kept moving with it, and trying to find gratification and satisfaction for my soul through other work in my "off" time.

However, the universe, my guardians, my higher self and my heart were not going to let that lie. I now understand that I'm divinely protected, and the divine will protect us—and redirect us—to soul alignment and our true depth. That kind of half-life I was accepting, that avoidance of my true desire and calling, was just not going to suffice.

Your higher self is the part of you that knows what it's doing. It's the part of you that's connected to God-Creator-Source. It wants the fullness of you, not your small ego idea of what you should do or what you're afraid to do. It will do what it has to in order to bring you into alignment with your soul's mission and who you really are.

If you deny it, avoid it, suppress it, you make it harder on the path and therefore yourself because you create blocks that have to be navigated around. When you resist, obstruct, and obfuscate, the universe has to bring you to truth in a harsher manner. The less connected you are with your higher self, the more suffering and sacrifice tend to appear in your life, because you're moving against the natural flow and order, "pushing the river." If you won't allow your destiny to unfold the easy way through the direct route, surrendering to it and meeting it, life will often push you to right livelihood and soul fulfillment via a more convoluted route—the hard way.

I was resisting my natural flow in the direction of spiritual work. I wasn't agreeing to give up my practice and transition 100% into the work of my heart and soul. Honestly, I simply thought I couldn't. But my higher self had different plans, and wasn't going to let me off the hook. I'm grateful for that now. But, at the time, it was turbulent.

THE AUDITS

We started to get a lot of audits of the business—specifically the billing. I didn't know where they were coming from. We were getting requests for folders, medication records, all sorts of files. I would go to Gabe and ask him about it, because he was in charge of all the billing. It's impossible for one person to oversee everything. You have to trust the people you're working with. It definitely was my error in trusting the wrong person.

Of course, as I was saying, now I know everything happened for a reason. But at the time, it was just a mess. I didn't understand what was happening. I spent a lot of money on lawyers getting through these audits. I listened to Gabe tell me about these honest billing errors that he had made, such as billing under the wrong practitioner for a service (the service was rendered, just under the wrong practitioner, but that's not okay to bill that way). There were also questions about the telemedicine paperwork, whether or not it had been done correctly.

He kept saying he had it under control, he had emails to prove it, and so forth. I still trusted him, and with the help of all these (very expensive) lawyers, I thought we were getting through these audits okay. Outwardly, the practice was still running very well, as far as client treatment, client care, quality of care. I'm not saying it wasn't stressful; it was. We got into some really big fights over the audit. But I was just stretched too thin to put 100% of my energy into it. I was trying to salvage my own joy and happiness, spend time with my children, have a life…

WHO'S YOUR DADDY?

When Gabe and I stopped being intimate with one another in 2015, I started to think that it really might be over. I had tried everything I could think of. I brought him to Cancun on a beautiful all-inclusive trip—still no romance, no lovemaking. I came back from that trip defeated and thought, "This is something that may not work out." But I still muddled along for some time after that with the way things were.

During that year, Sean and I would still message each other via Facebook periodically, and he was always putting out there that he was thinking about me. It felt good, but I was too stressed, confused, and disheartened to take it any further or wonder what it meant.

One day I was out with a friend, though, and I was drinking a little bit, and I was thinking about the lost baby. Now, I'm not somebody who felt like she had to have four children. I already had three wonderful kids I loved, and I felt very fulfilled in that way. Certainly I felt a deep emptiness about the loss of any real connection with Gabe, and about this split in my vocation—the "double life" I was living with my work and the sense of being trapped in my career—and I obviously had self-love issues as I've discussed. But I was definitely happy with my kids and my family, and I felt lucky to have them.

Yet I missed that soul who had miscarried or been taken. I knew that soul was important. There was something about that soul. I knew she needed to come in. And I remembered what the guardian parents had told me in Peru—that Sean was to be the father.

So I had a little bit too much to drink (or maybe not), and I rather recklessly and boldly messaged Sean, "How would you like to be the father of my child?"

He immediately messaged me back and said, "Yes, let's do it."

I was extremely shocked. I hadn't really believed he would take me seriously. I mean, I had only seen him a handful of times in my whole life. I never expected him to say "yes" to such a crazy, intense, random question.

But he did.

Then I sat on that for a very long time—months and months. He didn't let it go, though. He would occasionally reach out and question me about it, and ask what his role would be.

As futile as it had been seeming, a part of me *still* thought that Gabe and I would be together, so I even mentioned Sean being a surrogate for this baby. I'm pretty sure that's not what the guardian parents had in mind; I'm sure they weren't keen on that idea. But Sean said, "Okay, whatever capacity you want me in this baby's life, I'll do." Incredible. He actually agreed to be a surrogate.

I started to scheme, "Wow, what if I have this baby and Gabe can have that feeling he's always wanted of a family" (at least that's what he was saying). "And I can make the guardian parents happy, the soul can come through, Gabe and I will be happy… Maybe this is a way to salvage the relationship."

Nineteen months had now gone by without Gabe and I being intimate even one time. In October 2016, I woke up one morning and Sean was energetically lying in my bed next to me. It wasn't a dream, it wasn't wishful thinking. He was *actually there*. His energy was right beside me. And I knew it was time to go visit him.

I wasn't even so much thinking about the baby. So many months had gone by since that exchange. I just knew I was supposed to see him. So I reached out and told him that I had a business trip where he lived, and asked him if he would be up for seeing me.

I didn't really have a business trip. I was nervous and I wanted to have an excuse to go. (I didn't tell him this till much later.) He said, "Yes, definitely." He asked me about where I was staying and when I was coming. I hurriedly made up a date that would work for me. I wasn't thinking too hard about the date. It was a date in late October. I would fly down and we'd see each other.

I took my best friend Sherry with me. We got on the plane, got to Michigan where Sean lives, we checked into a hotel. Incredibly, it had been at this time more than three years since I had seen Sean. The last time I had seen him was the theta healing seminar.

He came walking into the hotel and I saw him and thought, "Oh my gosh, this man is so good-looking." Every time I saw him I thought the same thing; "He's so gorgeous." My heart started beating. I could instantly see a whole reality open up where I was with him, and wanted to be with him. It was so strange how quickly I could tune into that.

We went to my room and lay down together. He looked at me closely, asked me how I was doing, and started touching me, ever so gently, hugging me and holding me. It felt so good and it was like no time had gone by, like I'd just seen him yesterday.

Within 30 minutes of seeing me, he said, "I thought you and I were supposed to have a baby together." I laughed nervously, but then I started thinking. I realized, "Oh my gosh, I'm ovulating!" I was ovulating *on the exact day I had decided to go down and see him.* That was *not* something I had planned, but it was a fact.

So I told him, I said, "Well, I am ovulating."

Before I flew to Michigan, through our Facebook messages, Sean had suggested at one point that I should leave Gabe and that he—Sean—and I should just have the baby together and be together. I didn't really know what to say to that, and I just let it lie. He didn't push it—he was never pushy, always so gentle and agreeable. He still seemed open to any role with the baby, but he did let me know what his preference would be.

But when I was with Gabe, I still felt stubbornly bent on making it work somehow—even though I know that to anyone reading this now (and of course, as I look back), Sean was so clearly the better choice and Gabe was just so much trouble (to say the least).

Now, here with Sean, it felt very natural and right to be with him, and so easy. As dogged as I'd been about Gabe, there were moments when couldn't really understand why I was so hell-bent on seeing it through with Gabe when I was getting so little and giving so much. This was certainly one of those moments. But then, I still didn't understand the ferocious power of the dark energetic spell that was working on me through him.

I had told my best friend, who was with me, about all of this—Gabe, Sean, the baby, the guardian parents, and their messages. She was so supportive and I was so appreciative. Before Sean showed up that evening, she said, "Okay, let's do some energy work on you. Let's get you prepared for this." I hugged her. I said, "I know this seems crazy! Yet I know it's right, and I'm so happy you're here." She's very gifted, very connected to source and divinity, and she worked on me energetically.

Sean and I went out that night with my best friend. We had a nice dinner and an enjoyable time. Then she went back to the hotel and I went back to his house. And we made love.

There were certain ways that I was told by my guardian parents to make love to Sean using the art of Tantra. These included making sure his third eye was open, and doing breathing techniques with him. My guardian parents had communicated to me that this baby needed to come in a particular way, through the breathing. The breathing opens up a higher frequency dimension that the baby could come in through, they explained. (I didn't tell him about this till after I was pregnant, and he just went with the flow of whatever I did. I didn't tell him about my guardian parents till later, either.)

It wasn't the same as when we had first been together. I enjoyed it, but I was not yet healed from the "spell" with Gabe, and it still felt like there was something in the way preventing me from having the feelings I should. I also had some hurt left over from the fact that I had "recognized" him on a soul level when we first met, and he had not. So that made me hold back. Still, it was good, and I had been kind of starved for intimacy by Gabe, so the connection was sweet.

The next morning when we woke up together, Sean looked at me and said, "Oh my gosh, you might be the mother of my child!" We were both sort of dazed, like, "We can't believe we even did this! This is maybe our fourth time seeing each other *ever*, and we might be pregnant."

We spent the day together—Sean, me, and Sherry. We had fun. We went to a festival with art and bands, dancing. I didn't want to leave. I wished I could stay longer. But it was time for Sherry and I to head to the airport to go home. We were running late. In addition to that, I thought we were flying American Airlines, so Sean dropped us off at that terminal. Once inside, we looked at our tickets, and we were on Delta! We had so much running to do. We arrived breathless to security, and one of the security guards pulled me aside and said, "Ma'am, I need to pat you down." He showed me the monitor, and my whole pelvic area was lit up orange on the screen. I asked, "What does that mean?" He replied "Usually, that kind of reading means you have explosives."

He asked if I wanted to get patted down right there or go into a private room. I said, "I don't have time to go to a private room, we're late for our flight. You're just going to have to pat me down now." He did, and of course I had nothing contraband, and he let me leave. But I'll never forget that moment when my whole reproductive system was lighting up to the point that you could see it on an airport security monitor.

My friend and I flew back, and I returned to that world I had been living in and trying to work with. I was looking at Gabe, thinking "What did I just do? Is it good? Is it right? What's going to happen?"

I was 41 years old at the time, so I wasn't totally confident I could even get pregnant at this point. It certainly wasn't a slam-dunk that it had worked. So we went about regular life for the next couple of weeks. But I was getting scared. Sean was messaging me, asking "Did you take the test? How are you feeling?" I took one test after two weeks, and it was negative. But I *was* having some symptoms of pregnancy. I wasn't feeling too well, and I was very tired. About a week after the negative test, I took another one—and it was positive.

Sean and I had made love one time, and the test was positive. I knew that was a divine sign. This baby was definitely meant to be—and it was definitely meant to be Sean's. Just like my guardian parents said.

VERY MIXED UP

Once again, I'll share the whole truth, as confusing or crazy as it might sound. The second I found out that test was positive, I was desperately wanting to be with Gabe. The thought of losing him completely was so overwhelmingly sad. I was going through so much. After the positive test, I pretty much ran into his arms, hugging him and telling him I still have feelings for him, and that maybe somehow we can still have a family together. He seemed to get excited and started to be sweet to me…for a few days.

It took me a few more days, but I finally worked up the courage to tell him that I was pregnant. He was definitely not happy that I had done this with Sean, even though we had talked about the baby surrogate issue. He had known I was going to see Sean. I was honest about it, pointed out that we're barely together any more, we're basically just co-workers and roommates in the same house, we're not being intimate, we don't kiss. I had told him, before going to see Sean, that I didn't see us having a relationship any more. And it wasn't my choice—I had tried, I had done everything I could to rekindle our intimacy. He knew that.

It took him a few weeks to get used to the fact that I was pregnant with someone else. But then he started to warm up to the idea. He decided that, yes, he could potentially act as the dad of this child and help me to raise her.

I had told Sean that, if I was pregnant, I would tell him face to face. So when the pregnancy test was positive, I didn't actually message him that, I just said, "I'm going to need to come see you."

I got a flight and went to see him again, just a few weeks later. We went to dinner, and I told him I was pregnant. He wasn't at all surprised. He said, "I felt it. I knew you were pregnant." He was so loving and excited. He was wonderful.

But, once again, it was like I was under some sort of spell. Suddenly, I had no feelings for him. I was spending the night at his house, because I had committed to stay there for a week. We would go on walks together; we did things together, we were in intimate, but I had really checked out.

We didn't communicate very well then, so I didn't talk about how I was feeling, and I don't think he knew.

Bizarrely, I just wanted to run back into Gabe's arms. I wanted to be where I felt secure, where I felt comfortable. So at this point, once again, I was extremely confused.

When I left, Sean said, "It's my turn to come see you." But he knew about Gabe, and he was still laying back, saying that he would play whatever role I wanted him to.

After I flew back home, I went back to life more or less as it had been. The beginning stages of pregnancy are rather easy. I kept working, dealing with those pesky audits that kept popping up, and *still* trying to salvage the relationship with Gabe, even though I knew deep down that it was deeply troubled, perhaps beyond repair. And yet…I thought "we *do* have a new life coming, and this is what he wanted. And maybe this is what we needed."

When I was about 14 weeks pregnant, I took a trip that to Seattle to see Dr. Richard Bartlett for his Matrix Energetics class. I had planned it before I got pregnant, and I saw no reason to miss it. In the middle of the first day of class, I started to bleed a little.

I have had two miscarriages in my life, and both had begun with this kind of spotting. I had never spotted with any of my full-term pregnancies. So I was really concerned. I was very afraid I was going to lose the baby. I left the room, where Dr. Bartlett was teaching to 300 people, called an Uber, and was waiting I the lobby for the Uber to come.

Suddenly I looked over my shoulder, and Dr. Bartlett was standing there. He asked, "How are you, Rebecca?" I was confused, like "Wow, where did you come from?" I said, "Actually, not too well. I think I may be having a miscarriage. I'm spotting."

He said, "Okay, let's see what's going on and what we can do." We stepped aside to a more private spot, and he tuned in. He tapped into my reproductive system, "went into" the womb, saw what was wrong, and fixed it right there with his energy work. He said, "Okay, you should be good. The vitality is good now." Wow—I was so grateful.

I still went to the hospital, though, because I wanted to get it checked out and just make sure. And just as Dr. Bartlett had said, the heartbeat was fine and everything looked good. I could not have felt more blessed. Dr. Bartlett would turn out to be a major godsend to this child, my pregnancy, and the way things unraveled (and they did unravel!) and then resolved for me in my life. I knew I was divinely protected, and Dr. Bartlett's perfectly-timed gifts were a prime example of this. I was meant to be in his class at that very time. And again I was affirmed in my conviction that this baby was *so* meant to be.

The confusing part around it all continued to be: who was going to be the "daddy" and help me raise the baby?

SEAN VISITS

About four more months went by, and now I was quite pregnant. Around then, Sean reached out to me and said, "I haven't seen you in too long! I want to spend time with you. Let's get together." So we did. He drove out with his dog, and we spent some time at Deep Creek Lake with our dogs and my daughter, and had a great time. I felt closer to him than I had when I had last seen him at his place in Michigan. With our dogs and my daughter around, and on my home turf, I felt more connected. He was very sweet.

But I still couldn't shake Gabe, either. Gabe was volunteering to go to ultrasounds with me. I had to go through genetic counselling, because of my age. He wanted to go to that so that he could be there to support me. He was showing me his support, telling me how excited he was to be part of this child's life.

I started having more contact with Sean, because he was the father of the baby, and he was really excited as well. During my fifth and sixth month of pregnancy, I would invite him to see me occasionally. I was hosting holistic fairs in Rockville, and he would fly out and help out. (Gabe was so out of it that he didn't even know that Sean was coming out to help me with the fairs.)

Although Sean was loving and totally supportive, our communication could have been better. He could've been more open with me about how he felt (which, I later learned, was that he really just wanted to be with me and the baby), and I could've asked him more direct questions, too. He didn't say "Rebecca, I love you, and I want to be with you and this baby," he was just going along with the situation. It was supportive, but also passive.

We didn't really talk too deeply about these things. Maybe it's because he knew how confused I was, or that I had to work these things out for myself. Maybe he was scared. And I don't know if it would have changed anything at the time if he *had* been more declarative. Even as I was having these sweet times with Sean, and even though he was the biological father, I kept pushing the relationship with Gabe.

DARKNESS DESCENDS...AGAIN

So around mid-pregnancy, I was having sweet times with Sean, and Gabe was being supportive also. It was still confusing at times and certainly an unorthodox situation, but we all seemed to be going along with that.

Then, as I got into the third trimester, full-fledged darkness starting to emerge from Gabe. Paranormal, deeply disturbing events began to occur.

I was probably about 7 months pregnant when I started to get very concerned. There were dark energies in my house that even my older children were seeing. My oldest child started refusing to stay there, because he said there were "eyes" staring at him. My second-oldest child said he saw something move into the house. I couldn't ignore this—I knew my kids weren't crazy. I had an eerie feeling too.

Gabe was still staying downstairs. We were not sleeping in the same bed, we were not being intimate. If we were any sort of couple, we were a platonic couple. We were never intimate after I got pregnant (and again, had not been intimate for 19 months before I got pregnant). I'm not even sure now as I think back on it *how* I thought we were going to work as a couple or family. I just really wasn't thinking clearly at all; I was just doggedly stuck on seeing through this *idea* of me and Gabe.

But even that started to crumble when I began to feel this dark energy—and my kids actually *saw* it.

And then, something even more chilling happened.

I started to hear him talk to the voices he heard. The worst part was, *I heard the voices talking back to him!* It finally dawned on me: it *wasn't* that he was schizophrenic and talking to voices that he *thought* he heard—he was *really talking to some kind of beings that were there.*

I put a baby recorder downstairs at one point and recorded what he was doing. He was talking to these beings and saying things like "Well, she's human. Humans have to do it this way." And whoever they were, they were giving him instructions. I heard a voice that wasn't his, and I was extremely scared.

I really didn't know what to do because, periodically, I would get angry and frustrated and tell Gabe to leave the house, and he simply absolutely refused to. He would get mean again, his eyes would change to that cold vacant opaque blackness, and he would say "I'm not leaving you." I felt helpless and trapped.

During this time, one of my best friends came over and was observing the situation. I didn't even really tell her exactly what I'd heard. Later she came to me and said, "Do you know that he's talking to Greys?" I was dumbfounded. "What?" She said, "Yeah, he's talking to Greys. I can see that stuff, and they're giving him instructions about what to do."

This was a lot to take. I still didn't know much about the whole alien or reptilian scene, although there is actually a lot of evidence. I wasn't exactly sure what Greys were, or what was going on. I'm still not 100% sure exactly who or what he was talking to. But *something* terrible was going on; he was talking to some kind of entities. I knew that much. I started to become truly weary, as well as scared.

COMING TO A HEAD

My next ultrasound was at WVU. When I received the test, they told me that the baby's head was going to be too small and that this might be a sign of mental retardation. I thought about that energy that appeared to be lurking in my house. And I knew that something had to change, because this was dangerous for the baby and maybe for me.

It just so happens that I had another Matrix Energetics seminar scheduled with Dr. Richard Bartlett a month after that ultrasound. Prior to that seminar, Dr. Bartlett had never worked on people individually in his hotel room. He's a very popular person during these seminars, and many people would love his help. But usually he just teaches the seminar, goes back to his hotel room, and we see him the next day in class.

Oddly, this time, he announced to everyone that he'd be doing private sessions after class. His secretary walked up to me and said, "Hey, Rebecca, do you want me to schedule you as one of the first people? This is going to fill up really fast." I was again feeling blessed at the timing and the support. "Yes! I do."

Also around that time I had hurt my knee. I had been hobbling around, so I needed that healed as well. With the situation regarding the baby's head being too small, I had focused my energy work on the baby. But I was wrapped up in my own ego at the time, and it's pretty hard to do energy work when you're not in your heart center; I had certainly lost touch with mine by then, to a great and unfortunate degree. I was too stressed and scared to be effective.

So I went to Richard's hotel room. He had a colleague also there assisting, and the colleague said, "What is all this emotional stuff that's going on? There's a lot of emotional stuff going on around you." I said, "Well, I have a lot of audits at work popping up out of nowhere. Based on the actions of the guy I'm with—the way he's billing and licensing his program. It's really stressing me out." And I explained about the baby's head as well. The colleague said, "Okay, that emotional stuff is in your knee as well. We need to get it out of there." They both worked on me simultaneously, and I felt my knee go completely back to normal.

Then Dr. Bartlett touched my womb and he said, "Okay, her head is going to be fine. I'm going to fix it right now." He put his hands on my womb area. At the same time, his colleague asked if she could give me downloads from a very high frequency. I agreed, and it was intense. I had never felt downloads like that in my entire life. They were going through my crown chakra, and my whole entire body was convulsing. I could feel "threads" of light and energy course through me. It was extremely high frequency. It felt amazing! But my whole body was shaking, and Dr. Bartlett was holding the womb space and saying, "This energy is going into the baby's crown chakra."

After it was over, I sat up. Even though I knew that everything that had just transpired was aligned with my guardian parents' frequency and was in my highest and best interest, for the greatest good—whatever that was—I felt what I can only describe as a sense of *doom*. I knew that whatever had just happened *was* going to help me—*but not in a way that I wanted*. Or at least, not in a way that my ego at the time wanted.

I looked at Dr. Bartlett and I asked him directly, "What will be the consequences of this healing?" And he knew what I meant. He only said, "You're going to be okay."

I knew my highest and best interest—and that of my child—would be served. What had to be done in that best interest, I was apparently unable to do on my own at this point. The universe would now do for me what I had lost the strength, clarity, and will to do. I could have and should have gotten up and left Gabe at this point (not to mention the work that I no longer loved), but I didn't. So it had to happen the way it did. It had to change—and it would. But I knew intuitively that it would get worse before it got better.

A couple of weeks later I went back to WVU for another ultrasound. They asked me, "Why are you even here? The baby's head is fine. They shouldn't have even scheduled you." I was so deeply grateful to Dr. Bartlett and his colleague.

I left there feeling like a million bucks. I then reached out to Sean and told him everything I knew at that point—about the baby's head, the healing with Dr. Bartlett, and the strange and terrifying happenings at home. He was extremely concerned about the dark stuff that was going on around me, but happy about the healing to the baby's head. He said, "You're more than welcome to come live with me, or I'll come there if you need me, just let me know." He still wasn't trying to tell me what to do.

LESSON

Once again, as I write I can see things that are probably very clear to you as a reader. Maybe you're saying "This was right in front of your face. Gabe was terrible for you and the baby, whatever was in him or whatever he was tangled up in. Sean was amazing. Gabe was toxic and destroying your work as well as hurting your baby. You didn't see this?"

But I didn't see it at the time, because there was too much right in front of me. Now, as I'm telling the story, it's obvious that my ability to think clearly—at least on certain levels—was wiped out at that point in my life. I could function day to day, obviously take care of my clients and patients and my kids, and to some degree, myself. But some key pieces of self-preservation were absent. I had huge blind spots about the harm that I was allowing to unfold around me, in large part due to the toxic spell that Gabe (and his entities) were weaving around me.

Whether you think you're dealing with dark energy and reptilian forces—or just a sociopathic narcissist—the key to staying safe and making healthy choices is to be grounded in your heart center and thinking with your heart, and to completely unconditionally love yourself. These kinds of toxic and nefarious energies can be powerful and even addictive. Many people who have been through this have the same struggle I did—not being able to see clearly or get away from it. It doesn't matter how many friends tell you, "This isn't good for you"—at some level you know that, but It's like you're in some sort of trance. Somehow, it feels like this toxic yet spellbinding, alluring "love" is the only love that is going to make you happy, and you'll go to any lengths—often to the point of total destruction—to hold on to it. You don't trust that there is a more pure, innocent, and true from of love that would come for you.

But if you already love yourself unconditionally, you're protected, because you can't be hooked into this sort of scheme. You're already filled up, so you have no need to look outside yourself for some kind of love—and you hold yourself in too high a regard to allow abuse and toxicity. Plus, sociopaths and narcissists have something common with more paranormal forms of darkness—they simply can't thrive around (or even get access to) a pure heart, a space of self-love and self-regard. There's no oxygen for the dark energies in that environment of goodness and truth. In a sense, your self-love and pure heart make you virtually untouchable. If you're truly connected to Light, that Light will put out the dark, or cast it away.

I came to learn and understand this, and I did find my way. Unfortunately, I did it via the hard road, and it was a rocky journey to say the least—although, ultimately, profound and triumphant.

Chapter Eight

I WAS COMING TO THE END OF MY PREGNANCY, and things were getting crazy and scary. I had been in a whirlwind of confusion and indecision, with a growing dread about paranormal and negative energies in my home. I was elated that my baby's head was going to be okay, thanks to the work of Dr. Bartlett and his colleague, but I felt like we were barely keeping ahead of the all the dark and toxic influences.

I woke up one morning at this time, and some clarity pierced through all the fog. I realized that it was simply not okay that Gabe was living with me while talking to heaven knows what downstairs—reptiles, aliens, dark energies, whatever they were. He was talking to *something*—and it was answering. I was pregnant with what was clearly a divine child, and I had my other children in the house (who frankly were divine to me as well). My daughter, especially, had heard him—and *them*—and she was really frightened. I had to get him out.

I knew he was going to throw a fit. I knew it was going to be a big ordeal. We were working together in the practice. And he had this completely irrational sense of entitlement that it was "his" house and that he had a "right" to be there. But finally, I worked up the courage and confronted him. I asked him to leave.

As I expected, he flatly refused. I told him, "Look, I'm scared! I have these recordings of you. I don't know who you're talking to. It's strange and crazy. I can't have this going on here. I really need you to leave."

And he wouldn't. He crossed his arms and said, "No way." He raised his voice and said, "I'm not leaving." No matter what I said, this man was not leaving my home. And he denied the voices. Even when I told him I had recordings—which made him angry—he denied it. He wasn't physically aggressive, but he was shouting.

In despair, I said, "I'm going to the police. If you won't leave, I'm going to have to have you removed." He simply ignored me and said, "I'm going back to my apartment." He had his own apartment in the house, basically—a mother-in-law suite. And he had all kinds of crazy rationale for why this was *his* house, *his* stuff. My daughter overheard all this too, and became even more scared.

That did it for me. That very night, I went to the police. I took the recordings. The way it works is you go to the sheriff's office and file a domestic restraining order. They sent me to the commissioner's office. The commissioner was a woman and she had gone through something similar—I mean, likely not reptilian energies, but a domestic violence situation. So she was sympathetic. She and the sheriff listened together, and they thought it was pretty alarming.

Of course they weren't thinking about aliens, Greys, or dark entities. It sounded like Gabe talking and then him answering himself in a different voice. But that was incriminating enough. They said, "Wow, that's crazy, we need to get him out of there." They were concerned enough to approve an emergency petition. It was really major.

I went to a hotel that night so I didn't have to be there when they came for him, My kids were with my ex. So I don't know what the scene looked like, but I'm quite sure it wasn't pretty.

When they removed Gabe, they actually brought him to a psychiatric hospital. That was a miracle, since it had been so difficult to get him committed previously. I immediately called his brother, who was still trying to help too. His brother talked to the doctor. I went to the hospital. I talked to some social workers who were not very experienced, trying to explain. They barely listened to the recording. I asked to speak to psychiatrist, who simply said we have to evaluate and see how he does. The psychiatrist didn't listen to the recording at all.

Gabe stayed for two days at the hospital. Then, incredibly, the psychiatrist told me there was nothing wrong with Gabe and released him. Once again, he had this astounding ability to fool mental health professionals, to seem sane. He could immediately shift. He had fooled so many psychiatrists.

After that, he went to live in a hotel. But he didn't have any money. His brother paid for the first ten days of the hotel. His brother wanted Gabe to come back to Santa Barbara where the rest of the family was. But of course, Gabe refused. He was insisting on staying in Cumberland, closer to me, even though couldn't get near me because of the restraining order.

After ten days his brother stopped paying for the hotel. The hotel called me. Some of the staff, bless them, has actually pooled their money and paid for a few more nights for him, because he was sitting in the lobby and it was raining and they didn't want to kick him out. They were the sweetest hotel staff ever.

Finally, though, they were going to have to boot him out. In desperation and defeat, I gave them my credit card. I was afraid if they made him leave, he'd just come straight back to my house, restraining order or not. They gave me a discounted rate.

The police informed me that they could not remove Gabe from the practice, from his place of work. They could remove him from my home, but not from the office. But after two weeks of him coming to the office from the hotel, it was clear he was mentally incapable of working, and I fired him. He didn't care at that point; he wasn't fighting for his job then. He was doing things like sitting and starting at the creek behind the hotel in a daze. So for the time being, I didn't have to deal with him at all.

At this point I was getting close to the end of my pregnancy. Gabe lived at the hotel for two more months, and I didn't see him.

CONFUSION, VACILLATION, ESCALATION

During that same two months, after I kicked Gabe out of the house, Sean stepped forward and said, "Okay, do you want to do this? Do you want to make this work? You and I can make this work. I can come live with you. I'll quit my job, find another job, help with the baby. We'll be a family."

I felt so torn, though I obviously shouldn't have. I mean, I had looked at Sean the very first time and fallen in love with him at first sight. I'd felt so strongly about him, had such a powerful response to him, such a feeling of fate and knowing him. Before all the Gabe stuff, Sean felt like "the one"—even though at the time, he wasn't returning the feeling. And now here he was, wanting to be with me—and we were having a *baby*, for heaven's sake!

Yet, at this point, I was just questioning everything. I had been through so much. I was overwhelmed. I was very pregnant. And significantly, I didn't want to be with a man who just wanted to be with me because we had a child together and he thought it was the right thing to do. I really wondered about that, because he hadn't actually come out and said, "I love you and want you, Rebecca." I mean, yes, he had said a lot of beautiful things to me at the theta healing seminar, but that was back in 2013. Now it was 2017, I was pregnant with his child, and although he had been very willing to go along with the whole plan and support me throughout, I still wasn't really sure he wanted *me*. I did worry that it was more out of duty and responsibility than love for me.

It didn't help that although he kept offering to make it work between us and be a family, he also talked frequently about his ex-girlfriend. It was extremely strange at the time, and it hurt, as I sat there pregnant with his child. I do understand now this was his way of putting up a barrier, keeping distance between us, avoiding getting hurt. This became a big issue later, as you'll find out. At this time, it was just so confusing. He was so great in so many ways, so attentive and attuned and caring in most ways—but then he would tell me he'd had a sexy dream about his ex.

I was in so much shock, going through so much, I just didn't say anything about it at the time. I didn't feel equipped to address it with him and figure out what was going on. We didn't talk through things as much as we should have, and it was a long time before we did. Years later, a lot of this emerged. We still had a lot to work out.

Still, in spite of my confusion and hesitation, I did actually accept his offer, because it was so generous and helpful and kind, and it did seem to make sense. So he made all the arrangements.

And then…I just got so scared. I felt like I couldn't go through with it.

I'm not going to lie, even though I know how it sounds at this point. Part of me was *still* thinking about Gabe. The only way I can explain it is that I was still under a dark spell. It *was* incomprehensible. Here I had just gone to all these lengths to have him removed from my home by the police, after he was talking to entities in my basement and even my kids were picking up dark energy. And yet somehow, I *still* thought, "Maybe, there's a chance that Gabe is going to come back. Maybe he's going to get better. If I have Sean in the house, then that's not going to happen."

So I told Sean he couldn't come after all. Understandably, he was extremely upset. He had quit his job and his bands, and made all the preparations to come and move in with me. He'd packed up his house. I felt absolutely horrible, yet I just felt like I couldn't go forward when I was so unsure. I tried to force myself to go through with it, but I just couldn't.

At this point, the baby was going to be born in just a few weeks. I was shocked when Sean still wanted to come for the birth of the baby. He would have been completely within his rights to walk away from the whole mess at that point. I had put him through an unreasonable amount. It says a lot about his love and commitment that he stuck with me on this. I should have been able to see that as real love—even if it wasn't all there yet verbally—but I was so mixed up at that point.

GABE GETS CRAZIER

Meanwhile, also to my shock, I was served with court papers from Gabe contesting the restraining order, contesting the fact that he "can't come live in his home"—and, outrageously, questioning the paternity of the baby. There was obviously no biological way that this could have been his baby. It was bizarre and mean and adversarial, but I had no choice but to go to court.

The judge upheld the restraining order, confirming that Gabe was not allowed in the home. Regarding the paternity question, it was so strange. I stood there extremely pregnant, ready to give birth in a couple of weeks, and Gabe was saying, "That's my child!" I stated to the judge, "Actually, this is not his child. We were not intimate for almost two years during the time I got pregnant, we know who the father is, and there is no way that this can be his child."

Of course, a paternity test would have confirmed this, if it had come to that. And Gabe had to know that—he had known all along the baby was Sean's. I could not figure out what his angle was here, or who he thought he was kidding. Was he truly going crazy? I'm still not sure, but I think at this point he really was crazy enough to think the baby was his—just like he thought the house was his.

Even though realistically the judge had no proof we hadn't been intimate for two years, he was pretty sharp. He could see who was sane—who was who and what was what. So the whole thing was resolved pretty quickly. He upheld the restraining order and said, "get out of here."

WHY DOES HE WANT THIS CHILD?

Although Gabe didn't succeed with his blustery ruse, what I started to see was just how overpowering his need was to be the "father" of that child. All along, I had bought his "I just want to be a family, family is the most important thing now" line. But he was so hell-bent on getting back into the house and with that baby, I finally began to suspect that there was more to it. I still didn't understand exactly what that was, but I knew Gabe's intentions were not exactly fatherly, loving, or benevolent.

There was something about this child. I knew she was special. She had a purpose here. She had been "taken" once, and my guardian parents had helped me get her back, and other angels (like Dr. Bartlett) had helped me keep her well through the pregnancy even when things kept seeming to threaten her. I knew she was probably going to have abilities. Did Gabe really want to be a dad—or did he and whatever he was mixed up with want to "use" her for something? It was dark and creepy, but it was starting to make sense.

I was scheduled to be induced on July 6, 2017 to have this beautiful child. Again, to my surprise (and utter gratitude), Sean drove down and was there by my side while I was giving birth to the baby. He held my hand. In spite of all the upset and drama about the move, it was a beautiful moment. She was absolutely breathtakingly gorgeous when she was born. Sean immediately took his shirt off and they bonded together, skin to skin.

Sean ended up staying for about two weeks after the birth. He'd gotten another job by then, but he took time off. It was remarkably cozy, considering how resistant I had been to him moving in with me. It was really easy to be with him, and he was so sweet with me and the baby. He was still very affectionate, even after the hell I had put him through. We were watching our favorite shows together, living as though we would live if we were a couple. We weren't intimate because I couldn't be after the birth, but he was lying in the bed next to me, cuddling.

I remember at the end of two weeks, when he had to leave, I was despondent to see him go. I had really started to feel like I was in love with him again. Yet that also still scared me tremendously. It seemed like whenever I felt that love for him, there was some sort of energy that pushed against it, *something* that did not want that. I remember feeling this huge block, like something immovable stood between me and him. It didn't make any sense, but it felt totally real. (And now, I think it *was* real.)

Unfortunately, after Sean went home, I did start to see Gabe again. We started talking again. I was still under that spell. It was indescribable and crazy. I was just not ready to let him go. I wanted to be, but I wasn't. I rationalized. I began to bring Willow, my new daughter, to see him at the hotel—just for about an hour, twice a week.

Gabe never wanted to be alone with her, and I wouldn't have allowed that anyway. He had no genuine fathering instincts. He was so awkward. He held her and said she was beautiful. But he obviously was not and would never be a good father.

Yet I *still* felt this pull to him.

Sean did come back frequently to visit, as much as he could, and I would bring Willow to *his* hotel. He would swim with her, play with her, care for her—he really was an amazing, loving father. He was trying as hard as he could to be a good dad and a good man. He would even bring his own dad down with him sometimes, Willow's grandpa, which was darling. His dad is phenomenal, and from the beginning he and Willow had an amazing connection. But we were never able to all be together as a family.

Sean was putting up with so much—more than anyone would consider reasonable. I was still uncertain about his feelings for me and mine for him, and I wasn't in an emotional, spiritual, or mental place to have a relationship with him at that time anyway. But he was good and kind, and I had loved him at one time, and had glimmers of possibility with him—and he was Willow's father.

Each time Sean went home, I would continue my life. I continued to work; I hired a nanny to help me. My sisters, mom, and 11-year-old daughter also helped. My daughter loved Willow, and they had a lot of special moments together.

Willow was the best, easiest baby. She started sleeping through the night in her second week. She always played happily by herself. She was easygoing, always smiling and laughing, so loving. She was always way ahead of her milestones—a sophisticated talker who could get up in front of a room full of adults and lead. I was totally in love with her, and I was really enjoying her.

WORK GETS WORSE AND HOME GETS WEIRDER

When Willow was four months old, I did something that I know will sound appalling and incomprehensible. I was still clearly locked in the "spell." I actually ended up inviting Gabe back into the house.

It was Thanksgiving 2017. I felt like I still loved him, and I felt like the dark energies were gone. When I would go see him at the hotel, none of that "talking to others" was happening. He talked to invisible people constantly when he was living with me. Now he seemed sedated at first, and then calm. *Almost* normal. Distracted, but I didn't sense those beings around him, and he showed no signs of communicating with them. (When I reflect back on it, I think they may have receded so that I *would* bring him back.)

I thought maybe now that the baby was born, and he seemed better, we could be a family. Of course, he sat down and looked at me and said that was exactly what he wanted.

But then he said, "I'm just scared about her father being in the picture. Maybe I'll fall in love with this child and then he'll come and take her, and that would just destroy me."

Stupidly, I actually decided that I needed to protect him from that. I thought, "Okay, I'm going to make sure that Gabe gets to spend time with Willow, that she knows Gabe as well as Sean." So, from the time she was four months old till she was about a year old, Gabe was again living downstairs.

But although I tried to encourage the connection he said he wanted, the fact is that his actual engagement was lackluster. In spite of what he said about wanting to be a family and falling in love with her, he really wasn't there. He wasn't like a father. He wasn't that interactive. He would sit with her on the swing set, and he sat with her at the hospital when she had RSV. He really helped her when she was sick. There was a part of him that I felt wanted to be family. He just didn't know how to do it.

Once he moved back in, we remained very separate, with him spending a lot of time in his suite downstairs. There was no intimacy. I'd get a kiss on the cheek, a hug. We would cook, do the dishes, watch TV. But once again, like back in Santa Monica, he was a robot going through the emotions. There was a little inflection, but a lot missing.

I made excuses for it, desperately clinging to hope still. I kept thinking: he's in shock, he has PTSD, he's trying to get himself back. I was in saviour mode. If I could just get him back…

He wasn't scary at this time, at least. The kids were going along with it. They thought he was strange, they even took a little advantage of him (like before, he'd take them anywhere they asked) but they weren't scared.

Meanwhile, Sean would still come when he could, but this arrangement made it awkward for Sean too. He didn't come to the house because Gabe was there. So I continued to bring Willow to him at a hotel for his visits.

You would think Sean might have objected to my bringing Gabe back in, especially in protection of Willow, but he was just not a "put his foot down" kind of guy. This actually would become a real issue for us—that he wouldn't tell me what he thought, or what I should do. The little we talked about it, he just said, "I can't stop you. And I trust you." But he tended to repress his feelings. He didn't have the ability to say how something hurt him. At the time, he seemed disappointed, but reluctantly went along with it. (This also made me think he didn't care that much.)

TRYING TO WAKE UP

After a whole year of this, I started to kind of wake up again a little bit. Once again, those doubts: "What am I doing?" "What is happening here?" It penetrated my awareness how strange things were. There was such a lack of connection with Gabe. It wasn't getting better. We'd go to an outdoor concert, and it was like he was just half-alive next to me. It was very lonely. I started to see that part of him was dead, and I finally realized it wasn't coming back.

One day around this time, I left my house and got in my car to go pick up Willow from Sean's hotel, and on the way there I called a psychic to whom I had been referred. I normally don't follow psychics who do future-type readings, because I believe we have free will and we can create our futures. In my own work, rather than simply foretell someone's future—which is not set, but rather based on the current trajectory—I also work with what the person *wants* to create. By healing trauma, opening certain doors, and learning practices, we can shift timelines and get you where you want to be. But if a psychic foretells your future and you believe it, you might create that future by default—simply by playing out your belief—when in fact you could actually manifest something different.

Nevertheless, a client of mine said, "you *have* to call this guy," and intuitively, I wanted to talk to this one. (This client was also the one who had recommended Richard Bartlett, so I was inclined to trust her recommendations—I believe both Richard and this psychic Nathan were sent through the client by my guides.)

Nathan was in England. I was blown away by how tapped in he was. He knows names of people in your life; he knew things he could not possibly have known. I was impressed.

I decided to have him read me romantically. It was very quick—because he was so expensive, it was typical to simply have ten minutes with him. He identified that I had two men in my life. He asked, "Who is the one with dark hair and tall?" That was Sean. He said, "You're going to end up with him. You will live in a lake house."

He didn't say much more in our short session. But oddly enough, when I went to go pick up Willow, I noticed right away when I saw Sean that I had feelings for him again. It was as if that prediction had opened a door, or granted some permission. Even Sean noticed the difference in me immediately—he commented that my hug felt different.

This all coalesced about the same time. I was feeling done with Gabe. I finally saw that it was going nowhere and I was getting nothing. He felt this, of course. And it began to bring out some of the old ugliness, the mean and dark side. When he felt that he was losing me, I believe that this was where the dark energy began rising up and coming out again. The malevolence was back in his eyes. It was scary, but I felt more determined this time.

MOUNT SHASTA

Right around then, I had a really good friend invite me to Mount Shasta to visit her. She's very spiritual, and it was like she knew that I needed to talk to her. I thought, "I could really use this break. I'll take Willow to Sean, and he can watch her while I go to Mount Shasta."

So I did that. When I left to drive to Michigan and drop Willow with Sean, I had a huge fight with Gabe in the driveway, I told him, essentially, that it was over. I said, "I can't do this any more. I'm supporting you and getting nothing out of it. There's nothing here any more." He was furious, screaming at me, "You're not leaving me!" There was no reasoning with him. I just pulled out and drove away.

Again, when I dropped Willow off with Sean, my feelings for him were a million percent stronger. Something had turned. We slept together before I went to Mt. Shasta. He was going to sleep in another room, but then he asked if he could just lie down with me. I said yes, and he cuddled a bit. I rolled on top of him and said, "I've missed you." And he said, "I've been here the whole time." I didn't say much else about what was changing in me now, and I'd said a lot of things that didn't pan out—but I think he got that things were shifting. I was showing him, more than telling, that I was ready.

When I was with my friend Lara in Mt. Shasta, she asked me what was going on. I caught her up, as it had been a while. I poured it all out, explained the whole entire situation—Sean, Gabe, Willow, the dark energy, the voices, the audits. She listened intently. She was especially keyed in on the part about Gabe talking to the voices. She asked, "Do you have those recordings of Gabe talking to these voices?"

When I said yes, she continued, "There's a guy named Simon Parkes in England who deals with these reptilian Grey energies. I want you to reach out to him." She said he normally has a three-month waiting list, but she suspected that if I sent him this information and he heard the recordings, he might get me in sooner.

So I emailed Simon right away and sent the recordings, since I had them on my phone. Not even three hours later, I received an email back from his secretary saying Simon wanted to have an emergency session with me. He wanted to do it that night, but with the time difference, I was sleeping when I got the email. By the time I got back to them the next morning, we couldn't get the actual session scheduled for another week.

REVELATIONS

Directly from my visit in Mount Shasta, a week later I went straight to Baltimore for a meeting with my lawyer at the Attorney General's office.

All through my pregnancy, the audits had not only continued but gotten worse—more and more frequent, and also more secretive. I didn't quite understand what was going on any more. The Attorney General's office continued to asked for documents, but their purpose became more oblique. I felt like something was going to be revealed, and I had no idea what it was.

Now this court date had been scheduled by the Attorney General's office. I really didn't know what to expect. I was a little nervous, but still not overly concerned. I felt like my attorney had a handle on things and that nothing too serious could be wrong, even though the extent of the audits had become unnerving. It seemed like it was just a paperwork snafu, so we thought we'd be okay. I knew from my lawyer that I was going to sign a guilty plea at this meeting, but the offense as I understood it was small—administrative.

Willow was still with Sean. I arrived in Baltimore, went to my hotel, and settled in. I was scheduled to have my call with Simon Parkes right before the meeting with the Attorney General's office. So this was going to be a very big day.

Bigger, as it turned out, than I had imagined.

As soon as we had introduced ourselves, Simon immediately asked, "Rebecca, show me a picture of this guy Gabe." We were on Skype, so I pulled one up from my computer. He took a long look at Gabe's photo and said decisively, "Rebecca, this man is practicing Dark Magic." That's what he called it—Dark Magic. A chill ran down my spine and I felt cold inside.

He continued by speculating that Gabe had given his soul up to these reptilian energies for some sort of purpose. He suggested that these energies had probably been attacking him and feeding on him for quite some time, which would be why his skin had turned to leather that time. There was probably a time when Gabe actually had fallen in love with me, Simon conceded. But that would have gotten him into trouble, because he probably had a mission to accomplish with me, and love was not part of that mission.

He concluded by saying, "You need to stay away from him, Rebecca. You're not going to help him. I'm telling you, it is a matter of life or death. You *have* to get away from this man." It was chilling.

He also stated that Willow was extremely gifted and that I would start seeing her major abilities by the time she was five, and that she needed to be protected.

I knew that Willow was gifted. She was born with a very interesting birthmark on her forehead. I'm certain it was the result of those high frequency downloads that had been given to her through Dr. Richard Bartlett. The birthmark would activate when she was emotional or crying or if she was in water. It would turn purple and her forehead would start pulsating. My other daughter, who was 11 at the time, used to say "Mom, I'm not watching her when her forehead does that," because it was so bizarre.

One time, I had given her a bath and put her on the bed, wrapped her in a towel, and walked out to get her bottle. This is a king-size bed, and there's no way that baby was moving. She couldn't roll over, she couldn't scoot. She was two months old. I came back from preparing her bottle and the towel was unwrapped, and she was lying on the ground, doing tummy time. She was crying in irritation, because when babies are two months old, they don't like to do tummy time.

I was stopped in my tracks. What had just happened? How did my baby get from the bed to the floor? There was no one else in the room to have moved her. I stared at her in disbelief. I even took her to the doctor a few days later because I was worried she might have fallen, and I wanted her checked. He examined her and said, "No, she absolutely did not fall off the bed." He grinned at me, probably thinking I was tired or half-crazy, and he said, "Maybe she'll tell you what really happened when she's about 16 years old."

I've always remembered that incident because I'm pretty sure that she actually levitated off the bed. I remember telling Sean that and he laughed, but he said, "I believe you. I believe it happened. It's just unusual." It *was* unusual. But he was really supportive with Willow about her abilities, right from the beginning. That was another great thing about him.

I had some other interesting things happen to me early in my journey with Willow. I had a healer from Rhode Island call me out of the blue and she said she psychically knew I was pregnant. This was about the time I was close to giving birth. She became extremely interested in me, offering me a large amount of money to come and help her heal. I remember being puzzled and suspicious that she wanted to pay me that much money just to come and do some healing work. I didn't understand what was going on. I declined to do this work.

Another woman, Melissa, who used to travel with me to various energy and healing seminars became very interested in my pregnancy and the baby. She was even advocating against Sean, telling me that Sean had "dark energy" and she didn't think he'd be a good father. I knew better. There was no question that Sean would be a good father. And unlike Gabe, there wasn't a dark thing about him. I just didn't understand why she was so against him, what her angle was.

After the baby was born, I was supposed to meet with Melissa for a meeting about creating a business together. I wasn't totally interested, but I was curious, so I agreed. I had a sitter watch the baby while I was driving to the meeting, which was 40 minutes away. She called me while I was on the way and asked, "Is Willow with you?" I said, "No, she's not." And she cancelled the meeting on the spot. She didn't want to see me unless Willow was there.

Those are just a few of several unusual circumstances where it seemed like the reason people wanted to spend time with me was because of Willow.

Through all of these experiences, along with Simon Parkes' assessment, I slowly and uneasily started to start to take a more sinister view of why Gabe was so obsessed with being an influence in Willow's life, even though he was far from a natural parent and didn't seem like he connected that well to human beings generally. I had allowed myself to believe that it was because he had such undying love for me, and wanted a family—as he'd professed.

But as Willow's gifts emerged and others commented on it, paired with the dawning ugly realization that Gabe really *didn't* care about me that much, I began to suspect that he—or that dark energy working in him or with him—thought it could *get* something from her. Or, worse, that wanted her... not there. Or wanted her not fully functioning (as with the smaller head). Even at this point, I wasn't sure of this (now I can see it much more clearly). But the seed of this idea started to grow, and it added to the unease.

FROM CHILLING CALL TO COURT

Meanwhile, I had to go to court straight after that call with Simon. My head was spinning. I felt sick and scared. "What have I done? And what am I going to do?" It was like the whole world was coming undone around me.

And the unraveling was not finished that day.

At the meeting, I learned that the Attorney General's office was going to press charges against me for not having the telemedicine program licensed correctly. Because of this incorrect licensure, every single service we had rendered via telemedicine was called into question because it wasn't technically licensed. Even though the people got treatment and medicine, it was considered fraudulent because we didn't have the right licensure. Gabe had been in charge of that licensure.

Furthermore, there were billing errors in the doctor's program that Gabe was overseeing. Gabe's name, however, was not documented on any of this. Everything was under my name. Everything on paper was signed by me. As I've explained, we had decided it was easier and faster this way. Gabe ran it, but I signed off. He would bring paperwork and have me sign it.

Even now, with these charges, my lawyer did not seem to think I was going to get into much trouble. He did not think the punishment would be severe. He thought he could explain the whole situation. With as much evidence as I had, all the employees at my practice who knew everybody's roles, we could demonstrate that it was an honest error rather than intentional fraud.

My attorney had known all along that I would have to plead guilty to one count of fraud. But he said that intent matters, and in this case there was no intent to harm or conceal. Real services were rendered to real clients. It wasn't like I had created a Swiss bank account to squirrel away funds, or faked services. So we expected a slap on the wrist of some kind—maybe a fine.

This plea bargain meeting was July 2018, not long after Willow had been born. This was the meeting where we agreed on the plea. In September/October, there would be a sentencing date, and that would be when I would learn exactly what the consequences would be for this charge.

In spite of all he had put me through—and the fact that I was dealing with all of this due to his negligence—in my spellbound caretaking and "love," I didn't want Gabe to get in trouble either. I didn't want to bring his name into it. It's kind of a classic "protect your victimizer" complex, but I was willing to take the heat for him even now. I still felt like he needed to be taken care of, and his mental health had been questionable since the psychotic break. I didn't want him to get nailed. But I didn't want to take the hit either. I just wanted the whole situation to go away.

I did bring it all to Gabe's attention when I got home. Unpleasantly, my care and worry for him was not at all reciprocated. He didn't seem to care that his mistakes and negligence had gotten me into so much trouble. He didn't care that I had just paid $50,000 to a lawyer because of his incompetence or carelessness. He really was just focused on himself and defending his own needs. He was especially obsessed with keeping his job. He kept saying, "You're not firing me. This is my job, I'm keeping it. This is what I do, this is how I make my money."

I told him, "You just got me into a lot of trouble. They're taking me to court for this. I'm going to be explaining what happened. I don't want to get you in trouble, but I'm going to be explaining what happened." He had a one-track mind. He just said, "Do what you have to do, but you're not taking my job!"

So I flew back to Sean's to get Willow and brought her home. When I got back, the weight of all of it finally whacked me straight in the forehead. Something broke. The audits, the court case, this man in my home who didn't seem to care about me even though I kept caring for him to an over-the-top degree, all the darkness in my home which now I sensed creeping back once again. I *finally* stopped in my tracks and said, "Something has to give. Something has to change. I'm miserable, I'm not even in love. I need to get out of this situation."

The power that Gabe had over me was something I've never felt before. The inability to permanently get away from this man was huge. I didn't know what it was going to take for me to get away from him. I just knew something had to change.

But once again, Gabe wouldn't leave my house.

ESCAPE

Now I was really stuck.

Here was Gabe, apparently practicing dark magic and heaven knows what. He had kept me tethered to him in spite of the fact that it had really been quite miserable for some time, and his supposed intentions for being with me and my family didn't really make sense or play out. He once again had no intention of leaving the house, and I had foolishly invited him back in after the restraining order. It had been hard to get him out in the first place. Now the police would not take me seriously, because I had become one of those women who "takes the guy back" after a restraining order.

I knew more than ever that I had to get out of this situation, and get Willow and my other kids out of this environment, and clean up my practice and work too. But I felt frozen, locked into a prison that I knew I had allowed to build around me.

Between the Mount Shasta trip and the September sentencing date, Gabe and avoided each other in the house. He wouldn't leave, and I was too ashamed and hopeless about bringing the police back into it. I just wanted to get past the sentencing and then figure out my next steps.

Since it was a 6,000-square-foot house and he had his own suite, as awkward and scary as it was, I was able to steer clear of him. Plus, I visited Sean a few more times during that couple of months, when my kids were with their dad. I was realizing I did love Sean, and this felt like it changed things. I was also in contact with Gabe's brother, who I hoped could help.

But I still felt trapped about how to get out of this mess with Gabe. He was mumbling to himself again, and after Simon's declaration about what he was doing, I began to be quite scared about how I would escape.

Remarkably, I was actually doing very well with my spiritual practice and energy healing work during this time. Even amid the craziness around me, my work was pure and good, and it was taking off. I remember thinking, "If there was ever an opportunity where I could completely get out of the mental health and primary care business, it would be now." Yet still, I didn't want to disappoint or hurt my family, and all the people working for me. I didn't even want to hurt Gabe, even with the terrible legal mess he had gotten me into and the threat he presented, which Simon had gravely warned me about. I was caught up in some terrible martyr game, sacrificing so much for so many others.

THE UNIVERSE FORCES MY HAND

Everything came to a head a few weeks later.

After that meeting with the Attorney General's Office, a court date for sentencing had been set for September 24. I trusted my attorney; I felt I had really good counsel. He was telling me not to worry too much about it. He had explained, "You've pled guilty to the paperwork being wrong, to errors that you were not aware of, which an employee made without your knowledge. Everything is going to be just fine. This will be a light sentence."

I hoped he was right, but of course, I was nervous. It was on my mind constantly. All the while, I was trying to watch Willow, somehow manage living with this cold angry dark man downstairs who I no longer wanted there, protect Sean from the absolute mess that was going on around me, and love Willow and my other kids in the way that they needed me to.

I will say that through all this, I did manage to be a good parent. I was very protective of my kids and especially Willow. My mother love was strong and centered. But I was stretched thin for sure, in all other ways, almost to my breaking point.

Finally, the court date arrived. That's when everything came to a head. That's when my life turned inside out. That's when my guardian parents stepped in and took over, when they said, "Enough is enough! This will not continue. We're going to change your life one way or another. If you're not going to make the changes you need to, as your highest self, we'll do it for you."

They did. And it was going to be a ride I could never have imagined.

LESSON

I had stopped listening to my guardian parents some time ago. I hadn't listened to them since the time they told me that Sean was supposed to be the father of the baby. I couldn't hear them any more because I was so in my ego. If you're lost in your ego, even if your guides are talking to you, you won't hear. They helped me anyway, as much as they could; they did put Nathan and Dr. Bartlett and Simon Parkes in front of me. Sometimes, your guides will go through other people to help you, even if you can't hear them or you dismiss them.

I did get pregnant with Sean's baby, per their instructions, but after that I was riding very hard the idea that Gabe was going to be a father figure to her and raise her as his own. That was not their guidance. That was my own will, and very out of step with the highest good. The guardian parents kept trying to guide me, but I was no longer paying attention. A higher aspect of myself had been trying to get me out of this situation in a healthy way, offering rescues, opportunities, and avenues. I had been stubborn and obtuse and confused (and spellbound). I had not taken any of the "outs."

Perhaps you've heard this parable: A man was stuck on his rooftop in a flood. He was praying to God for help. Soon a man in a rowboat came by and the fellow shouted to the man on the roof, "Jump in, I can save you. The stranded fellow shouted back, "No, it's OK, I'm praying to God and he is going to save me." So the rowboat went on. Then a motorboat came by. "The fellow in the motorboat shouted, "Jump in, I can save you." To this the stranded man said, "No thanks, I'm praying to God and he is going to save me. I have faith." So the motorboat went on.

Then a helicopter came by and the pilot shouted down, "Grab this rope and I'll lift you to safety." To this the stranded man again replied, "No thanks, I'm praying to God and he is going to save me. I have faith." So the helicopter reluctantly flew away. Finally the water rose above the rooftop and the man drowned. At that point he got a chance to discuss the situation with God, and he asked, "I had faith in you but you didn't save me; you let me drown. Why?" To this God replied, "I sent you a rowboat and a motorboat and a helicopter, what more did you expect?"

If you don't pick up the cues and signposts the universe gives you, it will get louder and more insistent. I recommend paying attention and doing all you can to heed the guidance that you're given—and take the hands that are offered you out of a bad situation, if you can discern that they're benevolent. It's hard work to surrender to guidance—or *distinguish it from that of your ego—but a spirit-driven rather than ego-driven life is so much more authentic and satisfying.*

I refused a good few boats and helicopters before I awakened to what was really going on . God, or source or the universe or my guardian parents, had to get a lot louder. Although it was hard, I'm grateful that they took matters into their own hands and pulled me to safety so I wouldn't drown—even though at the time, it didn't exactly look like a rescue.

Chapter Nine

IT WAS A BEAUTIFUL DAY IN OCTOBER. I REMEMber thinking how amazing it was outside. I was looking at the fall weather and breathing in the fresh air, and feeling *so* lucky at that moment that I could be in such a beautiful environment.

This was the day of my final court hearing in reference to the case against me brought by the Attorney General's office. The charges were fraud for not having the telemedicine program licensed legally and properly. Not having the right licensure allegedly made fraudulent every single service that we had rendered through telemedicine over a period of time. As previously mentioned, Gabe was in charge of and had set up that licensure. There were also questionable billing errors in the doctor's program that he was overseeing.

Yet his name was not documented anywhere—everything was under my name. Everything on paper was signed by me, because he had brought me paperwork and I had signed it without looking closely, so distracted at the time and foolishly trusting him.

Again, my lawyer thought he could explain away the situation, given the evidence I had and the employees at my practice who knew everybody's roles. He believed he could paint a clear picture of what had happened, and that I had been foolish but innocent.

I was not completely innocent. I knew that. I should have done many things differently within the practice. It was *my* practice. I should have taken care of all the paperwork myself, or looked at it all more closely. I knew Gabe was at loose ends. I felt repentant and ashamed. Still, I actually was not that frightened of the legal case or its ramifications, because I knew that I personally had not done what I was being accused of, and that I'd had no ill intent.

Before the court hearing began, which was a sentencing hearing, I understood that I would be pleading to one guilty charge of fraud. The paperwork that backed up the licensure was inaccurate, compromising the legitimacy of the billing of all of the services under the telemedicine umbrella. The services had been rendered, but the documentation was inaccurate. So I had pled guilty to having allowed that, and I had signed a sentencing memorandum that formally entered my plea.

On the same page I had signed to enter my plea of guilty to that one charge, there was also a list of other charges that were inaccurate and untrue. My lawyer had told me, "You're pleading guilty to one count of fraud, and that's all. It doesn't matter if you sign that paper, because you're only going to be charged with one count." So, I signed the document and was prepared to go forward with the court case.

In the courtroom that day, I looked around me and I was stunned to think of how many people were there because of me and the decisions that I had made up to that point. The prosecuting attorney, my attorney, the judge, a few other people from the prosecuting attorney's office. My friends, my family, even my students and my previous clients were there to support me.

For a moment, I felt terribly stupid for not doing things differently. I had been acting like a lovesick child in middle school, and had behaved irresponsibly just to keep the attention of a person I loved. An overwhelming surge of guilt came over me, as well self-loathing for being here at this time. I could see there was a great deal of shadow work to be done in the future, and I vowed to myself to do it.

Even after all of this, and the fact that his errors (along with my own carelessness in allowing them) had landed me here, I was still thinking of Gabe in the courtroom too. Oddly, I wished that he were there with me. Then I received a message—as always, in a very clear, sort of telepathic thought form—from my guardian parents that I was going to be safer after this court date than I'd been for a very long time.

So although it was an uncomfortable, embarrassing place to be, I felt confident that things were going to go pretty well for me.

The all-day court hearing was pretty clearcut. The prosecuting attorney made his case, my attorney made our case, everybody agreed that the paperwork for the telemedicine program was inaccurate, and I was guilty of fraud because my name was on everything and I had signed off on it. That was undeniable. The judge expressed concern that I had spent so much time in California, accelerating my spiritual growth and career, when my practice on the East Coast was suffering and being run by someone other than myself. He stated that that was irresponsible and neglectful. He asked me about my thought process at the time, and I was honest. I told him that I was not happy in that career, and I was developing a spiritual practice that I would eventually go into full-time.

My family, my friends, and even one of my students were sitting next to me. Several people testified on my behalf and referenced the amazing changes they had experienced in their lives because of my work. It was very emotional for me. My older sister even got up and testified, and said some things that I didn't even know that she felt, which were overwhelmingly sweet.

Since I had pled guilty to one count of fraud, there was going to be a sentencing at the end of the case. We were dismissed for about an hour and came back in the courtroom for the sentencing. All of us (my family, friends, clients, students and I) assumed I would be walking away with a very light sentence, barely any punishment. I was completely unprepared for what was about to happen.

When the judge sat down, I "saw" my guardian father etherically "walk into" the judge—like, my guardian father's spirit sort of amorphously merged into the judge's body. I thought for a second that I was just completely delusional from stress, but the student next to me leaned over and whispered "Did you see that?" I said, "Yeah, I did." And she said, "Oh my gosh, everything is going to be okay. You're going to be okay." I smiled. I agreed, because I knew that my guardian parents always looked out for my best interests. I knew that this was divine intervention.

But divine intervention doesn't always look like we think it will. When we don't listen to ourselves, when we don't follow our hearts, when we function out of fear and guilt and self-loathing and not loving ourselves, divine intervention sometimes has to take place in ways that sometimes are not immediately palatable to us, and may even seem counterintuitive—though you can be sure divine intervention has its reasons.

The judge looked right at me and pronounced that my sentence was one year in prison.

To say that everybody was stunned is an understatement. A wave of shock went through the entire courtroom. I was dumbfounded and aghast.

What's more, they were prepared to take me to jail right then. My lawyer stepped up and said, "She was definitely not expecting this, we're not prepared, we need time." According to my lawyer, what the judge did next is very rare (normally, the court will allow you no time to leave and return on your own recognizance; they will insist on taking you into custody). The judge stood up and said, "You have three weeks to prepare for incarceration." In three weeks I was to report back directly to that courtroom and they would put me into custody.

I was obviously incredibly upset. My friends, family and clients were hugging me and telling me that everything was going to be okay. But at that moment I felt like my world had been turned upside down. It was two days before my son's 16th birthday. I had a beautiful home with beautiful children and two beautiful dogs—with only three weeks to move out of the house, arrange custody for my children, and find someone to take my dogs. All the while knowing that I was going to be incarcerated.

One of my very best friends drove me home from the court hearing that day, and I barely remember the car ride. It was a two-and-a-half hour drive to my home from the courthouse. On the way home I called Sean, in tears, and told him what had happened. He told me that he would be at my house in the morning to support me and do what I needed. I remember my heart swelling because he was going to drop everything and drive for eight hours just to be there for me. I'd already put him through so much.

THREE WEEKS TO MOVE MOUNTAINS

A significant support that got me through the next three weeks of my life was microdosing on psilocybin. The night of the court hearing, I remember going to sleep exhausted and waking up, wishing that it had all been a nightmare. But quickly, I remembered it wasn't just a bad dream. I got up and started doing what I needed to do to make it through this. I think about that now and realize how important the microdosing was at that time.

When you microdose, you're in the here and now. You can focus on what you need to do. You're not thinking about your fears, and the shadow energies just seem to disappear. Plus, it opens up gateways to conscious manifestation. Mother Earth gives us so much that we need.

As I previously stated, I had a 6,000-square-foot home that I needed to sell after living there for 10 years. I had no desire to keep the house after all the dark energetic stuff that had happened there. I needed to put everything in storage. Sean agreed to take one of my dogs, and the breeder for my wolfdog agreed to take him for the year that I would be in jail. This breeder lived in Miami. My ex-husband agreed to take our three children full-time, and Sean pledged to create a loving home for Willow and live full-time with her. All of this, miraculously, ended up working out in just three weeks.

For the next three weeks, things went as smoothly as could be expected under the circumstances. I was even able to contact Willow's future doctor and daycare, and begin the paperwork and process for children who chose to be unvaccinated. Sean and I had agreed not to vaccinate Willow, and that was extremely important to me.

My children were remarkably supportive, as was my ex-husband. My family came up to help me every day, to pack and get prepared. I realized how loved I was by my mother and four sisters.

The morning after the court hearing, Sean showed up at my house, and this was the first time that he and Gabe had ever come face-to-face. Sean walked in and Gabe immediately confronted him and told him to leave and get out of his house. Sean said, "This is Rebecca's house, and she wants me here, and I'm going to stay." After staring each other down for quite a while, I goaded Gabe, "Go ahead and punch him!" knowing that it would have the opposite effect. Immediately Gabe backed down and walked down the front steps and outside.

He came back later, and he kept to himself. The house was ginormous and Gabe stayed in the downstairs living area, and Sean stayed upstairs for a few days after the sentencing to help.

Predictably, Gabe was not supportive during this process. He was only concerned about where *he* would end up and what *he* would do while I was in jail. By this time, I was his sole caretaker. So in spite of the monumental, arduous task and journey before me, during this three weeks that I had to rearrange my entire world, I made it my duty to take care of him right up until my incarceration, and to plan for his future as well. This is pretty much the epitome of martyrdom, and capped off the extreme subjugation I had allowed for years in this relationship. I don't recommend it, and I would never do again.

The day that I was supposed to turn myself in, Gabe came up to me in the morning and said, "I really need you to go shopping for me before you leave," and gave me a grocery list. It was such a stark, crazy, jarring wakeup (not that I should have needed another one!) about what his priorities were and how checked out he really was. It really helped to put things in perspective. He cared only for himself, and he wasn't even rational.

A WAKEUP CALL ABOUT THE MEDIA

This is also the event that showed me that the media is allowed to exaggerate and be dishonest. This realization ended up helping me drastically during future world events.

What precipitated this awakening was being smeared by one of my ex-employees, a nurse I'd had to fire because she and the lead practitioner could not see eye-to-eye and were fighting in front of the patients. She had been extremely angry at me for that decision, and now she took it upon herself to write her version of these events to the prosecuting attorney. My local newspaper then printed what she wrote.

I live in a very small town. When anything like this happens, it's front-page news and it's aired by the local radio stations. Of course, we all know the wrath of Facebook and other social media. When I signed the document pleading guilty to one count of fraud, even though there were a lot of other items on that paper that were inaccurate and my attorney said it didn't matter, my signature gave the prosecuting attorney's office permission to publish those events in the newspaper. The disgruntled nurse was very creative in what she wrote to the prosecuting attorney, and did a very good job of exaggerating what happened. This tested my faith and my own boundaries greatly.

My 16-year-old son said, "Mom, I didn't even read it. I know you, I've lived with you, I love you, I know how beautiful you are, I know what an amazing person you are, I know what you're capable of." My two other older children were standing next to him, and all three hugged me. I knew I had the respect of the most important people in my life. Still, the public slandering hurt.

TURNING MYSELF IN

My entire family and Sean all rode the two-and-a-half hours to Baltimore with me to the courtroom that day when I went to turn myself in. We said goodbye with a sense of gravity and trepidation, but everyone was also thoroughly supportive. Everyone promised to keep in touch and encouraged me, "you're going to get through this." We hugged and it was hard not to cry.

I was handcuffed and I remember looking back at my family as I was led away, thinking that I would not see them for quite some time. I wondered what my life was going to be like. My family looked very concerned, loving, and sad. My mom would literally have taken my place if she could have. That moment will be forever etched in my mind.

From that point on, I was treated like a criminal (which I guess, according to the system, I was). I was first put in a holding detention center that was absolutely crazy. I will publicly say that that place should be shut down for many, many reasons. I can't believe, to this day, that women are forced to live this way—no matter what they had done, no one deserved to be treated that way. There were women in that place who had not been outside for more than two years, because of the way it's designed.

It's meant to be a detention center where you're held before you're moved to a permanent placement. Or you could be there awaiting trial. Some of the women in this detention center have been awaiting trial for over two years. It was like an oversized gym, filled with bunk beds side by side. Often the guards were too scared of the inmates to even walk up and down the floors and check on things.

I was so humbled by this environment. What I experienced during this process was absolutely traumatizing to me at the time. This was inner-city Baltimore. I had grown up in a very small suburban town, in an upper-middle-class family, an incredibly privileged situation where my comfort and safety was always ensured. We did not lock our doors at night. We could leave our bikes in the yard. I was extremely sheltered. I used to call hotels ahead of time to make sure that they had down comforters. I was very picky about the type of bedding I slept on, the type of conditioner I used for my hair, and so on.

Yet here I was faced with a room full of screaming women that looked like they were going mad. I remember thinking, "I don't know how I'm going to survive this."

But many, many things happened that were paranormal and magical during this process. And as terrible as this situation seemed, looking back now it's very clear the purposes it served and how I was protected and supported, as well as given ample ground on which to work out my lessons.

When I first entered this "holding pen," everybody was lined up for fingerprinting. After you're fingerprinted, you're supposed to leave within the next few days to go to your permanent facility. I was very tired; I had been up for a couple of days. A woman guard walked up to me and said, "Oh yeah, you've already been fingerprinted."

I *hadn't* been fingerprinted, but I didn't argue with her. I was so tired, and so out of it, I just let the comment pass. I had no idea at that moment the significance of that oversight and what it would lead to.

The next few weeks at this detention center in Baltimore actually changed my life forever. I started off very isolated. I remember hiding whenever I could on different bunks. Everybody was assigned a bunk, but the guards were too scared to actually enforce these assignments. So people would take your bunk when they felt like it and, if you didn't know the ropes, you were just kind of left to fend for yourself. That's what my first couple of days were like.

Than as I sat alone one day at a plastic table, writing, I heard my guardian parents in my head say "Go ask that girl if you can sleep above her." They were referring to a tall, tough-looking woman who looked like someone you definitely would not mess with. I said to my guardian parents, "I don't think so. I'm not going to ask for that." But I kept hearing it in my head, "Go ask her if you can sleep on the top bunk, go ask her if you can sleep on the top bunk."

I had learned my lesson regarding not listening to my guardian parents. So, as outlandish as it seemed, I listened to them this time. I walked over, very nervously, and I asked the woman timidly, "Do you mind if I sleep on your top bunk?"

She looked at me and her faced opened up in a beautiful smile and she said, "Oh my gosh! God must have answered my prayers!" She said she had been praying and putting salt around her area, commanding that all the negative energy be cast away. She was calling in positive energy. She said it was then that I walked over and asked to sleep on the top bunk.

Her name was Ashley, and to this day I still keep in contact with her. She was literally one of those angels you meet in a bad situation. She was in there because she had been raped and she had kicked the rapist down the stairs and he died. She was facing murder charges.

The first night that I slept on that top bunk, she made sure that I was extremely comfortable. She knew the ins and outs of that place. She got me the clothing that I needed; she even made me earplugs and eye covers so that I could sleep well. She was drawing beautiful art that she put around my bed. She told me not to worry. She said that she had been told—by *her* guides—that she would protect me, and that I would be okay.

Through this I realized that, despite my frustration, my sadness, and many other feelings and emotions, I was still being divinely protected, and this process would end up miraculous for me. However, I still did not expect what would happen the next morning.

I woke up the next morning and, as I looked at the women in this holding center, I saw their stories as though they were on a television show I was watching. I knew why they were there, and how to work on them so that they could have the best possible outcome to leave that place. I had never been so psychic in my entire life.

The general theme of all stories I saw had to do with women trusting men and giving themselves away to men—to a point that had driven them to a situation *this* undesirable. (Of course, that was true of me as well.) There were stories that were unbelievable. One woman had driven her boyfriend to a 7-Eleven and parked the car. She was unaware that he was going to rob the place. He got caught but because she was driving the car, she was an accomplice and was put in prison. Another woman was a yoga instructor whose boyfriend had sent guns and explosives to her yoga studio, so that he could pick them up at a "safe place." Because it was her studio, she ended up being the one charged with the crime.

These were the general themes of the "movies" I was "seeing" all around these women.

With one woman, I saw a baby that had been miscarried. I told her, "Your baby was miscarried and this was about three months ago." This was a pretty tough woman, and she looked at me in awe, and said, "Yeah, that's correct." I said, "This baby wants to come back. But the baby knows that you're thinking about going back with this man, and the baby is not going to come through until you figure out a way to love yourself enough to let him go." She was in tears and so thankful for the healing that I was making possible with this information.

Of course, through talking with these women, sharing what I was seeing and helping, I ended up becoming extremely popular in this place where I had been extremely scared just 24 hours earlier. I genuinely wanted to help in any way I could, because the movies that were appearing around the women were a gift, and not one that I had had before going into this place. I knew that I was supposed to help them.

Very quickly, I had lines of women lining up for help and information—to the point where my bunkmate, Ashley, actually started managing my hours. She would say "You can't bother Rebecca after 6 p.m." or "You can't bother her during dinner."

Others began to look out for me as well. I was put a situation where I was able to get lunch easily and effortlessly. The woman who was in charge of the phones actually came up to me and she said, "I don't believe in this stuff but I want you to do a reading and healing on me." After I was done, she said, "You can have any spot in the phone line that you want." At another point, I was holding my hands over my ears because people were screaming and yelling. It was about 2 o'clock in the morning, because there was no such thing as going to bed there. One of the women I had helped walked up to me and said, "Are you okay? If you want, I'll make everybody in here shut up." I said, "No, no, that's fine."

I believe my guardian parents, my guides, gave me this gift to help people—and at the same time, the gift was helping me, offering me protection. It wasn't a pleasant experience, it still wasn't easy, but it made me realize that my being there at that moment was important for my growth and the growth of those around me. I remember thanking the Universe, giving gratitude that I was given the gift of this sight so deeply and intensely, and that Ashley was put in my path.

Finally, after a few weeks, I realized that it was not normal that I wasn't being moved to the permanent place I should be going to. Everybody kept saying that when you got out of the holding center, you would be in a facility where you got to go outside and things would become a little bit more livable. So I was eager to be able to leave, even though I had connected remarkably well with the people around me.

One day, I walked up to one of the guards about two or three times asking about this, and finally she listened to me. She looked at her paperwork and said, "You've never been fingerprinted. You can't leave until you're fingerprinted."

So my not paying attention that first day when the woman thought I had already been fingerprinted had caused me to be there for a few weeks. Yet I also trusted that this has happened for a reason: so that I could stay there for as long as I needed to help these women, and also to learn what I needed to learn.

But the most important reason was yet to be revealed.

The next day I got fingerprinted. That same day, a woman named Danielle checked in. She was very quiet, kept to herself, and seemed like she didn't have much of a memory left. I began talking to her, and as she started to warm up to me, she became more coherent. She told me that she had overdosed on heroin about a year ago and had died. She was lying dead in a crack house when someone came in and resuscitated her. Ever since then, she said, sometimes she just "knows things." And she said, "You and I will go to the same place. Not only that, we're going to be put in the same cell." I said, "How can you know that?" And she said, "Trust me, I do."

It was the day after Halloween that I was lying in my bed and I heard my name being called, and I heard her name being called at the same time. I hugged Ashley and many other women that came up to give me a hug. I got my stuff and I was preparing to leave. One of the guards looked at Danielle and me and said, "Jails in Baltimore don't have any space left for women." They explained that Danielle and I would go to Jessup, which is a maximum security prison in Maryland where murderers are held.

Danielle looked at me and said, "Don't worry, I've already been there. I know that place inside and out. You're going to be fine." But I was extremely scared. I know what goes on in maximum security prisons, and I didn't know if I was prepared for what was about to come.

Before traveling to Jessup, our hands and feet were shackled as though we were Hannibal Lecter. We were put in a police car, and we were transported to the prison.

Danielle explained to me on the way that she had been in prison a couple of years back because she was on heroin and she was detoxing in a prison cell where they had put her for the night. As she was coming off the heroin, she had decided to steal one of the guard's clothes and escape. She said, "I was thinking irrationally. I was coming off of heroin, and I knew deep down that the plan wouldn't work." But she jumped on the guard and attacked her anyway. This earned her one year at Jessup. She had been put on probation after a year, but had violated her parole, which is what led to her being sentenced to more time in prison now.

Because she had previously been in Jessup for a year, she knew all the guards, she knew a lot of people, and she promised I would be okay and that she would watch out for me. So, if you can possibly feel better in a situation like that, that definitely helped me to relax a bit.

LESSON

IF WE DON'T LISTEN, THE UNIVERSE WILL INTERVENE

Lingering on with Gabe far, far past when I should have exited, I was stuck in a situation that I refused to get myself out of. I dug myself into a very deep hole by refusing to extricate myself from such toxicity and darkness. I wasn't listening to my guardian parents, I wasn't listening to my own intuition or my own channeling. When I look back at it, I can see how my insecurities were so deep, and my lack of self-love was so severe, that I couldn't let go of a toxic relationship that was literally ruining my life.

If we don't learn to love ourselves, the Universe will continue to bring us a mirror to show us the work we need to do. And if we don't listen to our higher selves, and what our heart knows to be true, then the Universe has no choice but to intervene in whatever way it has to in order to make sure that we are okay and safe.

For me, the resistance was so fierce, my lack of self-preservation so profound, and the spell or "dark magic" so gripping, that I literally had to be sent to prison in order to be separated from a toxic relationship that was going to destroy me. As harsh a move as that was, it was the wakeup call I needed to rise from the depths of my unconscious insecurity and self-aversion.

It didn't happen quickly. I still had a lot of waking up to do, even in prison. The paranormal events that happened while I was in prison were so intense and extraordinary that it took me a few years to be able to even process them.

I also learned that if you choose to worry about what other people think of you, that's going to put you in a place where you're unable to move forward. At the end of the day, the most important person to love you is you. There is not one person who says on their deathbed, "I wish I would have cared more about what others thought of me." And when you learn to release these shadow energies of unworthiness, self-loathing, and guilt, you will feel the people who truly love you come closer and closer to you. But it all starts with you.

The most important judge that we have is ourselves. Not our family, friends, teachers, students, or the judge in the courtroom. The person who matters the most is you. You ultimately can be the judge who sets yourself free. It took me a while to learn, but what you think of you, living up to your authentic self, and doing what your heart knows is right is what will set you free forever.

When clients talk to me about difficult times in their life and look at me as though I don't understand, because I seem successful and happy, I always refer them to this time in my life where I couldn't even see more than one inch ahead of me. Which—although it may sound strange—was actually a great way to live in the here and now, and to get through what I needed to get through.

What I can tell you—and I'll say more on this in future chapters—is that if you're going through something that you don't feel like you're going to survive, the best thing to do is to live in the exact moment that you're in and get through that exact moment, and then move on to the next thing that you have to do. You cannot think too far ahead of you, because your fears, your predictions, your programs, and your paradigms will get into the way of you consciously creating and having an outcome that could be miraculous for you. It will also cause you a lot of stress and suffering about things that haven't even happened yet, and you can't afford to drain your energy with imaginings of an unknown future—when you have so much to deal with in the present.

Chapter Ten

As Danielle and I pulled into the parking lot of Maryland's Maximum-Security Prison for Women, everything felt so surreal. I was floating outside my body as though it wasn't happening to me.

The first thing we did was line up to get prison clothes—pink jumpsuits, in this case. The next thing we had to do was extremely shocking for me. We had buckets of a chemical solution dumped over our heads to kill any potential lice. Finally, we were escorted to a section of the prison where new inmates go for the first six weeks to get oriented.

I felt like I was on a different planet. My surroundings were utterly different than anything I'd ever experienced.

Thankfully, just as Danielle predicted, we were put in the same cell for those six weeks. After being held for these six weeks, we would be assimilated back into what's known as the "general population." During the first six weeks, we would only be allowed out of the cell for breakfast, lunch and dinner, plus one 20-minute break during the day to walk up and down the halls and to use the phone and shower.

I had a lot to learn.

On my first day, right before the shower, I noticed that I didn't have any conditioner. I was pressing a button next to the speaker that was in the cell, but nothing seemed to be happening. I was trying to call somebody for help. Danielle looked at me and said, "What exactly are you doing?" I said, "I'm trying to call somebody. They forgot to give me conditioner."

Danielle literally fell on the ground rolling around in laughter. She said, "You just made me laugh for the first time in a very long time." Then she explained, "There's no reality where you can push a button and call for conditioner in prison. In order to get conditioner, you're going to have to get it from somebody in here by getting into their good graces."

She added, "Let me see what I can do for you." Like I said earlier, she knew everyone from her previous stay here, and a lot of people were here for life, or at least a very long time. Danielle came back from dinner with the conditioner. I asked her how she got it and she said she was able to trade a pair of jeans for conditioner.

The mind, body, and spirit seem to adjust the way they need to in order to survive something like this. Waking up the first morning in prison, I felt like it was a nightmare and I just wanted to close my eyes and go back to sleep. But, somehow, I was able to adjust and deal with it. One thing became clear again, just as it had in the preparatory weeks leading up to turning myself in: in these kinds of scenarios, you can't look much past the moment. All you can do is survive the moment you're in, and keep moving.

I was so thankful that I had Danielle. She was like an angel to me. She was very well respected and somewhat feared, because she had the attitude that she didn't have anything to lose and that nothing bothered her. She would not back down from anyone or anything. That's just in her personality. So, by association, I was protected too. Most everyone left me alone and I was mostly not bothered. I can only imagine what it would have been like if I had not been with Danielle.

Over and over again people stopped me to say, "You don't look like you belong here. What did you do to get in here?"

I also heard from quite a few people that, since I was only sentenced for one year, I would likely only have to stay for a short amount of time. That gave me hope beyond hope. On the other hand, everyone in the administrative system at the prison seemed extremely disorganized, so you never knew what was happening. Every day you were left with unanswered questions. So I couldn't be absolutely sure of anything, including when I would get out.

It took me a couple of days to realize that I was not receiving psychic messages from people here, and I was no longer able to read people. All my life, I've been psychic to some degree. I had always been able to go to psychic fairs, have people line up, and give them psychic readings and healings by tapping into their energy fields. As I mentioned, the peak of this ability came in the "holding place" where I had been just prior. That was an extraordinary new level. But I had been psychic before then.

Now, I wasn't receiving anything at all. This really threw me off, because this gift was something I often relied on as a way to connect to people under stressful conditions. Obviously, an ability to "tap in" to people and read them makes a really good icebreaker and a way to build trust with people. It had certainly made everything so much easier and better for me at the "holding place."

Now, I asked my guardian parents, who I knew had blessed me with that extra degree of perception at the "holding place" for the gifts and protection it provided, "What's going on?" The reply was that now, this would be a time for me to learn "who I really am," to tap into my inner self and my inner child and learn that I could get by with my own personality, by just being me.

For someone who grew up leaning on my psychic ability to get along and be liked and respected, interacting without it was like being naked in front of everybody. I had to learn how to cope with that.

Of course, I missed home terribly. I missed my children and I missed my family and Sean. But being in this situation and needing to fight for myself made me stop thinking about Gabe real quick—especially because his carelessness and lack of real concern for me was at least in part why I was here. For the first time since I had met him, he barely even crossed my thoughts. It was as if the spell was finally broken. It was only later that I would realize that it had taken something this extreme to actually break that spell, and that perhaps this was one of the functions my imprisonment had served. It was a wakeup call on numerous levels—and it was also how far I had to go to finally escape Gabe's orbit and energy.

On the other hand, I found myself missing Sean a lot. With some distance, with the spell broken and outside the context of all that craziness, I was finally really able to see our whole relationship in perspective. I was astounded at how much he had done for me and had tolerated, and I could finally feel how much he actually really meant to me.

ALWAYS PROTECTED

I knew I had lessons to learn. But during even such a harsh lesson, I also saw that I was divinely protected. And I will keep saying that—because we *are* divinely protected even through our roughest times in life.

As I mentioned, Danielle was one of the clearest and biggest sources of divine protection at this point. For those first six weeks we were held in the "orientation wing," I would wake up to inspirational sayings and positive quotes Danielle had written on the walls. She was always singing and laughing. In spite of her challenges, she had a really great personality.

Danielle had actually grown up in a very loving family; sadly, she had just met the wrong person at the age of 18 and gotten heavily into drugs. It was one of those situations where her parents stuck with her as long as they could. They tried to help her. She had two children with a guy who was also an addict. Her parents had to take the children and, eventually, allow her to go into her own journey, hoping that she would find healing.

At this time, she was 36 years old. There were many days and nights when she talked with me about her future and her desire to get off drugs and stay clean. She actually told me many times that I was pivotal to that desire. She told me that when I was around, she didn't want to do drugs. Drugs are very easy to get in prison. I never saw any, but a lot of people in prison are on them. She had every opportunity to get them, as she could seemingly get anything she wanted, but she never got drugs the whole time we were together in prison. She told me that as long as she was with me, and was talking to me about these types of things, she was able to say "no."

Danielle had her own angel in the form of one of the guards. Mrs. Carlson, the main guard who oversaw where we were held the first six weeks, was very fond of Danielle. She knew Danielle from her previous stay there. Danielle had minor cognitive deficits, due to her heroin overdose, so Mrs. Carlson was extremely grateful that I made sure no one took advantage of Danielle and that I was able to help Danielle at times that she needed it.

Because of Mrs. Carlson's care for Danielle and, by extension, of me, she walked up us one day and asked if we wanted to go to The Purpose-Driven Life. The Purpose-Driven Life was a six-week course run by a pastor who came in and talked about spirituality and faith and hope, and gave inmates exercises to do. Access to The Purpose-Driven Life is generally only allowed if you're in the general population, but she said that she would allow us to go, as long as we behaved ourselves and got back when we were supposed to.

The pastor who ran Purpose-Driven Life was Mrs. M. I had met some very psychic people in my spiritual and energy healing work, and as I've said, Gabe had early on impressed me as profoundly psychic. But Mrs. M was a whole new level of powerful—truly one of the most exceptionally gifted psychics I had ever encountered. She called herself a prophet, and I believe it. I knew it to be true when, on the very first day, she singled me out and spoke to me about something she couldn't possibly have known.

There were about 35 people sitting in the room. Mrs. M and I had never had a conversation. She looked right at me and said, "Sometimes the darkness can get through the people we love the most. It's not your sister who did this. It's the darkness that was coming up behind her to try to get to you."

I got chills all over. My favorite sister and I hadn't talked for four years because of something that happened in my practice involving Gabe and the eventual audits of the billing. Without going into all the details, let's just say I was upset with her for something I thought she had done, not knowing Gabe had orchestrated it. I had suspected this after a while. He was so jealous of my relationship with my sister. But when Mrs. M looked right at me and communicated this message, it confirmed what I had come to suspect. About a week later, my sister sent me a beautiful letter, and I sent her a letter back—and ever since we've mended our relationship and continue to be the closest of sisters.

Mrs. M would have us stand in circles and she would read us psychically. She would relay messages to us and touch us and give healings. Everyone wanted to know why it seemed like she singled me out me a lot—and she really did. She would come over and whisper things in my ear like, "This is your time of waiting. This is your time of patience. This is your time of seeding. Everything's going to be okay. You're going to create something beautiful out of all of this."

Whenever she would touch me, I would get a download. Waves of heat would come over me. I could feel my body start to shift as these downloads were assimilating. She was immensely powerful. I would go to the class once a week, and each week I would get these amazing healings and messages from her. These experienced sustained and saved me just as Danielle did. It picked me up, and was something I had to look forward to. It kept me connected with the Divine.

She also had us make vision boards about what we wanted in our lives. Vision boards are extremely powerful when you clear the blocks around them and when you believe that you can manifest what's in them. She taught us all of this. After the vision boards were created, she taught us how to bless them and release them to the universe. She taught things that I had learned in spiritual classes that I had paid good money for. She did healings at least as powerful as those in spiritual classes that I had paid good money for. And the vision board I created while I was in there has since all come true.

All of this was happening in a prison environment. Not just any prison environment, but a maximum-security prison environment.

After I got out of prison, Mrs. M. was one of the first people I looked up, because I wanted to donate money to her church. I wanted to try to repay everything that she'd done for me. But she was nowhere to be found. I couldn't find her anywhere in Baltimore, where she said that she had her church. I looked on Facebook, Google, everywhere. It made me wonder "Was she even real? Who is she? Where did she come from?"

Although Danielle and Mrs. M. made things much better for me, it's not like everything was peachy. On a daily basis there were fights, people screaming, people kicking, being woken up by people who sounded like they were in agony. Some guards would be mean for no reason at all. That leads me to my next story.

There was a TV show I had loved called "Once Upon A Time" that has a complicated fairy-tale plot, but the relevant aspect here is that whenever one character would write the story of what happened to him or to other characters, it would come true. In the show, this happened when he wrote in "squid ink" and the ink was the magical part—but the truth is, writing your story down is powerful no matter what kind of ink or instrument, and that's a principle I still use and teach to this day. In prison, it became quite a remarkable tool for me.

In prison it's common that if you get a guard who doesn't like you, for any reason, you can lose privileges—for example, you can miss getting your shower. One time there was a guard who didn't let me out for my 20 minutes, my phone privileges and my shower, which is a huge deal. You wait all day for that. I remember crying and crying as she just looked in at me and smiled, like she was so satisfied.

After crying for a while, I thought about that show and writing down stories that would come true. I took out some paper and a pen and wrote "Rebecca gets out to get a shower and use the phone tonight." About two hours later, another guard came right up to our cell and said, "Hey girls, did you get out for your shower and phone privileges today?" It was extremely unusual for one guard to come up and make sure the previous guard had let you get a shower. There was no real reason for them to them to question that you already got your shower as you were supposed to. Of course, I said, "No, I haven't gotten my shower and I haven't gotten my phone privileges today." And I was able to go out and do that.

After that, I started writing little things down all the time, like, "Rebecca gets to go to breakfast early" or "Rebecca gets to go to the library." Whenever I would write these things down, as if I were writing my story, I would get to do the things I wrote down. Part of this was intention, and part of it had to do with the energy of surrendering, which takes you to the field of the heart.

SURRENDER

When you surrender, you're letting go of all of your future and past. You're not thinking about your fear, guilt, doubt, or shame. You're not thinking about what bad things can happen to you in the future. All you're thinking about, when you really let go, is the here and now. When you're in the here and now, and in the flow of the heart, you're vibrating at a very high frequency—the same frequency as unconditional love and forgiveness, the Christ consciousness frequencies. You're connected to Source, God, or Creator. And when you write your own story—basically, intend and visualize what you want—while you're vibrating at, aligned with, or connected to this frequency, your ability to create is supercharged. You have so much power. This is a technique that I highly recommend to people, even now.

It's interesting how fast you're forced to surrender when you're placed in an environment like the prison situation I was in. And when you can actually surrender like this, you see miracles unfold around you.

People often ask, "But *how* do you surrender?" It's really hard to teach the "how" of surrender. In most circumstances, surrendering is something you do when there's nothing else to grab onto. You don't have the ability to control with your mind or actions. It's not like I could pick up a phone and demand myself out of prison. I lost all external control as I knew it. Surrendering was just taking a deep breath, letting go of everything I thought I'd had control of, all of the visions I'd had for my life, all the ways I thought things had to play out, all of the expectations. Just letting go of it all. Just breathing into the moment, and allowing. That is the best way I know to describe surrendering.

I learned a lot about myself during the surrendering process. I had to face the fact that I was in this horrific and extreme circumstance because I had been scared to lose love with Gabe. I did whatever it took to be loved, which is a ridiculously low-frequency shadow energy that I needed to release. As I've said before, we must learn to love ourselves the most. We have to put ourselves first. We don't have to put up with anything less than what we deserve. This was a huge lesson for me.

It doesn't take a clairvoyant or psychic person to surrender into to the field of the heart, or to align with the frequency of source, love, forgiveness, and the present moment. At this point, I was no longer able to read people, my psychic abilities had been put on pause, but I was still able to surrender into the flow of love and the heart, surrender to the moment and to Source, and create things around me that were extremely beneficial.

THE GENERAL POPULATION

When we were in the "orienting" holding space for the first six weeks, I was not exposed to anybody who had committed a serious, violent crime. It seemed like the women who were there with me for the first six weeks were those who (like me) were supposed to be in jails, but since the women's jails were closed down or full, we were in this overflow situation. Most of the people around me at this point had committed "lighter" crimes—violated probation, written bad checks, that kind of thing.

So I got kind of scared when the six weeks was nearing its end and we were going to be assimilated into the general population. There were six different places in the prison where you could be placed while you were in the general population. The place we heard the worst things about was the area they called "192B." Danielle, who had spent a whole year here before, said that she had been in an area called A-West. She said A-West was good and B-West was good, and a few others were okay, "but 192B is very scary. It's the section where the murderers and gang members are all placed."

I didn't feel *that* scared because I knew Mrs. Carlson was in charge of placing us in the general population. I knew she liked us both, and at one point she walked up to me and said, "I'm going to try my best to get you placed with Danielle." It's unheard of to be able to request a cellmate in prison. But because she saw how much I helped Danielle, and she really loved Danielle, she said she would try her best to get us put in the same section. That made me feel so much better.

The morning that the six-week hold was over, after I woke up Mrs. Carlson came over to us and said, with obvious dismay, "You and Danielle are going to 192B." We were shocked.

"Why?" I asked, stricken. She said, "That's the only place that's open."

And it was time to go. We each received two large trash bags in which to load up all of our stuff and began our journey over to 192B, which was about a quarter of a mile walk. We packed everything up. I was trying to carry these huge trash bags. A trash bag tore. The only laundry detergent I had started leaking out. It was just very discouraging from the beginning.

When we arrived at 192B, I was even more disheartened. It looked like an extremely old metal warehouse. It actually looked like hell. The other parts of the prison were modernized and rebuilt. This seemed like it hadn't been touched in a century. It was very dark, and it smelled bad.

As we walked into the hall, there was a group of guards in the center, One of the guards came to us and said, "Okay, I'm going to put you guys in cells right now." He started to put Danielle and me in two different cells. I spoke up. "Well, you know, Mrs. Carlson said that she and I could be in the same cell."

He laughed at me like I was insane. He sneered, "You're in the wrong place if you think you can make requests and tell me who I'm going to put you with." But Danielle piped up too and said, "Rebecca's right. It's true. You have to call Mrs. Carlson." Somehow, by the grace of God, the guard called her. When he hung up, he glared at us and snarled, "Okay, I'll put you two in the same cell." He added, "I never do this. This is nothing like I've ever done before."

Once again, I had dropped into the field of the heart, and remembered: "Okay, through all of this, you are divinely protected." I kept reminding myself.

They opened up the cell that Danielle and I were assigned to, and it was completely disgusting. It had mice in it. It was so run down that it looked like you were just sleeping in an alley. Someone who had been there before us had put gruesome sayings on the walls, the polar opposite of the positive quotes Danielle had put all over the walls in our previous cell. We sat down, and the energy was so heavy. It was so depressing. A couple of cells down, people were making a lot of noise and screaming.

But I sat there and I closed my eyes and did my best to go into the field of the heart, and started looking for ways to make this positive.

This first cell that Danielle and I went into had showers in the hall without any type of curtain. As women were showering, other women were making comments about them. This really bothered me. There were actually male guards there, too, which I thought was extremely strange. In spite of my determination to stay centered in my heart and surrender, I felt like "Oh my gosh, I just don't even know how I'm going to survive here."

About three hours later, a guard came to our cell and said, "You're moving." We were to stay in 192B, but now we would be in a different wing. Someone in a lot of trouble needed our cell, and we had to switch cells.

So, we gathered all of our stuff once again, and we moved to a different wing of 192B. It was still the same kind of dungeon atmosphere, but this cell was much nicer and the people around it seemed to be a lot more quiet. So, Danielle and I went into the cell and we started to get ourselves acclimated.

Thus began our journey into the real prison environment.

AN EXERCISE IN TRUST

My Guardian Parents were still giving me messages, even though I couldn't read other people. One of the messages they had given me recently was that I needed to do 1000 jumping jacks a day. This was fine with me because I really wanted to trim down anyway, and I thought "If I'm in prison, I'm going to exercise."

So, I was doing 1000 jumping jacks a day, 100 sit-ups a day, pushups, stairs. I climbed up and down the chair that was in the cell. Eventually, through my whole prison experience, I ended up losing 40 pounds. But the jumping jacks were especially important. Even now, I teach how to open portals through movement. At the time, I realized that as I was doing jumping jacks, I was opening up energetic portals to my own intentions. Those jumping jacks turned out to be a lifesaver for me.

On this first day in 192B, I did my first set of 1000 jumping jacks, took a rest, and went to get a shower. The shower was not nearly as bad in this new wing as the shower near our first cell. I came back and then something shocking happened. It was like something right out of the TV show "Orange is the New Black."

There was a big black woman in the cell literally across from ours. Her name was Jerry. She stopped me in the hallway and said, "I like you." She said, "You seem pretty innocent and pure, and that's unusual for 'round here. You don't seem like the type of person that would do drugs."

She added, "I'm going to give you a present." She went into her cell and came out with a black bra and underwear. Just then Danielle walked up next to me. I looked at Danielle like, "What do I do?"

This woman was in prison for life because she had murdered her husband 18 years earlier. She was a bail bonds person who had used her connections to have her own husband murdered. She had her own prison cell because of how dangerous she was to other people; she couldn't share a cell.

Now she said, "I've had this bra and underwear for 18 years. I haven't given it to anybody. I've been waiting for the right person to give it to." All around us were people who had committed horrible crimes, hardcore people around me. But when she brought out that bra and underwear, Danielle froze and everybody else around me froze too and just looked at me.

I whispered, "Oh my gosh, what do I do? I can't believe this is happening to me!" Danielle urged me, "Take them. Take the bra and underwear." I said, "Are you sure?" She said, "Yes." So, I took the bra and underwear. I thought, "Okay, maybe just taking this bra and underwear will put me in good graces with this woman." I went back into the cell with Danielle.

Then, across from the hall, she said, "I want you to put them on." I looked at Danielle and muttered, "I do not want to put this bra and underwear on. Everybody's looking at me." And Danielle said, "Rebecca, this is beyond me, but in my opinion you should put it on."

So, reluctantly, embarrassed, I put the underwear on. I didn't know what else to do. Jerry just looked at me from her cell across from us. And that was it. I took the bra and underwear off and changed into my own clothes.

Then the real hell began with this woman. She hit on me constantly. If I sat down to use the phone, she put her hand underneath my butt. She would say things like, "We can take it slow." I was in a huge bind. I felt like I was playing a high-stakes game and I didn't even know the rules. I was really, really scared for the first few days this was happening. Even Danielle went from being overprotective of me to "Oh no, this woman's going to try to kill me because I'm your cellmate." Even Danielle, who normally took no crap from anyone. was scared about what was going to happen with this woman.

As it turns out, this would come to a head and turn out to be one of my most important lessons of the prison experience.

 LESSON

Even at the worst of times, it's possible to see that you're divinely protected and that something is happening not to you, but through you and for you. Even in a maximum-security prison, I managed to find a friend who offered divine protection, and a prophet who gave me messages and energetic downloads (and hope). What were the chances of that? Even in the most surreal and bizarre and painful environments, good things happened, and I was able to create. I had to trust, and wonder at the design of it all—because although much of it was terrible, there were too many fortunate things to count.

The "writing it down" exercise proved very powerful throughout the rest of my time in prison. You don't need "squid ink" to make this practice work. If you want something to happen, try closing our eyes, dropping into your heart, visualizing it, and then writing it down as if it's already happened. Start with small things so you can play and test it out. But make it something that you can definitely point to if it happens, so you know that you created it. You'll be surprised at how quickly this intention experiment can work.

Chapter Eleven

It had been only six weeks since I had been in prison, but it seemed like forever.

I was dealing with life on a moment-to-moment basis. I was thinking about things, worrying about things, and doing things that I had never imagined. Obviously, I missed life outside of prison terribly. What kept me sane and protected was cultivating faith and hope, and practicing community creation.

When I look back on it now, I definitely see why my guardian parents took away my psychic abilities for the time I was in this facility. I couldn't fall back on those skills to impress, forge connections, or navigate. So I was able to—*had* to—connect with the women I was meeting on a level that I hadn't connected with people on since childhood. It was just…me and me. In prison, no matter how much money you have, no matter what abilities you think you have, or what you had on the outside, it's just going to be you and your personal capacities that get you through that experience.

The woman Jerry who had given me her underwear when I first arrived at this block of the prison continued hitting on me. The entire rest of the time I was there, I felt like we were in a game of cat-and-mouse. She would try to sit with me at lunch and talk to me in the common areas, and she would make insinuating comments. Thankfully, after that tense "underwear handoff" situation, I was able to avoid her a fair bit, especially with the help of other people who were hip to the situation. There were still some uncomfortable situations with her. But, for the most part, I felt like I was being divinely protected with this, just as in other ways. My goal was to navigate this carefully so that nothing major would get incited before I could leave.

The women I ended up hanging around with the most were women who were there for about the same period of time as me, and who had been convicted of similarly "minor" crimes. They were there for infractions like violation of probation or minor drug crimes. Believe it or not, one woman was actually there for writing too many bounced checks. This was because, again, jail space for women was in an overflow situation in Baltimore. I was supposed to be in a jail, not a maximum security prison, but this prison was all that was available.

Jennifer, Rabbit, and Rock were the three women I spent the most time with besides Danielle. (To this day, I don't even know Rabbit and Rock's real names—a lot of people went by nicknames in prison.) We sat together at every meal and hung out together whenever there was common time during the day and evening. We held each other's places in the phone lines, hooked each other up with commissary items, and played card games.

In Danielle's opinion, the best thing you could do to make the time pass in prison was to work in the kitchen. She told me that the first year she was there, she spent most of her time in the kitchen, working morning till night. She said, "As soon as you got there, it felt like you had just left. When you were done, you'd be so tired you would just go back to the cell and sleep." She actually liked it.

But most people dreaded that knock in the morning when they were told that they had to work in the kitchen that day. Many people got called for kitchen duty, and most of them tried to hide or otherwise avoid it. I wanted time to go quickly, so because of how Danielle experienced it, I actually felt excited to get called for kitchen duty, or at least find some kind of work.

So I went on a journey to find a job. But oddly, I couldn't seem to find one. It was so ironic. Almost everyone around me was hiding from jobs. The kitchen staff would come find people and make them work. Some women would pretend they were sick, and the kitchen staff wouldn't believe them and would make them go work anyway. But I actually wanted to work—and I was unable to.

One day, I walked into the kitchen during lunch, because Danielle said she would introduce me to people she knew there. She told them, "This is Rebecca, and she wants to work in the kitchen. She wants a job." The guard looked at me and yelled, "Get out! If we want you, we'll come and get you."

I left the kitchen, took a deep breath, closed my eyes, tuned in, and I heard my guardian parents and spirit guides. They said, "This is not your time to distract yourself." And I realized in that moment: working was what I had done all my life outside of prison to distract myself or not be present. During my marriage, I worked constantly as a way of escaping. During the whole mess with Gabe, as things were unraveling, I threw myself into my practice—both of them actually, the medical one and the spiritual one. I ran myself into the ground, providing for myself, my family, my employees—and at the same time not facing the darkness that was eating at me and my life. Being busy and being tired were great diversions.

My guides were saying, "This is not your time to escape, Rebecca. This is your time to deal with your inner child, your true self, and get to know who you really are."

And it was so divinely paranormal that I was unable to get a job. Everybody was asking me, "How is it that you're not getting a job, and everybody else around you has to work?" I just said, "I really don't know."

The only other women who didn't work were those who got to attend school and finish their education. The prison did give inmates that opportunity. I already had a graduate degree, so that wasn't an option for me.

So I stayed as present as I could to the day-to-day routine, without much to distract me. I slept about 12 hours a day. I tried to go to bed around 9, 10 or 11, and actually sleep for 12 hours. I read practically every library book in the library, especially the ones on spirituality and the paranormal. I exercised for about an hour and a half to two hours a day. I meditated. The rest of the time I just spent with the women that I met.

A major reprieve for me was the ability to walk outside. When I was held for the first six weeks, before being integrated into the general population, we weren't able to go outside. They didn't know us well enough, so there were no outdoor privileges. After you're in the general population, the guards and staff get to know you better, and they decide whether or not you can walk outside. If you're lucky enough to have the privilege, getting outside between lunch and dinner is the best recreation you can get. I was so grateful that I was allowed to do it.

Walking outside, you had to be very careful who you approached. Some women were ostracized because of the crimes they had committed.

I was told that walking up to those women or talking to them, even out of compassion, could get you attacked. And I saw it happen.

STORIES

The stories I heard in that prison were just indescribable. Some I heard secondhand, from women I hung out with, who knew the stories of other inmates. Sometimes I heard stories directly from the women who had experienced them.

There were gang members in prison who had gotten initiated by killing people. Drugs are often associated with these crimes. I heard many stories connected to meth, crack, and heroin. I believe that these drugs are portals to very low-frequency, dark behaviors. Sometimes while I was in prison it seemed clear that if there were no drugs, practically the whole prison would be empty. That's not an exaggeration.

At the same time, prison is not the place to go for help with drug addiction. There is absolutely no mental or emotional help there for people with addictions to drugs or to anything else. The system is extremely antiquated. From what I could see, no one was really getting rehabilitation. As a mental health professional, this was particularly shocking to witness.

For example, if you said that you felt suicidal, you were put in a sleeveless outfit that looked like a burlap bag. Your hands were handcuffed behind your back and you were put in a cold room for about 48 hours to be observed by the guards. It was almost like you were being tortured out of being suicidal. It was also hard to get a counseling appointment, yet easy to get psychiatric medication.

Some of the stories were terribly triggering, almost sickening—these tended to be the inmates who were avoided or ostracized. One woman who had been ostracized had been a foster parent. She wanted to keep the money for having foster children, but she didn't want to take care of them. Apparently she killed the foster children, put them in the freezer and, in order to get rid of them, chopped them up and fed them in food to her husband. This went on for quite a while before she was caught.

I found this out by sitting with some women at lunch who had been there for a while. They were praying over and blessing their food. I thought that was really cool, until they told me why they were doing it. "You definitely have to do this, because the person who is making our food is the person who killed the foster kids and fed them to her husband."

Another woman had been a prostitute while addicted to meth and crack at the same time. She had a three-month-old baby. While she was prostituting, she had a client who was complaining about the baby crying in the crib. Reportedly she put the baby in a pillowcase and slammed it against the wall until it died.

It was painful to hear the stories of women who were in there for life. One woman had taken the rap for her son because he had murdered someone. She accepted a lifetime in prison to protect him. A 23-year-old girl had killed her boyfriend because he had broken up with her. Oddly enough, she seemed incredibly sweet, not like someone who would be prone to snap like that. But she was facing the rest of her life in prison because she had.

There were many more stories like this. I'm not going to share all of the gruesome details, because it's not the point of this book, and there's no point in gratuitously traumatizing people with these tales. But I did make it a point to talk to people with whom I felt safe who were facing life in prison, whose stories were so unbearable that I couldn't even imagine how they were living every day. It did seem important to understand how these people went on living, especially with so little if any support for healing.

They all said pretty much the same thing about how they managed to go on. "You learn to take one moment at a time. You learn that you can't control the past, and you learn that you can't control the future. The only thing that you can do is just survive that one moment. You live in that second. And when you accept being able to live in that second, you can start to live in the next second and then the next second. Then your mind, body and spirit just adjust accordingly, and you begin not to worry." This is another way I would define surrender, which I talked about in previous chapters.

Even though back then I still was unable to imagine being able to surrender that way if I had been in their shoes, I saw these people doing it. They actually looked happy at times. They were laughing and dancing and talking to one another and decorating their cells, preparing to live the rest of their life in harmony there. It reinforced the lesson I had already been picking up so extra vividly since my sentencing: that the ability to live in the moment is everything. It can get us through times of ultimate trauma and suffering, times that we might think we would be unable to get through. This is how we get through them.

Still to this day I encourage myself and everybody else to practice this kind of surrender and acceptance. We don't have to come up against situations where we're forced to do it. We can practice on anything, and as we do it will build our capacity to surrender more deeply and dwell more readily in the heart.

How can you practice this daily? As you live your every day, if you start to worry or feel yourself pulled into anxiety, come into the present moment and find perspective. Take a deep breath and notice, "Hey, I'm okay. I'm perfectly fine right now in this moment. I'm here. I'm alive." Focus on the here and now, keeping your attention as riveted there as possible—not on the past or the future. Just this moment. Build that to the next moment and then the next moment. The more you can sustain this level of mindfulness and presence, the more you'll reside in a frequency of joy. Aligned with that frequency, you'll start to manifest accordingly.

(I know this may sound facile, especially if you feel like you have really serious, heavy problems or circumstances. But even if you do, this can still work. In fact, it's especially important to do this if you have serious challenges! This can help. Trust me—almost no one has harder, darker circumstances than most of these women I was in prison with, and over and over again they told me that this practice of keeping your attention in the present moment, the here and now, is what got them through and kept them sane—and even happy to be alive in spite of it all. It did for me too, and it still works. It's the core of mindfulness, which is extremely powerful and is even backed by scores of research regarding its effect on happiness. Try it!)

GUARDS

There are guards everywhere in prison. Whether you're at meals, walking outside, or any time you go from point A to point B, there are always guards looking at you. They have no idea why you're there, and they don't really care. You get treated like every other inmate, no matter what you may have done. Whether you're someone who killed a child or someone who wrote a bad check, the guards treat you the same. You're just another inmate, another prisoner—which they mostly didn't even seem to regard as human. I found the lack of human respect to be very hard to take.

One day in the cafeteria there was an older woman sitting at a table. When it was her table's turn to leave the cafeteria, she couldn't get up. I don't think she was able to—she was having some leg or hip difficulties. She wasn't able to push herself up. There was a guard there that day who was quite egotistical—you could tell just by looking at him. This guard went over to this poor older woman and started yelling in her face and then he took her arm and actually started to pull her up.

One of the other women there, someone who was known to be kind of a badass, was so outraged by this guard's treatment of the older woman that she tore the guard apart. She started yelling at him, calling him a weak pussy. Things that really would trigger a lot of men. She glared at him, turned around and started to walk away.

He just snapped. He ran after her and started strangling her from behind. I really think he would have killed her. Her face was turning red. All of the other guards ran up and pulled him off. It was tremendously unnerving.

Later that day, I heard that he was put on administrative leave, which I thought was good. But a few days after that, I mentioned to someone, "He must have been fired." The person replied, "No, they put him up in the towers."

The guards in the towers were the armed ones, like you see in prison movies. They look to make sure no one's trying to escape, because if you're trying to escape they're actually empowered to shoot you. I thought, "That is the worst place to put that man who is so out of control and unhinged—armed with a gun on a tower, where he can shoot anybody."

I remember feeling really on edge with that level of decision-making in the prison. It was another one of those things you just had to breathe into each moment and surrender to, because it was so out of our control.

FAMILY

When you're in a situation like prison, you appreciate things in life that you might have taken for granted before. Even if you appreciated them before, you appreciate them at a whole new level.

I was exceptionally fortunate. I had a tremendously loving family. I had four sisters and my mom, my children, and Sean, all of whom would come to visit me. Some people didn't have any support, not even phone support. You could hear them being put down when they were talking on the phone. Many women didn't have any visitors, ever.

We were allowed to have visitors twice a week. Even though it took my family three hours to drive there, and it took Sean an hour and a half flight and then another 40-minute drive, all of them came to visit me often. My best friend came also. And they brought the kids. I was so thankful for all of them.

The visiting room was painted to look like we were in the most cheerful place ever. That was definitely false advertising. We had to be searched before we went into the waiting room and after we got out of the waiting room, because drugs were so prevalent in the prison and the administration suspected that drugs were coming in through the waiting room. (Although rumor had it that they were getting in mostly through the guards—some of the guards actually got in trouble for that.)

My youngest was still just a little baby, and I missed her so much. When Sean brought her, I would hold her, and she would be so still in my arms and hug me, and it put me at ease so quickly. I remember thinking she was extremely special. That she knew on some level what was going on. The energy exchange that she gave me during that time was such a loving act.

Sean would tell me during these visits that he wanted me to come and live with him afterwards. He told me that I didn't have to worry about money, that I could live in his home, that he would take care of me and I could get back on my feet as I needed to. That meant so much to me. He didn't know that I had plenty of money saved through work and investments. I thought it was extremely sweet that he was so willing to take care of me.

That put to rest one of the things I had questioned about our relationship. I had always wondered, "Is he with me because he thinks I make a lot of money? Does he see a style of life that he wants to be a part of?" Turns out, that wasn't the case at all. He saw me in prison, as far as he knew I had nothing left, he had no clue what was going to happen after I got out—and yet he was willing to completely support me, unhesitatingly and unquestionably.

That was one of the things that really shifted my feelings for him—besides the way he showed up with such loyalty, the way he pitched in when I had to coordinate a nearly impossible amount of rearranging before I went in, the way he showed up for visits, the way he took care of Willow, the absolute insanity with Gabe that he had navigated around—all without judging me. It was tremendous.

Then there was my son, whose 16th birthday fell on the day I was sentenced. Three weeks after that birthday, he had to say goodbye to his childhood home, a dog he loved dearly, his new baby sister whom he had enjoyed. He had to go live with his dad full-time. I was concerned that he would just be full of anger and resentment—and frankly, I wouldn't have blamed him one bit if he had been.

But he wasn't. The first time he came to visit me, he looked me in the eyes and said, "Mom, this is giving me the ability to step back and to see what I had in my life. Like, all of the Christmases that you made for us, sending the elves, the way you organized Santa coming, the Easters, waking up in the morning and having breakfast. All the things in my childhood that I took for granted, now I realize that not every kid has. It just makes me feel so grateful!"

I can't even begin to put into words how blessed I felt that my son said this to me. There were so many different ways he could have taken this. He could have been angry, traumatized, anxious, depressed. Instead, he found gratitude. I was proud of him—and I have to admit, a little proud of myself for having raised such a remarkable young man. My own gratitude was overflowing.

My family would comment every time they saw me at visits about how rested I looked. It's interesting because of course on the one hand, every day I woke up wishing that I could just get out. I missed my "outside" world so badly. I missed my family, my work, and normal everyday life. On the other hand, here again was my opportunity to surrender into that moment and take care of myself the best that I could, regardless of my situation. And I was doing that. Despite the many stresses and sometimes downright horrors of prison life, I focused on my chance to get 12 hours of sleep every day, an hour and a half of exercise every day, and the leisure reading that I was doing. This was my chance to realize that it's not as much about where you are, it's about how you're treating yourself with love.

I was talking to my youngest sister every day, because she was taking the initiative to reach out to my caseworker at the prison and get my parole hearing organized. By law, you have the chance to be released on parole after one-quarter of your sentence time. That one-quarter of my sentence would be three months for me. But in the prison world, everything moves so slowly. It would be almost miraculous to get a parole hearing scheduled that soon after getting into prison.

But my sister had worked with me at my therapy practice and we were very familiar with Maryland agencies and paperwork. We knew how to be on top of things and that was her role at my practice. So she would call my caseworker at the prison and ask where my paperwork was. The caseworker would say, "I just sent over documentation to xyz agency and they need to fill it out." Then my sister would get on the phone with that agency and prompt them to find the paperwork and get that going. When they sent it back to the caseworker at the prison, my sister would be back on the caseworker's radar. My sister was following the paperwork trails like a detective, and putting them together to try to expedite the process.

The key was to get the parole hearing scheduled as soon as possible so that I could be released as soon as possible. I spent a lot of time thinking about that and organizing that, and I was forever grateful to my sister for taking all that on. Without an advocate bird-dogging this, your paperwork could get lost in red tape for a long time.

GHOSTS

One day, Danielle and I were outside walking on a beautiful fall day. My favorite season is fall, and it was such a relief to be outside walking and to breathe fresh air. That hellish section we were in had such stagnant energy, it was always so freeing to be outside.

In the area where we were allowed to walk around outside, we were surrounded by old abandoned buildings. That prison had been there since the early 1900s, and those buildings had been used for other purposes in their early days. As I was looking at one of the buildings that day, I saw a woman with long blond hair who was wearing a white dress with long sleeves, and she had her hands tied in the front. Not handcuffs—her hands were tied. And she had her head down.

At first, I thought that she was a real person. I hadn't seen dead people in a while and as I've mentioned, my psychic abilities had been put "on pause," so I assumed she was real. But then I realized she was a ghost. And suddenly, I heard in my head that her name was Rose. And I also knew that she had to be crossed over.

(What does it mean to be "crossed over?" There are a lot of different thoughts about this, and different spiritual practitioners might describe it differently. To me it means being allowed to "go on" beyond this world, rather than being stuck or attached here by something incomplete or unfinished. Some souls feel like there's something they haven't accomplished or that they can't accept. Sometimes they stick around trying to get resolution; sometimes they get stuck doing the same thing they were doing the day they died, just replaying. I was able to see ghosts when I was very little, and I saw this a lot.

To cross someone over, you give that ghost unconditional love and understanding. You tap in and see what it is they need to move on. For example, maybe someone had to see she that was a good mom. You give them that. Then they can allow themselves to go on into wherever is next—which of course is another spiritual question. Personally, what I learned in an ayahuasca journey is that you can go where you want to. Your own idea of heaven could appear. You might also decide where you need to go for your next life. You might say, "I need to live in the 1860s now," even if you came from 2023. You do this until your soul learns what it needs to learn. And then there is the idea that we return to oneness, to Source, to All That Is. But that's another discussion…)

At any rate, I didn't do it right then, and I didn't say anything to the women around me. I'm used to keeping such things to myself because mostly people can't see what I see, and if I tell them what's going on they don't believe me and might even think I'm crazy. That wasn't the case in the "holding facility" before I was moved to prison, where I became very popular for my visions and abilities, but I'm still not inclined to openly share what I'm seeing the moment I see it.

But that night, when Danielle and I were going to bed, I decided to go ahead and spend my before-sleep time crossing Rose over. I called Rose into my awareness and I was connecting her to the light, and suddenly I felt extreme resistance. Rose did not want to go.

Then Danielle said, "Rebecca, what are you doing and who do you have in here?" I was stunned. I knew Danielle was gifted, but she still amazed me sometimes. And I hadn't ever had anyone see in exactly the way I could before. I said, "You can see her?" Danielle said, "Yes," and proceeded to describe Rose perfectly. She said Rose had a long white robe on, long blond hair, and her hands were tied in the front. It was astounding.

She said, "Rebecca, I have chills. This doesn't feel right. This woman doesn't want to be crossed over. She's very angry."

Just then, a guard walked up. Danielle—because this was just how she was—said to the guard, who was a woman, "We have a ghost in here! We have a ghost in here!" You could tell by the way the guard looked at her that she didn't believe her—but then the whole door (it was an electric door) started making sounds and shaking. The guard looked scared. She didn't say anything and just walked away.

Danielle and I spent that night crossing Rose over. (Or so I thought. Later, I found out something else, as you'll see in a later chapter.) In the morning, I went to breakfast and the woman guard was there. She saw me and came over and asked, "Is everything okay?" At first I wasn't even sure what she was talking about. I said, "Yeah, everything's okay." She said, "No, I mean about the ghost. Did you get rid of the ghost?" I was amazed that she took it seriously. She still seemed spooked, and remarkably, she had trusted us to do something about it! I said, "Oh yeah, we took care of that."

TEACHING—AND READING—DANIELLE

That experience confirmed for me how open, clairvoyant and intuitive Danielle was. She had known we were going to be placed together. I believe that I was detained for that few weeks at the "holding place" so that I could be with her for this part of the journey. I felt she had abilities that could be expanded and refined, so I decided to spend some time teaching her energy work, how to read people, and all of the techniques I had experience with. I knew that Danielle would be good at it and that she would really enjoy it.

Danielle had an infectious personality. When she walked into a room, the whole room would light up. She made people laugh. People just gravitated towards her. But of course, when I met her, she wasn't on heroin. I do understand that there are two different people: the one on heroin and the one who isn't. So I understood the frustration that her family had had with her. But I could also see her gifts. I feel that a lot of drug addicts are naturally very empathic and intuitive. They have a yearning for passion and joy, and some turn to drugs because they think that they're going to get that god energy they sense and seek.

I also believe that Danielle had the veils open between the two worlds because of her overdose; a lot of people with near-death experiences have that kind of opening afterwards.

At one point, when I was working with Danielle and teaching her some energy techniques, I was holding her hand and my guardian parents gave me the ability to read her. As I've explained, for the most part this ability had been stripped while I was in this prison. While my guardian parents had done this for the reasons I've mentioned, I believe they gave me back this ability for just long enough to try to help Danielle.

When I was reading her, I distinctly saw two roads in front of Danielle: one was to the right, and it was dark and black. One was to the left, and I could see her laughing and playing with her children, having a good career and a really good life. Danielle was only about 35, so she still had her whole life ahead of her.

She felt me reading her. She asked me point blank, "What are you reading about me?" It was hard to tell her what I saw, but I wanted her to know; I wanted this brief reinstatement of my psychic ability to be a gift to Danielle.

I said, "I'm going to tell you the truth. If you go back to drugs, you will die and you're going to die fast. It's very important that you do what you have to do now to get yourself straightened out, enough that you can keep away from the drugs."

Danielle told me, "It's about the environment." She said that when she left prison this time, she could not go back to Baltimore and the same people. She wouldn't be able to do it. She told me that being around me, even being in a prison environment, it was easy to stay off drugs.

She explained that her mom, who was once very loving, was extremely frustrated with her at this point. I understood that side of it. I asked her if she wanted me to talk to her mom, and she was really thankful for that. I spent quite a few phone calls with her mom, explaining things and supporting both of them. I told her mom, "I'm helping Danielle through this." It helped that I had experience in counseling, that I had worked in mental health and was a professional.

Her mom was on board. She actually began making phone calls to get Danielle set up with transitional rehabilitation houses in Hagerstown, quite far away from Baltimore. She wasn't ready to accept Danielle back into her home, but she was willing to make a financial commitment as well as offer emotional support to help Danielle through this. I was grateful for that, for the chance to mediate and help reconnect them. I told her mom how grateful I was that Danielle was able to make me feel moments of joy and laughter in a place like this. I wanted her mom to know Danielle really was special, in spite of how brutal her drug issues had been to deal with.

FUN WITH DANIELLE, AND SURRENDER SAVES ME AGAIN

One time, Danielle and I were bored and she got the idea, "Let's fill out a grievance." Danielle had no difficulty expressing herself and being authentic. She would say what was on her mind. She didn't really have a filter.

She definitely had some attraction towards the male guards, and she let them know it. They would come to look through the window at us, to make sure everything is okay, and she would bend over and shake her butt at them. She had been there before and they knew her, so they would just laugh at her and walk away. Somehow, she made it kind of innocent.

There was one guard nicknamed "Boomie" towards whom she had a major attraction. So in this play grievance, she wrote a complaint about him being too sexy. It was just a joke to make us laugh. It got kind of perverted, but it was something to end the night on a funny, positive note.

That next day, as we were going to lunch, for some reason Danielle put the grievance on my desk. I remember thinking, "We need to get rid of that, because that would not be good if a guard saw that." We went to lunch and then Danielle had go do something so we parted ways.

I went to leave the meal area. Coming back from meals, there was a desk monitor you had to pass by to get back to your cell. Boomie was there. He stopped me and said, "Your cell has been chosen to be searched for drugs." This was normal. Cells were randomly searched for drugs, because drugs were so prevalent there.

I wasn't concerned about drugs, of course, but I knew that grievance was on my desk. There was a hundred percent chance that if Boomie saw a grievance about him, he was going to read it. I felt the blood drain from my face. I could not look innocent. I could feel my expression changing, and my breath caught.

He saw my face and he said, "You have drugs in there, don't you? You look really guilty." I stammered, "No, it's not drugs." He looked at me sharply. "You have something to tell me." But I was speechless. I literally could not form words.

Then I took a deep breath and let go. For me, the way this feels is there's a whole lot of heat, like when Kundalini is rising. I felt myself drop into the center of my heart and…it's not like you give up, but it's letting go.

It's dropping into trust. You give it over. It's acceptance and faith. There's nothing I can do in that moment. I was just like "whatever."

Right after I did that, he looked at me oddly and said, "You know what, you're lucky that Danielle is your roommate, because I'm just going to sign off on this like I've searched your cell." He signed off and let me go.

Moments like those, I was using what I teach in the most critical of ways. Surrendering to the field of the heart changed my outside reality—and it happened instantaneously.

LESSON

There are times in life when there's nothing you can say or do to control the outcome. This is very scary for us as humans because we have no choice but to let go and let fate take over. However, fate can tell when you truly let go and surrender. In my experience, circumstances can radically and drastically change when you drop into the field of the heart, open your hands up and say "Okay, this is beyond me and I am calling in the angelic forces." Have you ever tried this? Is there something in your life now that makes you feel cornered? Practice this strategy and observe what the universe can conspire to do for you.

Chapter Twelve

NOW IT WAS VERY CLOSE TO CHRISTMAS. ONE of the hardest moments of my whole prison journey was being there through the holidays. I grew up with a very festive family. We very actively and enthusiastically celebrated Halloween, Thanksgiving, Christmas—we were like a Hallmark family. I had been making the best of prison that I could, being resilient, and using all my practices to create what good I could from the situation. But being away from my children was exceptionally dispiriting at the holidays. Christmas Eve and Christmas Day were especially very hard days.

On Christmas Eve, people spent some time decorating inside "the unit." People were putting effort into decorating and getting some Christmas spirit going. They were trying to be jolly. But the duality of energy really showed up in that scene. As much as prisoners tried to brighten up the holiday energy, these efforts also seemed to bring up negativity.

You've probably seen this to some degree even in normal life at the holidays. Having been in the field of psychology and counseling, I knew that the holidays definitely brought out depression, anxiety, and other dark feelings. Although loneliness, money and time pressures, and family conflicts can be a few common and obvious triggers for negative feelings at the holidays, I also look at it energetically. I believe that these holidays can bring out people's shadow energies and lower-frequency energies. It's a function of duality—as spirit goes up, as people get happy and jolly, depression comes out too.

That phenomenon was definitely on display in the prison environment. As people were decorating and getting prepared for Christmas, a lot of bizarre things were happening.

For one thing, on Christmas Eve, one woman tried to kill herself by somehow using a battery to set fire to her bed. Imagine a place that already looks like a big dungeon warehouse. Very dim, stagnant energy, people behind bars. All of a sudden, there's fire and smoke everywhere, and people screaming and yelling in agony, and running every which way. It was like a scene from literal hell. Then water spraying everywhere as the sprinkler system came on. .

In the middle of this commotion, there was also an incident in which, when the cell doors came open automatically as they do during a fire, one inmate took the opportunity to exact some revenge she was apparently plotting. She seized the moment to run into someone else's cell with a pencil and stabbed that girl in the eye. So amid all the confusion and panic and raging fire, this poor girl was bleeding from her eye. It was a lot of intense negativity to digest—and certainly nothing like the idyllic loving holidays I was used to!

After this incident, we were all removed from the area and ushered into the gym, where we sat for hours and hours. I was just sitting there in shock, thinking "Wow, this is a really horrible Christmas Eve."

Then, in an effort to create something good out of this, I got my journal out—I was already writing this book—and started writing. I began to journal about techniques like breathwork and other practices I was using to be able to deal with situations like this.

While I was writing, everybody in the gym around me was talking. I kept hearing people discuss what they should have done differently to avoid being in prison. But it wasn't about rectifying their behaviors so that the crimes or incidents wouldn't have happened. It was about how they could have strategized differently to get away with the crime. Like, "When I killed this person I left them there. I should have put bricks on them and dumped them in the lake. Then I wouldn't be here."

This was the type of conversation I was hearing around me. It was dark, negative energy.

Writing that journal at that moment was a powerful experience for me. I remember thinking that even through all this, I was able to tap into god/creator/source energy and know that no matter what was going on, no matter where I was, I still had the ability to access that. In doing so during this nearly apocalyptic Christmas Eve, I calmed myself down and continued being the author of my own story. I wrote about my upcoming parole and my upcoming release from there, even as the inmates around me were perpetuating the same darkness that had landed them in this spot.

THE BEST PRESENT EVER

That was a terrible Christmas, yet I made it through. And the very day after Christmas, I got really good news. I finally received the date of my parole hearing, which was January 11th. It had taken only a little over two months from the time I entered the system, which was unheard of. I actually had many women come up to me and ask me how I was able to manifest this sort of thing in my life—to get a hearing so fast and have things go so smoothly.

In answering them, I talked about the administrative aspects of what my sister and I had done, but also the spiritual aspects of manifesting and writing your own story. People are very receptive to spiritual ideas when they can see real-life results working for you.

But it was also really hard for some of these people to shift into a self-loving, high-vibration spiritual energy that would allow them to manifest good things. There was so much self-sabotaging behavior going on around me.

One of the women I've mentioned who I hung out with some, whose nickname was Rabbit, was sentenced for a very short amount of time. She was there for violation of probation. You can get out rather quickly when you're there for a violation of probation, even without a parole hearing.

Yet, with only about a week remaining in her stay, Rabbit decided to take some drugs that were floating around the prison. Someone ratted on her, and she was drug-tested. As a result, she was put in what they call The Hole for six weeks. She had been so close to getting out, and she messed herself up.

You could see the subconscious at play in situations like this. Rabbit had told me about how she would be going home to her father, who she didn't think loved her. She didn't really have anybody on the outside that she felt would accept her back. So clearly, a part of her knew what she was doing. A part of her didn't want to get out, and purposely sabotaged her leaving that prison. A part of her felt safer there than at home, and that is what she manifested.

DANIELLE LEAVES BEFORE ME

The day after New Year's I got some more big news—and this news shocked me and left me rattled a little bit. I was in the shower and Danielle came running up to me calling "Rebecca, Rebecca! I'm leaving! You have to get out of the shower. Hurry up, I'm leaving!"

Something about Danielle was that her paperwork was all messed up. We didn't even know when she was eligible to get a parole hearing, according to the system. When you look up someone's case in the Maryland judicial case search, you can see all the details of the case. Searching Danielle's name, you could see that she should have already been out a couple months earlier, because they technically couldn't hold her past a certain day.

When they found out that they should have already let her out, they were going to have to pay her for the time they had made her serve that she shouldn't have been there. Therefore, the day they found that out—which was the day after New Year's—they wanted her out immediately. So they walked right up to her and said, "Get your stuff, you have to leave."

I rushed out of the shower and asked, "What's going on?" She said, "They just walked up to me, they said 'You have to get your stuff. You're out of here!'"

She hadn't had time to set up anything for herself on the outside. Her mom hadn't finished arranging where she was going to live in Hagerstown. None of that was planned. She was supposed to get all of her stuff together, get dressed, and get put on a bus. She would be dropped her off wherever she wanted to be dropped off.

But the only place she knew of to go were the places in Baltimore that she had previously hung out. This was a heart-wrenching situation for her and for me. I could see the fear in her eyes. She was half-excited to be getting out, but I could see that she was also terrified about where she was going. We had talked about how important it was that she not go back to Baltimore, and what would happen if she did. And we had been so close to getting something else set up.

She left some stuff in our cell, like she thought she'd be back. She said, "Don't worry, I think I'm going to come back and get this." I looked at her thinking, "I don't think you are." But I let her leave it there, and I told her, "Don't worry, I'll definitely be in touch with you when I get out." We hugged and then she left.

I felt so bereft and empty when she left, like, "Wow, my angel has left. The person who has guided me through this whole entire situation is gone." But what I realized was that she left me standing with my own torch. I was able to take what she taught me, and her good vibe and the way she looked positively at everything and her sense of humor, for the remainder of my time there. I was able to stand strong, even though I was nervous about who I was going to be matched with as a cellmate.

I spent that night alone. But, when morning came around, my new cellmate was a 24-year-old young woman whom they had nicknamed "Toe" because she had a tattoo across her cheek that said, "Toe." She explained that she was dating a guy named Joe who had wanted to tattoo his name on her, and they somehow spelled his name wrong and used a "T" instead of a "J."

She spent much of her time trying to get her high school diploma, so for the little bit of time that I was in there with her, I worked on getting her up in the morning to get to school. She was nice enough. We played card games and chatted a little bit. There wasn't much to say because of the age difference, and such a difference in our interests. But she was an easy cellmate, and I was still very fortunate and grateful to have her.

Toe was in there is because she was into drugs—meth and heroin. When she got caught, she was tased by the police officers and she fought back. So she ended up getting charges pressed against her for violence against the police. I actually heard quite a bit of that in prison stories, about people who are on drugs and the police trying to get them under control by tasing them, and they would fight back and hit the cops and then get charges pressed against them for that as well as the drugs.

At this point, I was just passing each day waiting for January 11th. I was so excited that this intense, surreal period seemed to be coming to an end.

On the day of the hearing, I was extremely nervous as I went before the parole board. You hear stories about how you had better say the right thing, or you'll be denied. And about how if you happen to get the wrong person, they can just deny you for no reason. I was so afraid this would happen, and then I'd have to wait God knows how long before another hearing might happen.

I walked into the room and there was a gentleman sitting there who I could tell was the lead, and plus two other people. He looked at me and took a deep breath. I was waiting to speak and preparing to say what I needed to say, and he said, "Are you ready to get out of here?" I replied, "Yes, I am." And he said: "You're leaving."

I was shocked, because I hadn't even said anything. I said hesitantly, "I don't have to say anything?" He countered, "Do you want to say anything?" I responded "No."

Then he picked up a stack of letters. He said that so many of my clients had written letters to the board. Clients I had helped, and clients especially writing about the children I had helped. He said that, after reading the letters, understanding what I had done for the community and how many people I had helped—especially sexually abused children—he said that there was no question in his mind that I was leaving as soon as administratively possible. He said that as soon as they could get the paperwork together, I was out of there.

I was stunned, and so thankful and happy. I can't even begin to describe it. I nearly skipped out of the place. I was all smiles. Now, I just had to wait for the paperwork to go through.

I called my youngest sister, who had been helping me with this, and I told her to do whatever it took to get that paperwork moving as smoothly and as fast as possible. She did, and within a few days we knew that my actual release date would be February 12th. I had just a few weeks to go.

In spite of my gratitude, knowing that I was going to get out actually made those weeks drag on even more slowly than normal. I did my best to stay present and make the most of my remaining time. I hung out with the women that I was used to hanging out with, tried to stay out of trouble, exercised, read, called home, and worked on staying healthy, preparing for my release.

FINAL SHENANIGANS

And then something happened that I didn't expect— not even a week before my actual release date. I got set up, which was extremely scary for me. It had to do with Jerry, the big black woman in the unit who had a crush on me. I thought she had given up on that, especially since she knew I was leaving. But there was to be one final, potentially destructive incident.

A woman from one of the cells who had quite a bit of time ahead of her had a television. She came to me and said, "I really would like to have some commissary, get some snacks. Why don't you trade me some food for watching my television for a few nights? That'll help you get through the rest of your days and distract you."

I did not know that this was taboo. I just thought, "Okay, that's a good deal." She gave me the TV and said, "The only thing is, I need this television back working. Don't break it. I really need this to work when I get it back." I said, "Don't worry, I'm not going to break it."

So she gave me the television, I gave her the commissary. Then I plugged in the television that night…and it just didn't work. I knew right then that I had been set up. This woman was not going to get her television back working because it didn't work. And I would be on the hook.

What I found out later from some of the other women was that Jerry had set this up. Jerry had suggested to this woman that she trade her broken TV for some commissary, and that I might be interested. She definitely was setting me up to get into a fight so that I'd end up having to stay.

I knew I was in big trouble. I just had to figure out what to do about it.

In a few days, when the woman came back to get her television, I did the only thing that I knew to do, which was to be honest. I explained to her that the television was not working when she gave it to me, but that I would do my best to find somebody who could get the television working.

That didn't work. She became so angry. She was acting really aggressive and I could tell she was somebody who just didn't care. She said, "I want that television back working. I told you that it needed to be working." She said, "When I get back from lunch, I am going to kick your ass. We're going to fight." She also added, "One thing I can tell you is that you and I are going to The Hole." She pointed out that she had nothing to lose. She said, "I'm in here for at least another six to seven years. Six weeks in The Hole is nothing to me."

What she knew was that if she and I got into a fight, the guards were not going to spend time figuring out what it was about and who started it, who was right and who was in the wrong. Eventually, they do that—but first, they take both parties and put them in The Hole for at least four to six weeks before they determine who was at fault.

I was getting out in less than a week. If she came back and fought me, it would ruin my entire parole.

She went to lunch. I skipped lunch, just trying to figure out what to do. I could have gone up to some guards and explained to them what had happened, how I'd been set up. But that wouldn't have gotten taken care of in less than an hour. When she got back, she would have still tried to fight me. Guards didn't act that fast. You can't really get anywhere in prison by tattling. It just doesn't work.

I decided that was the moment I once again had to practice what I had been preaching about surrendering, staying in the heart, letting go, and trusting source. This moment was so extreme, the stakes so high. I was incredibly excited about getting out in less than a week and I knew that if I didn't change my reality in less than an hour, I would not be getting out.

I went to my bed and lay down. I surrendered and relaxed into my heart space. I remember feeling a floating sensation, as though my body were on the bed, but I was expanding through my heart and becoming a part of everything that existed. I started to perform a technique where I was releasing any guilt, shame, doubt, fear, self-loathing—any of those shadow energies that cause bad things to happen for us. I did the

Ho'oponopono prayer: "I'm sorry, Please forgive me, Thank you, I love you." I was scrubbing my insides, scrubbing my soul, and giving myself an immense amount of self-love. Being in the here and now; basking in love, forgiveness, peace, all of that high-frequency energy. Releasing the shadow energies.

I spent all of lunch hour doing this—doing everything that I teach in what is now the AWAKE Academy.

Right after lunch, the TV woman came back to me as promised. I took a deep breath and looked right at her. I was ready for just about anything. I knew I had done the very best I could have to prepare for this.

She looked at me for a long moment. Then she pulled me to her, hugged me, and said, "Don't worry about it. It's okay. I forgive you. Maybe we can figure something out later." She walked out. I heard her talking to somebody.

It was done.

At that moment, I *knew* that everything I'd ever learned or taught spiritually was real. I knew that this work could change any circumstance in our life. This was all the proof I've ever needed. That moment changed my entire life. The power of the here and now, of surrendering into the energy of unconditional love and All That Is, the One source energy that connects us all together—my faith and belief in this potential was sealed.

After that, everything went smoothly. On my release date, I was able to get out and be reunited with my family.

Sean was in Michigan and I was in Maryland, so at first I spent some time at my oldest sister's house, which was a beautiful experience. During these first few months, while I was living with my sister, I was focused on reuniting with my family and creating living space where my children and I could all come together once again. Sean came to visit me from Michigan quite often, and I visited him quite often. We were getting very close.

And then something happened that was extremely disheartening, something that made me cry for about three days straight.

GOODBYE, DANIELLE

After I'd been out for a little while, I looked up Danielle. She was only about three hours away from me, and I really wanted to see her again and thank her for everything that she'd done for me. I didn't know exactly where she was, but I knew generally her whereabouts. I knew her first and last name, so I Googled her. When I did, her obituary came up. She had died about two months after she got out of prison. Of an overdose.

That was the crossroads I had seen when I had held her hand and read her energy. I had known that if she went back to the place in Baltimore that she had come from, she would die. I had told her that. She knew it too. Yet there was nothing I could do to stop it.

The grief I felt was overwhelming. Right then and there, I pledged that I was going to do whatever I could do for humanity to help with addictions. We had lost an amazing angelic being with two beautiful children. She'd had tremendous light around her, an infectious personality. The loss to me, and to the world, was immense.

I really did cry for about three days straight. I was unable to get out of my bed. There was so much sorrow. I had bonded with her so much. To this day, when I am conducting natural plant medicine ceremonies with people who have addiction issues, I feel the essence of Danielle come in and help. So I know that she's an angelic being, still at large in the angelic realms, and I do call upon her often.

As a side note, as soon as I got out of prison and acclimated back into life, I noticed that my psychic abilities—the ability to read people, tap into energies—came back, but even more so. It was at a new, deeper, more powerful level. That day that I had surrendered in the prison cell, regarding the television and the risk to my release, must have opened up something. Or maybe it was just the whole experience. I think I realized how little use the brain and human ego are to our overall creation of life. Regardless, my ability to channel and to receive information was strengthened manyfold.

LESSON

Let's not lose track of the fact that this is a book about twin flames. Yes, I'm talking about lots of events in my life that may not seem related to significant others or relationships. But everything you do in your life is part of your twin flame journey, because a twin flame is a reflection of who you are.

You're only going to manifest a twin flame based on where you're at in your growth, awareness, and self-love. So, if I love myself 50%, then I'm going to attract someone who shows me love 50% of the time. If I have guilt, doubt, shame, fear, and self-loathing and feel insecure about myself, then I'm going to attract someone who treats me accordingly.

What I believe after my experiences is that the twin flame is an essence, and it can actually travel through different people.

I believe the ultimate union in life is the union of self-love—honoring yourself and getting to know yourself on a deep soul level and unconditionally loving who you are. When you love yourself unconditionally like that, you'll be in a space where you can be alone and be just fine. The cool thing is, you won't be alone when you're in that space. When you love yourself that much, that's the frequency you embody, and the Law of Attraction kicks in and you receive that love back.

In that sense, everything in our life is essentially a twin flame journey. People often ask "What's my purpose in life?" There's only one answer to that question. Your purpose is you. Your purpose is loving yourself on a soul level, no matter what. Honoring yourself so much that you allow yourself to be in joy and to live your heaven on earth. When you do this, your light body will activate and you'll heal everyone around you just by being you.

No matter what I talk about, no matter what I'm going through, I do call this my twin flame journey. There are branches to my journey that may seem off the path, but everything in my life, and everything in your life, is a journey of self-discovery and self-love.

UPSIDE DOWN MIRROR

Chapter Thirteen

SO I WAS LIVING WITH MY SISTER, REORGANIZING my life, getting things together, and going back and forth to Sean's house in Michigan. He and I were spending quality time together, finally getting to know each other on a much deeper level. I was also spending quality time with my family and my children.

Finally, the time came when I was preparing to move from my sister's house and get a place of my own. I needed to go back to the house that I had let go, that I had lived in with Gabe, to get some things. The house had been sitting in foreclosure since I'd gone into prison, as there was no selling it in that market at the time—it was an enormous house, and I'd paid more for it than it was worth at that point. Cumberland is actually one of the poorest towns in the country, and I had bought one of the nicest homes there. I'd paid $485,000, and it was now appraising at $200,000. Foreclosure was the only solution.

Foreclosure takes forever, and although we'd cleared out a lot of my stuff and my kids' stuff in the reshuffling that took place before I went for my prison stint, we'd left some things behind that I now wanted—Christmas decorations, bikes, stored stuff from the huge attic. I wanted no part of that house any more, with all that had happened there with Gabe, but I did want some of those things.

I knew that during the first couple of months after I went to prison, Gabe had stayed in the house. My mom had been checking on it, and she had told me he was there. Being my mom, she even brought him food! But after a while she stopped going, and I honestly assumed that his brother had come and gotten him by then. I was so busy rebuilding my own life, I really thankfully hadn't given him too much thought.

After I'd been out of prison for a month or so, I was starting to look for a place of my own and wanted to see what I still had at the old place. When I went back to look at the house one day, planning to grab a load from the attic, I found something shocking: *Gabe was actually still squatting in the house.* There was no electricity there any more (my ex-husband, who understandably loathed Gabe, had worked hard to make sure the electricity was cut off when he learned Gabe was squatting there—it's harder to get the electric company to shut off power than you would think, but they had finally done it).

I walked in the door, and just as soon as I did, I felt this eerie feeling. And then he appeared out of the shadows, literally. I gasped when I saw him. He was like a skeleton. It turns out he had lost almost 100 pounds after I had consciously let him go. His eyes looked vacant. He reminded me of a wet rat. He actually *slithered* as he walked. His energy was very dark and damp.

He came up to me as if he has been expecting me and said, "Oh, Rebecca, I missed you! I thought about you every day. I've been waiting here for you this whole time."

I shuddered. I had already come to realize how much he never cared about me. I'd asked my mom, several times from prison when I knew she was bringing him food, "Has Gabe asked about me at all?" And she would cast her eyes down and say "No, he hasn't asked about you." So I wasn't under any illusions now that he was actually glad to see me or had been waiting for me. I quickly gathered what I had gone there to retrieve. As I was doing that, I could hear him once again talking to people that I couldn't see. He spoke in a robotic voice telling whatever these entities were to leave him alone. It was as creepy as ever.

As I was leaving, he came up to me and, of course, he asked me for money and food, and wanted to know how long I was staying and when I would be back. I just said, "I can't get you anything right now. I have to go." He followed me to the car, looking to his right at one point and asking the entities not to follow him. I got in the car, waved goodbye and sped away.

I still had to be very careful of this energy. He was repulsive now, not at all attractive, but this dark reptilian energy will try to pull you in any way it can. Even if it's "Oh, look at him, he's lost 100 pounds! He needs help. He's living in a house without electricity!" Now, after all I had been through, and finally having truly let him go, I realized these were his choices.

And I knew that the worst mistake I could make, after all I had been through and the extremes it had taken to detach fully from his energy, would be to go back into giving any time to him, *anything* to him, and feeding that dark energy. The best thing to do is literally starve it. I knew that my guides were saying "Hey, Rebecca, no more of this."

So I walked away. He ended up getting kicked out of the house. My ex called the police, and they gave him 30 days and removed him. He ended up getting bounced back to the same hotel as before. Some neighbors actually paid for a few days for him. Then when he was once again kicked out in the rain, I did finally do one last favor. I got him an emergency interview at the YMCA, which let him in. I talked to staff there, and did some paperwork.

After that, I just completely walked out of his life. He would call me occasionally; I would make the conversation extremely short and hang up. There was even one time he came to the door of my new rental and my son answered the knock. My son slammed the door in his face, and I stayed in my room. I still had other work to do—but this spell, finally, was broken.

A GOOD LIFE

I spent quite a lot of time in Michigan at this point. I was really getting to know Sean in a way I'd never gotten to know him before. And I was living in *his* life for the first time, rather than him always having to live into my life. I was working from home. He would go to work at about 4 a.m., come home, clean the house, make dinner. I went to his band gigs, So I got to really see the way he lived.

We were also having a tremendous time with Willow, our daughter. Everything seemed to be going really well. And the more time I spent in his environment, the closer we got. I realized, finally, "I truly love this man." And, "This is a really good life."

I felt like I had passed some sort of initiation. I remembered Mrs. B coming up to me when I was in prison and saying "Amazing things are going to happen to you. You are seeding. You're preparing for something large." I felt like now I understood what she was talking about. I felt that happening. My field felt very expansive.

I was also doing natural plant medicine ceremonies at this time to heal what I had been through. We had scheduled a trip to Miami, Florida, because I was going to go get my dog Casper, a magical mix of timberwolf, Siberian husky, and malamute. I'd had to take Casper back to the breeders when I had gotten the prison sentence. I was very close to this dog, and I was so excited about being reunited with him.

We scheduled a vacation at Miami Beach to coincide with this excursion, as well as an ayahuasca ceremony with a shaman I had worked with previously in Peru who would be in Miami during this time. Sean agreed to go with me to the ceremony so that we could work on ourselves individually as well as on our relationship.

After an 18-hour drive to Miami, I was so thrilled to finally get my wolfdog back. When I walked into the breeder's house, Casper saw me and started jumping up and down, doing his dog dance, licking me on the face. He rolled over on his back and I scratched his belly. What the breeders told me next really made my heart melt. They told me that about 30 minutes before I even got there, Casper started going to the door and sniffing and acting excited. They told me they were positive that he could sense me coming.

Knowing that he could sense me, knowing that he had missed me, knowing that he remembered me—it taught me an important thing about relationships and love. I understood how, with dogs, they don't perceive time the way we do. Even though it had been close to a year since I had seen Casper, for him it was like no time had passed. He remembered me and my scent, he remembered my energy, and he was just as loving as before. My heart broke open even more.

Next, we went to a resort in Miami. We were planning to stay for a week. It was a big family vacation. I had my mom with me, three of my children, Sean, and of course my dog. My mom offered to watch Willow and the kids and dog while Sean and I went to the ayahuasca ceremony.

I had gotten a message from my guides that I needed to heal trauma while in this ceremony. I was uncertain as to what trauma they were talking about. I speculated that they meant everything I had just been through. But what happened was far more surprising.

Sean and I sat through the ceremony for eight to nine hours. I did process through a lot of what had happened to me, purged, reached a balanced state of being, focused and centered my energy.

And then, when it was time for us to leave, we were to go to a room where we were staying with three other people. (In a traditional ayahuasca ceremony, you're generally in a large round room with all the other participants—it can be from ten to eighty people!—in a circle. You're with a shaman, who gives you guidance. This can go on for nine hours or more. When you're dismissed by the shaman, you usually go to a room to "come down," integrate, and rest or sleep it off. There will usually be three or four other people in that room.

I was used to all this, from previous ceremonies, but Sean was not. And we had this gorgeous resort to stay at, where the family was. So after the shaman sent us to the room where we were supposed to spend the night with three others, Sean was saying "I don't know, I really want to leave. I want to go back to the resort. I just want to spend time with you. I don't want to stay here with other people."

I said, "Okay. I just need to get my stuff and I need to go to the bathroom first. I'm feeling a little queasy." I told him I felt like something was still trying to come out of my body and I wasn't sure what it was.

I went to the bathroom. My body started vibrating and shaking a little bit. All of a sudden, I went to purge into the toilet and, of all things, what came out was the Blond Girl I had crossed over in the prison environment! Or, at least I thought I had—apparently not.

It was an indescribable feeling. I felt like something was ready to detach from me. I was swaying back and forth. It's certainly not unnatural to be queasy after ayahuasca, so I was bent over the toilet, ready to puke—and her *head* came out of my mouth! It was beyond shocking. It was like a translucent ghost sort of apparition. I could see her face and her hair. All of her, the whole translucent spirit, just sort of emerged out of my mouth, then swooshed down the toilet and was gone. No words were spoken.

I stood up, dazed at the strangeness of this. *Nothing* like this, in all my psychic and paranormal experiences, had ever happened to me before.

The first thing I noticed was that I could see more clearly. My eyesight had been a little off since prison, and I just figured I was getting a little older and my vision was not what it used or be. I had no inkling that anything like this was in me! There were no other signs.

Well, except for one—after this incident, I noticed that Sean looked me in the eyes more. I had noticed that often Sean would look in my eyes and then look away. That was something else that had worried me a little about our relationship. But after the Blond Girl left my body, that didn't happen anymore.

I have no idea what she was doing in my body and why she "hitched a ride" with me, other than maybe she knew I was getting out of prison and saw it as her way out of that place. Maybe when my guides told me I needed to get rid of trauma, this was what they meant. She was trying to leave me, and perhaps the ayahuasca allowed her to go to a better place.

At any rate, I walked out of the bathroom and told Sean, "I need to tell you something. You're not going to believe what just happened to me." Of course, he was really getting used to bizarre things happening to me at this point. I told him what had happened, and he was like "Are you okay?" I said, "Yes, I'm perfectly fine." I actually could see better, I could sense things better, I felt more like myself then before.

After that, we had some fun because weren't really supposed to leave. You're not supposed to just walk out of the ceremony, you're supposed to go to the next stage in the shared room. But we were completely okay at that point. We felt fine to leave but we didn't want to get challenged or jolt anyone else. Sean said, "Okay, I'm going to start the car for about 10 minutes, get everybody used to the sound of the car starting, and then you can get in the car and we'll go back to the resort."

And that's what we did. We stopped at a grocery store on the way back, because our suite had a big kitchen and we were just getting settled and I knew that everybody would be hungry. My mom had planned to take the kids out to eat, but I was pretty sure she hadn't gotten groceries yet. It was funny shopping like that, because were wearing all white and the shaman had drawn symbols on our foreheads with chalk while he was going around the room at the start of the ceremony. So we looked a bit unusual.

Then, right when we got to the hotel, everybody was standing outside. Apparently, there had been some sort of fire in the hotel, or a fire scare where there was smoke. We got out of the car at valet parking, and all the hotel guests and staff were there outside. My family saw us and came over. My son looked at us, all in white with white symbols on our foreheads, and he was like "Mom, you look like you're in a cult. What are you doing?" He knew we were going to a ceremony, but he didn't really know what it was all about. This gave me a chance to explain to him better what we really were doing.

We were outside for about 20 more minutes; then we got the all-clear and we were able to go back up to our suite on the 37th floor. We loaded in our groceries, made a great meal, ate and enjoyed ourselves.

IT'S BACK!

Then another fascinating thing happened. You might remember that quite a while back, years earlier when I was still back and forth with Gabe, I had been disappointed in Sean sexually because his I thought his penis was very small. Not the first time we were together, but subsequently. I didn't know if I could be with a man who had such a small penis.

Now, I was lying next to him, having just received a huge healing from ayahuasca, and we were cuddling. One thing led to another and we began to get intimate. I reached my hand out and I put it on his penis and…it seemed to have grown about *five times*! It was size I remembered it being when we were first intimate that night we met. I was shocked. How was this possible?

I looked at him and said, "What did you do to your penis?" He said, "I don't know what you're talking about." I insisted, "No, really, what did you do to make it grow? Did you take a pill? Did you do something?" He looked at me strangely and said, "Rebecca, I actually don't know what you're talking about. This is the size my penis has always been."

Then it hit me. I had been under a spell, which I already knew. But that spell actually extended to my perception of partners' penises!

My perception of Gabe's penis at first was that it was huge. And then there was that time later in our relationship where it had shrunk. For quite a while he was complaining and fretting about his penis shrinking, and I myself saw that and was quite disappointed. As Simon Parkes had suggested, perhaps he didn't fulfill his contract with those entities and they took everything away.

But at that point, the spell was also of my own making—my own martyr stuff. It was having been in love, trying to help someone who was sick, holding onto what I remembered, not wanting to let go, being in obligation and fix-it mode, giving my life away. It was guilt, shame, fear, and attachment, which still created portals for shadow energies.

But then, I was given the perception that Sean's penis was super small—presumably, so that I would want to be with Gabe and not Sean, and maybe allow Willow to be raised by Gabe (giving the entities access to her). Or maybe I just couldn't see clearly through that entire mess.

Now, I told Sean about all of this. Sean thought it was pretty funny. "You thought I had a small penis?" He just started laughing. But I was astounded once again by the power of the spell I had been under. Such a powerful energy to give me a false perception like that.

It seemed that this ayahuasca healing had finally cleared the last of Gabe's energy, so I could see Sean as he actually was. And when you actually get rid of that toxic false twin flame energy, what's right in front of your face is amazing.

The way I was connecting with Sean now was so powerful, too. I was so invigorated. I felt, "Finally, I have someone who treats me well! Someone who truly loves me. And I love him—and I love myself. Things are really working out." I felt like I was finally truly bringing my Heaven to Earth. Everything I had been through was for a reason.

This is when Sean began talking about marriage. Even on the way home from the Miami trip it began to come up. He started to mention it. Sometimes, it was in unromantic ways. For example, one time he brought up the fact that I could get on his health insurance if I married him. I said, "I don't want to get married because of insurance." He just laughed.

Other times, we would approach the subject more gracefully. Either way, we were getting very close as a family, and I was extremely happy about that.

CONFIDENCE

Even now, though, I was still working on confidence issues. Even with all he had given me, how he had stood by me, and all he was showing me now, still I was looking at Sean wondering, "Does he really want to marry me? What does he think about me?" There was still more that I needed to work on.

Something important to remember is that when you're dealing with any toxic energy, it always attaches to your shadow energy. Your shadow includes insecurities—lack of self-confidence, guilt, doubt, shame, or fear. Anything other than completely loving yourself is how these energies can attach.

I obviously had a lot of this work to do, or I wouldn't have been vulnerable to Gabe and his spell. And then, while all of it forced me to do a lot of work, it also put me through so much. When I was in prison, one time I told Danielle, "I'm sure I'm never going to get married, because who would want to marry me, knowing that I've been in prison?" Danielle just laughed. But I was serious.

Then one week visiting Sean in Michigan, I started to feel Gabe's energy in Sean's bedroom. It felt like something was staring at me from the corner of the room. At first I thought, "Okay, it's just me. I'm imagining things." But I was still kind of scared. I would take a shower and I'd feel the energy in the bathroom.

I told Sean about it and he got a little upset, saying "I really wish that we could be done with him." I felt abashed, and I understood how he felt; he'd been through enough of Gabe. It was crazy that even after all the world I had done, this could *still* permeate all the goodness and positive energy we were creating together and as a family. So I didn't say anything else.

But that night, when I went to sleep, there was a monster face in my dream, coming right out of my third eye. I knew then that I wasn't imagining it. Still, I was determined not to bother Sean with it any more.

The next day, though, my suspicions were confirmed by Willow, and Sean couldn't dismiss it. Sean and I were dressing Willow, and I was very aware of that energy still in the room. But I wasn't saying anything. Suddenly, Willow looked at us and said, "Shhh…" and pointed to the corner of the room where I was sensing the energy, and she said, "Scary monster."

Every single hair on my body stood up. Then, of course, Sean looked at me and said, "Okay, there is definitely something going on here."

I realized I had to take charge of this energetically and clear this from our space. I had Sean and Willow leave the room. I commanded the energy or entity to leave. And I began to work on myself, whatever was attracting and allowing this energy still to attach. I realized that this energy still gaining access to me because of my lack of confidence and loving myself. Those lower-vibration feelings were creating portals for negative energy to enter. I knew that I had to go full force on ridding myself of that.

For the next few weeks I spent a lot of time doing my integrative holistic energy work. I focused on nurturing myself energetically and with self-love. I worked out, I meditated, I spent time with Sean and Willow and my other children, I went to social events that made me happy. I focused on living a joyful life. And the monstrous Gabe energy did not return.

As time went on, I began to trust more, too. I realized that Sean was looking at me with such love in his eyes and such admiration. He told me, "I admire you for everything you've been through and your ability to just come out and get right back into the groove of things." He told me that he'd always believed in me. And he told me that from the first second he really saw me, he knew that someday that we would be married.

So finally, I began to feel really good about the situation—deep down to my very core, with no doubts lingering. I felt good about myself, I felt good about the way I looked, I felt good about my spirituality, I felt good about my emotional state, I felt good about my relationship with my children and my family. Finally, I was in a state of true empowerment. And the negative, dark, reptilian energy had no access, nothing to attach to.

AWAKE

Then one night when I was sleeping with Sean, something happened that changed my life forever. I was sleeping, but it was one of those sleeps where you're actually awake, but in a different dimension or parallel reality. I'm not even sure what exactly was going on, just that I was both asleep and awake.

I woke up and I saw a being in my room, actually a few beings but one in particular was really prominent. It reminded me of the movie Scream. It was an oval face, slanted eyes, very tall. The figure was in all white.

At first, I was really scared. I guess I watched too much Scream, because I was thinking he was going to stab me with a knife. But then I looked at him more closely, and I said, "I know you." And he smiled.

It was my guardian father. I had not seen him since that time in Peru when he and my guardian mother had appeared to me in the ayahuasca ceremony.

What he did next was absolutely phenomenal.

About four years prior I had gone to a river clearing ceremony in New Jersey with a very powerful shaman named Forest Speaker. After the river clearing, he came up to me and he drew an image of portals on a piece of paper and handed them to me. He said, "These are for you. I think you're supposed to get these tattooed on you."

I wasn't really that into tattoos, so I got two *invisible* portal tattoos, with invisible ink—one on each forearm. I trusted that someday these would be useful, but I didn't know for what. Sometimes when I meditated, I could feel light go in and out of these tattoos, but other than that, nothing significant had happened—until now.

Now, my guardian father took hold of my arms where the tattoos—these portals—were, and he transmitted into them what felt like a warm, sludgy substance. Then I felt my body vibrate and start shaking. I was receiving downloads into these portals.

All of a sudden, I *really* woke up. I was in shock and a little frightened. I don't know why. It wasn't really a scary experience, but it was unusual (not that I hadn't been through and seen plenty that was unusual by then!). Sean woke up too, and I told him everything that had happened. I said, "I want to sleep with the light on."

He said, "Okay, we will. But I think you're okay, because you know this being as your guardian father. You're going to be okay."

We went back to sleep. And then, all of a sudden, a couple hours later, I sat straight up and I said, "AWAKE: Academy of Wealth, Alchemy and Kinetic Energy." Then I grabbed my phone and started taking notes. Because I knew then what my guardian father wanted. He had said to me, at the end of the dream or vision earlier that night, before he left, "I'm going to be bringing our children to you. Starseed children. You must teach them, support them, and empower them to find their magic and do their own work."

So, I was going to develop this Academy through the downloads that they had given me. In prison, I'd really had to tap into the power of deeply understanding how we're all connected, how being in our hearts and scrubbing ourselves clean could create miracles, how we can create or dis-create events. This had opened me to something I could share. That incident with the TV, for example—that surrendering had allowed me to open a channel that I'd never opened before.

Now there were messages and codes coming through me that I would have been unable to hold before. I had reached a degree of purity where I could hold, could *be*, these transmissions from the guides. And I was very honored and excited to begin the process of creating the AWAKE Academy.

The energy that my guardian parents, these star beings, wanted me to transmit to students is a very powerful energy. I had to do it in a way where students could receive and hold the messages and codes themselves. Since we live in a 3D reality, I designed an academy where I teach different energy healing techniques that I had learned over the previous twenty-something years. I put it all under an umbrella in which people could get certified as Integrative Energy Healing and Holistic Practitioners.

That's the practical container for the process. But behind each video is an energy that is way more powerful than the words I'm saying or the techniques that students are learning. During the meditations that I recorded for AWAKE, I would go into a trance. To this day, I still don't remember the meditations, because it really wasn't *me*; I wasn't creating them, I was a channel or vessel for them. They came through me, from the star beings.

That's why AWAKE students often tell me, "While I'm listening to your meditations, I'll start convulsing, my body will start shaking—what is going on?" Those are DNA activations from the codes. When you change your body on a deep energetic level like that, you're having quantum shifts, and your body has to regulate.

I felt very honored to be given that gift to transmit to other people. This started a whole other career movement for myself and my family, and it's been absolutely amazing.

MARRIAGE

Meanwhile, Sean still officially lived in Michigan. I got my own place in my hometown, which was about seven hours from Michigan. During this time, I was consistently working on AWAKE and living my life with my kids and family. (I had allowed the primary care practice to dissolve—I didn't want anything to do with it any more.) Sean still had his engineering job and was travelling back and forth. We were both watching Willow. For the most part, Willow stayed with me and when I went to visit him on the weekends I would take Willow with me. Things felt smooth and good.

Then I started talking a little bit more seriously about marriage. Sean is English, and while I don't want to stereotype, for the most part English people have a difficult time expressing how they feel. Especially men. That became a little bit of a problem for us when we would approach the subject of marriage. He would do it in a way that a bit cagey and back-handed, and definitely not romantic. It was making me feel like "Does he want to do this? Does he feel obligated to do this?" Even though I had done all that work on my confidence and really knew now that he loved me, I still wasn't sure how serious he was about marriage.

My guides had given me the message that they wanted me to get married at the age of 44. That number is also a portal, and it's a magical age. Age 44 is when a lot of the magic happened for me, and when I really shifted to become who I really am.

The guides also specifically wanted us to get married on February 20, 2020. So this also put a bit of pressure on.

Around September 2019, he texted me, "When are we going to get married?" I texted back to him what my guides had told me they wanted. Then he kind of backed off a little. I had the impression he felt like "Hey, that's way too soon." So I just completely let it go. I wasn't really stressed about it. I thought "Okay, in a few years' time, we'll get married. It's no big deal. The guides will be okay with it."

Then, only about a week later, he sent me another text saying, again, "When are we going to get married?" I said, "I guess in a few years." He messaged back, "I thought you wanted to get married this upcoming year." And I said, "Well, you didn't seem like you wanted to." He said, "No, I do."

So that's basically how he asked me to marry him. Kind of over text, which wasn't the most romantic way. But I was really okay with that—at least, I thought I was, or told myself that. Things were going really well. I felt secure and happy. I didn't have big expectations about how I would be asked, because I was at a new level of self-love that didn't require that external validation. However it happened, I would be grateful.

We penciled in the date of February 20, 2020. I didn't have a ring yet, so I had to remind him, "Hey, I'm not going to marry you if you don't get me an engagement ring." He kind of joked, "Oh, I have to do all of that stuff?" I said, "Yeah." Once again, this felt unromantic, even though he was such a sweet, loving guy and as I said, I felt pretty okay with however it happened.

So I did what I had to do. I went on the Internet and found the ring that I wanted. I remember looking at it thinking "I don't want it to be too expensive." There was a higher-quality version of the ring, but I thought "Oh, he's not going to want to spend that much money." So, I picked the lower-quality version for myself and gave the link to him so he would order.

Then it came in the mail, and for a couple weeks it just sat there in his kitchen in the box. I knew what it was. He knew I knew. But there wasn't a time when he actually planned a proposal.

Finally, one day I said to him, "Are you just going to let that box sit there forever?" We were standing in his kitchen (and I specifically remember the kitchen being really messy at the time) and he got the ring out of the box when I said that, and got down on his knee and asked me to marry him. In the kitchen! It was very unremarkable, but I thought "Okay, this is better than nothing. I do want to marry this guy. I know that he loves me."

Of course, I said, "Yes." We kissed and hugged—and then we went about the rest of our day. I swallowed my disappointment that it wasn't more romantic and dramatic and momentous.

Then we started actively making plans. Our family thought it felt kind of rushed, because 2-20-20 was only a few months away. But we didn't want anything big. I was more concerned with the things that I knew my guides wanted us to do during the wedding than I was with any traditional trappings or customs.

I knew we were supposed to get married inside some facsimile of the infinity sign. I knew I was supposed to stand in some representation of the feminine, he was supposed to stand in a representation of the masculine, and we were to say "I do." I also knew that one of my best friends was supposed to marry us, because of how she embodied the complex Lilith energy connoting sensuality, sacred yet edgy feminist energy, and the importance of shadow. Really integrating the shadow is so important, and she embodied that energy and sensibility.

About two weeks after we officially knew we were going to get married, Gabe called me from the YMCA. I still answered the phone when he called. I just wanted to know if there was an emergency. This time, he was just asking how I was, probably wanting to see me. I told him, "I'm getting married." He was shocked. He began to yell at me. "You're not getting married. You're not getting married. You can't do this!" I remained calm and steadfast. "Yes, I am. I'm getting married to Sean." Then he got nasty, sneering, "That was awful fast." He then continued to demand that I not get married. Obviously, this was not something he had any say in, but as usual he was delusional. I said, "Well, this is my choice," and hung up the phone.

QUIT YOUR DAY JOB

During the December before we got married (a few months before the date), I received another message from my guides. The message was that the twin flame energy is very important to our union and mission, and that the divine masculine and divine feminine open up magical portals of healing. When I got the codes for the AWAKE Academy meditations and was channeling all that material, I felt like I was beginning to fulfill that mission and role. Now, I feel like people who come to the Academy are also on that twin flame journey and also part of that movement to unite the masculine and feminine. The truth is, I think *any* journey to true health and wealth—as well as love—is a twin flame journey, because in all of it, you're moving towards love and intimacy with yourself. That is the ultimate and core relationship from which all else emanates.

The guides also told me how they wanted our marriage to reflect a greater possibility than normal relationships. "Because of the way the world is today, it makes relationships hard. Two people wake up, go their separate ways, come home, they're tired…" My guides said, "We don't want that for you. We want a family unit where the two of you can work together, open up the divine feminine and masculine portals, and help humanity." So our relationship, our marriage and union, truly had a higher purpose.

In service of that, they told me that Sean was to quit his engineering job. This wasn't something that made sense to him at first. He was making a decent amount of money. I told him what the guides had asked, and he just looked at me and chuckled. I explained, "The guides told me that if you quit your job, they're going to at least double my income."

He said, "Well, why don't they double your income first, and then I'll quit my job." I replied, "That's not the way it works. We have to have trust and faith. You need to quit your job and then my income will double."

To my surprise, he did grasp that idea, and actually made plans to quit his job February 5, a couple of weeks before the wedding. He was putting trust in the guides at this point. That made me happy.

CAT AND MOUSE

As close as we had become, and as smoothly as things were going, a phenomenon occurred as we got close to the wedding date that I think can actually be a common pattern or dynamic. As the moment of deepest commitment approached, I felt like we both came up against an instinct to run—to withdraw, retract, recoil. The dynamic this can set up in a relationship is a push-pull of fleeing and pursuing, Once there's a "runner"—one person begins to step back—the other person can feel this, if not see it, and tries to step in closer, to pursue or chase or bring the other person back into connection. And this can switch back and forth, so when one person gets really close, the other person may run, and then vice versa.

This dynamic is very common in twin flame relationships because we're dealing with deep vulnerabilities and intimacy. But really, everybody gets caught up in it to some degree. If you're human, you're probably going to have intimacy issues to some degree. Every single human is working on deep self-love, and to be able to accept deep love from someone else. So whenever you start to attach to someone, it can be a little bit scary. You might make up reasons why you don't like the person, or reasons why it won't work. Expressing yourself and discussing your relationship with one another will always be extremely important.

Sean and I did experience some of this push-pull going both ways before the wedding, and resolving it would turn out to be as interesting as everything else had been.

LESSON

I believe that the twin flame push-pull is a reflection of your own "push and pull" inside. Part of me still felt like Sean was doing me a favor by marrying me, that he didn't truly love me and that the proposal was a reflection of this. But that doubt was really being fueled by something much deeper; inside myself, I was questioning my own worth. This then played out in our external reality.

Can you identify times in your life where you harbored conflicting feelings in your internal reality that reflected in your external reality? This is a very powerful concept to master because it allows you to step into your power even during times when you perceive someone is treating you badly. While it's easier to project our experience onto the other, and indeed others do play their role, the fact is that our own selves and our own experiences are the only ones we have any agency over. When we transform inside, especially our beliefs, the world can change around us—more than we might imagine is possible.

Chapter Fourteen

IT WAS SIX WEEKS BEFORE OUR WEDDING. SEAN was in Michigan and I was in my hometown. We were, once again, seven hours apart. We did not see very much of one another at all. Over the previous month and a half, we had seen each other just one weekend, when we did go out and pick out wedding rings. But with everything else, we were falling behind—from getting his suit to tying up last-minute items.

I noticed that he was taking a lot of band gigs during that time. I could tell that he was starting to get a little bit antsy about changing his life. He was planning on moving to my hometown, so he was going to have to quit the bands he was in. I could see how he was kind of holding on to the last vestiges of his own life in Michigan. Scheduling more gigs, becoming very busy.

The truth is, I was getting cold feet around that time, too. For me I think this was mostly because I wasn't seeing him. It felt strange and wrong to me that I hadn't seen my future husband for six weeks.

He was supposed to come up a little over a week before the wedding, stay with me until the wedding, and then we would get married and start the moving process. We had a small honeymoon planned, and then a larger one within a couple months, to Costa Rica. When he finally showed up that week before the wedding, he walked in the door and gave me a kiss on the cheek. I looked at him and said, "You know, that's how my grandfather used to kiss me." I wanted him to kiss me on the lips.

I realized we had a problem with kissing. I loved French kissing. And I see kissing as very important. If you want to say "Hey, how was your day, honey?" you touch tongues. The tongue is at the end of the vagus nerve, and the vagus nerve is the vessel of Kundalini energy, so you get energetic updates from connecting there (I call them "software updates" or "codes" or "Kundalini updates"). You can feel a sort of melding and, though you may not realize it, you're getting information that way. That's why so many people enjoy it, even if they don't know exactly why. It's very powerful. If you're not kissing on the lips or touching your tongues for at least five seconds a day, then you're missing out on that person's energy.

So all of a sudden, I got really scared. I was like "I can't believe I'm going to get married to someone who doesn't like to French-kiss." And yet, I also knew all was not lost. Our first kiss had been absolutely phenomenal. It was probably the best kiss I'd ever had in my life. But I was wondering why and how we had somehow gone backwards. What had changed? I'd had that in my mind for a while, actually, and I was sort of keeping it in a "file" to talk to him about.

And then I didn't do it. I had welcomed him into the house, we started talking about wedding plans, and the kissing conversation never happened. Now here I was, about to marry a man who didn't seem to be into this kind of kissing that I felt was incredibly important for connection and communication.

That Friday was February 14th. We were getting married on Thursday, February 20th. So we had Valentine's Day, and then we were going to get ready for the wedding. In spite of my letdown and little freakout about the kiss on the cheek and our "kissing problem," I started feeling really good again. I looked at this extremely amazing, gorgeous, kind man, who had supported me so completely through so much, and remembered what I loved about him and how lucky I was.

That surge of contentment and gratitude didn't last long. Shortly after he arrived, he announced, "By the way, I can stay here for one night, but then I've got a gig in Michigan that I have to go back for, on Valentine's Day. Then I'll come back."

That just crushed my world. I felt like "Wow. He just got here. The wedding is in less than a week. We haven't even finished everything up, we haven't seen each other in six weeks, and he just came to stay *one night*?" He was going to leave the next day to play a gig? Not only that, but a gig with a female singer with whom he had been gigging with for a long time. It was at a very small bar that would probably have about 20 people there watching them. How important could this be? What was the message here?

I was extremely upset. I looked at him and said, "Look, these are telltale signs. Something is not right. I don't feel like you're really into this wedding. Your priorities don't seem right to me. We haven't seen each other in six weeks and you get here and you want to go back to Michigan right away. It seems like you're really in denial about this wedding."

And that's when I brought up the kissing. Maybe it wasn't the most relevant or fair moment, but it just spilled out along with all my other misgivings. I said, "I also noticed that you don't even really kiss me. It doesn't seem like you want to do that with me. You don't seem to be interested in us touching tongues or French-kissing."

He denied this. He said, "I love kissing you!" He just didn't understand.

I was so disheartened and distressed about the way this was going that I said, "Okay, you know what? We're going to postpone it." We had just a small gathering planned. Most of his family was in England. He wasn't really inviting his close friends because it was a Thursday and a lot of people worked. So it was mainly my family and his dad and brother. It wouldn't be a big deal to call them and say, "Hey, we're going to postpone this wedding for a while."

He looked at me in shock when I suggested this. He said, "No. We're getting married. I want to." I said, "No, we aren't. Not now. I want to make sure I'm marrying someone who really wants to marry me." He just stood there dumbfounded, and I walked away to go to bed.

The thing was, I wasn't even angry about it. I just felt like, "I think we need some time. I think we need to iron out these things before we get married."

It seemed like the best course of action, but it also kind of broke my heart. I was grieving. I went and I lay down in my daughter Ariel's bed. Her presence was always soothing and healing. I was laying there and getting ready to go to sleep for the night with her. I had come to terms with the fact that we were just going to postpone the wedding for a while and I was going to be okay with it.

Then Sean walked into the room and he said, quietly so as not to wake Ariel, "I cancelled the gig. I'm not going."

I felt an overwhelming sense of guilt. Now, looking back on it, it's not something I should have felt guilty about. Right there is a sign of me *still* not loving myself in the way I needed to—even though I had done so much work and come so far. Still, I felt guilty. I was like "No, I don't want you to do that. Just go play the gig."

He said, "No, Rebecca. I do want to get married to you. And I want to do it this Thursday, February 20, like we planned. I don't want to do the gig." He said that it took me calling it out and being upset about it to realize how off base it was for him to rush back to a small gig days before the wedding. He said, "Please, please, please, marry me." He had tears in his eyes.

Well, I couldn't dismiss a heartfelt apology like that, nor his willingness to wake up to something, become aware, and see things differently. He was so sincere, of course I forgave him. And it seemed clear that he *did* want to get married.

So the wedding was back on. I went back to the bed we had made up for the two of us.

Here's the thing, though. Even though he pleaded with me to marry him and was telling me how lucky he was, when I look back on it now, I remember still somehow feeling almost like a burden in these days before the wedding. I felt like a nag or a pain in the butt, just asking him to get done what he needed to. "You have to get your suit, you have to do this, you have to do that." I still had some sense of guilt, like, "Look what you're putting him through, Rebecca."

Where was this coming from? Why should I think that the ordinary, necessary tasks of preparing for a wedding were too much to ask of my loving future husband? I had been so strong through so much; I had been given and had cultivated such remarkable psychic and spiritual powers. I had worked so hard on self-love. And I had come such a long way. But shadow energies may need to be worked through in layers; they can be persistent and have all sorts of tentacles into various parts of you and your life. Apparently it still had some in me and mine—and this would create more situations and require more work for me and for our relationship in the future.

THE WEDDING

The night before the wedding, we followed tradition. The bride and the groom are not supposed to see each other. I went to Deep Creek Lake, where we were going to be married and which was about 50 minutes from my hometown, and spent the night with my friend who was an ordained minister and was marrying us.

Sean was watching the dogs and finishing up some last-minute things. My sisters and my mom drove up to Deep Creek Lake as well, and they were getting the wedding site ready.

Where we were getting married was very important to me. It was the first place I had ever seen Sean. I remember walking into that bar, looking at him, and it was like my soul knew him right away. Even though it had been such a long, meandering, and often confusing road after that, it started right there with absolute clarity. And as it turned out, though I hadn't learned it till much later, he had had that clarity too. So I had decided I wanted to marry him on that very stage where I first laid eyes on him.

It was a cute little bar. They'd never had a wedding there, and they were excited about the story and to be a part of it. My family and friends were very open to the way that I wanted to get married. They were decorating the stage according to the way my guides said that it needed to be.

It was set up beautifully. We had a figure eight—the Infinity symbol—that was outlined by roses. One side of this figure eight represented the divine masculine, the other represented the divine feminine. We would be standing in the center, the zero point, when we said our vows. I had written the wedding vows myself, talking about how we had come full circle on this journey together. I thought the vows were beautiful.

That night before the wedding, the friend who was marrying us spent the night with me at a cute cabin in the area. We talked about and finalized the wedding vows, we edited them a little bit, and then we went to sleep.

I fell asleep fine, but in the middle of the night—maybe not surprisingly—something paranormal happened. I had a dream that I was levitating. I got really scared, because I couldn't get down. I felt like some sort of force was holding me up in the air. One of the teachers who worked with me in AWAKE at that time was on the ground, telling me to step into my power. She said that I could come down. But Gabe was there, and for some reason I was thinking "He's the only one that can get me down." I was screaming, "Gabe! Help me! Help me!" My co-teacher was shouting at me, "No, Rebecca! Stay in your power! You can do this!" And then I did. I came down and I was able to stop levitating.

What woke me up from the dream was a fire alarm in the cottage that started blaring. I know that my dream (and the frequencies in that dream) set the fire alarm off.

So I didn't sleep too well that night. But I got up the next day and I was excited about getting married. I loved my wedding dress. Willow looked absolutely adorable. She was the flower girl. And my older daughter, who was 14 at the time, was also one of my bridesmaids. It was a very special experience for me. I was getting my makeup done, my friends were there, my mom was there. I was trying on my dress, drinking champagne, and feeling relaxed.

Finally, it was time, and we were to make our grand entrance.

I was taken to a small room just off the main one, and then we heard the wedding music play. The couple who played the wedding music were Sean's good friends. He had been in one of their bands. He had known them for about ten years and was very close to them; he was so happy that they had come all the way from Michigan to Maryland to play at our wedding.

He went up on the stage, and I walked down the aisle. I remember looking at him and thinking, "I'm definitely making the right decision." He was looking into my eyes as we were saying the vows. The way he looked at me, I could tell he was saying to me, "This is what I want. I'm serious. I'm going to devote myself to you for the rest of my life." I saw it in his eyes.

Then we said, "I do" and he kissed me and everybody cheered and threw rice and blew bubbles (we did have some traditional wedding rituals too).

And then, when everything had calmed down, we looked at each other…and then he looked past me right at Willow and said, "She's absolutely stunning." Which was fine, because she *was* absolutely gorgeous. But he didn't say that *I* looked beautiful in my wedding dress. That kind of stung me in my heart. I felt like "Oh gosh, he doesn't like my dress. He must not like the way I look."

But I quickly let that go as everybody started to come up to us and congratulate us. Then we fed each other the cake, and we slow-danced to a song that I had picked out. His family was there, my family was there. Everybody had an amazing time.

At the reception, I talked to the husband of one of my best friends. He had been a wedding planner for about 12 years, and he said he had never heard vows so beautiful. He said, "Rebecca, that was a very unique wedding."

Then, just as we were about ready to wrap up and get going (we had rented a resort cabin close by, and had plans for skiing the next day) we went to go say goodbye to his good friends who had come from Michigan. What happened next shocked me. It shocked me so much that I couldn't even speak up about it.

He looked at his friends and said, "Why don't you guys come over tonight and hang out?"

I thought, "But…it's our wedding night." Yet I didn't say anything. I was so deeply in shock that I was speechless. And then, I just let it go. I told myself, "Okay, pick your battles, Rebecca."

I decided that if his friends were coming over, then I was going to invite my sister. I walked over to my sister and said, "Hey, why don't you and Todd (her husband) come over and we can hang out?" She looked at me like I had fifteen heads, and she said, "Rebecca, this is your *wedding night*. I'm definitely not coming to hang out with you." And she smiled and hugged me.

Then I *knew*. I wasn't just being petty. It was *not* normal that he had invited his friends over.

So we went back to the little cabin, and his friends came over. Then his dad came over, and his brother came over. I was sitting there thinking "Okay, we're still going to have *our* night after this, after they leave." I had bought some cute skimpy sexy lingerie that I was going to wear. I decided that it would still be okay—after this little visit, we would have our real wedding night.

We ordered in some pizza, we talked a lot, we went to the hot tub. But then 11:30 came and I was getting very discouraged. The wedding had been over since about 6 p.m.. I started to think, "Okay, well, we're just not going to have our wedding night together." I was getting really tired. I just looked at the TV and felt really sad.

Suddenly Sean noticed me feeling dejected. He looked at me and asked, "What's wrong?" I just looked at him like "What do you mean, what's wrong? This is my wedding night and I'm watching TV while you're talking to your friends."

He got this look on his face like it registered, and he quickly said, "Okay, guys, it's time to wrap it up. Rebecca and I are going to get ready for bed." And then they left.

Unfortunately, it was too little too late, and his last-minute kicking out the guests didn't lead to a beautiful wedding night. I was so hurt and frustrated by then that he and I bickered about it. We weren't even intimate. Finally, after we had struggled for a while, he said in defeat, "We'll just do that tomorrow." And I thought, "Yeah, but tomorrow is not our wedding night." I felt stricken, like something had been lost that we could never get back. We might have a nice night tomorrow, but our one wedding night was over.

We went to bed, and we still cuddled. It was sweet, after that, although it still wasn't what it could have been and should have been. Once again I tried to swallow my disappointment. I was still doing that "making myself small" thing. I was settling, and trying not to ask too much. I told myself, "Rebecca, this is really nice, really beautiful. Don't be so picky." Yet again, I look back on it now and I see that I was not treating myself like a queen. And I was allowing myself not to be treated like a queen.

THE MORNING AFTER

The next morning when we woke up, we decided to go skiing as planned. In spite of the previous night's dismaying, underwhelming letdown, I was excited for the day. I love skiing. I was going to ski and Sean was going to snowboard. And, after all—we were married!

We got ready to go, had breakfast, got all of our gear on and left. We didn't talk about the night before—I figured we'd just start fresh that night. In spite of my deflation, I was ready to reset and have a great day. We were affectionate and things felt better. Of course, I was repressing a lot at this point, but I was really trying to make it work.

And then…before only our second run, as we were getting off the ski lift, I went to the left, he started to go to the right, and he fell and hurt his ankle pretty badly. An ambulance came up and got him in an emergency snowmobile and they took him off of the mountain. He ended up having a sprained ankle. He really couldn't walk on it at all.

I thought, "Energetically, what does this mean?" Because that's the way I think. As in, "Why did he attract a sprained ankle the day after our wedding, and the first morning of our honeymoon?" It felt avoidant, especially in light of all the other dismaying incidents leading up to and through the wedding. The push and the pull, the leaning in and running away. It was still happening. I actually did point this out to him. The fact that it happened just seemed like yet another forestalling of a full, wholehearted embrace of our union.

And now I had to do everything myself, such as walk the dogs, get dinner, take care of him.

Yet fundamentally, I was still extremely happy being married to him. And I know, in spite of these hiccups and stumbles, he was fundamentally glad too. The big picture felt good and right. Many nights following the wedding, we would lie in bed together and just say how happy we were that we married one another. We even joked about the ankle and me having to do everything: "Okay, this is married life!" It's just that these incidents were adding up to the fact that there was still work to do.

For one thing, we were still working on the kissing. Before we actually got married, during that brief window where he wanted to go home to play a gig on Valentine's Day, when I brought up the kissing in my distress, I told him, "I'm going to schedule an emergency session with a Tantra specialist, to intervene here!"" Because I couldn't seem to get us kissing by myself.

Well, after scheduling a $500 kissing session, he decided to take it seriously and promised me that he would work on it. And he did…but it still felt very robotic. I could tell he still wasn't into it, not like he was the first time we met. So, that was still in the back of my mind, too, along with all of these wedding-day and wedding-night slights—even though I knew he loved me.

These things were adding up. Not telling me I was pretty at the wedding, feeling like I was a burden during the wedding and all of the planning, inviting friends and family to our wedding night, not having sex on our wedding night, and now the ankle. The list was growing and I was feeling it, but I still wasn't saying much, other than the bickering on our wedding night and the kissing discussion before the wedding. I was just letting a lot of it bottle up inside of me.

I decided we needed to do some major Tantra. Of course, I knew Tantra very well. So I told him, "I'm going to actually create a Tantra video series. But when I do it, you and I are authentically going to go through it to demonstrate. We will be teaching Tantra to others, but we'll also be healing ourselves."

He seemed very open to this, which was encouraging. I knew this would help with intimacy and vulnerability and bringing us closer. I was sure it would be healing.

GOING INWARD

Right after we got married, Covid hit, so the whole world shut down. We were in our homes. We would have been anyway, because I worked from home and at that point, Sean had quit his job. (By the way, remember how the guides said my income would double if he quit his job, and he was skeptical but thankfully he trusted them and went with it? Well, my income actually tripled after he quit his job, within a little over a month. It was a great example of how the universe will reward you for your faith, and I had the same faith that if we worked diligently on our relationship, it would yield comparable results.)

So, we decided to get a cabin in the middle of nowhere on a beautiful river. We found a great place in Berkeley Springs, West Virginia, and we stayed there for almost five weeks. The plan was not only to practice Tantra while we were there (and simultaneously create the video series for my Academy), but also to do ayahuasca together during this time as well, to enhance the process.

That time in that cabin was profound. It shifted us in such powerful ways. I will never forget it. The cabin was surrounded by nature, and I made the ayahuasca myself, doing the downloads and using local plants. Enjoying the plant medicine with him was very, very rewarding and we had many deep experiences.

At this point, Sean already knew that paranormal events happen in my life on a regular basis. He had been acquainted with this early on, from the guardian parents telling me that he was to be father of my child, to us conceiving after just one lovemaking when I was over the age of 40. But the time in the cabin really opened his eyes—not only to my gifts and spiritual connection, but to a whole different side of Willow and the gifts that I knew she had come into this world with, which had been hinted at by Simon Parkes and others.

This was the first time that I had done ayahuasca with Willow around. She was about two at the time. I had done ayahuasca when I was pregnant with her, but never in her vicinity once she was born. This was a pretty big deal, and a new experience for us all, thought it felt perfectly natural and comfortable for me too. My mom was with us to watch over Willow, just in case we needed her, knowing that we would be taking ayahuasca.

When we first took the medicine, we had gotten in a hot tub. Willow got into the hot tub with us and the ayahuasca started to kick in. When you're in water, things can be accelerated or intensified. The heat began to overwhelm me. At some point I started saying, "Wow, this is really intense, this is really intense!" Sean was sitting beside me, and I was saying "Wow, I think I need something!" He said, "How about I get you some ice?" I said, "yes, yes, please, go get it."

So he got out of the hot tub and hurried to get me ice. And then Willow turned to me, took her binky out of her mouth, looked me directly in the eye, and suddenly it was like she was twenty-five years old. She said, "Go to your heart space, mama."

I did—and all of a sudden, I saw visions of the movie *Frozen*. And the feeling that I was having, this intense heat that was overwhelming me, just dissipated. She healed me by doing that.

She put her binky back in her mouth, Sean came back, and I said, "You're not going to believe what Willow just did." Of course, he looked at me like "Oh come on, you're under the influence of ayahuasca." She just sat there innocently, looking like she hadn't done anything.

After the hot tub, we went into the living room and I noticed that I was speaking to her in a different way, almost telepathically. She was talking to me through her thoughts and communicating with me. Then she began speaking Light Language, or Star Language, and I understood what she was saying on a soul level. She was talking to me a lot about the whole experience with Gabe and how she had felt kind of resentful that I was going to have Gabe try to raise her. I was hugging her, and apologizing for that. I bonded with Willow amazingly during that time.

Then she reached behind my ear, and there was a sort of nodule on my ear that had never been there before. She pushed on it and then *I* started speaking Light Language. It was all incredibly and intensely paranormal. I was seeing different worlds that you can't see when you're in a normal 3D reality.

Sean was just observing us. The whole time, I was thinking that he was really connecting to us, really getting what was going on. But when I said something to him about it later, he said, "Yeah, you seemed pretty out of it." Which was not the case at all. I remember feeling great disappointment that he still didn't really get what was going on.

Still, even though he was still not totally on board with where Willow and I could go, he and I also bonded more deeply during this stay. We talked through some important things. We breathed each other's breath. We shot videos every night for the Tantra series. In this regard, he was amazing at participating. He did very well with helping me on the series. And it really helped us too, just as I had hoped. It created a deeper connection and it also allowed to us to create our future more intentionally.

SEX MAGIC AND MANIFESTATION

One of the videos were created for the Tantra series during our time at the cabin was about sex magic. Sex magic involves thinking about orgasm as life force. If you think about it, we wouldn't be here without orgasm. Orgasm is creation. It's the beginning of something new. Harnessing this energy can be very powerful for manifestation. With sex magic, you use Tantra and orgasmic energy to manifest.

When you tie your manifestation into orgasmic energy, you're creating a new beginning. You're creating a new life. As a practice or ritual, the idea is to consciously create and intend what the two of you want created together, and then make love. Through that orgasm, you bring your manifestation into creation. Of course, I went into this in depth for the Tantra series, but that's the gist of it.

We did the process to demonstrate but we also developed our creation in the course of doing that. We wanted to create a magical life together. We decided that we were going to have a house on Deep Creek Lake, because that's where we met, and we wanted to live there. We were going to own a property in Costa Rica and learn surfing. We put all of this in our manifestation, as well as of course the blossoming of our deep love and being healthy and our children being healthy. Pretty much everything you'd want in a manifestation, we included. We orgasmed through it, and that was our sex magic.

Now, through this, Sean was really beginning to see a whole new side of me and my spirituality, and how connected I really was to everything in my belief system.

What happened the next night after the sex magic process really threw both of us for a loop. Willow had become really attached to this one room in the cabin. She was hanging out in there a lot. One day she took my hand and said, "Here, mommy, come in here." I walked in there and it felt very...shadow-like. Not bad, just....different. I thought, "This is a place where you would definitely be able to work on your shadow energies." It felt eerie, but I just smiled at her and said, "Yes honey, I like this room." I knew we had shadow work to do, and she was leading us to the right space.

That night, Sean and I were sleeping in our bed. She was sleeping in that room she liked, and all of a sudden she woke up crying. Normally, Sean just gets right up and goes to her. He's conditioned to do that. But I looked over and he was still sleeping, so I thought, "Okay, I guess I'll go to her." I went to the room, and she said, "Mommy, lie down next to me." I did, and she went right back to sleep.

Then, all of a sudden, I felt my third eye open and I felt some kind of energy at the end of the bed. I looked down and it looked like a huge mantis at the end of the bed. Without my conscious will, my legs spread open, my sacral chakra opened up, and then the mantis energy...*combined* into me. I could almost say "It was like the mantis had sex with me" but that's not really exactly what it was. it was more like energetically combining with me. It's hard to explain, obviously. It didn't feel bad; it felt extremely powerful. But it was shocking, and just that fact of how strange and different it was scared me. So after a few moments I flew from my body into the room where Sean was, where we had been sleeping together, yelling "Help me!" I didn't *physically* go back into Sean's room—I astral-traveled. Then I came back into my body, woke up, and I was staring up at the ceiling of this "shadow room" that Willow was so enchanted with.

Sean walked in then and asked "Are you okay?" I said, "Not really. I think a bug just had sex with me." He just looked at me like "Okay..." He was, as I said, getting used to the paranormal around me, but this was pretty out there. He said, "Why don't we just go into the other room?" I followed him back to our bed and I tried to explained what had happened. He did listen and was very open, which I appreciated.

Willow slept through the whole thing. It was like it was her job was to get me into the room for that experience, and when that was done, she contentedly drifted off.

I wasn't sure why it happened until the next day. I took ayahuasca again (for the second and final time that trip). During that journey, I began doing movements that...well, humans just can't do. I was contorting in ways that most people can't contort. I was stretching in ways that I've never been able to stretch before. My skull was cracking. My head was cracking. I was guided to do this in what I now called the Shadow

Room. And as I did, I was working on shadow energies by enacting these flexible movements.

It felt so profound that I did it for thirty-some hours. I also went in the hot tub during this time and did some of these movements, because I needed the water to warm me up. Later, Sean told me, "When I saw what you were doing, I just left you alone, because there's no way a normal human being could move like that, so I figured you were doing something very important."

At the end of that journey, after all those other-worldly movements, I had a near-death experience. A beautiful darkness came over my pineal gland. It felt like I was in vast darkness, but it wasn't scary. It was very peaceful. Suddenly, that darkness turned into a big, beautiful, bright light. At that moment, I knew that I could go anywhere I thought about. But I realized that what I wanted was to go back into my body; I wanted to be where I was. I felt like I now understood personally what a near-death experience was.

The really bizarre thing about this experience is that before we went to the cabin, it flitted across my mind that I was going to get into a car wreck and that I needed some sort of seizure to happen, like a near-death experience (NDE), to get where I needed to go spiritually, to expand my consciousness. Parallel to that, one of the teachers in AWAKE Academy at the same time entered my dream and said, "Rebecca, I keep seeing you having a car accident." So I was thinking "Okay, I'm going to have a car accident, then I'm probably going to have a seizure. I'm not really going to die but I'm going to have a NDE, because that's what I need."

I believe that the mantis helped me do these ultra-flexible, bug-like movements to purge what I needed to purge and to be able to have a near-death experience, but very peacefully, without having a car wreck. My daughter helped with this by leading me into the room and to the mantis, thereby changing the timeline so that I didn't have to expand by having a car accident and seizure. This was a much safer and gentler way! I am extremely grateful to this day that it did happen this way.

I can imagine that all of this was probably a lot for Sean to handle. I'm the type of person who wants a husband to be a best friend, so I wasn't going to hide anything from him. I wanted him to share in all this. As I was telling him everything that was happening to me, he would get this look on his face and nod and occasionally say, "Yeah, I believe you believe it." Which felt just a little condescending—although I knew he was trying—because it meant "I see you believe it, but I'm not sure I do."

And I really wanted him to get it. I could tell that he was starting to see some of it that he couldn't deny. For example, I flew out of my body and woke him up that time when I was laying with Willow and the mantis energy happened. He woke up and heard that I needed him and came into the room. He was starting to accept some of this into his life. But he was teetering.

Meanwhile, I had known from the beginning that Willow was gifted and magical, and as I've shared, there had been plenty of moments from the time she was a baby that she demonstrated those gifts. So that wasn't surprising. But during this time I began to see just how psychic she was. She would do things that she knew would later really benefit us.

For example, something happened during the cabin time that helped me realize that Sean, for all of his kindness and goodness and sweetness, still had quite a bit of work to do (not that I wasn't suspecting this, with all the kissing avoidance and the wedding resistance). I was sitting on our bed and thinking "Everything is just really good." Right then, Willow came up and handed me his phone. It was very random. It wasn't something she would normally do. She just went and got his phone and brought it to me.

Of course, I don't look through Sean's phone. I would never think to do that. But I looked down at it, and the phone was open to Facebook Messenger and I saw that he was messaging a woman. I looked at the messages quickly and there were some inappropriate things. She was talking about sex—not in reference to him, but about her life, and he was responding to her about it. It was not appropriate for a married man. It was 2 o'clock in the morning, at one point, where they were messaging back and forth. He wasn't hitting on her, but the lines were definitely blurred, and I did not feel at all good about it.

I also didn't like that he seemed or be venting to her the way you would to a best friend—it was like she was his confidante. For example, he shared complaints about the cabin with her that he had not shared with me.

I thanked Willow and then I confronted Sean about it. I told him about how Willow had "alerted" me, because I always wanted him to see how gifted and intuitive she was. Then we had a conversation about it.

At first he was defensive, saying they had been friends for twenty years and that it was no big deal. But when pressed, he also admitted that they had slept together in the beginning, before they agreed that they were better as friends. I explained why this was not cool, especially at 2 a.m., and I said, "Can you see how this kind of behavior could lead to you eventually cheating on me? He said he could see that, and he agreed not to do it. At the end of the conversation, I trusted him.

Our time in the cabin ended near Easter, so we celebrated there. We hid Easter eggs for Willow all over the property, and she ran around with her Easter basket finding them. And we had a lovely Easter dinner.

It was a nice, simple, mellow way to end a pretty momentous and rich time of growth.

After we left the cabin, I felt really fabulous. Doing all those amazing movements, doing the ayahuasca and purging so much shadow energy, being with my husband and doing tantra, seeing Willow's gifts and bonding with her so deeply—it was a profound healing experience.

Now, we were going to take all this back into the real world.

LESSON

Sometimes our shadows are so deeply ingrained that there's no conscious way of letting them go. No matter how much our brains want to release the guilt, doubt, shame, fear, and insecurities that we embody, they seem stuck. This is because they're held in not only consciousness, but at subconscious, genetic, and soul levels. We're carrying the stories of our ancestors and humanity as a whole. Energy work, movement, and breathwork allow us to release and purge those energies once and for all.

However, this release can happen in layers. We need to be aware that when we purge these energies, material might start reappearing in our lives so that we can navigate through it. Thankfully, because these energies are on their way out, you can often process them out quickly if you're aware and diligent! (And you can do it without a "Shadow Room" or "sex with a bug"—these extremes were very particular to my journey. You must find the practices that work for you.)

At this time I was purging a lot of shadow, and many layers of shadow were yet to appear in my life to be further worked through. But the healing was worth it, because each layer that lifted allowed me to manifest a little more of what I was truly here to create.

Chapter Fifteen

NOW WE WERE BACK IN THE REAL WORLD—and it was the world of Covid. I had never been a big fan of conventional medicine, and I had learned from doing a ton of plant medicine ceremonies that the reason that people get sick is because an illness attaches to shadow energy. Illness is low frequency, so it can only attach to areas of you that are low frequency. So, if you did a lot of spiritual and healing work, and were raising your frequency, the stagnant energy of illness would not be able to attach to you. Being in your heart space and raising your frequency is the best prevention.

If you do get sick, it's a perfect time to focus on purging shadow energies. If I get sick, I always ask, "Okay, what am I holding on to? What is this Illness about? What do I need to release, to let the illness release?"

With these perspectives, I wasn't scared of Covid like many people were. I spent a lot of time walking the dogs in the sun and being in nature. I got Vitamin D shots and took zinc. I really felt like I was protected by everything I was doing. And I was teaching my family to do the same.

Likewise, the people who were drawn to AWAKE (The Academy of Wealth, Alchemy and Kinetic Energy) were not scared to get together because of Covid. Most of the students in AWAKE think the way I do. So we didn't really have a problem with Covid when we were doing natural plant medicine ceremonies all through 2020.

Financially and career-wise, this turned out to be a secure time for me as well. I was extremely fortunate because I created AWAKE way before Covid hit. But in the Covid era, it really took off because people were looking for online classes and that became a very popular thing to do.

With that success, we decided to start acting on our manifestation that we out forth during the sex magic process at the cabin. It's very important when you manifest that you actually do take action as well. The universe will show up for you miraculously, but you have to apply focus and action along with your intention.

LAKE HOUSE

With that in mind, we started looking for land at Deep Creek Lake, where we had met and gotten married, as we had planned. It happened quickly. Just a couple of days after we decided to step into action, about a week after we had gotten back from the cabin, we actually put a contract on land that we had found. It was absolutely perfect for us. It was lakefront and had a dock with it. It had state land around it, so there would be no other house near to us. It was beautiful! We knew right away that this was where we wanted to live.

The owner accepted our offer and we started preparing to build a home on the land. Because Covid hit right when we were supposed to go on our honeymoon to Costa Rica, the honeymoon was postponed until Costa Rica was allowing people to fly into their country. So it was a good time to be focusing on the new home instead.

For the most part, I woke up every day thinking about how lucky I was. I woke up in gratitude, excited about my life. I had amazing work, family, kids, home, financial security, and so many possibilities. Sean and I were working on our relationship—doing Tantra, talking. The kissing was definitely not yet where it needed to be, but I could tell he wanted it to be.

I was realizing, though, that this was about way more than just kissing. It was something deeper. As he became more and more attached to me, it was harder for him to allow his heart to open, because he was getting vulnerable and he was struggling with that. I can step back and see that very clearly now. But at the time, this was harder to see. When you're going through it, your own insecurities can play on you. In spite of my contentment in so many areas, I was getting kind of upset about the ways that his resistance to attachment and vulnerability were showing up.

One of the ways this played out was when he would make these amazing dinners—which on the face of it, sounds fantastic, right? He had lived in Italy for six years and learned the cuisine, and he would cook incredible Italian dinners for us. This could have been so romantic—except once he had made the meal, we'd be sitting at the dinner table, and he would pull out his phone and look at it for a lot of the dinner.

At first, in that way of wanting to focus on the good things and not be ungrateful, I would think, "He made this great dinner, I don't want to be a bitch and complain." Yet it was still starting to really get on my nerves. Whether or not he had made the beautiful meal, it was rude that he then spent the meal on his phone. It's kind of a well-known fact how even the presence of a phone destroys intimacy and connection. I finally said something to him about it, and he did listen—he started to put his phone away at meals.

But what I started to notice was that he seemed to want to be on his phone *all the time*. It was a way that he distracted and distanced himself constantly. When he wasn't on his phone, it was because he was scared that he was going to get in trouble with me, not because he wanted to be present with me—and that kind of missed the point.

The avoidance and distancing showed up in other significant ways too. I would go to bed at night and it seemed like he would purposely stay up and read or play guitar. He would always come to bed later than me. That made me feel really lonely and sad. For me it didn't make sense at all for a couple to go to bed at different times.

So I told him, "I think going to bed together as a couple is extremely important. It's our talk time, our bonding time, and physical intimacy time. But it seems like you really want me to be asleep when you go to bed." I pointed out how during the day, we didn't spend a tremendous amount of time talking, because we each were doing creative projects. I was always in my office, creating, which I loved doing! But evenings were our family time and couple time.

When I talked to Sean like this, he would give me a "deer in the headlights" look. I would grill him, looking for answers—"What are you thinking? Why do you do this?" But he couldn't really articulate anything substantial. It was just "No reason." He would listen, he said he understood, and he'd promise that he would change. He did say that being with me was important to him, and that he wasn't meaning to avoid me. I would be briefly mollified—but then the behavior would continue.

And even when he did modify a little, it felt like it was only because I had had asked to—like he was trying to do what I asked, do what I wanted, "be good." But I didn't want to be a checklist item—that didn't feel good either.

Another example of his holding back was really quite hurtful. During this time, we had decided to take salsa lessons together. When Sean had lived in Italy, he'd learned to salsa dance, and he really loved it. It was a passion of his. I wanted to take lessons and have us do it together, because I wanted to be his salsa partner. I took some salsa lessons individually, and I told the instructor, "I really want to be the one who dances with my husband." And I expected that, when he came with me, we would practice together. But what happened was a whole different scenario. He came to class, but he seemed very disinterested. And I ended up dancing with the instructor instead of him.

So here is a man who loves salsa dancing, and he has a wife who wants to salsa dance with him, and is taking lessons so she can do that. I thought he was going to love that. But I asked him to come back to another lesson so we could work through it, and he said, "No. You go by yourself." That was another huge disappointment.

Again, looking back on it, it's very clear what he was struggling with, this resistance against attaching and being vulnerable, and all the ways it was showing up. But at the time, it just felt terrible. It felt like, "He doesn't really love me that much. He doesn't want to be with me."

DISTANCE AT WORK

During this time, I was doing a lot of natural plant medicine ceremonies with the AWAKE students. Willow and Sean would come with me, because I wanted us to do this as a family.

One especially magical ceremony that I did was in Kentucky, with two students who had graduated from AWAKE and had excelled so much that they were now helping me with the Academy. We got to know each other pretty well. These two students each brought their husbands to the ceremony, so it was three women and their husbands at a beautiful Airbnb in Kentucky for a healing weekend. We had Willow there, and Willow thrived in that environment. She absolutely loved being part of these ceremonies. She would tune in very fast, and actually help us heal, and she would even speak Star Language. It was like a dream job, just absolutely perfect, to be doing this with my little girl and such wonderful colleagues and clients.

Except for one thing: again, Sean's distance was casting a shadow on an otherwise beautiful and light-filled situation, dimming my dream and my joy. When I would get together with people and do these ayahuasca ceremonies, he would hang back and withhold himself. And what I really wanted, and what my guardian parents had said they wanted for me, was a partner to work with. I felt that we were supposed to open the divine masculine and feminine portals during the ceremonies, as part of the healings, and I needed his divine masculine to come forward. I felt that it was our responsibility to have that divine connection together, to open up these healing portals. Yet instead I was seeing my husband act like he didn't want to be there, playing on his phone and practically running away from these magical events.

When we were in Kentucky, for example, there was an absolutely gorgeous moon one night as we were all sitting around the circle doing healing on one another. We decided to go out and look at the stars and the moon. Sean was off doing his own thing in another room. So I was sitting outside with the two women and their husbands and Willow. One of the women said to Willow, "Go get your Dad! He has to come out and see this beautiful moon!"

So Willow went and brought him to the door and said, "Daddy, come out! Look at the moon!" And he said, "Uh, no…" I also called, "Sean, please, come out!" And he was like "No!" He absolutely refused to come out and look at the moon and stars with us.

My heart just sank. What was this? What was going on? It was lonely and embarrassing and confusing. So I went and asked him, "Why is it that you're not with us right now? Why won't you come out?" He said, "I just don't want to be around people who are doing *that*." Meaning ayahuasca.

This was news to me. We were not *out of it*. With ayahuasca, you're not inebriated.

Eventually, I would learn what his resistance was—it had to do with fear surrounding his "rave days" and other drugs he had taken in the past. But it would take a while before all that came out.

Meanwhile, during this time in Kentucky, we worked amazing, profound, magical, life-changing healings on one another. Sean was in a separate room and didn't see all this magic. I would later explain it to him, but it wasn't the same. I felt so disconnected from him. I also felt envious of the other two women and their husbands, who were willingly and completely a part of this. As dearly as I loved Sean, I was starting to have doubts at this point. I just couldn't see being married to someone who didn't see and understand the work I was doing, and who didn't want to be part of it.

There had been times where he really seemed to "get it," like he saw me and admired me for what I did and how I worked. But since getting married he seemed to have become resistant and closed.

Of course, Willow always steps in at the right time.

During the last night in Kentucky, Sean was sleeping, and he was having a dream. In it, as he later described, a whole bunch of politicians were on his back, and he had a big set of keys to try to get into a garage, but he couldn't get in. The politicians wouldn't leave him alone until he could find the right key to get into the garage. He was trying all the keys, but he couldn't open the garage door.

He woke up, and Willow was there staring at him. She said, "Daddy, where are your keys?" He came out and told me about this. "Rebecca, that was absolutely insane! I didn't talk in my sleep. She was staring at me and she was reading my dream!" Finally, once again, he started loosening up. He started remembering what he had seen about me, and about Willow. He once again realized that the spiritual and psychic work we were doing was "real."

We drove home from Kentucky in good spirits. But I still had a mix of emotions. Obviously, there were some things I wasn't happy about. I loved Sean, and he was an amazing husband in so many ways. He did so much around the house, loved our daughter, and I knew he did love me. It's not as if he was doing drugs or drinking or cheating on me. For the most part, I was thinking, "You have a really, really good man."

But I had high standards. There were gaps, areas of resistance, nagging feelings that something was missing. I knew I was supposed to have my Heaven on Earth, and it was supposed to be complete. I was supposed to have a man I was in love with, who was working with me to help the world. And often I felt like it was me trying to help the world…while he sat in a corner and looked at his phone.

I was having tremendous success in my career. I was bombarded by students and clients who were offering testimonials of miraculous healing. It was my dream come true to know that I was finally in a place where I was super passionate about what I was doing, and it was healing the world around me. I wanted Sean to join me in this mission, in this work, and I had thought he wanted that too. At times, he had seemed willing. And I knew that it was what the guardian parents had intended for us.

I just wasn't sure where to go with these areas of unrest in our new marriage.

BACK TO THE LAKE HOUSE

We were now in the summer of 2020. Back home, I was looking for house designs to build. We were finishing up with the bank, getting prepared to receive a loan to build the house of our dreams. I was reviewing over 250 house designs, until I came across the perfect one. I would be submitting it to different contractors within a few weeks.

There was another powerful technique I used to get the land on the lake. I've explained how we did the sex magic process for our manifestation. But right before we actually found the land, I was staring out my window (in the place that I had gotten right after moving from my sister's) and I was staring at a brick house right next to me. I thought, "I want to be looking at the lake. Rebecca, do you have any belief systems where you're unable to look at the lake? Why are you looking at a brick house instead of the lake through your window?"

And then beliefs started coming to the surface, beliefs such as "It's going to take time." "It's too soon." "You're going too fast." "It costs too much money." "Only really, really rich people can live on the lake."

And just as I had done when I was in prison, to dis-create the event of the inmate beating me up, I started "scrubbing" myself clean of fear, doubt, and guilt. I dug deep to find my blueprint of negative beliefs and to authentically connect with positive ones. (This is much deeper work than simple affirmations where you "paper over" your negative beliefs with statements you don't necessarily believe—that doesn't work. You have to get to a place where you really believe the new beliefs.)

I needed to actually change the paradigm I was in—the one most people are in. My sister said things like, "Don't you think living on the lake is a little too much? You just got out of prison. Maybe a year from now." Almost everyone has—and repeats—these ideas: "Money doesn't come that fast." But with intention, rooting out your limiting beliefs, discovering where they lurk in you, and consciously shifting, you can create a different reality from the ordinary paradigm. This is very powerful work to do when you're trying to create and manifest in your life. I teach this practice in AWAKE Academy as well.

I leaned into what was really true for me. "It's a beautiful lake. You deserve to look at it just as much as anybody else. In heaven, you're not going to be looking at a brick house, you're going to be looking at beautiful bodies of water. You're bringing your Heaven to Earth. You can do this just as much as anybody else. Stand in your power."

We had another AWAKE ceremony coming up that summer. This next natural plant medicine ceremony was in this beautiful hangar on a mountain. It was owned by a retired couple who had been pilots. They had a plane and after they retired, they turned the hangar into an event site for weddings and such.

For some reason, I got on the Airbnb website and I said, "Guide me to where we're supposed to go for this ceremony," and I was guided to this place. When I was reserving the Airbnb, the woman casually inquired, "Can I ask you why you decided to come here?" I said, "Well, really, I was just kind of guided here. My guides told me." And she chuckled and said,

"This site is on the 37th parallel highway, where we often see aliens and things." She added, "I think that the land really needs to be cleared here, so that might be why you guys are coming."

Once again, the ceremony that we had there (it was a two-night ceremony) was absolutely beautiful and transformative. So many healings were happening. And we had so much fun. In this ceremony, we weren't just healing participants—part of it was also about healing the land around us.

Yet again, that pang of disappointment simmered inside of me. Once again, Sean stayed distant from everybody. He wasn't trying to be a part of what was going on. He once again sat separately, looking at his phone or staying upstairs.

I wanted Willow to be a part of all this. I want her to grow up able to facilitate ceremonies, because she already had such natural and innate gifts for it. She was doing it at such an early age, and she loved it. She already brought her own magic to it. Sean was there ostensibly to watch Willow. She was so magical, and even in his resistance he couldn't help but see this at times, like when she saw his dream.

We were in a situation where we were conducting a plant medicine ceremony in a location normally designed for wedding receptions. It was decorated with beautiful lights. Someone had connected a Spotify playlist on their phone to the speakers. At one point the first evening, all of a sudden, Willow screamed "Mommy!" and I came running to her, wondering what was going on. She was standing right on what would be the dance floor outside, underneath a gorgeous crystal light. Then she screamed "Daddy!" and he came running too.

Right then, the most beautiful romantic song came on. And Willow pushed us together, so we danced. It was honestly better than our actual wedding dance. It was magical. I looked up at him and said, "You can't make this shit up." And he smiled and hugged me.

So, he knew. At times like this—as with the dream about the keys—he would see how powerful our beautiful little daughter was. I just wished he wouldn't keep forgetting and withdrawing and retracting.

The next day, we were in ceremony until around 5 p.m.. We were getting prepared for the sunset, and then we would be leaving. I had an intuitive hit, and I told everybody, "Something is about to come on the horizon. It's extremely important, and it's a reward for the work we've done here."

I actually have a picture of what happened, and it's absolutely breathtaking. Pictures don't usually do things justice, but you can see it in the picture. What came was just miraculous. It was like a whole new earth came forward. It was as if the clouds were coming forward, but the clouds turned into castles. They looked like castles in the sky, with horses. It looked like heaven was coming forward. Everybody just sat there and stared at it and took pictures. It was absolutely undeniable that we had worked so hard on that land, and that this was our affirmation and thank-you from the land.

I have a magical picture of Sean and I hugging each other, looking at these castles coming forward in the sky, that one of the students took. That picture is hanging up in our bedroom to this day. That photo means so much to me because it was one of the moments that he let in the magic of my work and my world. He said, "It does remind me that magic and miracles are real."

HOME AGAIN

We journeyed back home, and now it was time for me to interview the contractors about the house. This was an interesting part of the manifestation. I wanted a beautiful home but we had a budget, of course. The first few contractors who saw my house plans just handed them right back and said, "There's no way that's happening on your budget."

Then, out of the blue, a real estate agent called me and said, "I have a contractor's name. I think you're going to like him." So I called him. He didn't work in Deep Creek Lake, but in a neighboring town. We met for lunch, and I showed him the plan. He looked it over and said, "Yes! I absolutely can do this for the budget that you're asking."

That was wonderful enough. But there was even more synchronicity. Sean had given up all of his bands in Michigan to come in and live with me. I knew that was a loss for him. I kept telling him "I really want you to start playing in a band again. I know you miss it, I know it would feel good to get back to playing." He had said, "Well, I would do it as a substitute."

During that lunch date, when we were showing him the plans, our contractor mentioned, "I'm the lead singer of a band and my bass player often gets sick." Sean plays bass. So, there we go! Sean actually ended up substituting for his bass player several times. I thought at the time, "The universe is really handing things to us on a silver platter at this point."

We were having miraculous things like this happen to us all the time. Everyday life had magic in it. Especially after that ceremony when the castles in the sky came forward. We just noticed really synchronistic events were happening. Even Sean couldn't help but notice it.

Sean was intermittently opening more to the world that I lived in and the way I was working and creating, and those moments would lift my heart and give me hope, but there was still an underlying resistance from him that was palpable and showed itself often. And it was starting to eat me alive. I had this very successful academy that he didn't seem at all interested in. He had been working with me a little on it at first, but now that we were married and it was taking off, he had pulled back in this deeply distressing way.

I thought, "If my husband had created something as big, beautiful, lucrative, and magical as I have, where he was healing a ton of people, I would totally want to know what it was all about! I would want to listen to the meditations; I would want to look at the videos."

I realized he hadn't looked at any of my content. He hadn't listened to one meditation, and he didn't watch any of the videos. When I asked him about it, he would just say that I hadn't offered it to him, or he would give some other kind of vague excuse. I told him, "Well, if it were me, I would be curious. I'd want to know about what you were doing."

At one point, I worked with a man in an ayahuasca ceremony who completely healed from chronic traumatic encephalopathy (CTE), which is a brain disorder associated with repeated traumatic brain injuries (TBIs), including concussions and repeated blows to the head. Many sports players, especially in football and boxing, have suffered greatly from this condition; depression, rage, and dementia are among the symptoms. It causes the death of nerve cells in the brain, and it's a progressive and fatal brain disease.

This man did an eight-minute testimonial for me, talking about his healing. He talked about how through this ceremony with me (which of course was really Spirit working through me), he experienced a complete healing. I was so proud and so happy about this, because a healing of such a devastating and incurable conditions is a *huge* deal. It's powerful testimony to this healing work, and it's such a joy to help change a life in this way.

After I viewed this testimonial, I actually walked right over to Sean and asked him to look at it. I just really wanted to share it with him. I wanted him to see what this work could do, and to be proud and happy with me. I said, "I really want you to watch this. It's eight minutes long, so tell me if you can actually do it." I didn't want to be disappointed, and I didn't want to get into a fight. I just really wanted him to see it.

He said, "Yes, I can." So I turned on the testimonial. Within literally 30 seconds, he was walking out the door, saying something to the dog.

My heart was crushed. I burst out, "Why can't you just listen to anything I do? Why don't you want to know anything about me?" As usual, he made an excuse. "Oh, I didn't want the dog to run away." I said, "No, this is so much deeper than you not wanting the dog to run away. This is becoming a huge problem for me—and for us."

That night, when I was lying in bed, the guardian parents sent me a vision. The guardian parents are always right, so I knew by now to take this seriously. They showed me a man from the waist down, and he had work boots on. I knew he did something with his hands, with construction. I didn't know where he was from, but Montana is what came to me. And I knew this man was coming into my life. I didn't know in what capacity, but I knew the guardian parents really wanted me to work with the divine masculine, with a partner in that. They really wanted us to open these portals.

I actually told Sean about this vision. I told him what I thought it meant. I said, "I'm telling you that if you do not shift, this man is coming in." I felt like he brushed it off. He still didn't completely believe everything that came from my guardian parents was real, even though he had seen the evidence over and over again right in front of his face. And maybe he just thought I was threatening him.

But this vision was probably a warning for me too.

ANOTHER CEREMONY, A FINAL WARNING

A few months after we got back from the ceremony where the new earth came, we had another ceremony with those two beautiful women from AWAKE and their husbands—the ones we had worked with in Kentucky. Two other students from AWAKE joined us. It was a beautiful ceremony in Sedona—a truly magical place on earth. We got a stunningly gorgeous house in the mountains with an indoor pool. We made our own ayahuasca brew. We went hiking. And once again, we had paranormal, magical events happening all around us.

At one point, we went hiking, and I was microdosing on psilocybin. This was right before we actually made the brew for the ceremony. I was so in the moment during that hike, I could feel and hear the trees. I was completely one with nature. And when you're that in the moment, magic can happen.

Back when I was in prison, I was writing a novel. My guides had told me that there was a reality where you can give a sample of your blood to the forest, and the forest can make a berry based on your blood and it will be exactly what you need to heal you. Mother Earth can do that for you. When that came to me from my guides, I put it in the book. But I had forgotten all about it.

Now, as I was walking on the hike, I suddenly felt like something pushed me from behind. But there was no one there! I ran into a cactus and I cut my leg, and it started bleeding. "Ow!" I wondered, "Why did that happen and what pushed me?" And then I heard my guides say "You're going to come across a berry that looks like it doesn't belong. You need to take that and put it in the brew."

I kept walking, and suddenly there were trees with silvery branches. A sort of red-red berry stood out clearly against the silver of the branch. I knew that was it. I took that berry back with me to put in the brew.

We went back and we were having an amazing time making the brew. When you make ayahuasca brew, what you put in it is so vital. The brew is everything to a ceremony. It's important to have beautiful, positive intentions.

Some of us went out to the store after starting the brew, to get some groceries for dinner, and we told one of the women's husbands to watch the brew. He was doing work on his computer, but we told him, "The brew needs tender love and care. The brew needs to be spoken to lovingly." He was a sweet, caring guy, and he agreed to watch the brew, but as it turned out, he didn't really get it. When we came back, the brew hadn't cooked down, and it had been cooking for two hours. He said, "I don't know why the brew isn't cooking down."

All of a sudden, two of the students—this couple who were 22 years old and quite powerful, worked together really well—started chanting "Om" and doing hand movements. With an ayahuasca brew, you need to open to Spirit and give the brew what it asks for. You can't control it, you just open space and invite downloads to come. If you're in a space of unconditional live, it will come, and the brew will receive what it needs.

So this young couple connected and opened and began offering, and we could see the brew rapidly cooking down, right before our eyes. It was so magical! The man who was supposed to watch the brew was floored. He said, "I can't believe I saw that! That cooked down in 20 seconds more than it did in two hours!"

When we started to actually take the brew and do healing work, one of the husbands talked about how he was stuck in a situation at work. He said, "I've got to get out of this. This is my intention. I've got to get through this situation at work." Now, the thing about ayahuasca is it's almost all about the purge. When you have stuck energy, you feel sick, and you feel like you're going to throw up. Many people throw up on ayahuasca, and it's extremely cathartic.

Willow was out in the living room, and wise little shaman that she is, she came over and grabbed his hand. She said, "You need to come out and look at the moon." He looked at us for confirmation, and we said, "Yes, follow her."

So he went outside with her, and she pointed to the moon, and he looked at it, and suddenly he purged everything he needed to purge. When he came back in, he said, "That was absolutely magical! I feel so much better! I feel like I just transcended the biggest problem in my life." And he gave Willow a hug.

At that moment, I realized that my husband was once again not part of this with me. He was, as he so often did now at these ceremonies, sitting on the couch just looking at his phone. Not even seeing his own daughter help heal people. Not seeing the brew go down. He didn't witness or even listen to the story of the berry miracle that had happened to me.

He was so on the outside, so separate from all that was going on, that I just couldn't handle it anymore. I was distraught. I felt like, "I can't believe I married this man. This is not the man who is going to open up healing portals with me."

I walked over to talk to the two beautiful women who had come with their husbands, and I said to them, "I don't know how much more of this I can take." Then I went over to confront Sean. I said, "Look, why do you keep looking at your phone? Why don't you want to see what's right in front of you? What we're doing here, the magic that's happening? Why are you even here?" He didn't answer. He just gave me an exasperated look.

I looked up at the stars through the massive floor-to-ceiling windows and skylights of this palatial home, in the magical star-studded sky of Sedona. And I said decisively—not as a threat but knowing to my bones that it was true—"If you don't change, there's a man who's going to come down from the stars to help me fulfill my purpose in life." I'll never forget that moment...because of what happened next.

⋘⋙ LESSON ⋘⋙

If there's magic happening all around you except in one area that seems stuck, the most powerful place you can look is inside yourself. I was having incredible success in my work with some of the most magical ceremonies I could ever imagine. Synchronicities, powerful healings, and miracles were unfolding all around me. Sean would open up to it when it was undeniable, but then shut down again. The window would open a crack and then slam shut. Something about who I was being allowed for all the magic and healing, but something was also blocking. While Sean definitely had his issues, which emerged over time as we worked things through, I also had to look at why this element of sharing my work with him—which was so crucial to me—was meeting such resistance.

I can look back on this now and see that if I had been fully standing in my power, fully unconditionally loved myself (even more than I had already worked to do), had realized that I did deserve everything I was expecting and wishing for, that I had no need to apologize for those expectations ...none of this would have had to happen. Had I been fully owning all of that—that I am the queen of my castle and I deserve to be treated like as such—my reality would have reflected the way i feel about myself. I get that now. But this is how it was occurring for me at the time.

Where might you be holding back in your own self that creates blocks or resistance in your life? Where does your reality reflect the way you feel about yourself?

Chapter Sixteen

IT WAS BEGINNING TO BE QUITE A CONFUSING time for me. Clearly, Sean had intimacy issues. I was trying to create our heaven on earth, and I felt bogged down by this struggle with intimacy. At the end of the Sedona ceremony, I was feeling pretty devastated. I wasn't seeing much hope for a future in which Sean and I worked together in the capacity that I *knew* I was meant to work with my husband.

Yet, around me, magic was still happening, The foundation to our beautiful lake house was starting to be built. Costa Rica had opened up its borders, and we were ready to go on the honeymoon that we had been waiting to go on.

I *was* grateful to Sean for agreeing to do Iboga, another natural plant medicine, during our honeymoon. We both knew that we had work to do. So we decided to do Iboga for part of the time, to support this processing, and then go to go to Nosara for the other part and have a magical honeymoon.

A few days before we left for the honeymoon, I walked into the bathroom and laying right there on the counter was his phone—once again, with Facebook Messenger open to a chat with the same woman he had been talking to previously, the one he had promised to back off and tone down after our time in the cabin with Willow.

Again, I don't seek out his phone or try to sneak peeks at it, but it showed up like this (which is also interesting, almost as if he wanted at some level to be caught). Once I saw it, and saw that the message on top was inappropriate, I felt justified in picking up the phone and scrolling through the messages.

What I saw next actually made me explode. I'm a big investor. I invest in cryptocurrency, and Sean knew I was extremely passionate about it. That was another journey he had refused to embark on with me, saying it wasn't his thing. Well, this woman apparently was taking up investing, and he actually had written to her, "I'm going to send you some money to invest." Even worse, after that she started calling it "our money."

That just made me so angry that I thought I was going to explode. I took the phone to him and asked "What is this? You should be investing with your wife! Not with this girl that you actually used to date. 'Our money?' Are you kidding me?" And then I added hotly, "Why are you even talking to her? I thought that you were not talking to her anymore."

He was so evasive. He sighed and said, "You know, I tried not to talk to her, but then…we just started talking again." He had really nothing to say.

At that moment, I was stunned into crystal clarity. I knew with absolute certainty that I was worth way more than that. It was a defining moment. I said to myself, "Rebecca, I don't care if you're building a billion-dollar house. You'll never be happy unless you can feel secure that this man you love is truly in love with you, truly committed to you, truly partnered with you in life and on the path. You cannot go on until whatever is going on here gets fixed. And you simply cannot tolerate being treated like this. There is absolutely nothing wrong with what you're asking for or expecting."

I was so angry, so clear, and so resolute. It was a good thing. I gave him a steely look and said, "I'm out of here," and I turned on my heel, grabbed a few things from the bedroom, and left the house.

I stayed at a hotel for a few nights. I stopped by my sister's house during this time, and I talked to her about it. She pointed out that he wasn't cheating on me. It was inappropriate, but not officially cheating. Many people would look the other way and say "good enough." Most people would look at Sean and say, "He's such a great guy!" A lot of people settle. Most people in their relationships don't really have a connection where they're working together on all levels. They're used to going their separate ways.

Obviously, I had higher standards that that. I wanted my heaven on earth. I wanted a connection where my husband is my best friend, where we can read each other's minds, we get each other, and we work together to make the world a better place.

My sister said, "Well, Rebecca, I don't know if you're going to find the guy you're talking about. I'm not even sure that guy even exists." I just said, "You're different than me. I know most people don't think they can have that man. I know I can, and I will not settle until I do."

After talking to my sister, I checked out of the hotel and went back home. Sean was in his music room, and he was in tears. He said he'd been throwing up, that he was sick to his stomach. He said, "I realize how much I truly, dearly love you, Rebecca, and I'm so sorry. I told her that we can't talk anymore, and I got my money back. I just really want to move on from here." I weighed his words, studying him, and I knew that he meant it.

He also added, "I don't know what's wrong with me. Maybe I do have some intimacy fears." I sat down with him and we talked through that a little. I was so grateful he was opening up. We made love. I thought, "Okay, I'm hopeful now that we can move forward with this."

IBOGA

So we went on our honeymoon. We got to Costa Rica, and started off the trip with the Iboga ceremony. I felt like that went very well.

If ayahuasca is the loving mother, then Iboga is the stern father. Ayahuasca is like an internal counselor. She teaches you, showing you what you need to see, for the most part in loving ways. Iboga, on the other hand, is kind of "in your face." It can be almost apocalyptic. What it showed both of us essentially was "Death, death, death." The point being, "Live while you're alive, because there is death."

But what it also taught me was that with death there's rebirth. We're always recycling. Energy never dies. Iboga also said something very interesting to me. It said, "You don't even know how many times you're being recycled. If you had died in a car accident yesterday, you could be back where you are today, in a slightly different reality. Sometimes that's what déjà vu is." I felt like that made sense.

The journey had a real impact on both of us, and was transformative on many different levels. It deepened our sense that life is worth living, and the importance of living in joy and not fear. Sean seemed to see even more clearly what he had and how lucky he was. He said to me, "I just kept thinking, Rebecca, how much I love you, and Willow, and our family, and how I want us to bring our heaven to earth, like we talked about."

After our journey, we flew to Nosara. We fell immediately in love with that quaint, peaceful Costa Rican town. The beaches are incredibly beautiful there. It's laid-back, less touristy than other Costa Rican destinations, friendly, and a big yoga and surfing spot. I told Sean, "Let's look for land here. Let's look at Nosara Estates and see what we can come up with."

As you may recall, owning land in Costa Rica was part of the manifestation we created in our work at the cabin, when we did the sex magic process and articulated all our dreams and intentions. And here we were, already falling in love with this stunning Costa Rican locale of our honeymoon.

We had brought $5,000 in cash to Costa Rica. We didn't know what that would get us, but we wanted to see what we could find. We had preplanned a real-estate tour where a company selling property in an emerging gated community called Nosara Estates would put you up at a nice condo, give you a chef, and assign you someone whose job it was to drive you around and show you properties. A very nice gentleman kind of took us on, wined and dined us, and showed us pieces of land. I told him our budget, and what I had in mind.

The first piece of land we came to, you couldn't even see the ocean. I asked, "Where's the ocean?" He pointed through the trees. I said, "Oh, no—we need land where we can see the ocean." He didn't say anything, but looked like he was trying to hide a smirk, like "Yeah, right." He continued driving. Then we drove by another lot and I lit up. "That's it!" I shouted! He shrugged. "That's out of your budget." I insisted, "No, I want to see it."

So he took us in, and it was absolutely perfect! It had a mountain view, *and* you could see the ocean. There was a little cliff, where I knew the infinity pool would go. I can be pretty bold when I know what I want. I said, "This is it. This is what we want to get." I told the guy our financial plans, and how we were building another house back in the States. I was very resolute. I knew exactly what we could do. I explained, "I can put this much down right now, and then once we get home, I can put this much down within two weeks, and then we can put the rest down within the next year."

He just looked at me, I think impressed by my confidence and resolve, but also skeptical. He shrugged again. "I'm not so sure she's going to go for that, the owner of this land." And I declared, "Well, this is what I want to manifest." He shook his head. "You guys are very different than the people I usually show property to," he said. I don't doubt that!

Daniel, our guide, took us back to the condo we were staying at, and then Sean and I went to a nice meal at a restaurant. Sean had loved the larger lot too, but he was also skeptical about our ability to afford it. He was suggesting we go smaller, just get a little piece of land with a little two-bedroom house, keep things simple.

The next day, Daniel came back to see us, his eyes wide. He said, "Rebecca, you're not going to believe this. I didn't even have to tell her what you said. All I said was, they want to come up with a financial plan. And she said, verbatim, what you said to me. This much now, then this much in two weeks, and the rest over the next year." He said it made the hair stand up on his arms.

So it was done. We went back up to look at it, excited and overjoyed. When we went back, we saw white horses on the land. I just felt like, "Oh gosh, we are such in divine timing right now. We are so protected. We are in such a magical place in our lives right now."

We played in Costa Rica for about another week, going back to the land on ATVs, which are a big way people get around Nosara on the dirt roads. We ate in some nice restaurants, took some surfing lessons. Then I had to go home early because Willow had Covid and my mother was worried about caring for her alone. Sean had to stay behind due to a snafu with his passport, so we actually flew home separately.

But we left Costa Rica having contracted to buy our dream piece of property there. At the same time, we were still in the process of building our dream house on Deep Creek Lake. We had manifested all of this through the sex magic process we had done at the cabin.

And now, Sean and I were really working on ourselves and the relationship. We were trying to figure out how to get into that space of ultimate joy and to sustain it and how to open the divine feminine and masculine portals to do the healings that we wanted to do.

By now, Covid had set in a little bit more, and investors who wanted out of cities started buying up properties all around the lakes. Building supplies kept going up in price—the costs hiked up three times during our build, so I kept having to give more money to the contractor. It was hard for contractors to find employees. Home builders were desperate for employees. This definitely created challenges for our project.

What I noticed, though, was that when the contractor would come to me and say "I need an extra amount of money beyond budget, because such and such material cost just went up," the universe would give me that money. The universe also gave me enough money to pay off the Costa Rica land. I believe this is because I had so much faith in our manifestation. When you go into your heart space and manifest in this way, if you invest in yourself, the universe will invest in you. That's what we were seeing all around us. Even Sean couldn't help but notice the magic, and he commented on it with awe.

ANOTHER CEREMONY

A few months after the honeymoon, I was contacted to do another ceremony with some new clients. I had actually reached a point where I felt like giving up on Sean participating in these, and I was ready to do it without him—but once again he came forward and said no, I do want to be part of this. So we agreed that since he's a musician and loves music, he would DJ at this one. I thought that might be fun for him, keep him engaged throughout the process.

I was hopeful things would be so much better this time. I had every reason to believe it would. He had really broken open after the blowup before the honeymoon, and we'd had the Iboga ceremony and that had opened him up even more, and we'd been really working on ourselves. He had been seeing and acknowledging the magic around our new lake home and our Costa Rica land purchase. I was hoping that we could really do this now, that he could finally see how important this was, how beneficial to everybody, and participate with me fully and joyfully.

So we went to the ceremony. This one was in North Carolina. Once again, we were at a location where weddings and receptions were often held, so it had a huge outdoor area where we were able to do ceremony and play music. In preparation, I explained to Sean, "The way this works is that we activate our light bodies, and it's the activation of our light bodies that heals everybody around us. It's not us personally. Our light bodies are conduits for God-Creator-Source energy, which actually heals people." I felt that because we, as a family, were conduits for healing, we really needed to be grounded and oriented in this work, very clear and whole. This was why it was so important to me that we be intentionally together in this endeavor.

So the ceremony began. In the middle of the ceremony, different client participants were having different experiences. Sean was playing the music, from a good psychedelic playlist he had found and had on his phone, and I was tracking what was happening with everyone.

At one point, I knew that someone in the group needed us to play the song "Let It Go" from the movie *Frozen*. At that point, Sean was playing Kundalini music, a long piece of music that had been going on for a while. I was looking at a girl who was struggling, she was crying, and as I often do, I just knew what she needed.

For some reason, I just knew that he wasn't going to do what I said. He was going to resist me. I don't know why. I walked over. He was looking at his phone, glanced up at me, and looked back down. I said, "Please, trust me. I need you to play this song." And he didn't play it.

I felt like my head was going to explode. A rush of sick dismay that we were, after all our work and breakthroughs, here again. I took a deep breath, and I said, again, "Play that song, please."

He muttered something under his breath, looked up the song, and finally he played it. When it came on, all of a sudden, Willow went out into the middle of the group, opened her arms and began singing along with it. The girl I was concerned about began releasing, still crying. She was letting go of what she needed to let go of—at the very level of her DNA. Willow was belting out the song, the girl was transforming, and everyone else was swept into the energy of that transformation as well.

Sean saw it. He saw the whole place around him transform because of that song. Afterwards, I went over to him again and I asked him, "Why didn't you play the song when I asked you to?" He responded, "Well, I didn't know that all *that* was going to happen!"

But what did he need to know in advance? What did he need to know in order to play a simple song that I requested, when he knew I was intuitive and that I did this work extremely successfully? I demanded, "Why don't you trust me at this point?" He said, "You didn't give the Kundalini music a chance."

I was furious. He was being childish. Was this about petty withholding? I said, "The Kundalini music had been playing for an hour. And I had a premonition. I *knew*, through my channeling, that that song had to be played. Why don't you trust me? Why can't you see what I'm doing?"

His response to this was to roll his eyes. I was so fed up with his attitude. I grabbed his phone and I threw it as far as I could, into the field beyond he courtyard. I said coldly, "That's what I think of your phone."

Then he knew not only how deeply distressed I was, but that I meant business. He said, chastened, "Okay, Rebecca. I'm going to take part in this." Of course, he had said this before a number of times. There had been numerous contrite reconciliations, and I was starting to grow weary of promises and breakthroughs that kept reverting back to the same old obstinate turf wars.

But for a little bit after that, he actually was dancing with me and having fun. During that time, I felt the energy shift all around us. And the thing is, it was amazing the difference it made when he did participate. Willow started playing with the people we were working with. She was so gifted that she could play with six people at a time and heal all of them at once. They would bring their child selves out, and she would heal them.

For example, Willow told one young woman, "You know, you and I have to go trick-or-treating." Later, I found out that her family never let her go trick-or-treating as a kid. Willow somehow knew these things, she just "got" things about people, and she would bring them right to the surface. In interacting with people around their wounded parts, with her support and the support of the plant medicine, they would heal. When Sean and I were connected, Willow was doing this more; she was truly in her element. When he and I weren't very connected, she wasn't doing this nearly as much.

I tried to point this out to him, to get him to see the difference this made. I said, "See? This is what I'm talking about. When we open these divine feminine and masculine portals, miracles happen!"

He got it a little bit more at this ceremony, but in the end, he still retreated. He even left early. He said, "I'm going to let you work with people, I'm going to get out of your way." I said, "No! That's not what I want. I want you to work with me, whether you're doing the music, or just dancing with me—I just want you to be a part of what we're doing." But he still didn't really understand.

With all this going on, I felt that this ceremony was going to be the catalyst for some major shifts that were about ready to happen in our relationship.

PORTALS

It was also during this ceremony that i first learned how to open up portals. This would change my life forever. A portal is an opening or vortex that leads from where you are now to where you want to be. It's all about intention and focus. When you open up a portal, it's very important to be in the field of your heart and to have pure intentions. You have to be clear and grounded.

It all started when I and a group of four other women in the ceremony were dancing. I was taking some stagnant energy in my hand and moving it, using my hand to open a channel to God-Creator-Source energy. My intention was to open a portal to true love. As I was doing this, my arm started acting as a pendulum. The women around me began doing the same things with their arms and their legs. They were moving with the energy to help consciousness expand. You could feel the energy around us open, and all of this expansion happening.

All of a sudden, I heard a thought in my head: "You have to have your clothes off. You need to be doing this in the nude." Immediately following that, my reaction was to think "that will never happen," so I just pushed it out of my head.

But shortly after, one of the other women i was dancing with suddenly said, "we're supposed to take our clothes off." I was like, "oh my gosh, I know! I just got that message as well." We just looked at each other and shrugged, knowing we weren't going to do it.

About 15 minutes later, *another* woman went into a trance-like state and, believe it or not, took her clothes off. She was doing what she had to do to open up the portal as needed. And then she started speaking Light Language. But it was a different kind of language I'd never heard before. Very unusual and extremely powerful. As she was speaking it, I could feel my DNA start to shiver, calibrate, sort of…quantumly shake. It's extremely hard to describe; I'm using the best words that I can.

She kept dancing, and I could feel the energy around us expanding bigger and bigger, deeper and deeper. I began getting messages from my guides. One of the messages I got was "Are you being judgemental?" I thought, "No, I'm not being judgmental." The guides said, "Actually, you *are* being judgmental, because you're not going over and dancing with her."

I let this message resonate for about 30 minutes, and then I surrendered to it. I walked over to one of the other women, and I said, "We need to go dance with her." I explained to her that I realized we were holding judgment because she was dancing naked. I said, "I heard my guides say that humans were put on this earth naked. Keeping your clothes on is fear of exposure. If you're too scared to go dance with her, and let go and expose yourself, how do you expect to open a portal to love and heaven?" I knew my guides were right. So I went to dance with the naked woman, and the other women joined me.

The coolest thing happened when we went to dance with her. She turned around and she started doing these special movements, and we were naturally mimicking her movements. We were synchronized. These were the movements needed to finish opening this portal to true love.

Once this was done, the energy in the room was *literally* spinning. When someone would walk in, they would say "Why is the room spinning?" There were even people purging. I understood that what they were purging was any energy that stood between heaven and the 3D world. Whatever you were holding in your DNA that kept you back from heaven needed to be purged. There was a lot of throwing up going on that night. That lasted for five or six hours before the woman who started us off naked came out of the trance.

I knew that the portal we had opened was a portal to true love. One woman who was dancing in that portal met her twin flame a day after we opened it, and she is still with him to this day. Everyone who was part of that portal was aided in their twin flame journeys.

POST-PORTAL

Once again, post-ceremony, we got busy with life. We were focused on the lake house being built, we were busy with Willow and her school, we had our work. I was still creating in AWAKE; Sean was doing his music. We had also gotten a boat, and we were out on the lake every chance we could get.

So things were going pretty smoothly. I was happy for the most part. But I still felt that burden of Sean not being fully engaged with my world, my work, our mission. I loved my husband so much, but I still felt things had to shift.

During that time, one of the contractors who was building the house quit. Even though there were five contractors building the house, he must have been Superman because when he quit, everything just seemed to go on pause. I went there day after day and asked "What got done today?" And it just seemed like nothing was getting done.

Since I'd now learned how to open up portals, I used that skill. I said to Willow and to Ariel, my other daughter, "We're opening up a portal for this house to get done." I used music, choosing the song Purple Rain, because Prince was very powerfully connected to Spirit and that song is one of my go-tos for spiritual openings. My incantation was "This house is going to get done. This house is going to get done. This house is going to get done." And then I connected the portal to the heavens. I even saw eagles around the portal. Then Willow, ever the attuned soul, said, "Mom, you have to do *this*." She started doing some movements with her hands. So I copied her, because I trusted her instincts and intuitions.

The thing that's important to understand as you learn what emerged from this portal is that while getting the house done was on my conscious mind, in my subconscious mind I was wrestling with this issue with Sean as well—about having him join me fully in work and life, being my partner in every way that I wanted. I wasn't thinking about it consciously, but it was in my energy field. This is important because as I opened the portal, my concerns, longings, and desires were getting mixed in and pulled in to what I was also consciously declaring I wanted to create. We can't necessarily stop this from happening.

That was on a Sunday. On Tuesday, I received a call from a man who was interested in going through the AWAKE Academy. His name was Ryan. He said, "I'm a contractor, I'm from Missouri, and I just got done with my job at the union. I'm in between jobs and I'm really interested in going into this work." But, he added, "I don't have that kind of money for the tuition."

At first, I offered him a scholarship and he still said, "I just don't have that right now, being between jobs. I have to save my money." So I just said, "Okay, if things change, call me back." I hung up the phone, and I heard my guides. They said, "You need to barter with him. He's going to help you with your house."

Well, this was very out of the ordinary, not only because I didn't even know the guy but also, you don't usually go find subcontractors when you have a main contractor; they want to do that themselves. But I texted him at the number he had called from, and said, "Actually, would you be interested in bartering? I have a house that I'm building in Maryland, and one of the contractors quit, and we really need help." He texted back, "Yes, I would be."

Then we talked on the phone, and he told me he could wrap things up in a week or ten days, hop in his car, and be in Maryland. Initially, we said four weeks of work, but then he said, "I can actually be there longer. I'm open."

After we arranged that, his wife called me. She also wanted to come. Now this I did not feel good about. I was getting this feeling of "Eh…not so much." I trust my intuition and I just knew that she wasn't supposed to come; I just had a bad feeling around it. But I said, "Yeah."

I hung up the phone and then I started thinking "Oh my gosh, I just opened that portal!" Willow, Ariel, and I just opened that portal Sunday, and now it was Tuesday, and we had a contractor coming—on a barter deal! I was excited and grateful for the power of that portal, for bringing him in, and getting help with the house. Sean was all for it, too. He said, "If you trust this guy, then I'm fine. Let's get this house done."

Ryan and his wife showed up at the beginning of July. I was in the house when they pulled up. They got out of the car and came up to the house, and I greeted them. Immediately, with Ryan, I felt this very pure energy, but with her, I just immediately just… didn't really like her. And I don't say this about many people. I just felt this really dark energy. Of course, I didn't say anything. I invited them in, and I told Ryan everything that needed to be done. He was totally on top of it, totally competent, and excited about the work. He said, "I can work with the main contractor, and I'll start on Monday."

Ryan was a very hard worker. He knew what he was doing. As I began having conversations with him, I also could see that he was spiritual. He was in the moment, and very interested in bringing conscious creations into his life, which is why he wanted to be part of AWAKE.

Everything was going smoothly with the work, but more started to be revealed about his life. It turns out that he and his wife had been separated for quite some time and she had been addicted to drugs. Ryan, too, had once been an addict, but he had been clean for years; his wife had not done so well at that. So they had been together on and off, and he had just decided to give her another chance. He told me a little ways into the work, "I didn't expect for you to let her come." But, he added, "She's here now, so I guess we're going to try to give her another chance."

It didn't work, though, with his wife. She kept finding drugs and getting into trouble. So my instinct about her had been spot on, and it eventually came to a head. He got very upset with her and put her on a plane and sent her home.

Ryan also had a daughter who was now in his mother's custody, because of the drugs in his past. A lot of things were coming to the surface for Ryan that he was clearly ready to work through. So I suggested "Why don't you come and do an ayahuasca ceremony with me? I think it's really going to help you." And he said, "I would absolutely love to do that."

RYAN'S FIRST CEREMONY

One of the students from AWAKE, her husband, Ryan and I all met in this little cabin where Sean and I were living (while the house was being built) to do an ayahuasca ceremony with Ryan. Ryan's intentions were to clear his energy field, and heal his shadow energies. He was also interested in finding out more about his own twin flame journey, and to purge the relationship with his soon-to-be ex.

Something really funny happened at the beginning of the ceremony. We were preparing and doing the sacred rituals, setting our intentions, and all of a sudden, we heard screaming outside of the window. We ran to the window, and this completely naked guy was running down the road. He looked like he was in a trance too. Then, his family was following him in a minivan, screaming at him to get back in the car. It was so strange! I had never seen anything like this. It took me a while to get over the whole shock of it all and realize that, just like "getting naked" needed to happen in the last ceremony to open up those portals to manifestation of true love, so did some instance of "nakedness" need to happen for this one. i couldn't help but think it was very synchronistic.

Ryan had a transformative journey with his first experience of plant medicine. He decided that this was going to be a profound journey, and that he would be also using this to unleash his purpose in life for himself and for others. He then expressed interest in attending as many AWAKE natural plant ceremonies as he could, so that he could heal himself and begin to learn to heal others as well. Seeing his affinity for this work and his earnest intentions, I said, "Okay, we're having one in Colorado next, and I would love to invite you." He accepted.

Up until the Colorado trip, he worked very hard on the lake house. I saw him work so hard that I felt kind of guilty about it. I starting feeling like I should feed him. I never saw him take a lunch break or anything. I also knew that he was going through a lot emotionally and personally at the time. So I tried to be supportive, check on him, bring him lunch sometimes.

Willow took a liking to him right away. She was kind of doing work on him, in her way, as soon as they met. She would do her magic in a child's way, but it was still powerful. She was not an aggressive child, but once she hit him with a piggy bank, because that was for prosperity, which he struggled with. She bounced on his solar plexus to open something up. She ran circles around him, and most people would think she was just being silly, but I knew she was weaving magic.

I also began to see that Ryan was kind of supernatural or paranormal. For example, every single photo of him that he had or that we took featured a sort of spaceship-looking light body around his crown and his third eye. There were other unusual features in photos of him too—like he was shape-shifting. I thought, "He is definitely a Starseed."

THE COLORADO CEREMONY

During this time, right before the Colorado trip, Sean and I were actually getting along very well. I was feeling like "Okay, I'm in love with him and I think things might just work out." I had done my best to put all the differences and "missing connections" behind us. I told myself, "I'm happy! I have this house and we have the place in Costa Rica and we're both doing creative projects." Sean wasn't engrossed in my life like I wanted him to be, but I was for the most part actually quite content.

For the September trip to Colorado, we all flew there, and it was once again another magical ceremony. Miracles were happening, people were healing, and i felt like I was with my soul tribe. Sean played music, but he was still very much on the outskirts of the ceremony. I would have these amazing magical things happen, and he would be in the bedroom not really paying attention. He would pay attention to Willow, but that was about it.

This time, I just kind of accepted it. I thought "Okay, that's fine. This is just the way it's going to be and I'm going to be happy about it. At least he's here with me, I'm here with AWAKE, and everything is going well."

At the end of the second night, it was a long night, I was about ready to go to bed, and I was actually thinking, "I cannot wait to get into the arms of my husband." Then, two of the students came up to me at the door of my bedroom and said, "We really need you downstairs." I said to them, jokingly, "Really? I'm getting ready to go to bed with my husband." They looked at him and one of them said, "He's asleep, he's not going to know. You can come down for a little while."

I sighed. I had a responsibility to my students, my participants. I said, "Okay." I went back down the stairs and looked around to see what exactly they needed. Sitting there were a few students—and Ryan. One of the students said, "I need to give you and Ryan an activation. I've been told to." I sat down warily, a bit puzzled. I looked at Ryan, and he looked at me and shrugged. The student said, "Okay, let's do this."

She gave us the activation, and I felt a surge through my third eye and then my eyes started rolling in the back of my head. When it stopped, I gasped, "Whoa! What *was* that?" She said, "I gave you his Star, and I gave him your Star, because you guys have to remember some things." I just looked at her. "Okay...." I had no idea what this was about, but it was powerful.

Then she looked at us, and she said, "Cuddle for a moment!" I thought, "Well, that's awkward." He looked at me, obviously thinking the same thing: awkward. But gamely, I lay down, he lay down behind me, and he put his arm around me, and we cuddled for just a moment. Then I got up, talked to another student, and walked back upstairs. I went to sleep, and I didn't really think too much more about it.

The next morning, we were cleaning up the Airbnb, getting ready to leave. Everybody got on their flights. We got home. Everyone was safe. Life was back to normal.

Then, about two days later, I was sitting in the exercise room after a workout, and all of a sudden out of nowhere, I missed Ryan. I was thinking about him in a way I'd never thought about him before. I felt like, "Why am I thinking about Ryan like this?" I didn't feel this when I first met him. Not for one moment.

So I texted the student who had given us the activation. I said, "What was that activation? And why did I have to cuddle with Ryan?" She texted back, "I told you, I had to have you guys remember some things; you needed the Star Activation." And then she sent me a screenshot of a text that Ryan had sent her an hour earlier. It said the exact same thing I had said. He asked her, "Why did I have to cuddle with Rebecca, and what was that activation about?" And, "I can't stop thinking about her." We both felt this bubble up at about the exact same time.

Immediately, I thought about two things: that vision that my guardian parents had given me of a guy from the waist down with work boots on. And me looking up at the stars, angry at Sean, saying "If this doesn't change, some other man is going to come down from the stars to do this work with me." Of course, there was also the portal that I had opened up.

In that moment, I felt a little bit panicked. I wondered if perhaps I had manifested a little too well.

Chapter Seventeen

SO RYAN AND I HAD RETURNED FROM THE CEREmony in Colorado with feelings for one another that we had not had before we left, thanks to the Star Activation that one of the AWAKE students had been guided to give us.

I say that I'd not had feelings other than friendship for Ryan before that activation, and that's true. However, there is one odd experience that I had put out of my mind until after the ceremony.

I had been talking to Ryan at the ceremony in Colorado—*before* the Star Activation—and suddenly I heard my husband's voice in my head say *"This is your husband."*

At that point, I definitely did *not* want that to be true. I actually felt panicked. I excused myself, ran upstairs to our bedroom at the Airbnb, and found Sean. I asked, "Hey—are you happy to be married to me? Are you happy that I'm your wife? Do you still want to be married to me?"

He started laughing. He said, "Yes, silly. Why are you asking me this?" I just said, "No reason. I just got this weird feeling downstairs." Reassured, I went back downstairs and went back to work.

Now that we were home from the ceremony, it was time for Ryan to get back to work and finish the lake house. At this point, he had already fulfilled his end of the barter, and he was done working for the Academy, but he said that he would stay on and be committed until the end of the project. That made me really happy, because he was offering an extremely good deal for his services.

There was also something even more important to me than the excellent deal, which was that as he worked on the house, as he was building the foundation, as he was doing *anything* in the house, I knew he was putting energy work into it. He was putting love into it, and he told me he was doing it with intention. This was an even better deal: not only was he a skilled contractor, but he was also good at energy work. He was putting the two together, which is really a dream come true if you're building a house.

Meantime, we had this new energy between us. We were choosing not to talk about it at first. But I began to notice more and more about the kind of person he is. He would notice the smallest things. For example, I had been looking at fake flowers on the Internet for hours, because I wanted to buy flowers for the dining room table that looked real, and I was looking for ones that look like they had water in them. It took me hours to choose these flowers. They arrived and I put them on the dining room table, and Ryan came up to me about a half an hour after I put them on the table, and said, "I really love those flowers. I like how it really looks like there's water in there; they look very authentic." He noticed the carpets I picked out, the curtains, my design ideas. We talked a lot about design.

I thought, "Wow! Here's a guy who's in touch with his divine masculine *and* his divine feminine. Not only is he out there building with his muscles and working hard, he's creative and artistic and he can express his feelings and discuss things."

He and I started to spend time together after work. It started out with just him, my best friend and I doing healing ceremonies. We would go downstairs to my basement and just work on one another. I couldn't help but notice that the connection he and I had was indescribable. It's like he just understood, on the deepest level, what I was talking about. To be quite honest, I had never met *anybody* in my entire life who so deeply understood what I was talking about,. Everything to me is energy. If my car breaks down I'm thinking about what was in my energy field to cause that breakdown, so that I can address it so it doesn't happen again. It was so unusual for me to be around someone who was in a similar type of flow, who had that kind of perspective.

At this point, I had not told him anything personal about Sean and I. I only bragged about our relationship, talking about the Tantra and how much I loved my husband. Ryan knew I loved my husband; I didn't keep that a secret. I would kiss my husband in front of him all the time. He didn't know any of the things that Sean and I had gone through or were struggling with.

So it's really the universe at play that he would go up to my husband and say things like, "In video number three, listening to meditation number five, such-and-such happened to me." He would tell my husband how gifted I am and how I had changed his life, just through The Academy and its modules.

That touched me so deeply, because as I've said, my husband wouldn't even listen to the modules. Yet here was Ryan, benefiting so much from my work and generously acknowledging it. Here was a man (who to this day I could swear is beyond merely human) who came into my life from the stars and was telling me how great my creations were.

Plus, he was working beyond our barter agreement to complete my house. He worked so hard that even Sean noticed. Sean actually walked up to me one day and said, and said, "Do you notice how hard Ryan is working? Do you see what he's doing for you?" I said, "Yeah. I do."

I did see—and I also saw how it was bringing up my own deepest intimacy fears. I realized that the situation was reaching a point where once again I needed to do some more work. I keep coming back to this concept of the mirror. I've been talking about all the things Sean was doing, but here I could also see the same resistance in myself. Ryan was burrowing deep into my heart, the way he was working on my house and working with me, the way he looked at me. And it was getting to be more than I could take. I felt myself start to constrict around such love and devotion.

Often in a Twin Flame relationship, when you get to barriers you think it's because you're with the wrong person—but it turns out to be that your own heart is closed. You're the one not opening up.

Ryan was not only showing me what Sean "should" be doing—what I said I wanted him to—but also a window into why it wasn't happening with Sean. Because when Ryan gave to me in that way, openly, it felt intense and uncomfortable. Sean had his own intimacy issues for sure, but in the mirror I could see that I did too. He was reflecting my own inability to accept that much love. It was a messy realization that would need resolving, but the universe said, "You want this much love? Do you love yourself this much? Here's the guy." And I needed to resolve it or figure it out.

THE WINDOW

Then something happened at the house I had previously rented, before the lake house was being built. At the end of the lake house build, we had started living in it even though it was under final construction. Willow had started school near there. The contractor was still working on the last pieces. We started building in August 2020, and we moved into the house in September 2021.

Soon after we moved out of the temporary rental, one of my sisters took over the rental, since it was a great place. But something strange happened with a door lock there. Heidi had accidentally locked it, and there was no way in. I'm not sure why she thought it was that important, but the cleaning lady (who had come to clean before Heidi moved in) broke the window to get in.

When she called to tell me what had happened, I told my sister, "I could probably have Ryan come down and fix it." He was at my house working at that moment. So I asked, "After work today, would you ride down to the old house with me so we can get the window fixed and my sister doesn't get in trouble with the landlord?" He said, "Sure."

The old rental was an hour from the new house, and by the time we got there and Ryan measured the window and figured out what he needed for the repairs, it was late. We needed to go to Lowe's to pick up some supplies for the fix, and they had closed.

Even though it wasn't absolutely necessary, we decided to just spend the night at the old rental. We sort of reasoned that it made sense, since we had to go to Lowe's in the morning. An hour away was a significant drive; it would have been some wasted time to drive home and come back again in the morning, but it also wasn't so far away that we couldn't have done that. We kind of used it as an excuse—it was obvious we wanted to spend the time there together, even though we didn't admit it.

The house was empty at that point; my sister hadn't moved in yet. The cleaning lady had been coming in order to prepare it for her to move in. There was no furniture yet, so I found some blankets and we got down on the living-room floor camping style.

It was obvious that we were both feeling so much that had been building up. The unspoken energy was palpable. We talked for a while, and then we were quiet. We were just laying on a blanket staring into one another's eyes.

Finally, I asked him, tentatively, if he was feeling the same energy that I was. He started laughing. "Absolutely!" He added, "But I don't want to hurt you or Sean or Willow, I love all of your family. I didn't expect this to happen." I said, "I didn't either."

The rest of the night, we lay there holding hands, looking into each other's eyes. Near the end, we held each other. He clung to me. We lay there together in each other's arms and I felt like I had known him for eons.

I rolled onto my back and started at the ceiling, thinking, "I can't believe this is happening! Who is this guy? Where did he come from? And what am I going to do with this?"

We slept a little and then got up, too full of feelings to really put anything into words, quiet but still very connected. We just kept looking at each other. We got ourselves together, went and got some coffee, grabbed the supplies from Lowe's, Ryan fixed the window, and we went back to the lake house.

When we arrived back there, the other construction workers were definitely looking at us like, "Hey, something's up." And of course, something was—and I'm sure it looked very strange that Ryan and I pulled up to the house after being gone all night.

Sean somehow managed to ignore it at first, or else he was totally unaware. At first, in general I could see he wasn't bothered by me being around Ryan so much. In fact, he seemed relieved, because Ryan would do things with me that Sean didn't want to do. If I wanted to go on a boat or ride around on jet skis or do something else playful, Ryan was all for that—and Sean wasn't so into that at this point. He had been into the boat at first when we got it, but then he kind of lost interest. He would say, "Okay, yeah, you guys go do that." He didn't seem worried about me spending time with another man.

That is, until things got so intense that Ryan and I could not stand to be apart. I have never felt that way in my life, where I couldn't stand to be out of someone's presence. It was bizarre. I can't even explain it. It's like I imagine it might feel being in the womb with a twin and then suddenly being separated, and feeling a sense of abandonment. That's how I felt when I was not with Ryan, and he felt the same.

When things got that intense between me and Ryan, Sean finally started to notice. Ryan would start to come over at 6:30 a.m. instead of 8:30 a.m. to start work, and he would bring me a muffin or coffee. Sean finally came to me and said, "What is going on? Why is Ryan standing in the driveway this early?"

I didn't really have much to say. I made up some excuse. But I could tell that my husband was curious about what was going on, and suddenly he was paying a lot more attention.

OUT IN THE OPEN

One day, it all came out. I had invited Ryan and my best friend again to do some healing work. But we'd gone to a neutral place outside of the house this time. We were doing a ceremony together, and doing healing work on one another. During this ceremony and work, what I had bottled up from the wedding finally came out. I think it was because Ryan was seeing me in a way I had never even seen myself. He actually looked in my eyes at one point and said, "Rebecca, I can see you." There was a piercing energy in my soul, and I knew how much this man loved me. I felt it.

This provided a safe container for me to start purging what I needed to purge about that time—all the sadness, frustration, hurt, and loss I had stuffed down related to the wedding. We had been married for almost two years at this point. I finally started *really feeling* the hurt around him planning an out-of-state gig the week before our wedding, inviting his friends over on our wedding night, spraining his ankle the next day, and generally all the nagging I had to do to keep him moving on wedding prep. How it felt like he didn't really want to get married, the way that he had proposed to me (how the ring I had picked out sat in in the kitchen for weeks, and he had to be prompted, and how he got down on his knee in a dirty kitchen).

All these feelings of not being worthy came out. I was saying, "I don't think he really loves me, or why would this have happened? Why did things go down the way they did?" I was angry and hurt not only at how he had behaved, but also that I had accepted it, swallowed it, believed that it was all I was worthy of. With Ryan holding such a safe, loving, and all-seeing container, all of this finally emerged and purged.

Because there was no way to conceal this now, I went home to Sean and told him all that was going on. I said, "Do you remember that ceremony in Colorado?" I told him about the activation that happened there. And I reminded him about the time in Sedona that I said a man was going to come down from the stars if things didn't change. I told him about the vision I had been given of someone with work boots, and about opening the portal. I told him how unseen and unloved all his actions had made me feel, how angry I was, and how seen and appreciated Ryan made me feel. I said, "I think I'm in love with him."

When I told Sean all this, I was sitting in the bathtub in water. At first, Sean just looked at me horrified as all this tumbled out. But I would never have expected what happened next in a million years. He got into the water with me, hugged me, let me cry on his chest, and said, "I'm going to be here for you, Rebecca. I'm going to be your best friend through this. You can talk to me about this."

I was surprised, and grateful, but I pressed forward. I told him, "I can't be out of his presence. You can't kick Ryan out of this house. Ryan still has to work on this house. He has to finish it. It's very important that he finishes it. It's very important that he's in my life right now, energetically. I need him in my life. Don't make me choose. If you force me to make this choice, I will end up going with Ryan."

Remarkably, my husband heard me, listened to me, and let Ryan continue to come to the house and work. He knew what was going on, and he just went with it for the moment, as he had promised. He let it be unclear, he let it be confusing, he let it unfold.

Ryan had his own relationship trials parallel to mine. As Sean and I were working through this, and Ryan and I were just allowing this to be whatever it was, Ryan was also periodically going back to Missouri to process with his (soon to be ex) wife. He would have all kinds of feelings for her and about her. He would go and purge, process, come back, and talk to me about it all.

He would be completely honest with me about what had happened with her. So I was dealing with what was going on there, and also between us.

We were both fairly confused. We knew what we felt for one another, but he had a wife and I had a husband. We weren't really certain what to do with it.

Willow absolutely adored Ryan. She laughed and played with him; they healed one another. That takes nothing away from Sean, because Willow and Sean had—and have—an absolutely magical relationship too. Willow would laugh and play and have a great time with Sean as well. As it happens, Willow has never known a man in her life who has treated her as anything other than a princess. Willow to this day believes that men love to play Barbie dolls, because no one ever refused her that. In her reality, her grandfather, Sean, Ryan, and my sons will all gladly play Barbies with her. So Willow has a very different perception of men than what I had when I was growing up. I am so grateful for that, and for how I've been able to give her an absolutely magical and wholesome environment that nurtures and honors that magical child she is.

Ryan's love for me felt so pure and authentic. He would say amazing things to me. One time, he was putting together a new bed for me, which came from a company where the instructions were in Spanish. He had to figure out how to put together the bed without instructions. I said something about having to sleep on the floor or on the ground if we couldn't get the bed together, and he looked at me and said, "I wouldn't care where I slept as long as it was next to you." I loved these completely soulful expressions of devotion. They were so much of what I had wanted from a partner.

At this point, as I said, Sean was finally seeing and hearing me too. All those times I had told him about the connection I desired, asking him not to be absorbed in looking at his phone, I wasn't getting through. But now, with this unfolding in front of him, it was definitely getting through about what I wanted—and what I could be getting from someone else.

I had warned him back in Sedona, and it was happening. And he finally woke the fuck up.

Suddenly he was cooking me omelets in the morning, bringing me coffee, doing chores that I know that he doesn't like to do, catering to me in very possible way. He was trying to give me as many orgasms as he could, so I wouldn't want any more orgasms. He was attentive as I'd wanted him to be.

But at first, I didn't totally trust it. I felt like he was just doing it because Ryan was in love with me. If Ryan hadn't been in love with me, then Sean wouldn't be showing up this. I told him as much. He said, "No, Rebecca. I really love you and I don't want to lose you."

Regardless of how it was coming about, this is what I had wanted—and Ryan had clearly been part of the impetus, the stimulus. And that had been predicted, apparently part of the plan. I had declared it, and the guides had shown me. Maybe it had to happen this way for all the lessons—for all of us.

THE MIRROR—AGAIN

After I got through a phase of having to be around Ryan all the time, not being able to stand being apart from him—after I let him in to the point where he could truly see me and read my soul—I started to reject him coming around all the time. After he would do the things he needed to do on the house, I would make up excuses not to see him. I started to spend less and less time with him. He started to feel it and was distressed about it, asking, "Why aren't you spending time with me?"

Here again was the mirror. This was me not being able to go deeper into my relationship with Ryan. Again, I eventually came to see that this was why I couldn't expect Sean to go deeper—because I couldn't go deeper either. I *said* I wanted it, I pushed for it, demanded it—but when faced with someone who was ready and there, I pulled back. Everything I was experiencing with Sean was a mirror of myself. Now I was the runner.

On Halloween, things came to a head. We all decided to dress up and go out—me, my best friend, Sean's best friend (a woman he used to play in a band with), and Ryan. We all went out to a place on the lake where there was a Halloween party.

I told Sean, "Okay, we're going to microdose on some mushrooms and I need you to go deep. I want to know why you invited your friends over on our wedding night. I want to know why your proposal was so unromantic if you really wanted to marry me. I want to know why you didn't tell me that I was beautiful in my wedding dress. I need to know the answers before I can move forward with you. I don't want a superficial answer, either." I felt I had a better chance of getting the depth of answer I wanted by using plant medicine, so I insisted on the microdosing.

At this point, Ryan's ego was flaring a little bit. He was treating me a bit like territory. I said to him, "This isn't going to work. You need to back off. Everybody here is going through a process. We all need to do this work." We had all been going through it: I was working it out with Sean, I was going through a process with Ryan, Ryan was going through his process with his wife, uncertain of what was going on there and how it would turn out (though they did end up splitting). And Ryan was dealing with what was happening with my husband and me.

It sounds like a mess, I know, but this is the sorting that was happening to us and through us and all around us. It may sound crazy, but I truly see now that it all did need to happen in order for each of us to work out our intimacy issues.

We were actually having a pretty amazing Halloween night, in spite of this. We were all dancing. Sean and I were dressed up as a Mr. and Mrs. Vampire. He was Dracula and I was a female vampire, and we looked really good together. Meanwhile, though, I kept telling him "You need to think about this. You need to give me answers." I continued to press him about those questions.

His best friend Cece (a singer he had been in two bands with previously, many years before I met him) said, after a while, "Let me talk to him. I think I can get him through this." She spent 45 minutes with him off to the side. Afterward, she called me over, and she said, "I know why this all happened."

I was waiting for a profound answer. She said to me, "Because he was stupid." I waited for her to continue, but that was all she said. I was stunned. I said, "Wait, you just talked to him for *45 minutes*, and that's all you got? He gave you the answer that he was stupid—and you accepted that?"

She looked lost. I shook my head. I said, "Maybe that works for you in your relationships—well, I don't think it *is* working for you actually, but that's not my business. For me, that is not an acceptable answer."

I walked away. And then I had a wild idea. I went back and I said to Sean, "I know everybody at this place and I'm going to go on stage between sets, take the microphone away from the singer, because she'll let me—and I'm going to tell everybody what you did to me on my wedding night. I'm going to ask people to raise their hands and give me suggestions as to why you did that."

He looked petrified at that prospect. He stammered, "Okay, okay, just give me a little bit more time." He walked away.

About 15 minutes later, he came back up to me and he said, "Okay, here it is. I don't think I was crazy in love with you when we got married."

Well, that just made everything so much worse. I was absolutely devastated, heartbroken. I was sure that when I married him, I *saw* that he was in love with me. I could see in his eyes that he was really in love with me. But at that moment, I was doubting everything. I was doubting my guardian parents (my higher guidance), doubting my messages, doubting who I should be with, doubting what love even is. I was in tears.

And Ryan was right there, willing to step in at any moment and take me for life. But I had to step into my power, step up and work through this. I told Ryan I need to go home and deal with this. He was acting confrontational to Sean at that point, and I told him, "You need to stay out of this right now, and let me deal with this on my own." He listened and backed down.

Sean and I drove home together in silence. I was angry. I wasn't speaking to him. I went up into my office. I was sitting and wondering what to do, crying. He went and took and shower, and then he came and found me. He was shaking his head. He said, "Rebecca, I didn't say it right. At all. Let me try again."

He sighed. "I was thinking about what I told you and what I meant to say. You have to understand, Rebecca, I can't express my feelings that well. I can't even feel them like you want me to." He went on, "You're the first person who's ever made me even think about feeling this deeply. And to go this deep is really hard for me."

I listened impassively, guarded, wanting to believe what he said, wanting to hear something authentic that would make sense, wanting to open to him but not wanting to be hurt more.

He took a deep breath and looked into my eyes. "What I *meant* to say was, I don't think I even knew what being in love was when I married you. Of course, I loved you, but I'm so much deeper in love with you now than what I was when we got married. It's like it wasn't even the same type of love. I wasn't allowing myself to feel that deeply, because of everything that I had been through in my life. It had nothing to do with you. But you're the one who's been breaking all that down."

My eyes filled with tears. I couldn't help but believe him because I *knew* in my soul, in my cells, that he was speaking the truth. And then he kissed me passionately...and I *felt* that kiss. I felt that kiss like I had wanted to feel him kiss me since we had been married. It was the same as the kiss from the night we met each other. It was deep, it was profound, and it was telling a story.

At that moment, I felt like "Okay—NOW I have my husband." We had a really good night. It felt very powerful energetically.

...EXCEPT FOR THE ENERGY WORK

But there was still a holdout. I asked him, that night, about the time I heard his voice inside my head say that Ryan was my husband. When I had come to him and asked him if he was happy to be married to me. He thought about it for a minute, and he said, "If I could have it my way, he would be kind of like your ceremony husband. He would be the one who does energy work with you."

Once again, my heart sank. Because the energy work I talk about isn't actually *work*. It's a *space*, energetically, where someone connects and opens up a healing field. And my husband *still* wasn't getting that. He seemed to actually wanted to give me to another "husband" for that "work" and then enjoy me for "the rest of life." But to me, "the rest of life" wasn't separate from that space, and that energy and healing was something I yearned to share with my husband.

So, even with this huge breakthrough, I *still* felt that there was more to work on.

Despite the strong connection I had with Sean, the energetic connection I had with Ryan was still on a whole different playing field. Ryan and I both felt we had never seen two people work together or just exist together the way he and I could.

And despite what he had said about Ryan being my "energy work husband," Sean also started to get a bit fed up with how much Ryan and I connected. Somehow, I think he thought Ryan and I could segregate the ceremony and energy work from everything else. Sean felt at this time that the ceremonies were hard work, and he wanted Ryan to handle that. He was glad to hand that off. He wanted Ryan to do everything he was uncomfortable with. Then he wanted me to come home and do everything else with him.

But it doesn't work that way for me; it can't end there. For me, I always knew the person I worked with in ceremonies would be the person I'd be with. It needed to be the same person. Eventually, I had to be working with my husband—whoever that was.

Working with ceremony with someone is magical. You see magic together. You see healings. He was missing that, and I was sharing it with Ryan. To go home and say "guess what I did" just wasn't working.

But Sean wasn't ready to step up. And the more ceremonies Ryan and I did, the more connected we were and the more time we spent together. Ryan would sit at the house and watch me work. Sean would walk in and ask, "Why is he sitting there watching you?" Or, "Why is he with you at the dentist and when you're getting your hair done?"

So a couple of months after Halloween, Sean made a rule where Ryan was not allowed to come back in the house after the house was complete. The house had been completed around the end of October or early November. After that, I was "allowed" to go see Ryan outside of the house anytime I wanted, but Ryan could not come in the house.

I told my husband, "Ryan is like is a Star Brother. Like a best-best-best friend. Someone I could not imagine having out of my life." Our connection was so deep, it was beyond any stupid romantic notion. When I was around him, I healed on levels that I have never healed before. I could not yet imagine letting go of this. But really, it was brotherly.

That was something Sean seemed to understand. He even said to me, "I see the unconditional love that you and Ryan have for one another. I don't want to step in the way of that. But I want to be your husband, Rebecca. I don't want to stop you from seeing Ryan. I just can't let him in the house right now." That seemed fair, so that's how we went on for a few more months.

Sean was so supportive of my connection with Ryan—outside of the house—that one time when Ryan and I had had something planned and it had snowed, he got up to shovel the driveway so that I could get out to see Ryan. He was not suspicious or fearful of my spending time with Ryan outside the house. He even knew I cuddled with Ryan and held hands. He seemed okay with it as long as we didn't cross the line sexually.

One aspect of connection that never wavered with my husband through all of this was the sexual intimacy. It was always really, really good, and that's important. As I've said, the kissing had been an issue—and to me kissing can be even more telling than sex; kissing tells the story, whereas sex can sometimes be mechanical. But with my husband, sex was definitely not mechanical. Sean was able to express himself with me in the bedroom perfectly. By the way he moved, by the way he touched me, by the way the way he breathed. During lovemaking, we were always very connected. The Tantra was powerful between us. The thing that became clear was that Sean was having trouble putting that into words, or expressing himself outside of the bedroom.

I had not done Tantra with Ryan. I didn't feel like it was appropriate to cross that line, so he and I had never actively gotten together. There was Tantra energy that came through our relationship, because of our connection, but it wasn't a conscious choice like it was with Sean and I.

My desire when I got married, before I was married, and really ever since I was born, was to find that one person with whom I could have heaven on earth. I wanted that one person to be my best friend, my lover, my confidante. That one person should be the person who would play with me on the playground like a little kid. We would know each other inside and out, finish each other's sentences. My dream love was one person I could spend my life with, where we would build an empire together, and help the world to do the same.

So as I worked through this very tumultuous time with Sean and Ryan, every day was a bit torturous for me. The right thing wasn't entirely clear. I had two men I loved and with whom I had powerful connections, and they differed. It was not one person, as I wished. At the same time, there wasn't one day that went by where I didn't feel incredibly lucky, because I had two phenomenal men in my life. But I really was working on a way to make this into one person.

People around me, of course, were confused and somewhat judgmental. I understood that it was hard to understand. Even my children saying "Mom, it's like you have two husbands. What's going on?" My 17-year-old daughter said to me, "Jackson's mom (Jackson was her boyfriend) thinks that you have a polyamorous relationship because you're always with two different people." One of my sons said, "Mom, you're like a walking red flag. I would never let my wife do these things with another man."

I couldn't tell them much. I couldn't entirely explain it myself. And I didn't know how it was going to end. I just had to tell them the truth—that Ryan I had some connection, that I needed to see it through, and that Sean knew about it.

We all still had work to do, and things to learn. And we did. Because we stayed in the game and were willing to be in the "not knowing"—and to ultimately come from love—we were about to get a lot of help from the universe in seeing what we needed to see.

LESSON

Sometimes a person in our lives is there as a catalyst. I had been in a process for some time of healing a sense of unworthiness, an insidious apologism for everything I wanted in a partner. I had been seeking and demanding more and more of my husband, and was actually receiving more as he expanded, but there were still limits that frustrated me, and I veered between insisting that I could have it all and trying to accept that having "most of it" was "good enough." But the more

I healed, the more I realized that I was worthy of everything that I deserve and desire, and none of it was "too much" to ask (even though it's more than most people ask for or expect!).

As I began shifting internally, my external reality was mirroring my insides. Ryan came into my life as a catalyst showing me that there are men who operate on the level of intimacy, connection, and spiritual attunement that was increasingly my standard. He was showing me that the places I still wanted Sean to step into—that I wanted to complete my marriage—were places that another man could go. There are men who can read your soul, do energy work (and love it), and express in healthy and intimate ways.

Deep intimacy was a huge lesson for both Sean and I. We had been doing this dance from the start, and in spite of profound improvements that were gratifying, there was clearly still work to do. I wanted to have the ultimate deep connection with my husband on every level. At this point, Sean and I had powerful connection on many important levels, but we had not yet declared that we were "best friends." Ryan was emerging as my "best friend" on a soul and energetic level, and it was very compelling because it was what I knew was missing with Sean and still craved to have "under one roof."

If you have had the experience in your life of having deep soul needs met by more than one person, you know how confusing this can be. Do you have someone in your life who has been a catalyst for seeing that what you want is possible, and knowing that it's okay to expect it and pursue it? When does having this catalyst in your life create productive and constructive growth and healing, and when does it start to interfere or become too complicated?

Messy is okay; it doesn't help to judge yourself or others for exploring what is not yet clear. But it's important that you stay conscious in all your relationships to make sure the catalyst is not being used to avoid something rather than create something. It's okay to let it play out and see it through till it's clear, which is what I did. To allow just one person to see and experience everything that you are requires you to open deep space within yourself. It requires you to be truly vulnerable. This journey requires patience and openness.

Chapter Eighteen

SOMETHING HAD TO CHANGE. SOON AFTER THE Halloween blowup, Ryan and I decided we needed a separation. We both decided that that would be good for us. The energy was becoming stagnant. Things weren't shifting in the way they needed to.

After finishing his work on the house, Ryan had hung around Deep Creek Lake just staying at Airbnbs. He didn't have a job anymore, so he was just staying near me. When we both acknowledged that things were stuck, he decided to move to Florida and live with a friend for a while. Though I knew it was the right thing, it was hard when he moved. All the holidays were coming. We had been so close, and we both had a difficult time with the separation. We missed each other. We would talk on the phone or text, but it was still a shock to the system.

Before Ryan, I had been struggling with—but also kind of accepting—the lack of connection with Sean. And although I yearned for more connection with Sean, I definitely hadn't yet experienced anything like the bond I had with Ryan. Ryan showed me something that was beyond even what I had craved, and opened me up to new possibilities.

Ryan was someone I could lay next to on the living room floor and laugh with all night and talk with endlessly. If I was thinking something he would know it, and say "Hey, what are you thinking about? I can feel that." That was a connection I'd never actually had before with anybody (except for maybe my younger sister).

But having the separation also showed me how much things had shifted with Sean since Ryan. Sean and I had scheduled a trip to Costa Rica for the holiday season. We had gotten our land, so we would visit Nosara occasionally to plan the house, meet with the architect, and just get to know the place more.

Now, being there with Sean for the holidays, I could see that more had opened up. I felt more connected to my husband. The Tantra was flaring between us again. I loved him; I was in love with him.

Still, my standards were very high and my senses were super attuned, and I *still* felt that he and I could walk on the beach together and somehow not be *totally* together. With Ryan, I felt like if he and I walked together, whatever we were doing, we were always truly together. With Sean, I still sensed a separateness between us.

That bothered me still, so even though I was feeling the love and the Tantra was strong, we started to get into little fights in Costa Rica.

One in particular had to do with how he liked to make fun of the way I speak. He's English, and I'm from Western Maryland. He often teased me about my accent. It sounds harmless, but he would do it to a point where if I was trying to tell a story, then *all* he would do was make fun of me for the whole the story, and it was distracting and I didn't feel like he was listening.

At one point in Costa Rica, I was trying to show him a vehicle (I guess I say it "vee-HICK-le"), that I thought we should have in Costa Rica, one that would be good for the terrain. As soon as I said, "vehicle" he started making fun of me. He went on and on for what seemed like minutes as I tried to talk, interrupting me. Finally he stopped and said, "Okay, continue your story." At that point I shut down and said, "No. It's totally gone now."

Then Ryan reached out to me right in the middle of the trip saying that he "couldn't do this anymore"—meaning, he didn't want to be the "other guy" in my life any more. He was thinking of me in Costa Rica with my husband, and said, "maybe we should just stop." Meaning, maybe we should stop spending so much time together, being so close, connecting so deeply and entertaining these questions about whether we might be destined to be together. Because even though we had separated physically, we were still talking, Facetiming, and being pretty emotionally intimate.

I was upset with Ryan. I didn't try to hide my distress and hurt from Sean. I still felt like I could, and should, share just about everything with

Sean. So I told him how I was feeling. I said, "I don't think Ryan wants to talk to me anymore."

He didn't say anything, so I went on, all of my frustration bursting out, "It just seems like you and I are so disconnected that we can walk on the beach together, and we're still not really *with* one another."

Even now, Sean still didn't quite understand what I was talking about. He just looked at me helplessly. He didn't know how to do any better. We had existed this way for a while, and for him, it was fine. We were pretty close.

For most people, as I've said, it would have been more than enough—in fact, amazing.

But the exquisite, powerful, profound closeness I was desiring in a relationship was something unique, and even though most people don't have it, that didn't deter me from wanting it or being determined to get it. And now I had tasted it with Ryan, so I *knew* it was possible—and even though it scared me and showed me my own resistance, I still yearned for it.

CALLING IN DIVINE MASCULINE

I was exasperated after Ryan sent me that message, and equally by getting into all these arguments with Sean. I was fed up with the whole mess. In a huff, I went out to the beach by myself. I sat there just breathing and connecting and channeling, looking at the ocean.

Then I heard the voices of my guides. "Remember, you can't find things outside of yourself. Everything is a mirror. Right now, you're feeling like you don't have the divine masculine in your life. But you have to realize that you have it within YOU. Also, don't blame divine masculine energy for any hurt that a man has caused you. If you were hurt by your father or your ex-husband or an ex-boyfriend or a person who raped you, that is not the divine masculine's fault. That is ego. Men and women both hurt each other through ego."

I thought, "Wow, okay, that's a huge message." I vowed to embrace and love divine masculine energy, and not seek to find it outside myself, or to wrest it out of Sean or anyone else.

I continued to sit on the beautiful beach, and I chanted to myself "I love the divine masculine. I love the divine masculine. I LOVE the divine masculine ..." And I could feel divine masculine energy coming in, and how this allowed my divine feminine energy to relax, calm down and play.

I got up and walked back to the place we were staying. It just so happened that right then, I had to get my stuff together and take a short flight from Nosara to San Jose for a dentist appointment.

Sean took me to the airport. I got on the plane. Turns out somewhere during the flight, I had I dropped my wallet. I had hundreds of dollars in it. A man came up to me, in the most loving way, and said, "Hey miss, you dropped your wallet." He handed it back to me with a kind smile. I was like "Okay, there you go. I love the divine masculine."

After landing, I went to a popular coffee shop in San Jose while I was waiting for my appointment to start. I was looking around for a place to plug in my charger. All of a sudden, a man came up to me and said, "I see that you're looking for an outlet to put your charger in. Here, here's one." He pointed to it and walked me over to it. I felt like "If this isn't the universe showing me 'Look what happens when you embrace the divine masculine!'" I smiled to myself, "I love the divine masculine."

I saw how if we're not attached to divine masculine representing just one or two human beings, but instead embrace the divine masculine within you and everywhere, it will come to us from everywhere. So much protection, safety, kindness, compassion, and love. It's all available when you open to it, instead of trying to grasp onto it or force it.

After San Jose I flew back to Nosara. Sean and I went out to dinner. I looked at him seriously and earnestly, and said, "Look, we're creating a paradise here. Literally. A beautiful house on a mountain, overlooking the ocean. It's paradise. Except…it won't really be paradise *unless we are paradise together*. It'll just be us living in hell—in heaven. We'll be in an external heaven, but in an internal hell. In order to create heaven, it has to be within us first." I added, "For us to do this, we've got to really work on this connection issue."

He really tried to take this in. He listened; he nodded; he said he understood. And to his credit, he really tried. He was buying me jewelry from roadside stands. He was kissing and hugging me and showing more affection. But he still didn't quite understand how we were going to get to where we needed to get. Or why the level of connection that I felt with Ryan was something I didn't feel with him.

And maybe I didn't totally understand either. When I got too close with Ryan I would push it away, and even Ryan would push it away when the intensity got to a certain level. I knew I still had to do a lot of self-work. We all did.

RAZOR ROCKS

Soon after this, we went on a snorkeling trip—or we tried to. We got in a charter boat with a company that was supposed to take us to a pink sand island for snorkeling. The large sailboat would anchor offshore and then a smaller boat was going to ferry us to the island.

But then Sean told the boat driver that he can't swim. He can, so I didn't understand why he said that, even though I know he gets scared by big water—I'd seen him swim in the lake at home and he swims fine.

The boat driver said, "Oh, well if you can't swim, then you have to go somewhere special." He took us to a beach where we had to walk across razor-sharp rocks for about 30 minutes to get the water. The rocks were literally cutting our feet. I had no idea what was going on. The boat driver guy was running across the rocks, apparently with very tough feet, but we were so scared we were going to fall and kill ourselves. The guy was trying to lead us somewhere, and he kept encouraging us to follow.

We finally got to a place where the water was only two feet deep. The sharp rocks were everywhere. The guy said, "You who can't swim, you go here."

I was really mad at Sean now, because I had *really* wanted to go snorkeling and his comment about not swimming had led us to this crazy death trap. We couldn't even put fins on, because it was so shallow. There weren't any fish to look at, and we couldn't have looked anyway. All we could be concerned with was whether we were going to be cut up by the rocks.

We started looking for some way out—someplace where we might get to actual water that we could swim out in. The guy was looking at us nodding and smiling as if to say, "Oh, you're having fun!"

Finally, we came to place where the ocean was rushing in between two huge rocks. From here, about 300 feet offshore, we could see the big sailboat that we had taken off from. The water was pushing and pulling, very rough, at this spot. But it was a way back to the boat.

We either could go back the way we had come, thirty minutes across the razor rocks, or we could shortcut through the rushing water back to the main boat, and just pray that we survived the crashing surges. I'm a good swimmer, but I was thinking "There's gonna have to be a helicopter that comes and saves us." Sean looked petrified. I looked at him and said, "I have to go. I'm just gonna go. I'm gonna swim for it."

I swam out, and I felt the undertow, and I just went with the flow until I bobbed up. Then I swam as hard as I could to the boat. The guy who had led us to this shallow place ended up literally grabbing Sean's arms and swimming with him.

On the way back, it became clearer what was going on. It turned out that Sean had brought a ring with him that he was going to use as a sweet proposal, since his first proposal had sucked and he knew it. He told me what he had planned, that he'd thought it would be romantic to propose to me with the fish on a beautiful pink island, but obviously it had not worked out. The whole snorkeling adventure was a disaster. We were throwing up because it was so rocky. He was sick, I was sick, my mom (who had come with us to stay on the big boat and watch Willow) was sick, and Willow was sick.

Even he could see, as he told me what he had been planning, "It's like the universe didn't want that. The universe did not want me to re-propose to you." I said, "Probably because I would have said no. If I had known back then what I know now, I wouldn't have done it; I would said thought we weren't ready to get married. So that is probably why."

I left that trip in Costa Rica a little disheartened, thinking "Okay, we live in paradise in the United States, we're creating a paradise in Costa Rica, yet we've got this thing that is *not* paradise in our relationship."

We both actively continued to work on ourselves. There were some nights that were magical; we would talk and connect and the Tantra was amazing. And again, that was telling, because Tantra is not just sex. It's energy, and the fact that it was powerful between us meant that we had all this potential and connection. When Sean was on top of me and inside of me, he wouldn't even have to move—just his energy and my heart against his heart would bring us to orgasm. It was very explosive. So I knew that on a soul level, we were truly in love and connected.

But there's material from the soul all the way to the conscious mind. There's genetics, collective material, DNA, and more that has to be healed and cleared for our potential to express on all levels.

CEREMONY PARTNERSHIP CONFUSION

Meanwhile, my husband still did not want to conduct ceremonies with me. So I reached out to Ryan (who had totally walked back his "maybe we shouldn't do this anymore" sentiment) and said, "Do you want to do ceremonies together? Like co-lead the professional ceremonies with me?" He said, "Absolutely!" So we began to plan some ceremonies, and that started a whole other journey.

Ryan was a natural at working with plant medicine and conducting ceremonies. We worked together so elegantly; the energy just flowed. We didn't even have to talk. We intuitively knew what to do for the people we were working on. Together we created a beautifully loving, healing space.

First, we did one ceremony our house in February 2022. Sean said, "You guys can do your thing, I'm going to be downstairs, making music." I had invited a few people over with whom I had already worked, and now they wanted to bring their teenage children to experience the healing as well. We had a really good time doing that.

But during the ceremony, Sean came upstairs and one of the women looked at our wedding picture and said, "That's a beautiful wedding picture." You can tell that we were dancing when the photo was taken. She looked right at my husband and said, "Which song did you get married to?" My heart dropped, because I *knew* that he would not remember. His eyes got really wide, and I looked at him and said, "You don't even remember, do you? What song we got married to?"

The poor lady was mortified. "Oh my gosh!" she said, "I did not mean to cause something." I said firmly, "No, you're fine. It needed to come out. That's what the plant medicine does, it brings this stuff out."

The ceremony continued for the rest of the night, and everything went amazingly as usual. Then it was time for bed. I was feeling pretty feisty and activated by everything—the power of the work, the mounting disconnect between me and Sean about the work, the struggles that continued despite our efforts.

I came out with it. "It doesn't bother you that I'm doing this magical work with another man? He's doing with me exactly what I want to do with you. And I'm not just talking about healing, or taking the job as a healer. I'm talking about just connecting with me on that level, no matter what we're doing, that creates a healing space. Being *present!* Not on your phone. Being present with me in the moment and with whoever may be in the room."

I tried to articulate: when you're present in the moment, and you're in love with the moment, it creates magic and miracles around you. The presence and connection is everything. I said, "It doesn't bother you that this is happening right in front of your eyes, with a different man?"

He went into his whole spiel about how he knows that Ryan and I have unconditional love for one another and he doesn't want to get in the way of that. He just didn't want what Ryan and I had to be sexual. Which so upset me, because it was *so* false masculine and macho to be okay with whatever your wife does as long as it's not sex with another guy. I felt like he should be just as concerned—if not more so!—about the best friend part, the emotional intimacy, the spiritual connection. He should want that, and he should *not* be okay with me having that with someone else.

I told him so, and added hotly, "And what am I supposed to think about you not even knowing the wedding song that we got married to? It's like the universe is trying to point at us and laugh and say 'See how much you guys don't even really know each other? Or weren't present when you got married?'"

He looked at me helplessly. Finally he said, desperately, "Rebecca, I'm on your side."

I was stunned. I sputtered, "That was the name of our wedding song."

He looked confused. "What?"

I said, "We got married to "On My Side" by Lenka, and you just said 'I'm on your side.'"

He started laughing. So did I. He agreed that was pretty synchronistic. So we processed through that, and then we went to bed.

In this way, it seemed like we kept digging. I felt that, slowly but surely, we were making fits and starts of progress. Sometimes it felt like taking a little pitchfork and digging into a mountain of rocks. But we were getting there.

At the same time, working with Ryan doing ceremonies, I began to fall head over heels in love with him. The magic we created and saw was so life-changing. People were healing and thanking us; the changes we were seeing, that we were making in the world together—this was exactly what I had wanted in a husband.

This made things a lot harder with Sean, because I would see and experience the most miraculous things, synchronicities were lining up everywhere…and I would come home and try to tell my husband about it, and it didn't work. Both because it couldn't be described, and because he wasn't that interested. He just wasn't a part of the magic. He was just someone I tried to explain it all to.

So in this way, we went back and forth for a while. Sean and I would have little breakthroughs and start to get closer. I would stay away from Ryan until we had another ceremony to do together. And then…I would experience that healing magic, and the love that he had for me, and the love I felt for him. We would experience that deep connection, and I would come home confused. It was like a cycle.

Sean noticed it. He said, "The first three days after you come home from ceremony, you're very distant." But what did he expect? I had explained what I was getting at those ceremonies, what I was experiencing with Ryan, and I had been very clear that I had wanted *him* to step into that. I would remind him again, "Well, yes, It's because I'm creating magic with a different man."

The whole time I was puzzling over which man was The One. Who should I be with? Sean or Ryan? It was so confusing.

At that point, Ryan was experiencing the same relative to me. He was wondering if I was the one for him—or if I was just a catalyst to get him where he needed to be. He said at one point, "Rebecca, if I'm not with you, at least you're a reference point. I will never settle for less than what I have now with you." And then he added, "But I'll even have more, because I'll have *all* of that person, not just the part of her who's not with her husband."

We realized also the exact song that I used to open up the portal right before he appeared in my life—Purple Rain—was the theme of our relationship. If you listen to the words of that song, it talks about being weekend lovers. And that song played everywhere we went. One time we went to go see a bluegrass band at the lake, and they played Purple Rain. The synchronicities and messages were everywhere we went.

Ryan and I did a few more ceremonies together in 2022, including April in Sedona, May in Deep Creek Lake, and then another at my house with AWAKE students. In June, Ryan moved back to the lake, and rented a condo there since now he was now making some decent money co-leading the ceremonies. That way, he was near the ceremonies that we did in Deep Creek Lake.

COMING TO A HEAD—NEW YEAR'S EVE

Then a really big test came. New Year's Eve was approaching, so I said to Sean, "We have to invite him over. He's coming over for New Year's Eve. You have to accept that." Sean agreed to that.

New Year's Eve arrived, and we had a crowd. My whole family was there, extended family, lots of friends. We have a large swim spa, so our hot tub can fit 10-12 people easily, and that became the focal point for this gathering.

Around 11:00 PM that night, everybody was in the tub, and I was sitting there and I realized, "Midnight's going to come and my husband's going to expect me to kiss him." And I realized that I literally could not do that in front of Ryan. I couldn't choose one of them at that moment to kiss at midnight. I couldn't do that to either one of them.

So I tried to get out of the hot tub, but the universe conspired against it me. Willow was in the hot tub and didn't want to get out. Everybody else said, "No, let's stay in the hot tub! It would be great to be in the hot tub when New Year's hits!"

So it was getting close to midnight. Sean walked over in the tub (our tub is huge and you can walk in it), and I leaned over and said to him quietly, "I can't kiss you. I'm not doing that to Ryan."

And that is when Sean just broke down and layers came off of him. He said, stunned, "You're not even going to kiss your own husband on New Year's Eve because of another guy?"

People heard that, so then everybody hurried out of the hot tub—except for my best friend Sherry, Sean, and me. Even Ryan left, his eyes wide, taking Willow with him. Everybody disappeared into the house. And Sean and I had it out.

I said, "You've been okay with this all along. You said you were. You've been watching me create magic with another man, in this work, while you stay at home and isolate yourself and then you hope I come back and that you can make me happy outside that magic. I'm supposed to be okay with that. Well, I'm not. I'm telling you, I think I'm in love with him still. And I don't know what to do about it."

Unbelievably, it started to thunder. My best friend was still sitting there in the tub witnessing this, her eyes huge. I was hurling all of this stuff at Sean that was obviously going to be hurtful. And he just sat there and took it. Then I took off my rings, threw them deep into the woods, and said, "That is what I think of our marriage right now."

Then, all of a sudden, it started raining.

The universe was really playing jokes on us at this point. The funny thing is that since the first day I'd met Sean, I had told him that I think it's really romantic to kiss in the rain. That scene in the movie The Notebook, when they kiss in the rain, I bet every woman dreams about having a moment like that. And I love the rain. I'll walk in the rain, I like to play in the rain. And I think kissing in the rain is tremendously magical.

He had never tried to kiss me in the rain. As the years went on, I would actually point this out: "Do you know you still haven't tried to kiss me in the rain? And I always tell you I want you to kiss me in the rain?"

So, here we were in the hot tub, I had just thrown my wedding ring into the in the woods, I had told him I was in love with another man and I might still leave him for this other man…and it started pouring rain.

He looked at me straight in the eyes and said, "Kiss me."

But I was too irate and wrought up. I said, "You've gotta be kidding me. *Now?* The one time you finally want to kiss me in the rain is *now?* Absolutely not!"

We stared at each other. And then I said, "I don't know what we're going to do about this, but something has to be done."

Sean turned away then and left the hot tub. Sherry and I were in there alone. She was in a state of paralysis and shock. She was a bit traumatized; she said our fight had taken her back to when her parents used to fight when she was a child.

But after she had taken a few deep breaths and was able to ground herself, she said something that riveted me, and that I will never forget. She said, "Rebecca, Sean is divine masculine. The things you just said to him, the things that he witnessed, what he just endured—he stayed very calm, he stayed collected. He's still listening to you. He still wants to be there for you. This must be so hurtful for him. He must be grieving substantially. Yet I'm watching him keep it together as he's still feeling love for you. That is divine masculine. Trust me, he loves you."

I got out of the tub. Ryan was sitting in the living room. He said. "You know, I was just staring at your wedding picture and it's making me sad." I didn't know what to say. I felt sad too. He had been waiting for me, hoping I would choose him. I just said, "Well, you can sleep in Cody's room."

Willow got her shower and we put her to bed. And then Sean and I went to bed. I told him what Sherry had said. I acknowledged with appreciation that it was meaningful that he was going through this with his heart open, not getting caught up in ego, and that he was expressing divine masculine in doing that. We cuddled. I was not completely happy, but I was mollified. I knew Sherry was on to something.

SIGNS AND MORE SIGNS

The universe still was not done with us. Very shortly after New Year's Eve, my daughter Ariel, her boyfriend, and Sean and I went out to dinner. I hadn't told my daughter anything about what we were going through—not in any detail, anyway. She knew we were going through things, and she knew about Ryan. But she didn't know details like about Sean inviting his friends over on the wedding night, or the way he proposed to me.

I also wasn't wearing my wedding ring (even though Sean had actually gotten a metal detector and located my rings in the woods the very next day!) But Ariel didn't notice that.

We were sitting at dinner, just chatting, and then all of a sudden she randomly said, "Mom, you're not going to believe this. Alyssa's friend got proposed to, the other day, in a *kitchen*. And, of course, she said NO." (Alyssa was my niece, and my daughter's cousin.)

I looked at Ariel like okay, somehow she knows something about what happened with us, and this is a joke. But it wasn't a joke. She had no idea. She was just sharing this news and her reaction. She shook her head. "Can you believe that her boyfriend proposed to her in a *kitchen*?"

Sean just looked right at me and said "Okay. I get it." It was like the universe just slapping him across the face. He laughed and laughed. He said, "Okay. I believe you, Rebecca. This stuff is real. The guardian parents telling you Ryan was coming in, showing you the vision, you opening the portal, him coming through it—all of it. I believe it. I can see this all happening right in front of my face."

Of course, he had said this before—at ceremonies, at other times of synchronicity—and then checked back out, or gone back to sleep, or still not changed much. But each time, I think, he got it more. It just seemed like his awakening was happening in stages, layers.

Later that night, as we were going to bed, he added, "Why can't your guardian parents or higher guidance talk to *me* and tell *me* what to do?" I answered, "If you would be centered in yourself, grounded and trusting, you could hear them. You could hear your own, too. But you've got to go deep into yourself and trust yourself enough to be able to hear what they're saying." He said, "Yes, I get that. And I'm going to be working on it."

Then he said something that was absolutely amazing to me. He said, "I want you to know that I'm so thankful that Ryan has come into our lives. Because what has happened and transpired since he came in has made both you and I grow so much. We would not be healing in the way that we're healing right now without him. We would have waited till later in our marriage, until we were twenty years in, and be like 'Oh, we're really disconnected now.'" He said, "I am very, very grateful for Ryan. I want to let you know that know that this man has helped us. He's been a catalyst to our healing."

It was absolutely incredible that Sean got to a place of seeing that. I was so grateful too—to both of them.

But of course, we still weren't all the way there. During the next plant medicine ceremony, something happened that changed everything for good.

LESSON

If you're going through the push-pull of intimacy with a partner, confusion whether a person is a catalyst or The One, or other twin flame challenges (really any life challenges!), the universe will help lead you along the path—if you're tuned in and paying attention. In this period of my life, and in my relationship with Sean, the universe was giving us numerous signs. Even Sean could not deny this was true, as many of the signs were for him too. During this chapter of our process, many synchronicities encouraged us that we were on the right path, or led to rueful recognition of a truth. These synchronicities were like path lights, little breadcrumbs leading us forward.

There is no doubt that the universe offers us signs and synchronicities to unveil truths. Unfortunately, most people haven't cultivated the awareness to see these signs, and don't pay close enough attention to these often subtle cues so they can connect the dots. We all receive messages from our higher selves and angelic guidance, too—but again, it's not typical in our culture to develop the capacities we need to see and hear them. Programming and static get in the way of receiving these messages.

When you become more awakened to this level of communication from spirit, you'll start to distinguish such messages from mere thought; you can tell these "voices" or images are not something from the ego. This kind of guidance is so important when you're trying to consciously create your life, so I encourage everyone to explore and pursue the kind of healing and consciousness-raising work that cultivates our sensitivity to synchronicity and other messages of guidance.

Chapter Nineteen

I WAS DRIVING DOWN THE ROAD ONE DAY NEAR home and I looked down at my rings. As I mentioned, Sean had found them in the woods with a metal detector and had given them back to me. But they just didn't feel right.

On this day, very calmly and consciously I pulled over to the side of the road, took off my rings and I threw them, again, deep into the woods. It just felt right. I felt very relieved, actually.

When I got back home, I told Sean very calmly what I had done. I said I wasn't angry. "But, you know, that proposal and wedding isn't the way I believe that you and I should have entered into this union. So, if you decide that you want to stay married to me, then it's going to be completely up to you to buy me new rings, and to do it right. But I'm not going to stress you out about it."

He looked a little bit hurt. He said, "Okay, I understand." He took his ring off, too. He left it off for just a couple of days, and then he came back to me, and said, "I hear what you're saying. But for me, I just don't feel right without it. I want my wedding ring. I'm going to wear mine."

MEETING LIAM

About a month later, Sean got word that the wife of his best friend from England had died of cancer. He and Liam had been best friends since elementary school. Liam had met his wife when he was seventeen, and they married in their early twenties. Now he was 53, and he had lost the love of his life who he'd been with for 35 years.

This was devastating news for my husband, because he had been very close with both of them. He actually talked to Liam every day. We knew that Carrie had been sick. But her death was still crushing.

Of course, we cleared our schedules and we made preparations to go to England—Sean, Willow, and I—for the funeral, and to support Liam.

I had always been under the impression that all English people have a hard time expressing their feelings, showing affection or being vulnerable. At least the men. Sean certainly had been fulfilling the stereotype up to that point, and when he talked about his friends it also reinforced that impression. My sense was that they especially didn't like to admit when they were in love. Maybe because it would make them seem weak.

But when we made the journey to England, and I finally had the pleasure of meeting his best friend, I was so pleasantly surprised. He had a really healthy ability to communicate his feelings, including and especially in reference to his wife. We spent a long time talking about her and his feelings related to her passing, and about the afterlife. He was very much able to show his emotions.

When I was young—I mean, oddly young, maybe not even 10—I already believed the whole purpose of life was to truly be in love. I knew how important love was to every single human being. I knew that if you were truly in love with yourself, you'd be in love with somebody else. And I knew that if there was true love all over the world, no one would be focused on fighting. There wouldn't be war. And true love opens the divine feminine and masculine portals.

So, I just knew: true love is everything. And if I had my way, everybody around me would be in love. I try to prepare everybody in AWAKE for their ultimate true love relationships.

If I had a weakness—and I'm going to call it a weakness—it was seeing true love bring grief to somebody. That's been a vulnerability or soft point, or whatever you want to call it, ever since I can remember. As I was talking with Liam about his wife and their relationship, I could see that they had been very much in love, and they had created a beautiful life together. They had a daughter and a grandson. He had his passions, she had hers. They woke up every day looking forward to life. They had beautiful things, like a vacation house, but more importantly, just a life full of love. I was very happy to hear about their life together. But I also felt his grief deeply—more than I expected to.

When I went to the funeral and watched his expression, his reactions, his daughter's reactions, and listened to him as he went up front and talked talking about his wife and how she was his soulmate, how much he loved her, and how she's never going to be replaced— crying, and vulnerable—I could feel every single thing he was feeling. I felt all of the energy. Not only that, but it burrowed deep into my own worst fear, which is about being that much in love and then having that person taken away.

I left the funeral feeling kind of shellshocked, numb, overwhelmed by the emotions and energy, as if I were going through the loss myself.

That this deep connection to another's grief made me vulnerable is going to become highly relevant later, but I need to interject here that I believe Covid (or any illness, really) attaches to and tries to purge shadow energies. When your body produces an illness, your energy field has allowed it in through lower frequencies. Covid or other illness gets in through guilt, doubt, shame, fear, or any lower-frequency energy you're holding. Of course, in addition to the energetic perspective, we know those kinds of emotions are simply stressful to the body, and there's just plain good science showing the ways that stress biologically lowers your immune defenses.

I've been to a lot of funerals, and I was expecting a "normal" funeral, where I can walk out of the place and not feel totally like I'm falling to pieces. I hadn't myself had anyone close to me pass away. My dad had died, but he had been an alcoholic, and he and I weren't that close. My grandfather had passed away, and he and I *were* close, but he died of old age, and he'd had dementia for a while, and it was expected and we were prepared. I hadn't had any losses where I was completely griefstricken.

So this left me vulnerable, and given our travels and all the exposure to large groups of people, you might imagine what's coming next...

Meanwhile, we went to the reception after the funeral, and, as Liam and I talked there, he told me, "You know, you've made Sean a really happy man. I've never seen him this happy." Which meant a lot to me, because I didn't really know much about his past relationships, or what to compare it to.

On the other hand, as we sat together at a table later that evening, Liam also told me, "We didn't even get to see a picture of your wedding day. Sean refused to send us any pictures of you or him or of your wedding." I didn't know how to take that. Once again, I felt like "Oh my, he was ashamed!" I just looked at Sean a little confused, because everyone was laughing. His friends said they had wondered if I was real.

I turned to Sean and asked, "Why wouldn't you send them a picture of me?" His face turned red, and he claimed that he was embarrassed because he had thought he looked fat in the wedding photos. But it really fit with everything else that had been emerging about our wedding and early marriage.

SEAN'S MOTHER SHEDS LIGHT

I only had about three days in England, because I had to fly back for a ceremony (which I was going to lead with Ryan). Sean and Willow were going to stay for a few more days and fly back a little bit after me, because they wanted to visit his mother.

I did get to meet his mother before I left, and she was a little…different. She had a very hard time showing affection. At one point, she looked at me and said, "I guess Sean seems happy. And he does have Willow. And I guess he seems happy with you as well." It was very odd, very negative and ungenerous, almost as though she didn't want to admit that he was happy with me. I could tell she really didn't like the fact that he was with someone. In fact, on our wedding day she had made a post on Facebook saying how weddings don't work out, how terrible they are, how terrible marriage is. She did it on the exact date that we were married.

So she had a lot of resistance to me, and I could feel the insecurity she had that somehow I would take away Sean's love for her. But I tried not to take it too personally. It wasn't like we had to see her a lot. And I knew these were her issues, not mine.

We decided to take advantage of the couple of days I had left in Europe by making a side trip to France. We went to Paris, and had a great time there. We went to the Eiffel Tower, took Willow to see some other sights, had excellent dinners. The day after we got back to England, I got on an airplane and flew back to the United States. I was still feeling a lot of unusual grief from what I had experienced with Liam and his lost love.

At that time, you could not fly back from Europe to the U.S. without getting a Covid test. I took a Covid test within 24 hours of flying, and it was negative. I landed in the U.S., back in Maryland, and the next day Sean called and told me that practically everyone at that funeral had come down with Covid. He had it, all of his friends had it (including Liam)—the only person who didn't have it was Willow.

It made sense, because I knew how Covid travels through sadness, grief, and shadow energies. I could see how that was happening and I wondered why I didn't have it, since I myself had so much sadness around Liam and his loss.

At any rate, this turn of events meant Sean had to stay in England for 10 more days, when he and Willow had planned to come home in a couple of days. And because Sean was sick, Willow had to stay with Sean's mother.

THE INTIMACY CEREMONY

During this next ceremony that Ryan and I led, which was at my house on the lake, there was a general theme—which was, of course, intimacy. There were probably about ten people at the ceremony. One couple came in on the verge of divorce. The woman told me, "I don't even know if I want to be here. I don't think anything can help." I told her, "Let's just give this a chance." She agreed.

As we got into the work, the woman's husband had taken two or three glasses of ayahuasca two or three hours apart and still wasn't really feeling anything. Intuitively, I looked at the wedding ring on his finger and I said, "You need to take that off." He said, "Really?" I said, "Yeah, I'm just getting this feeling."

He took the ring off his finger, and within ten seconds of taking it off, everything hit him at once. One of the issues that his wife had was that he could not express himself. She thought of him as kind of a pushover. Didn't have much to say, not stepping into his power, not giving his opinions about things, being too submissive.

When he took the ring off, the medicine finally hit him and he had an enormous release. He broke down to the point where he was shaking, crying, and convulsing. It was as if he'd had the weight of the world on his shoulders, holding burdens and suffering and trauma for not just from his life, but for all of his ancestors as well. And all of his fears of not being the perfect man for her, of not being able to take care of his wife, came to the surface.

But what came to the surface most was how strong he really was—IS. When he was able to let go of the fear of exposing himself and step into his power, his wife was able to see his strength beyond measure.

Meanwhile, his wife had had a breast cancer pattern that we were working on. She was on the floor, and she was crying as she released *her* stuff. Finally, what felt most comforting and healing to her was when her husband came over and took her into his arms. It was such a magical, enormous transformation for both of them. It was another example of what's possible with these ceremonies and this medicine, even when people think there is no hope. They just went through layer after layer of healing, opening up more and more, until finally they said, "We're going to get remarried." And they did. They actually renewed their wedding vows after this ceremony.

During the whole process, Ryan and I were connecting and working together beautifully. And I was having those same feelings I always had in doing this magical work with him, those feelings of being in love with him. But on this night, after it was over, I looked in the mirror, and I really saw myself. I said to myself, "Wow, Rebecca, look at you and your fear of intimacy. *Your* fear of intimacy. This isn't Ryan's fault, it's not Sean's fault, that you're unable to get where you want to. It's you." I felt sick to my stomach, and I thought "Okay, it's really time to do something about this."

I was also starting to feel a little bit feverish. I could feel some symptoms coming on. I knew that I was open for Covid to get in. Not so much because everyone at the events in England had it, but because of the grief I'd been feeling. And my own fears about getting close to someone and losing them were coming to the surface as I processed what had happened to Liam.

After the ceremony was over, everybody went home. I was in the house alone at that point. My daughter and husband were still in England, and Ryan went back home to his condo. Things had simmered down between us, but I still had questions.

I was still feeling distracted by everything that had happened in England, and all the grief. Liam and his loss were on my mind a lot—more than I felt like made sense, and I would understand that better later.

And finally, I came down with full-blown Covid. I needed to purge this resistance to intimacy. So much had been stirred up: being at the funeral, attaching to the fear of the kind of devastation and loss that Liam experienced; then seeing that couple at the ceremony and how much they loved each other. Just feeling all of that brought up a huge purge within me. I knew that Covid was going to help me to release it.

Covid for me was not severe at all. It felt like I just needed to lay in bed and sleep for a few days and process. I was able to work through those energies that needed to come out.

CARRYING ENERGY "BAGGAGE"

When all of that purged, what was facing me next was my body.

I had noticed that, through all of this turmoil and upheaval with Ryan and in my marriage, I had gained quite a bit of fat. I was carrying about 50 extra pounds of fat at that point. I was seeing someone in the mirror who I did not even want to look at.

Having worked through all this, I'm now as fit and lean as I was in my twenties. The thing is, our fitness isn't just about the food we eat. It's also about energy, just like everything. Excess fat can be about fear of exposure, fear of attaching, fear of intimacy—which I was obviously struggling with. Our bodies also respond to our belief systems about what we eat, how we're feeling when we eat the food. Like money, food is energy and currency, and it works for you differently depending on the energy you have around it. You can use both food and money for unhealthy reasons, or for wholesome ones.

I came to learn that energy can actually be trapped in fat cells. Kundalini yoga and energy work are important to do when you're working on losing fat, to clear the energy, even as you do the fitness work alongside to reduce that fat itself. Revisit your relationship to food. Look at your relationship to intimacy. All of it is important. I began to do all this work, and eventually it all came together.

Meanwhile, though, on a related note, after about 10 days Sean and Willow came from England, and I looked at my daughter and was shocked. She was four years old at this point, and in the mere 10 days she had stayed with his mother, she had gained seven pounds. For a four-year-old, that's a lot.

I asked, "What happened to Willow?" He went into an explanation about, "Well, Mom didn't really have that much to do with her but cook, and she fed her a lot of snacks…"

But I knew there was more to it than food. Of course, food is part of it, but as with everything, so is energy.

Willow is a lot like I was as a child. My sisters were very skinny, but I was always on the large side, even though we all ate the same. Yes, we had different body types, but that doesn't entirely account for how much larger I always was than my sisters. I was a tomboy. I played football, rode bikes—I was really athletic, so there was no reason for me to be fat. Now I realize that I was so empathic, I was soaking in…everything. I was holding on to and storing so much energy in my cells. And Willow is equally empathic, if not more so. I realized that because Sean couldn't be there, and his mom was so negative, Willow had soaked in some of that energy. And that made her balloon out, just like I did as a child.

We had worked so hard on raising Willow to eat well and freely and have a healthy relationship to food. She ate well, but if she ate chocolate cake, we didn't make her think that was any different than eating an apple, because I think if you're constantly being told that this or that food is bad or it's going to make you fat, your body will take that on. We made sure Willow had a healthy balance. She could eat healthy food, she could eat chocolate cake, and she wouldn't feel bad about herself. She was healthy, happy and in good shape. But in ten days with Sean's mom, she was noticeably plumper.

This told me, too, that there was much more to Sean's relationship with his mom than I even knew. I knew his mother was not thrilled about me, or about him being married, and she was not a positive person. But whatever she had projected onto Willow added a whole new layer. Literally.

This shed even more light onto the intimacy challenge that we had been going through. Sean's mother didn't know how to give affection or say "I love you." She was distant and cold. Although he was more demonstrative and evolved than she was, Sean still carried some of that energy from his mom. She had also left him when he was 12, so there was an abandonment piece that no doubt played into the whole situation as well.

But the trip to England brought us closer in a lot of ways. Being around his friends and getting to see his lifelong relationships was powerful. He had five best friends who he had known since elementary school. When I watched him around his friends, he was so happy and authentic, and while in his own culture he was more affectionate to me. He enjoyed that I loved being a part of that. He would take my hand and look at my eyes and hug me, and just say how grateful he was that I was his wife, and that he was proud to be married to me.

All in all, the trip was eye-opening, and deeper layers of our intimacy issues were emerging, especially as I was trying to lose this fat.

Right after England, Ryan had come back to our hometown again to do some more work on the house. This also helped with my fat loss and body improvement process. Ryan, during our whole time together, had probably gained just about as much fat as I had—so had Sean, for that matter, but Ryan and I more so. He believed it was for the same reason I had—the intimacy blocks and defenses. He too was determined to shift this. Ryan began working out with me, and we both began eating a ketogenic diet. This gave me a good kickstart, and I began to see results after just a few weeks, especially when I also added in the energy work aspects. Ryan did the energy work with me as well.

STARS ALIGNING

The next ceremony was the transformational one that I mentioned at the end of the last chapter, the one that really blew things open.

Ryan had gone back home for about five days before we were to do this ceremony in Sedona with private clients. He was visiting his daughter in Missouri, which meant that he would also be seeing his wife. Every time he went back and saw his wife, he had similar experiences to the ones I had when I would return to Sean and remember how much I loved him, how connected we were, how hard he was trying, and so on. He would start to wonder if maybe he hadn't given her a chance, if maybe she *was* the one. So when we came back together after time apart, the energy between us would be different. It would take some time for us to really connect again.

We arrived in Sedona for the ceremony. Sedona is magical. When I look at the area, it definitely does not look like the planet Earth. I feel like if you were to step back and see Sedona from above, it would look like a pod that some sort of spaceship was supposed to be landing on.

Ryan and I had planned a few days to ourselves before and after the ceremony so that we could get prepared and then rest adequately before we went home. The energy between us started out a little distant, for the reasons I just mentioned. We were feeling a little dissonance. But we were still doing things together.

One of the really sweet things that happened on this trip was when we took a hike up to the Birthing Cave in Sedona. When we got up there, there was a tree with a sign hammered to it. I could hear the tree talking, and I could feel its pain. The tree was saying "Please, take this sign off of me. It hurts me." The sign said something very obvious, like "No arson."

The thing is, people who go to Sedona and hike to the Birthing Cave aren't likely to do the things that the sign warned not to do. So Ryan agreed that we would hike back down, go to the hardware store, get whatever tools we needed, hike back up, and remove the sign to help the tree. That was quite a journey for us, and I thought again what a sweet guy this was, that he would do that with me and for me—and for a tree. It was neat too, because after we did it, we could hear *all* the trees talking to us, and we actually felt a closer relationship with the trees.

Then the ceremony started, and we had the best four clients I could ever imagine. It was two couples. Once again, the whole theme was intimacy and getting closer. They all wanted to create their heaven on earth with each other, so it was completely aligned with what we were working on and trying to do for ourselves.

We were teaching these couples Tantra. With one of the couples especially, I had picked up that the woman had "baby" in her field. Before she even went and started to practice Tantra with her significant other, I talked to her about that. She said, "Well, Rebecca, I'm in my 40s, and I just feel like I'm too old to have a baby." I told her, "No, not at all. That is just a belief system. If you believe you're too old, then your body's going to start to act that way. There's so much work we can do around that." So she and I worked on fertility issues and her belief systems. Then she went off and she started to work with her significant other.

One of the things we do in ceremony, which I find absolutely magical, is that we put on a playlist and see which songs come up at which times. It's always uncanny, always perfect. We used to have a completely planned playlist, but now we put on an ayahuasca playlist from Spotify, with hundreds of songs (and we have hundreds of playlists). The universe will always pick the right song at the right time, and that's just part of the mystery. Happens every time.

At this ceremony, we were outside by the fire, just observing, waiting for the participants to do their work and come out as needed. The woman I had worked with about the baby came out, and she was all smiles. She said that the two of them had worked out so much about his ex and her ex, and what it would be like to have a baby together. As she was talking, over the playlist, came the words of a song where you hear the lyrics "Mommy! Mommy!" She was literally talking about how they were going to create this child and suddenly we heard from clearly all the speakers "Mommy! Mommy!" We just looked at each other, stunned. Then she said, "Oh my God! You can't even make this up. This is so, so magical."

She went back in, and they continued to work with each other. Then the other couple came out, and they told us all this magnificent stuff that was happening with them—how they were able to work on each other's bodies, reading each other's minds telepathically, practicing the Tantra techniques breathing each other's breath.

Then the woman of that couple looked at me and said, "You need to go lie under those stars right now." She added, "I don't know why, but I know it. The two of you have to go under those stars and look up at them." Normally, I wouldn't do that, because I'm always looking out for the clients. But she insisted, "We're all fine. You need to do this."

I had obviously been guided through ceremony participants to do things with Ryan before, and the result had always been powerful. So I went with it. We went out to the back of the house, and put down some blankets to lay on. It was April in Sedona, so not terribly cold, but still chilly at night so we covered up with more blankets. We settled down and we looked up at the stars, which are incredibly clear in Sedona's dark skies. I wasn't thinking too much. I was just doing what we had been guided.

Then, I heard the message "Find your Mothership star." I said, "How do you do that?" I heard in reply, "Go to the field of your heart, because your heart is your Mothership. Your heart is your command center. When you're connected to your heart, notice the star that shines for you."

My guidance, which is really my higher self, told me to do this and also to tell Ryan to do this. I explained to Ryan what we needed to do. Then I heard, "Okay, now put your intentions out there."

What were our intentions? Well, he and I were both trying to figure out what this relationship was about. Is he for me? Am I for him? Is he supposed to be my husband? Is he supposed to go back to his wife, or get divorced? We had all these questions. We wanted a clear life direction for the highest good, to bring true love into our lives, and we were open to how that would look.

Then, we heard, "Don't have any expectations, just put your intentions out there. There's so much that can happen that you're unaware of."

I surrendered to this. I had located my Mothership Star, and Ryan had located his. We set our intention, and we gave our attention to or respective Mothership Stars. All of a sudden, the most astonishing thing happened—*all* of the stars began moving very fast, like spaceships, in diagonal patterns all around our Mothership Stars. I'd never seen anything like it before or since. I gasped. I exclaimed, "Can you see this, Ryan?" He answered, "Yeah!"

Then I heard my guidance say, "This is what they mean by 'The stars align for you.' By connecting your Mothership—your heart—to your Mothership Star, you allow the stars to align right now, so that everything happens exactly the way it needs to." To this day, I now use this as a technique in my programs (and although I've never seen it happen as dramatically as it did for us that night, it still really works). Go to a place where you can really see the stars, lay down, open your heart, find the star in the sky to which you're most attracted, set your intentions, and watch what the stars do. Let the stars align.

This was such a magical, cosmic experience that I was jumping for joy. Ryan was also giddy. We went back in and I told the participant what had happened. She had been working on her intuitive abilities, so she was happy that her guidance had led to something so important. Then we continued to work with our clients.

When the evening was done, everybody went to bed. Ryan and I stayed up and got in the hot tub and listened to music and talked. We both noticed that since the "star alignment," we felt very different with each other. At one point in the conversation, I said to him, "Look at me and tell me if you think I'm the one for you." He looked at me, paused, and said, "No, Rebecca, I don't think you're the one for me." Then he added, "I don't think my wife's the one for me either. I think it's someone that's about to come."

I wasn't hurt. I felt relief, like some big burden had been taken off of me. We agreed that we still unconditionally loved each other, that we were still going to be the best of friends. But at that moment, we really saw that we were not the ones for each other. We were not two people that were supposed to be married in this lifetime. It seemed that the stars had done their job. Our intention to get clear about this question was fulfilled, and quickly.

The next morning, when we woke up, we still felt the same way. We cleaned up, said goodbye to our clients, and then stayed an extra couple of days, just to rest and sleep and wind down. We hiked, ate, talked, and enjoyed our time, but it felt very platonic. Then we each got on an airplane and went to our respective homes.

Both of us were still a little confused, though. We had stated that we didn't feel like we were the ones for each other, but we were still vacillating a little, still reluctant to let go. During the last couple of days there, he was saying things like "Well, when I said you weren't the one, I meant it at that time. But things can change."

So, we were still in a little bit of a gray zone. But we were definitely in a different space.

LESSON

The stars have so much universal significance and power. We've all heard the expression "the stars aligning for you" but until that night, I never took it literally. The fact is, they actually do literally align for us. My life changed so much after this experience with the stars, and I have never forgotten that night where so much in my life moved after seeing the stars move. It was so magical, and so powerful.

Try this for yourself. Go out somewhere where you can see the stars really well, in a place where the sky is dark enough on a clear night. Lie down if possible, or sit and look up. Relax with no expectations and drop into your heart space. Pick the star that stands out to you; let your heart guide you in this. That star will be your mothership star. Now, signal your heart's desire to your mothership star by thinking—or better yet, speaking out loud—a clear intention, request, or question. Trust that it is received. Get ready to notice changes and movement in your life. It will be helpful to journal the night you do this, and then continue journaling to track changes, signs, and synchronicities related to your intention.

Chapter Twenty

I'M GOING TO BEGIN THIS CHAPTER WITH A LITtle reflection. It took me years to get to this point in the book, this point of writing it all down. I used to think that was because I was still in a little bit of shock from everything that happened. I was taking time to really process it. Sometimes I thought I was procrastinating or making excuses, but what I realize now is that I'm divinely guided by Spirit. I always have been. I just know the right times to do things.

The timing of this transmission of my story is perfect, because it gave me the space and reflection time I needed to be able to relate it in a way that would help others. When you're in the thick of things, as you're going through them, the lessons can be more oblique to you. Now I have more distance to be able to turn these experiences into insight and wisdom. This can take time.

THE MARTYRING MUST GO

Once I got back from Sedona, I started reflecting on some patterns with Ryan that were showing me more toxic tendencies that I needed to release. One of the things I was working on releasing is martyring. I knew I had this pattern where I feel like I have to save everybody. No one's okay unless Rebecca jumps in and saves the day. I noticed how this pattern was playing out with Ryan. He was this wonderful guy, and we were connected and could read each other's thoughts and finish each other's sentences, but he always needed help with something. He couldn't afford to get someplace unless I paid for it. He was often stuck until I got him out of a situation.

I realized that this toxic need to martyr was rooted in the idea that that if I'm always the one who saves the day, then I'm never going to be alone. People are always going to love me, because they'll need me. I'm going to be their savior. This is something that I absolutely wanted to release. Instead, I wanted to be like a soaring bird. If you can soar as fast as I can, then come fly with me. And if I can hold your hand as we're flying, great. If you fall down in the dirt, I'll take your hand and help you up. But I can't walk for you, and I can't fly for you.

I had been realizing for a while now that the universe is going to show up for you when you love yourself enough, when you love yourself completely. It's very important that we release these toxic patterns within ourselves. We can actually release them at the level of our DNA, and this helps the collective as well. So this was very much in my awareness as I viewed the situation from this new place that Ryan and I were in.

EVOLVING COMMUNICATION

When I got back, I went back to everyday things, and life was really good. I was spending time with Sean and Willow and my other children, and working with the AWAKE Academy. Sean and I were creating magic; we kept making the lake house even more beautiful, our family more beautiful, and Costa Rica more beautiful! That manifestation continued to unfold in amazing ways. My guides told me that we manifested the money for Costa Rica in order to build a beautiful retreat center on that beautiful piece of land. Everything was flowing, and we were continuing to do this through Tantra, and through constant communication.

Let me give you an example of how our communication was evolving. One time, I had gone to Costa Rica for a couple of weeks for business, and he stayed home with the dogs and Willow. Now, I'm really a kind of go-with-the-flow type of person. If I drove across country, I wouldn't know what hotel I was staying at each night until 30 minutes before I stopped for the night. I don't have to be very obsessive or overly precise about airfare when I travel.

For Sean, this was often irritating. Sean wants to know what airplane he's going to be on, what hotel he might be staying at. He often chafed at the way I would tell him my itinerary at the last minute and, in his words, "make him follow me around."

So I was in Costa Rica, and for the first three days when I called home, he always allowed distractions during our phone calls. You could hear the dogs, Willow would come in, we couldn't have one conversation without an interruption. The fourth time that this happened, I said to him, "This is the fourth time I can't have a conversation with you without the dogs or Willow interrupting. I've been around you where you get an important phone call, and you stand up and leave the room immediately to take that important phone call and make sure you won't be disturbed."

He said, "Well, I thought you'd want to talk to your daughter." I said, "Yes, and I did already. And when you and I are done talking, I would talk to her again. But when I'm talking to you, I want to talk to you."

Then I added, "Here's an NLP technique that I learned: let's take the sound out of everything and just make this a video. You're a student, and you're watching this video. There's a man, and he gets phone calls, and he goes into a quiet room, and you can tell that he's attentive and he's listening. Then he gets another phone call, and now he's acting very lackadaisical, letting the dogs interrupt, constantly looking away from the phone, talking to others. What are you going to think? How are you going to analyze that? Then the instructor says 'Okay, what is the level of importance of each one of those calls?'"

Then he understood. He said, "Okay, I get your point." And now, in response, this opened up space for him to share his resentment about the lack of clarity about my itinerary, this sense of being in the dark. He talked about not even knowing when I was coming home from Costa Rica, my flight info, what time he was picking me up.

So in turn, I saw how I had not been listening to him. I said, "Okay. That's fair. I'm doing something disrespectful also, and I need to honor what feels respectful to you." He had been asking me for this, and I hadn't been responding. I'd kept doing my go-with-the-flow thing. I appreciated that he spoke up and told me. Then I started sending him all the information he needed, and he got to feel like "Wow, she listens!"

So we both clearly, non-judgmentally stated our needs and aired our grievances, and the other listened and conceded that there was something we needed to clean up.

This is the type of work we did every single day, and it *really* helps relationships. Clear, transparent, honest communication. Owning where we've been disrespectful and cleaning it up. These are things that a lot of couples ignore. They let them pass—but then they store up resentments. We were clearly sharing our concerns and misgivings before they snowballed and became toxic—at least, we were finally starting to. Then we were resolving them, addressing behaviors that weren't fair or honoring. What sealed the deal was the Tantra. This is how we could focus together and really start to create magical heaven on earth.

Something else I noticed, as I settled into this new place of letting go of Ryan, accepting that he was not the one, was how Sean was good at things I needed to grow at. With Ryan, we were either too much alike or I was too much his saviour. Sean was different from me in ways that were very appealing, that stretched me. Sean had such artistic gifts. He could play a melody with his right hand and the chords with his left on the guitar. He's great with foreign languages—he knows Italian and Spanish and he's learning French. He can draw. All these were ways that I could grow and stretch.

Sean bought books and said, "I'm going to teach you how to draw." He got me special earphones with a certain frequency to help me learn and retain Spanish more easily.

At this point now, we started back with the salsa lessons, and it was totally different than when we had tried before and weren't as connected, when Sean wasn't showing interest and I was struggling. Just because of how we were shifting now, we went from being horrible to being really good with each other. We can go out dancing now, and go to dances together, and we're laughing and having fun.

Before our connection got to this level, I could dance with the teacher but not with him. Even she was shocked at the transformation, because we weren't doing anything different logistically. It was just our connection that had deepened and clicked. Plus, I finally let him be my leader. In salsa dancing, there has to be a leader. Now, I trusted him. And he can lead me in the music realm, the language realm, the artistic realm. I want to be the best version of myself and learn things I've never learned before, and I'm open to it. I stopped trying to control and allowed myself to be led, and this opened up new doors.

This is why I suggest you be careful about judging whether someone is your twin flame or not based on how much you're alike or how much you have in common. While it's nice to have commonalities, and definitely certain core values and goals are important to share, "sameness" is not a sign of soulmate, per se. In fact, it can be a way of staying safe, doing the known, being the same, not evolving or stretching or growing. When you're gushing "Oh, we're so much alike!" …is that such a great thing? It's good that you're you. You're perfect the way you are. But what if there are entire other sides of you that you didn't know about that a person could open for you?

MAGICAL CAMPING

In June of 2022, I decided to give Sean a really special Father's Day present. We would go to an Electric Festival in Michigan. The festival was held in a forest, and included music, meditation, and healings. There were bands and workshops and the connection to nature. We would microdose with mushrooms to enhance the experience.

So we went. It was really crowded, and I wasn't sure how well that would work for me, but it actually was great. We went with two good friends, one a chiropractic doctor and one a bodyworker, and they're avid campers. That was perfect, because they knew what they were doing, and Sean and I really didn't. I used to camp a lot as a child, but I'd forgotten a lot. But these friend had our backs.

For example, we'd brought this big, heavy hammock. The chiropractor smiled and explained, "That's not going to work, because we have to hike to get to the bus that takes us to where the music is. You won't want to be carrying this big hammock." And he had these two little hammocks all folded up, and he said, "I brought one for you guys."

So we got to where the festival was, and got our camp all set up, and we were having so much fun. The site was beautiful, and you could feel how the earth was soaking up all the good vibes, the music and the healing. And it was funny, but it's the only place in any woods where I didn't see any bugs.

Sean and I were holding hands as we went around the scene, really connecting. I felt like "Wow! I'm seeing this man so differently."

Two really cool things happened at the festival that I think really changed us even further for the better. The first thing was that we had put the little lightweight camping hammocks up, and they were really small. Being tucked into the hammock together was like being in a mother's womb, and it felt like we were twins, cocooned in our little womb, completely enmeshed. And it was there that we finally, finally found our Tantric kissing.

We kissed for a long, long time. Deep, like the first time we had met. He was remembering me, I was remembering him. I was honoring him. I wasn't shutting down the parts of him that weren't like me.

As I said, kissing is a story. When you're doing Tantric kissing, you're saying "Tell me more." If there's no more to tell, the story is going to end, and the exploration of the tongues stops. Before, I was blaming him for stopping, for not being into it. Now, I was open and I was saying "Okay, tell me more about you. I like what I see." I was saying to him, through my kissing, "Tell me more about you." He was feeling that energy, feeling like "Oh, she wants to know more about me. She loves me. She sees me!

She likes what she sees." So then he opens up, and then the kissing gets deeper and deeper, better and better.

We did that for quite some time. After this beautiful Tantric kissing, we took a break and we went and danced. There was a light show, and the band was great, and hula hoopers were out with light-up hula hoops. It was a magical, perfect evening.

The next day, something else magical happened. We had gone to another part of the forest where everybody was settings their hammocks up to see a band, and I saw three big trees leaning in a way that formed a pyramid shape. I could see that the energy in the middle of this shape was very powerful. I do see pyramids where others can't see them—natural formations that are suggesting a pyramid shape, as well as their energy. Pyramids are powerful portals. They help with manifestation and transmute energy. I use them in my meditations, and teach AWAKE Academy students methods for using pyramids in meditation to help them create.

Trees often create pyramids in the forest that protect all the nature elements and beings of the forest. I often see them rising up from trees, and I see gold and light and energy. I could see that this one was extremely powerful and I knew our hammock was meant to hang right in the center of that pyramid.

I said to Sean, "I think we're supposed have our hammock between those trees over there," There was just one spot left in that space, and I knew we were supposed to be there. Just as I said that, our two friends took that spot for their hammock. The chiropractor friend said, "Here, we'll put you guys over there," and pointed between two other trees. I was disappointed, but I shrugged and said, "Okay, that's fine."

Now remember, this guy is an avid camper, and he knew what he was doing with hammocks and everything else. He hung up our hammock expertly, just the way he had the day before, and then he hung up theirs, and Sean and I climbed into our hammock.

The moment after we climbed in, the hammock fell to the ground. I fell on my tailbone, and it was a shock. My chiropractor friend was shocked too, and mortified. "I am so sorry!" he gasped. "You don't understand! This has never happened!"

I started laughing, and I said, "I think I know why it happened. I think we're supposed to be over there, where you guys set up. I don't know if you can see it, but it's a pyramid." He said, "Okay, okay, I'll put you guys below us." He hung the hammock so that we were right underneath theirs, and we all got to be in that pyramid. And not surprisingly, we all received a lot of energetic downloads and activations that night.

We didn't know what they were, but we could feel the energy moving through our spines and energy centers.

This is a great example of what can happen if you don't listen to your guidance. I *knew* that we were supposed to be in that pyramid. Because I didn't make sure that we heeded this message, I literally fell on my butt. It was as if the universe said, "Hey, wake up! You've got some grounding to do!"

It was a very happy trip. When we got home, we were in a great space, and had a nice time seeing our children playing on the lake together, going boating, and spending time with friends. Things were good.

MOTHERS AND PORTALS

Soon it was time to plan for a visit from Sean's mother. I knew this was going to be an interesting visit, just from the brief time I had spent with her on our trip to England for Carrie's funeral, and from what had happened to Willow after being with her for ten days. I was still wondering why Willow had plumped up so much while she was in Sean's mother's energy. Also, I had noticed that Sean purposely would make sure she and I were never alone in the same room together.

I actually had never seen Sean treat a woman as badly as he did his mother. I even told him one time, "If you ever talk to me the way you talk to your mother, we will be done." I did know that his mother had left him when he was 12, when she went off with a man. She had essentially abandoned him. While they were reconnected now, it wasn't exactly a warm relationship.

Of course, I could see the genesis of some of his intimacy issues in all this—in that abandonment, and in the cold way she treated me and the idea of marriage, and the unpleasant posts she had made about our marriage. So I had a lot to learn and understand, and this visit was going to be interesting. And transformative, as it turned out.

We planned it for the month of August. We had a month to prepare. During that month, I received a message or intuition that I should open a divine masculine portal in our backyard. I didn't know why it was divine masculine, but that's what I was told. I was also told to open it while listening to Nicki Minaj's Super Bass Song. The universe can be really fun and playful. The way I teach it and do it, you can get serious, deep energy work done and have fun at the same time, as long as your intentions are where they need to be.

I included Willow in the opening of the portal, as I had before at other times (such as opening the portal for the lake house to get finished). She's powerful and magical, and really gets the work. Willow and I were getting ready to open the portal, and I was getting out my playlist, and without my having told her about the message I received, she picked that exact song!

We did the energy work. When Willow opens up portals—and she's so gifted at it—she looks at all the trees and makes hand movements and then she tosses invisible energy "things" for me to catch. She calls them "stickers." I'm not sure what that means, but definitely the trees are giving them to her. She'll ask me sometimes, "What stickers do you want?" She tells me to throw them in the air and let them go.

So we worked together, moving energy and opening this portal, and when we were done and I stepped back, I was amazed. I knew to get my camera and I take a picture of it. I still have the photo, and I've shown my students the picture of the divine masculine portal that we opened. It was an energy field with little holes throughout it.

I left it like that for a couple weeks, and then out of the blue I heard the universe say to me, "Now it's time to put the divine feminine in." Sean was literally on his way to pick up his mother at the airport. I had taken Willow out to eat. I said, "Willow, oh, we need to open up the feminine part of our portal right now!" We left the restaurant to dash home and do it. I asked her, "What song do you think should we use?" Songs seem to be very important when opening a portal. Just as I said that, as we were pulling out of the restaurant parking lot, Cyndi Lauper's "Girls Just Want to Have Fun" came on the radio. I said, "Okay, there's our answer!"

We got home, and I said, "Okay, while Daddy's gone, we're going to open up the divine feminine aspect of this." She was excited, again intuitively knowing exactly what to do. Willow was throwing me her, "stickers," and I was activating them from the heart space with true love, highest intentions, health, and prosperity. Agaain, portals are all about intentions. It's extremely important to be coming from unconditional love when you open a portal.

Then I took another photo of it. Remarkably, it had now transformed from an energy field with little holes in it to a huge energetic third eye surrounding the house. You could see where the divine masculine had transformed when it was joined by the divine feminine. It was unbelievably cool.

I didn't understand *why* I had to open up this portal until Sean got home with his mother—even though I had known it was going to be an interesting visit.

Sean's mother is very unlike my mother. My mother was so affectionate when I was a child—always hugging, always kissing us, tickling us, telling us that she loved us. I was surprised when I first learned that not all mothers do that. Because of this upbringing, my sisters and I are all still very affectionate with one another, and my mother is too.

Sean's mother was the opposite. She didn't really know how to connect in that way at all. She was cold, stiff, critical, and didn't tend to say kind things.

During this time, I had still been working to get my body back in shape, to get lean and healthy and have my body match all the other goodness and magic that was unfolding. And as you recall I had been combining energy work to release toxic energy from the cells and my being, along with eating differently and bringing my relationship with food into healthy balance. I was doing really well with it, and I was happy.

I was eating when she first arrived and came into the kitchen, and she walked up to me, looked at me, and her opening line was, "You sure do have a hearty appetite." That was the first thing she said to me. I thought, "Wow, this *is* going to be a *very* interesting three weeks."

But before I could even think about being resentful of her, the way Sean treated her superseded anything I could have come up with. His treatment of her actually made me feel more compassion for her. He would not be in the same room with her. If she was upstairs, he would go downstairs. He disagreed with anything she said. He obviously had major resentment towards his mother. I was surprised he had even allowed her to come visit, since he didn't seem to want to be around her at all.

But it was time to heal this, and maybe that was why he had allowed her to come, in spite of himself. I thought, "Okay, this is the perfect time to work on all of this." And I trusted the portals to do the work.

And they did! The next morning after she arrived, she woke up and she was so sick. She stayed in her room throwing up and having diarrhea. She said, "I haven't been this sick in a long time, Rebecca." She was like that for two days.

The amazing thing is, I didn't even have to point it out myself—that's how awakened Sean was becoming. He named it. He said, "It's the portal, right? It's making her sick." The portal is love, health, joy, compassion, connection. If you go into a portal like that and you've got stuck, stagnant intimacy issues, you're going to purge them out. That's what ayahuasca does. Well, thanks to the portal, she was having an ayahuasca experience by just being in our house!

Something else completely magical happened right after we opened up the feminine part of the portal: an apple tree grew suddenly right next to the portal that had never been there. I saw these beautiful little apples, and I said to Sean, "That tree wasn't there before." He agreed, "No, it wasn't. I walk the dogs past there every day, and I've never seen it." That apple tree literally grew overnight.

Suddenly the neighbors were coming over, asking if they could use our apples and offering to bring us pies and cider. I asked Willow what she thought about it, and she said, "Duh, Mom, trees give us energy. The other trees were giving me the energy to put in the portal, and then that energy grew the apple tree."

So we starting eating those delicious little apples. They actually were healing, heart-opening apples. We had Sean's mother eat the apples. Eventually, AWAKE students ate them when they came to my house too.

Meanwhile, after two days of being sick, I was sitting with Sean's mother in the dining room and she was wondering why she had gotten that sick. I'm very authentic and I believe so much in the work I do. Even though she didn't know me well and I knew that so far, she wasn't enthralled with me, I was honest and earnest. I pulled up on my phone the photos of the portals, first the masculine, and then the masculine and feminine together. I showed her. "Do you see this?" She said, "Yes! Is that behind your house?"

I said, "Yes. Willow and I did that. We opened up a portal to true love before you came. So I think that everything that was not true love in you purged out through the vomiting and diarrhea."

I didn't really expect her to accept that, but shockingly, she did. She only said, "I just wish you would have told me that ahead of time, so I could have been prepared." And that was all she said about it!

Sean was over in the kitchen, beyond where we were sitting, and his face turned red, and he looked over at me and laughed. He said, "I think Mom is going to have an amazing time here." I felt like there was a lot to work through, but that this visit and this work was going to help everybody on every level.

LESSON

A portal is an intentional opening from point A (where you are, or where a situation currently is) to point B (what the desired outcome is). The opening acts like a vacuum, and can quickly create an outcome not limited by the rules of time, distance, or matter. It's crucial that portals be opened with frequencies of unconditional love and gratitude.

Portals are responsive to your body's movements as well as your intention. The 1000 jumping jacks that I did in prison helped to open up portals to my desired outcome, which I was already intending from my heart. The responsiveness of energy and spirit to flow and movement are so important. Yoga, qi gong, tai-chi, and many other energy and movement practices are rooted in this truth. Without flow and move-

ment, the energy in our quantum field can become stuck and stagnant. It's always a good idea to get up and do something physically different if you're feeling stuck. Along with cultivating continuous gratitude, and keeping your attention and intention grounded in your heart, this can radically shift your life for the better.

Chapter Twenty-One

WHILE SEAN'S MOTHER WAS VISITING AND purging out shadow energies (which was also helpfully clearing the DNA of my husband and daughter, because they all share DNA), Ryan was dealing with his own shadows.

Though we had concluded we were not meant to be a couple, Ryan and I were still divine friends. We still talked, and we had a ceremony planned in Mount Shasta a few months from this time. I was excited to still conduct ceremonies with him, even though Sean was stepping up to the plate.

But my ultimate goal was still to have Sean be my partner in ceremony. I still felt that my divine partner was one who would share everything with me, including the powerful magic of life-changing healing ceremonies for others.

Out of the blue, while Sean's mom was still visiting, Ryan called me and told me that he was fully committed to taking back his ex-wife. I was griefstricken to hear this. I knew by then that his marriage was a toxic environment, full of dark energies, drugs, and everything that he had worked so hard to free himself from. I was extremely disappointed, because I could see what was going to happen. His mom had *just* finally agreed to give custody of his daughter back to him—under the condition that his mom saw that he was staying away from his ex. By taking his ex back, he would again completely lose the custody of his daughter, a privilege that had taken him a long time to earn back. He was losing everything he had worked so hard for.

I was sad to do it, but I said, "I actually can't work with you in ceremony with these energies around you. When things shift, let me know." I wished him the best, and we didn't talk for a few months after that. I wondered why he had decided to take back something that had made his life so toxic, and that he'd done so much work to change and shift away from. But I wished him the best and stepped away. I told myself, "Who are you to judge?"

I had plenty to focus on in my own life. With Sean's mother visiting, although she had purged some energies and been surprisingly open to the reason it happened, there was still plenty of work to do. For one thing, we had to manage a lot of parenting stuff. She parented in a way that was very different from how we parented Willow, a manner that was not aligned with how we wanted to relate to our child or the energy we wanted her exposed to. I also knew that whatever she was doing with Willow had happened to Sean when he was a kid.

For example, if Willow was in the living room playing with her toys, Sean's mother would tell Willow what she was doing "wrong." "Don't make so much noise, it hurts my ears. Why are you doing all that? Don't put all those toys out at one time!" She was critical, judgmental and bossy, telling Willow what *not* to do—instead of getting down on the floor, playing with her, and connecting.

I was really proud of how Sean handled that. Pretty soon after that started, Sean walked into the room and said, "That's not how we do things. Willow will put her toys away when she's done. She doesn't need to be bossed around and told what she's doing wrong. You can leave the room, Mom, unless you're going to learn to play with her." His mother looked shocked, and said, "Fine," and she left the room.

I had suspected that something like this kind of energy, taking on this negativity, was likely what caused Willow to "plump up" during her time in England with Sean's mother. Now I knew we had to work on teaching her not to take on people's stuff, and to release it if she did. She was holding a lot. We told her, "You don't have to hold other people's stuff." To this day, we still have to remind her. "That's not yours to hold. Don't hold my stuff, don't hold Daddy's stuff, don't hold anybody's stuff."

There were quite a few episodes like this where things had to be reframed. I worked on Sean energetically, we talked, we talked to his mom, and things came out in the open. We had some very mature, healing conversations. So it ended up to be a very profound three weeks. And it gave me so much clarity. Between going to England and being with Sean's friends, and then visiting with his mother, seeing all of these different sides of him, I felt like I was really beginning to understand this man I had married.

I also now really understood what he'd meant when he said that the day we got married, he didn't really know what true love was. He had thought he did. He had tried to tell me this on the night of the Halloween party when I was demanding answers, and I got so angry at that answer. But I was getting it now. I could see how the influences of his childhood had affected him and colored what he thought of love, knew of love.

And now he really was loving me. He was hugging me and kissing me in ways that were so affectionate. One day he went out to walk the dogs and when he came back and he said, "I saw a shooting star, and immediately I wished that all of your wishes would come true, Rebecca." It was incredibly sweet and generous. He would have never said that before. He would have thought that was too corny. But now he could express himself that way, and it felt good to him. It felt good to me too, and I felt the same way. I was really happy with what was emerging.

SEAN STEPS UP

Since Ryan was out of the picture, I ended up doing the Mount Shasta ceremony with Sean and a colleague, a teacher from the AWAKE Academy. It turned out to be an incredible ceremony. The energy that Sean displayed during that ceremony was amazing.

We drove across country with Willow and our two dogs. We were really connected. We talked about music and art and meaningful things. We made a rule where we weren't allowed to just fill space by talking about other people. That's all gossip. We had to fill space by talking about creative things. This is a great rule to abide by when traveling with loved ones. Silence is good too, but if you're going to break the silence, do it creatively.

It took us five days to get to Mount Shasta, because we took our time on the drive. By then, we were really ready to get settled. We had made a beautiful ayahuasca brew from the headwaters in Mount Shasta. That was a three-day process. And the brew was absolutely perfect, as usual.

Sean was in a totally new place with the ceremonies. In spite of how much I wanted his partnership in this work, I had fully let go of having him do or be any particular way around ceremonies. I was done with martyring, done trying to make people anything they were not. I was no longer trying to change anyone. I took responsibility for my own needs and wants. If my husband had wanted to continue to sit in a corner looking at his phone during ceremonies, I would have probably eventually divorced him. But I was not going to yell at him or make demands or beg him to change. So there was not one part of me any more that was trying to get Sean to do anything other than what he wanted to do.

And in that space, which was so much more inviting and freeing, Sean stepped into his power. He played the music, worked on himself, and worked on other people. He told me that this was a connection he had always desired. He finally realized this had nothing to do with the psychedelics and raves he had done in his twenties. He could finally really see all the magic and miracles that were happening in these beautiful ceremonies. He had seen it in glimpses previously, but he would always lapse back into forgetting or resisting. Now, finally, he was truly getting it.

One example of portal magic that happened at this ceremony was related to the Airbnb that we had rented for the ceremony. The woman who owned it had for some reason locked the air conditioners. This was during a heatwave in Mount Shasta. It was nearly 100 degrees. People in their 40s, 50s and 60s were coming to the ceremony. We had up to four people sleeping in each room. This was untenable. I was calling students who were on the way and paying them to buy portable air conditioners, if they were able to find them. We ended up with two small portable air conditioners, which helped some, but that was not going to be near enough to cool this large home for everyone in the middle of such a heat wave.

So Willow, my colleague Paulina, and I went outside and began opening portals to the weather, asking for thunderstorms and rain and clouds. Then Willow said, "Yes, but we want stars, too." Willow did her special portal magic, giving us "stickers" for our intentions. Willow asked what else we wanted. Paulina said, "I want my own retreat center in Mount Shasta" because she didn't want to deal with having to rent somebody's house any more. Just as we had done in my backyard when we opened the portal before Sean's mom visited, we threw "stickers" and Willow did her arm and hand movements, used her feet, and we activated our intentions.

The next day, the students arrived. Immediately after they arrived, thunderstorms began. There was rain and lots of lightning. The weather changed drastically.

And the weather turned out to be more than just a cooling of the house. It was healing. At one point in the ceremony, a woman was feeling really stuck. She said, "Rebecca, I don't know how to get out of this." With ayahuasca, although you do get through it, sometimes you can go into a dark place in your own ego and get trapped there. You're there for a little while, maybe hours, struggling with your own shadows. This woman was in that loop.

She had her bucket and wanted to throw up, but she couldn't. She was rocking back and forth shaking. She was scared to go into whatever the shadow was that she need to purge. She became frozen. It had to do with her best friend's death, but we didn't know that at first.

She was starting to panic, because she felt sick and this trauma wouldn't unleash and she felt like it was stuck in her stomach.

Intuitively, I took her right out into the rain. Within five minutes, she had done a 360. In the rain, she threw up, and the water hitting her calmed down immediately. Her panic completely subsided. Tuning in and sharing what came to me, I said, "tell me about your best friend." She started talking, and there in the rain all this trauma processed. We did some energy work, and she was completely okay.

Then she went back inside and started healing other people. She started talking to people and doing hands-on work. (AWAKE students are different kinds of ceremony participants; they're training and practicing, thinking about facilitating, so they come to ceremony understanding that they will practice on one another.)

And before the end of the night, Sean was out there too, sitting in the rain, letting the rain just pour over him, right beside my beautiful wolf dog. I went out to him, and I held his hand, and I let the rain wash over me too. I looked at him and said, "I love you." He said, "I love you too."

Then something happened that had never happened before: we started speaking Light Language or Star Language to one another.

Light Language is a magical language of the soul, coming from our connection to the stars. It can't be translated into English. It heals with vibration and frequency, even though most of us on earth don't understand it. There are different dialects from different star systems. People may know at a soul level what you're saying even if they couldn't explain it. It can calm people down immediately. Not everyone is able to speak it, and we never had before (except when I had spoken it with Willow that one time at the cabin). Now we were fluently speaking it back and forth and kissing.

At one point, just as our lips touched to kiss, a huge clap of thunder sounded and a flash of lightning lit us up. A guy who was also sitting outside said, "Oh my God, you see that?" It was so magical!

Right then, I knew we were truly connected, truly soul partners. Everything had been for a reason. All the work had been worth it.

Sean ended up absolutely *loving* that ceremony at Mount Shasta. He didn't want it to end, and he could not wait until the next one. I looked at him and thought, "Okay, THIS is what I wanted." And it was as if he finally realized he could let this part of himself express and play.

I didn't find this out for a long time, but Sean had actually been a Reiki Master before he even met me. He had also been into Transcendental Meditation. For some reason, he had let that part of himself go dormant, and even resisted it, certainly when he was first with me. I had always assumed that the healer in him was something that *I* wanted to cultivate that I wanted him to express. But he wanted it, too—despite his resistance through those earlier ceremonies, and his repeated "forgetting" of the magic he had seen.

Now I know that Sean is a healer, too. He does it differently than I do. Once I let go of trying to make him do or be anything, the healer in him was able to emerge in its own unique way. Without being pushed or forced or demanded or cajoled, the healer in him could relax and find its way.

AFTER SHASTA

From there, we went back to our home at the lake and back to our everyday life. A couple of weeks later, I got a phone call from Ryan, telling me that he had made a really big mistake, that he knew now that he and his wife were completely done. She had stayed sober for three weeks, and during that time he realized he doesn't like her even sober. He had assumed before that it was just the part of her that was on drugs that he didn't like, but he realized that he wasn't able to resonate or connect with her even when she was sober. I could tell that he was serious. I could tell that he was done.

So he went through the process and obtained a divorce from his wife. That didn't change anything with us, but I felt really good that he was through with that energy. I felt like "Okay, he's crossed the path, now he's ready for someone who's going to treat him well." I knew that a lot of the work we had done together, personally and professionally, had helped him reach this point—even if it was hard and confusing at times. He even said to me, "I'm going to use our connection and everything I've learned with you as a reference point, so I can bring in someone really healthy for me."

Ryan ended up going back to live for a while at his mother's, where his daughter was. He and his mother and daughter were repairing, healing, and rebuilding a relationship that had been damaged for some time. His daughter was learning to trust him, and he was growing in leaps and bounds. I was extremely proud of him.

While we were talking, I told him about how I felt like I was at the final frontier of my fitness journey, losing all the fat and energy I had accumulated over my life from various experiences. There was a last phase where I felt that some stubborn fat was hanging on from a specific sexual experience as a young woman.

I suggested, "Let's do a fasting and energy work trip, where I come see you for three days and you work on me energetically while I fast." For some reason, I felt like I needed to be away from my house for this, and I knew he was gifted, skilled, and sensitive enough to do this work on me. I trusted him. I told him, "I'll pay you to do this as my energy worker." He agreed, and we planned it for a few weeks out.

The very next morning, I heard a clear, loud message in my head from my guides or higher self: "Go look at your husband's phone now." I was upstairs, and he was downstairs, sleeping on the couch. I went down, and the phone was laying on the ottoman.

I picked up his phone, looked at it…and that same woman Corinne who he had promised to stop messaging on Facebook had just responded to a message he had left her. His message was something like, "What did you dress as for Halloween?" She had answered and sent a picture of herself and "How about you?"

The dialogue wasn't the point; the point was that he was hiding these messages from me, *again*, and risking everything to do it. He could have stopped as we had agreed, as he had promised—*or*, if he really felt that it was an unreasonable request, he could have told me honestly, "Rebecca, you make your decision. She's a friend and I'm going to talk to her."

It turned out that what he had been doing the entire time was just deleting her messages.

I was absolutely devastated. He woke up then and saw me reading it. He knew instantly what I was seeing, and a look of shock and terror crossed his face. I told him my guides had told me to check this. Stricken and furious, I demanded to know why he was still doing this when he had promised to stop.

I was even more angry when he started minimizing and gaslighting me. He said, "I just reach out here and there. It's not a big deal. It's not major." I said, "But it is a big deal, because you lied! You promised!" He said, "Well, I waited a while and then felt the urge to reach out. I mean, she's an old friend, 20 years."

I was livid. I said, "You're excusing this when you promised? Now you have reasons why you went back on it? You could have discussed it with me if you wanted to change the deal. But we made an agreement. And you know what? She's inappropriate, she's trashy. Your conversation is inappropriate. You're not owning up. And this is a betrayal."

I was very cold and clear, and then I walked away. I said, resolutely, "I'm leaving now. I was planning on going for a three-day fast with Ryan in a couple weeks, but I'm out of here now."

I packed my bags in less than an hour and walked out. Sean stayed out of my way and didn't even say goodbye as I left. There was really nothing to say at that point. I slammed out, drove to Missouri, and started my three-day fast.

I was not crying or grieving. I was at a point where I felt very clear: "This is everybody's journey."

Once we were together, Ryan and I connected on the same deep soul level we always had. But I wasn't falling back into "Oh, now I think Ryan is the one for me." Not at all. I even said, "Ryan, I'm not coming to you to tell you I'm leaving my husband and let's live happily ever after together. This is not what this trip is about." He said, "Yeah, I know, I agree."

Magical things were happening, we were learning new energy techniques, and he helped me to release old toxic energy, but that was it. We weren't falling back into old patterns, only into our deep friendship.

We did the three-day fast together, and we did powerful energy work, including breath work, to clear me of any remaining stagnant toxic male energy. This had just happened with my husband again, so clearly I had to pull this out of my field. I had to get rid of this energy.

While I was there, Ryan and I did sleep in the same bed. Nothing happened, literally just sleeping in the same bed. We listened to music together, talked, and I met his mother. This was huge. Clearly I was on the "meeting people's mothers" path. As with Sean, I could see some of the energy and behavior that he had grown up with, dynamics that I knew that he was trying to release.

One example was that his mother would smoke inside the house around his daughter, and the cigarette smoke was even going into the daughter's room. It was quite toxic. I saw these dynamics and toxic behaviors, and I realized, "Okay, this is some of what he's been through. This is the type of connection he's used to. This is what 'love' was in his upbringing."

This made sense of some of what he and I had gone through together, and what he had gone through on his own. In spite of his mother's behaviors, I could also see that beautiful healing work was in progress as they lived together and sorted all this out. I was kind to her, and I hugged her when I left.

On my drive back home from this healing energy and fasting experience, I stopped at a hotel to spend the night. From there, I called Sean. I was very direct, not blaming or shrill, but strong and clear. I said, "There's something here that the universe wants us to look at, or this wouldn't be happening. I need to know what about this woman would make you risk your marriage."

He protested, "I wouldn't risk our marriage!" I said, "But you did. You promised to stop messaging her, yet you continued to. You were deleting messages. You've told me you hate liars, yet you lied. That's hypocrisy and deceit." He was silent. Then he protested weakly, once again, "It just wasn't that major."

I was fed up. "Everything we have been through together and everything we've been over and over about her, and you're still just saying the same things?"

We hashed it over a while longer, and finally, he conceded to everything I was pointing out. He promised, "I get it. I will never ever, ever, ever reach out to her again. I'm not even going to respond back to this message. And I swear on everything I love that this is true."

I felt that he was really telling the truth. I didn't quite understand why this had to happen with this woman, but I accepted that for some reason it did, and that maybe it had jolted Sean to new awareness. I finished the drive back home, we reconnected and bonded, and we picked up where we had left off.

DNA HEALING

Something else that happened when I went to visit Ryan illuminates something that I think is really important for us to understand about genetics. Something I had been noticing with my children is that their own relationships were repeating patterns that I had in my DNA. They were experiencing patterns in their relationships that were mirroring relationships I'd had before they were even born. We're born into our ancestors' stories.

My 20-year-old son had just ended a relationship of two years that reminded me greatly of a relationship I had gone through when I was his age. I would have done anything for that person, I was so open and kindhearted, so focused on compassion for that person, and he just trampled that love, took it from me and only gave back hurt in return.

Caden had a similar dynamic with this girl. Cruelly, she would look at him and say "Caden, you know you're ugly, right?" Bizarrely, I could remember that in the parallel relationship I had at the same age, the guy would make me cry and then say, "You're so ugly when you cry." There were many other things this girl said and did to Caden that were so comparable to what I had gone through with this old boyfriend.

When they finally broke up, Caden was thoroughly devastated—just as I was when I broke up with the man who did those same things to me. In fact, I believe I married my ex-husband (who was an adequate friend and partner, but I wasn't in love) because I didn't think I could be in love ever again. Caden, too, was feeling like he could and would never love again. He was like, "Mom, I'm done." He couldn't go to school, he couldn't even be around the same friends that they'd had. It was just overtaking him.

When I went to go see Ryan, in addition to the work we did on my past experiences and excess toxic energy that I needed to release, we also did a powerful healing technique to support Caden. I acted as a surrogate for Caden, and asked Ryan to help me heal Caden. The outcome of our performing this technique is such a striking example of how transformative energy work can be, and how connected we are, especially to our loved ones.

While I was acting as a surrogate for Caden, as a healing subject—I basically *was being* him—I did a scan of myself, and I realized *I didn't have a heart*. If you've ever seen that fantasy adventure series *Once Upon a Time*, where an evil witch takes people's hearts and puts them in boxes, then controls them by talking to the hearts and telling them what to do—it was like that. Something had my heart.

Not surprisingly, Caden had told me a few days before I left for Ryan's, when we went out to eat, "Mom, you don't understand. It's like she has a part of me. She has a part of me that I can't get back." Then, as his surrogate in the healing, I actually felt it. I realized he had literally given his heart to her.

In the energy work, I went and reclaimed his (my) heart, and I put it back into my chest. And here's the unbelievable part, but it's the truth. Minutes after I did that, I got a call from my ex-husband—we were still right in the middle of the healing—and he said, "Caden just called me, and he said he's having a heart attack. He thinks he might have to go to the hospital. He's at my mom's." He wasn't sure what to do. He asked, "Do you think it's anxiety over Grace? Do you think he's really going to have a heart attack?"

Just then, Caden called in too. I said, "It's Caden calling me, let me go talk to him, I'll call you back and let you know what's going on."

I hung up on my ex-husband and Caden was gasping, "Mom, Mom, I can't breathe, I can't breathe. My heart hurts so bad." I said, "Okay, Caden, listen to me. It's okay. It's because you just got your heart back." He was still gasping for breath. I said firmly, "Trust me on this. Your heart is just coming back, so you've got to accept it. Accept your heart."

Then I asked, "Was there ever a time when you loved Grace more than yourself?" He said, "Absolutely! All the time." I said, "Okay, here's the thing: you love Caden more than you love her. You love Caden more than anybody. Go into your heart and say that. Say that." We worked on it and worked on it, and he calmed down, and we got him to a space where he fully embraced his own heart. He took it back, and he accepted it. That very next day he let her go, and to this day, he has never talked about her ever again.

I share this not only as a powerful healing technique, but also as an example of how important it is that we shift and clear toxic patterns from our DNA. As I'm shifting my DNA and working on my toxic patterns, it's releasing patterns that our children are going to otherwise go through. If we clear them early enough, they don't have to live it the way we did. Otherwise, they're being born through our stories and then replaying them. It's very important that we clear ourselves; this is another reason to do our work.

So after all that, everyday life was good and stable. I was enjoying my work, Sean was enjoying his work, Willow was enjoying her life, my other kids were living their lives as well. We were now planning our next ceremony for Sedona, Arizona, which would be in January of 2023.

I stayed in touch with Ryan. We had a great and loving friendship. But Ryan was now reliving an experience of dependence with his mother that he really needed to release himself from—being in her basement, unable to financially get out. The reconnecting with his mother and daughter was good, but it was reaching a point where he was stuck in a pattern of "being mothered" that was unhealthy and that he needed to release.

I was trying to help him release it. I would say, "It's obvious that you're stuck in a mothering pattern, because if someone looked down at this scenario from the stars, they'd see that you're stuck in your mom's basement, without a car, without money, and without custody of your daughter. Whether this pattern is about abandonment, or people providing for you, I think it's a mothering thing."

When I said things like this, he'd get upset with me and argue, "No, everything is fine!" And then he would ask to borrow some money. I was seeing this pattern digging its heels in with him in a way I'd never seen before, but I was holding a place of non-judgment as best as I could.

Now the holidays flew by. I don't think too much of Thanksgiving and Christmas any more. I've lost interest in buying presents to prove I love people. I try to show my love in other ways. I think that thankfulness and giving should be every day, all year long, not confined to one or two holidays. So the season wasn't a super big deal with us. Willow had fun, though; she still believed in Santa, and she was in love with her Elf on the Shelf.

After the holidays, it was time for our ceremonies in Sedona. We were doing two back-to-back. It was to be the same facilitators as before: Sean, Paulina, and me. It was a good team, but I was thinking, "We need one more divine masculine facilitator," because I like to have an even representation of feminine and masculine when it comes to facilitators. I think it's ultimately most powerful when ceremony facilitators are couples who have harmoniously worked out their "stuff." Then their own light body activations can create a huge healing field for everyone to open up to true love, true health, true wealth, and finding their heaven and joy.

But I felt it was going to be good. We got to Sedona, and it started snowing, and we made the brew. We always put different things into the brew for each ceremony, it's always unique, and this time the brew ended up being extra powerful. It was much stronger than the brew at our last ceremony in Shasta, which told me that there were some big energies ready to work through.

Right before the ceremonies began, we decided to take a little side trip to the Grand Canyon. I'd never been there. Sean and Willow and I were hiking on a little trail, and we were just looking at the Canyon and how vast and beautiful it is. I was thinking "Wow, this could be life or death." I remember looking at it like it was a void. It could be anything that you wanted it to be, when you looked at it in a certain way.

Just then, my husband said, "Rebecca." I turned around, and Sean opened up a box and said, "Will you marry me?" In the box was a new set of rings that he had picked out. It was pretty magical, with Willow right there, in this vast gorgeous void of the Grand Canyon. I had let go of him re-proposing since I'd thrown my original rings. So much of the goodness that was emerging with us now had come through me letting go. He had thought of this all on his own, he had surprised me, I hadn't had to plan it for him. I was really happy. So of course, I said, "Yes!"

The first day of the ceremony held really good energy. We made sure to set the flow of the room. We had opened up divine masculine and feminine portals, so everything would be in balance. Everybody was having a really good time. There was a lot of profound, magical healing going on.

Willow had decided that it was very important that we open up a portal for a genie to come out of. She said to me, "Mommy, the genie is going to help you with all your aches and pains from working out so much." My muscles had been hurting from running so much lately. I just giggled, and she added, "And it's going to help everybody else find love."

So Willow was making everybody run around in circles and do special movements to get the genie to come out. Then she exclaimed that it had come out. "Do you see it, Mommy? Do you see it?" I didn't see it like she did, but I agreed, "Well, I can feel it." She said, "Yes, the genie is here."

The next day, I decided to go into a salt cave and get a deep tissue massage. A salt cave is a space with a generator that's activating Himalayan salt, and you're breathing it in and it's clearing you. As I was breathing the salt and the massage therapist was massaging my tissues, I thought, "Ah! This must be the genie Willow was talking about, relieving my aches and pains."

But then an amusing thing happened. This was a very small space, and there was a locker to put your clothes into; then you'd put on a towel and go lie down on the massage table. After I was done getting the massage, I couldn't find my pants anywhere. They weren't in the locker. The massage therapist and I were the only ones in there. He shrugged, "I don't know what to say, I don't know where your pants are either."

Sean knocked on the door, asking "Where is my wife?" I said, "Sean, I can't find my pants anywhere." Willow started laughing, and she said, "The genie thinks this is funny." I never did find my pants. I had to go back with Sean's coat wrapped around me like a skirt.

When we got back, we had another day of ceremony left. Everything went great. Then we had a day off, and we would be having another group of people coming in. This second group was going to be larger. I really felt like we needed some more help, and I felt very drawn to fly Ryan there to help. It was just in the depths of my knowing that he was supposed to be there.

At first I was thinking, "But Sean expresses himself so much more freely in ceremony without Ryan there; Ryan stepping back was when Sean came out of his shell." And then I thought, "You know what, Sean needs to step in his power whether Ryan's there or not."

So I made the executive decision for Ryan to come. Sean wasn't completely happy about it at first, but he accepted it—and then he actually drove to the Phoenix airport from Sedona to pick Ryan up, instead of having me do it. They apparently had an amazing, beautiful conversation on the way back, so it turned out to be perfect—all part of the healing.

When Ryan came in, everybody was really happy to see him. He started to work the ceremony with us. Sean said to me, "I actually missed Ryan." Ryan started playing with Willow. Everything was beautiful. I connected with Ryan again too, hugging him and saying, "Hey, I really missed you."

At one point, Ryan and I went out to the same place where the stars had aligned for us last time. We went out and looked at the stars again. We had come full circle.

The next day during post-ceremony integration, Sean actually asked to speak first. He was saying how he had missed Ryan, and how Ryan had been a catalyst to his own change. He was thankful for Ryan and thankful for everybody, talking about all the healing he had experienced. It was magical—truly an expression and example of pure, unconditional love as well as integration of the divine masculine and feminine.

By accepting divine masculine and divine feminine energy into my life, seeking it and working with it, I had created a container where the divine masculine could be so loving and trusting, without being competitive and aggressive. I also finally felt like I was in a position to accept this love.

LESSON

There are always more layers. You can always go deeper. The moment you think you're "done," the universe will show you that there is more. Sean and I had had so many breakthroughs, even to the point where he was finally showing up at ceremony the way I'd always wanted, and stepping into his power as a healer in his own right. Yet we still at times stumbled into more layers of intimacy and trust issues, and pockets of dishonesty that needed to be cleaned up. Ryan and I had become clear that we were divine friends and not destined to be partners—yet we still ran into bumps when he struggled with his own attachments and independence, and was experimenting with expressing his autonomy (sometimes clumsily, but that's how it can be at times).

Note that we worked through these things—Ryan returned to ceremony stronger than ever, he and Sean found a new depth of brotherhood, Sean and I confronted the ongoing issue with his Facebook Messenger friend. We were able to do this because I kept my own healing at the forefront. With Ryan, I had to stop martyring. With Sean, I had to be very clear about what I was and was not willing to tolerate, without drama. And I had to let go and stop trying to control it all.

The hardest thing to do when someone is triggering you is to look in the mirror and ask what in YOU needs to be healed. The next time you find yourself at odds with someone you love, see if you can turn that spotlight on yourself. It's not about "letting them off the hook"— no doubt they have work to do too. But you can't do theirs—only yours. And you doing it will make space for them to do it.

And when you hit that next layer, experiment with not being surprised. If you think the journey should be neat, tidy, and at some point finished, you're likely to be frustrated. Stay open to the twists and turns. They are leading you to the next breakthrough.

Chapter Twenty-Two

AT THE END OF THE SEDONA CEREMONY IN January 2023, Sean told me he wanted Ryan to be my Starseed brother. Ryan watched me hug Sean and Willow, and he smiled, telling me how happy it made him to see us happy and to see us grow. I was thinking, "I can't be a luckier woman than I am now. And now I have to give this love back."

There were a few more layers that I knew I had to work through. I wasn't exactly sure what they were yet. But I knew that as always, the work I needed to do would be mirrored by the people I love the most. Love always provides a mirror for the work we need to do.

Right before we left Sedona to return home, Ryan, Sean, Willow, and I decided to go see the Grand Canyon one more time. Another student from the Academy joined us. Since we had just come from ceremony, I was in the energy of "Everything is serendipitous, everything is synchronistic, and when you think something, it happens." Instant manifestation. That's the point that ceremony and this kind of energy work gets you to. We have that power within us, and we can learn to tap into it.

After a while, Sean was getting a little tired of driving, so he asked me if I would take over driving as we got closer to the Grand Canyon. I joked, "Oh, I'm not sure my brain is in a great state for me to be driving." I didn't have the plant medicine in me any more, or anything like that—it was just the after-effects of ceremony. But I added, "Okay, sure, we can take a journey into my subconscious mind." And I started driving.

Soon after I took over the wheel, I saw Exit 333. I said, "Oh wow, if we had time, I would just drive down that exit, because it's got to be a portal." No one else said anything, and I just kept driving. All of a sudden, the GPS said we were going the wrong way. Sean was like "What the heck is happening? We're not going the wrong way. Why is it wanting us to do a U-turn?" I said, like "Well, I guess maybe I missed an exit." He said, "No, you didn't miss an exit."

I insisted, "Let's just follow the GPS and see where it takes us." So I made a U-turn, and the GPS took us right back to Exit 333. It actually said, "Take Exit 333." Sean looked at me, and his eyes were so wide. He said, "Oh my gosh, Rebecca, this doesn't even really lead anywhere. I guess I'm going to have to drive. Because you're right, you can't drive right now because everything you think is going to start happening."

We all laughed, and Sean and I switched and he took over driving again, and we chatted about the energy of 333 as we went on our way. Numbers like 111, 222, 333, 444 and so on are notable and meaningful when we see them, and there are some different ideas about what they signify, although most agree they're some kind of message from Spirit or a sign. I also believe these numbers are portals. In this case, we talked about how 333 has to do with trusting yourself, putting your plans into action, and having personal strength. These also happened to be themes that had been present in the ceremony.

After the side trip back to the Grand Canyon, we got home and got settled, and one of the first things Sean said that first night home while we were lying in bed together was "Wow, we need to make another batch of ayahuasca." I started laughing, because we had just done ayahuasca for six nights, and that would be a little much.

But I loved that he loved it so much. I said, "Soon. Soon we will." He told me how much fun he'd had, and how he really enjoyed this being a part of his life now, and how he knows now that music heals him as it heals other people. He was telling me how much he has to learn. We were cuddling and kissing and talking.

And then something *really* magical happened.

Remember I told you that my guides had said that when a woman is fertile, if a man comes inside of her, she doesn't need to have a baby—instead you can create any life force you choose. You can create any kind of miracle or life creation (such as a project, home, health outcome, business venture, or other dream). Any manifestation, any vision can come to fruition if you employ "fertility" in this way.

Before that ceremony, even though I had explained this, he would have never in a million years allowed himself to orgasm while inside me because he thought I could still get pregnant. But that day I was ovulating, I knew it and I told him so, and still he said, "Okay, let's do it." And he has done that ever since. He never worries any more about me getting pregnant. He said he just clears his mind, connects to me, and wishes for our true love and happiness, and he knows *that* is what's going to be born.

MARTYR REDUX

In that last ceremony, I had been continuing my work on a deep layer of martyring. It had been underlying the whole entire time, and I had made great headway with it, such as with letting go of Ryan, but knew I still had more to go. I had to root out every bit. It had been a deeply rooted pattern for me, helping everyone out, being a savior, not just from joy or love (though sometimes that was part of it) but also guilt or obligation.

We cannot fully bring our true heaven to earth if we're still operating with any low-frequency energies. We'll just manifest *through* those low-frequency energies. And martyring is a very low-frequency energy.

One of the martyr scenes that was still playing out in my life had to do with my youngest sister, who's ten years younger than me. She was leaving a man, and I told her I would pay her rent and all of her bills for six months so she could get back on her feet. But it was her job to get back on her feet—and she could have. I made sure there was opportunity there. And that six months turned into a year, and after a year passed, I said, "Okay, what are you going to do now that I'm no longer going to pay your bills?" She looked at me and said, "I guess I'm going to have to take him back."

WOW! I knew right then that what I had done to enable her (when I thought I was "helping" her) was the perfect example of what not to do. It was such a big slap in the face. So I just decided to let go.

But then something deeper and more complicated came up when I told my sister, "Absolutely not! I'm not going to be that person that pays your bills anymore." It put me in a position where I needed to say no to my mother as well. I love my mother dearly, she's a very good mother, and I would do anything for my mother, and gladly. I would be in high frequency doing things for my mother. That's how much I love her, and how much she's done for me, and how it's an equal relationship.

But she started martyring for my youngest sister whenever I stopped. That meant that my mom came to me and said, essentially, "Please help me as I martyr for your sister, because I really can't afford to martyr for her, so you need to martyr for me." The way she saw it, "You're not doing it for your sister, you're doing it for me." Because she knew that for *her*, I would. And then I was really stuck in this whole knot.

I played into it for a little bit. Once again, there's a mirror there. At this very same time, Ryan was stuck at his mother's house, literally in the basement. She still had custody of his daughter. He somehow got his car taken away by his grandmother. I didn't even quite understand it. He appeared to be trapped in his mother's house with no way out. Of course, running my martyr trip, I started thinking "I have to be the one who saves him. I love him so dearly." And even though I had already had some experience of letting go with him and letting him do this thing, I actually started going back into that old pattern with him.

Then Paulina, a teacher for AWAKE, ended up manifesting that beautiful Mount Shasta dream home for ceremonies that she had asked for and created in that ceremony in Mount Shasta. She wanted me to fly out with her to sign the paperwork. She was so excited, it was incredibly beautiful, and I said, "Yes." But right away I thought, "I'm going to bring Ryan." I had two reasons: I missed him, and I had loved seeing him in Sedona. And, I thought this would be a great way to get him out of his mother's house. He had been really suffering with that whole situation.

I asked Sean if this was okay with him. He wasn't super excited about it at first, and I could understand why. But he said, "Okay, I guess I'll stay here. I don't really want to travel anyway. That's fine." I said, "It's only going to be for four days." And he held space for me to do that. We were in such a good place now, and there was so much trust.

So I flew Ryan out to Mount Shasta. I met with Paulina, and we all had an amazing time. She invited another friend as well. The house was truly beautiful, and we spent some time opening up portals there. My connection with Ryan even got deeper, if that was possible. I remember looking at him when he got there and feeling something different. Almost like an expansion in his heart. I could tell that he had done a lot of work on himself.

When we went to bed that night, I told him that we would be sleeping in separate bedrooms, and he agreed. This had gotten to a point where it was obvious who was going to be with who. I was going to be with Sean, and Ryan was completely, unconditionally accepting of that.

Yet then something really strange happened. This is going to sound cliche, but it really did happen: I was lying in bed in my room, and there was a dark figure there. I ran out of the room into the living room. I thought everyone else was in bed, but Ryan was sitting there. I said, "There's something in my room! A dark figure!" He laughed, but he said, "Do you want me to lie down with you?" I said, "Yes!"

He came back into the bedroom with me, and the dark figure had disappeared. We lay down together, and had a really good talk. He told me more about the situation with his mom, and I was doing energy work and giving him advice, and we started cuddling. I could feel that expansion in his heart, and I could feel the connection. I lay there in his arms, and we played some music, and talked about how much fun we'd had together, because we had been to the waterfalls at Mount Shasta that day. We just really started to feel that connection again. Even after all the decisions, all the growth. There was a little bit of me wondering how I could be so deeply connected with one person, even when I was truly in love with another.

He looked at me and said, "It's okay, Rebecca. Things are going to play out the way they need to. You and I can be divine friends, and this is the way it's supposed to be. You're supposed to live in a world of unconditional love." I was consoled by that. We eventually fell asleep together around 3 a.m., and the rest of the trip we work on the house together. Then we all parted for our homes.

Before he left, I gave him some money, because I knew he didn't have much and he was going back home to his mom. But I told him "You know, you've got to just say no and walk out of that house." He said, "I know, I need to do it." And I was realizing was that I needed to do the same thing—with my mother.

I got home and I started to have some conversations with my mother. Finally, I stood in my power. I didn't make up an excuse and say, "I don't have the money to help my sister" (I wouldn't want to say that to the universe because, mostly, whatever I speak comes true!) Instead, I said to my mother, "It's not that I don't have the money to help her, because I do. But if I had a billion dollars laying right in front of me right now, I would not help her, because of the energy of it. She's not helping herself. She's refusing to help herself. She's being a victim. And when you help her, you're investing in that energy. You keep feeding that victim energy in her. If you stop giving her money, if you stop feeding that energy—which is a monster—that monster will die and something else will grow. She'll step into another power, another energy, and she'll start to provide for herself. We have to help her grow, and claim her own power, not enable the victim energy."

My mother said, "You would do that to her children?" I said, "It's not *me* doing that to her children. *She's* doing that to her children, and that's going to be up to her."

After I made that decision, I got a repair bill from the landlord for lots of damages, and a very high water bill—I didn't know a water bill could even be that large. I couldn't fathom what she had done with the water. Whatever it was, the universe was saying "Here you go! Here's some final remnants of your martyring." So I told my mom, "No." And I told my sister, "Never ask me again. I'm not going to do it."

I had invited Ryan to join us for the Mount Shasta ceremony that was coming up. I had invited him before he and I left Mount Shasta on that short trip when Paulina closed on the new house. It had been a few weeks since that trip, and everything was going well in my life. Sean and I were continuing to grow. He was introducing me more into his world, and entering into mine through music and other creative resources. That expansion was profound (and it still is).

Well, around this time I got a jarring phone call from Ryan. He had agreed to work on a project at my house to pay back some of the money that he owed me. Now, he was telling me that he no longer would do it. His exact words were, "I'm just going to sit here and see what the universe brings me, and you can find someone else to do this job. In the future, if I want to do some work on your house I still can, because there's still plenty to do." It was incredibly arrogant—and not really like him.

Then, even more outrageously, he informed me that I would have to lend him money to get to Mount Shasta—that I would be paying for him to get there, as though it were my obligation. I couldn't even believe the conversation. I felt like, who is this person? But then I realized, "Okay, this is a test. It's something he needs to process, but it's also a way for me to test my strength and clarity about martyring."

I passed that test. I told him that I would be finding someone else to do the repairs in the house. I told him that I would leave an open space for him to come to Mount Shasta, where we would be conducting two kick-ass ceremonies. But I would not provide one penny for him to get there. Not even to pay him in advance for facilitating. Nothing. He would have to provide his own way there, show up for himself, and that was only way I would accept him back into my life. I told him that to be in my life, he had to show up for himself. That I was done having to make sure that everybody was taken care of because of my fear of losing them. I was willing to completely let him go and trust that if he was meant to show up, he would.

Ryan got very quiet when I said all this. He understand what I was saying, I think, even though he didn't back down during that conversation about what he had said. We just agreed, "Okay, we'll see what happens," and I hung up.

This was a really big decision for me, and it started to show up in such positive ways in my life. Even in my career, with people in the back end (when you run a business, there's a big back end), people started showing up for me who were in their divine power, who knew what they were doing, who were charging the right prices, and getting to the point. I wasn't having to go through any BS. Everything was aligning perfectly. The universe was protecting me and keeping me safe. In my love life, health, or wealth, I found that if I stood up for myself, dropped all the martyr energy, and was clean and clear, that's what the world mirrored back to me.

A BODY THAT REFLECTED MY TRUTH

At that point, I had my body also just where I wanted it. All that excess fat, which as I've said is at least as much about excess energy as it is about food, was gone. I had been absorbing it and holding on to it since I was a kid, and now with all this work, inside and out, I had released it.

So now, I decided to have surgery done to remove the loose skin that was left after eliminating all that fat. I wanted to really step into my divine feminine and feel see that part of me reflected in the mirror. I had worked very hard physically and energetically to get to this point, so this was my reward.

I made an appointment to get this done in Costa Rica. Costa Rica is a great place to do something like this, because their medical care is just as high quality as in the U.S., but much more affordable. Plus, they have amazing hotels that include 24/7 nursing care. My surgery would get done in a clinic, then I would stay at a hotel with overnight 24-hour care and be chauffeured around.

Sean supported my plan 100%, But I told him, "I'm not going to need you to go with me, because the universe is going to show up."

And it did. The whole trip was just amazing, from the food I was eating to the driver who picked me up from the airport. The hotel that I stayed at was wonderful. The nurse was very loving—this was a nurse who watched over you 24/7. I had a lymphatic massage after the surgery. Even the doctors who did the surgery were different. I remember calling them "My Galactic Surgery Team."

When the main doctor walked in to talk to me beforehand, he asked me, "What do you do for a living?" I told him, and he said, "Oh. That makes sense. Your energy is really different. I'm not used to being able to be in a room with a patient for much time. In my profession, I'm kind of in and out really fast. But your energy feels very calm and collected and you feel really grounded. I like that." I replied, "Thank you. I trust you." And he said, "Don't worry. We got you."

I was undergoing a five-hour surgery. I chose to go alone, because I knew that the universe would give me the best if I trusted the universe. If Sean had come (and he would have, even though he had things to do and didn't really want to travel), I would have felt obligated to tend to him when I was lying there trying to heal. That was energy I didn't want. I love him, and I knew he'd be there for me. My sisters would have been, too. So many people offered to come support me, but I knew. I said, "Don't worry, I'm going to be 100% taken care of." And I was a *million percent* taken care of.

One night while I was in Costa Rica, I was told by my guides to lie down. So I lay down in the bed and I started shivering. I knew that I was getting worked on by higher guidance, by the Starseed beings. I always get really cold when that happens, almost from the inside out. I started shivering, and they showed themselves to me as pure white light; they've said that when they work on people, they take this form.

They told me at first to lie on my back. They were doing some downloads, working on my DNA. Then they told me to turn to the right side, and they worked on me there, and they told me to turn to the left side, and they worked on me there as well. It was interesting, because they were putting something in my uterus that they said that was going to be born for me. It wasn't a child, but a creation of some sort.

They also were telling me about Ryan and that there's a larger picture with him that I can't see, because I'm too in my 3D thinking, but that I made the right choice there; just give it compassion and unconditional love, and not to worry. They affirmed, almost in a lovingly amused way, "Sean is the One that you keep referring to." Yet they also reminded me that I'm always going to have unconditional love around me. That's not one person. It's going to show up through men and women and whoever is around you at the time, if you allow it.

But that One person you keep growing with and growing with and growing with, they were affirming to me, "Sean's going to be that person." Then they put some downloads in his crown chakra, and they were showing me that. They said, "When you get home, make sure that you make love and he comes inside of you again, because he's going to be fertilizing this creation that we just put in you, and something really big is going to be born for the both of you." I was very excited to see what that would be.

I came out of the trance of this "psychic surgery" and, right then, got a text message from a student from AWAKE who said they had just seen me in a situation where I was going to rebirth something. They outlined exactly what my guides had told me. I thought, "Whoa. You definitely cannot make this stuff up."

THE HEALING EXPANDS TO EVERYONE

About an hour after that, I got a text message from Ryan saying "Hey, I'm sorry. I will come and work on your house." I replied, "No, that's okay." I told him, once again, "I'm saying this in the most loving way, I'll always love you, the door's open for you to come and facilitate with us, but you have to be able to show up for yourself and you have to be able to get there. I'm leaving that be, and I trust that. I have no attachment to how that's going to end up."

My old self at that point would have been a little clingier to Sean after that, given that I had just potentially let go of Ryan forever. My old self was like "I've got to have somebody." Instead, the opposite happened. And suddenly I knew another layer of what I had to do. I had to let Sean know that I could not control who his friends are. That I trust him, so if he wants to Facebook that woman Corinne and be her friend, he can do it. Just don't hide it. We should be truthful with one another, open about our friendships. He appreciated that and agreed.

After getting that "psychic surgery" done by the guides, even more shifted in my life. My son called me before I came home. He was in the room with my ex-husband's mother, and I was talking to him, and he said, "Mom, I got to go, Nanny's here." And I said, "So? Why do you have to go?" He hung up the phone.

The issue there was that he wasn't allowed to talk to me in front of his Nanny, because she gets mad when he talks to me or any of my family. She's very controlling like that, to the point of just about having borderline personality disorder. So now, I texted Caden, very lovingly, "You should be able to show your love to me in front of anybody. You should be able to scream it from the rooftops."

And then I heard from my guides, right then, that this was not something to work on right now directly with Caden. It was something I could work on indirectly, through my own work and with others. Then he and I could talk about it later.

So intuitively, I called my ex-husband, and I told him what had happened. I said, "I just want to tell you that I understand a lot of things that went down for you in your childhood." I asked him to tell me how he felt in those situations when he was a kid. He willingly talked to me about it, saying, "Well, I felt trapped, and I felt like I was in jail, because that's what my mom has always done to me."

Darrell's mom was so possessive and disordered that our kids weren't even allowed to play with my sister's kids when they were growing up, or he would have gotten into trouble. He had to hide it from his mother when our kids played with their cousins. It sounds crazymaking, and it was actually kind of crazy. Part of it was that she was jealous. She didn't ever want my mom watching the kids; she wanted to be the only one watching the kids.

This is the kind of controlling, smothering "love" he grew up with. He told me, "To me, love is prison, and I just want to be free."

Darrell and I divorced in 2008, and he had not had one girlfriend since 2008. When he and I first got together, I had just exited a horrible relationship and I didn't really want to connect with someone, and he definitely didn't want to connect because he didn't want to be trapped. In that way, we were a strangely perfect match at the time. So that relationship played out how it had to, even though we did love each other in our ways and we got our beautiful children out of it.

During this conversation, as I was listening to him share about his childhood, I was working on him energetically during the conversation and giving him downloads. I was telling him, "Love is not a prison. It doesn't have to be." He kept saying, "But I just like being alone. I like being free."

Then I said, "Imagine being with someone who's your best friend. And when you're with them, they make you even *more* free, because they support the passions and freedoms you love, and they just amplify your freedom. Can you imagine that?"

He said, "Well, I never really thought of that but… Yeah, I guess I can." I did more work on him, so much work that I wouldn't have time to explain it all here. But at the end of the conversation, I said, "I think someone's coming into your life. I'm guided to tell you that." He said, "Really, Rebecca? Your messages are usually accurate." I said, "Yeah. And it's very important that you listen to what I'm saying, and take this opportunity to be that person's best friend, and be their lover." He was so moved. He said, "I really, really appreciate this, Rebecca. More than you know."

Then, he and I agreed to be beacons of light for our son. By shifting our DNA, his DNA would shift. He would get through what he needed to get through with this situation and with all situations. And, for the first time since we had divorced, I said, "I love you." And he said, "I love you too, babe. Thank you so much." We hung up the phone. So much healing!

SCARS

I flew home from Costa Rica the next day. My plan was to stay at a hotel in Pittsburgh on my arrival back in the U.S., so that the very next morning I could meet with a surgeon there who did laser therapy for scars. That was part of my surgery plan: to go to Costa Rica; get the loose skin removed, and then immediately meet with a professional who had amazing reviews on his website about a new technology that was removing scars with lasers.

I arrived safely back in Pittsburgh after long travel from Costa Rica. I was still recovering from the surgery, though doing well. At 7:00 o'clock the next morning, I woke up and got ready for my 8:00 o'clock appointment with the laser surgeon. I got there on time, waited about 30 minutes, and then the doctor's secretary came in. She did a pre-assessment, taking notes, and then she would takes notes on what the doctor said to me as well.

During the pre-assessment, she told me about the noticeable difference that the laser would make after about four weeks. We discussed my scars and post-op care, and then she said, "Okay, the doctor will be in soon." I waited for another 30 minutes. Then a tall, very healthy-looking doctor came in, crossed his legs and looked at me like he was really going to give me attention.

He said, "Okay, so I hear that you got this surgery and you're looking for scar removal." I said, "Yes!" I told him about what I had learned from all the research I had done, how there were two lasers and the combination was even more effective than either one by itself.

He told me, "We got rid of those two lasers a long time ago. We now have an even better laser that offers better results." I said, "Well, I saw the before and after pictures, and the results look amazing."

Then, all of a sudden, he seemed to go into a trance. He shifted gears. He said, "Actually, you can't believe those before and after pictures. If these machines worked as well as they supposedly do, a lot more plastic surgeons would be using them. A lot of plastic surgeons could be including these lasers in their healing package, but they don't because they're not that helpful.

"The truth is, at the end of the day it's up to your genetics as to how this scar heals. And you'll probably heal just fine on your own. I could give you the laser and then when you heal you would treat me as a superhero, when the truth is you could have done it yourself."

Oh, this was 100% him channeling Spirit.

The secretary stopped typing and looked at him dumbfounded. He then explained a bit about how lasers work—how they create a deeper injury to the skin under the scar and jolt the body into accelerating healing in that area, ostensibly healing both the new micro-injury along with the existing injury.

Then he said, "I don't know why I just said all of that. Everything that I was thinking in my head just came out of my mouth." His secretary continued to look at him in wonderment. He looked at me and said, "I know I've probably confused you and you have a lot to think about. But if you want to continue, then you need to put 5% down to secure the date." He shook my hand and left, and the secretary and I sat there staring at each other.

I said, "So wait, does this laser machine work or not?" She said, a bit dazed, "Well, I thought it did."

Suddenly I realized that what he had told me is essentially what I'd been telling all my students. A scar represents suffering. It covers up a trauma. If you heal the trauma, you heal the scar. I realized, again, that now was the time for me to continue to heal my own DNA—which would heal my skin along with many deeper layers of trauma, patterns of suffering, This theme of healing at the DNA level was coming up from all sides.

I couldn't thank the universe enough for that one.

It was a long day. My husband came and picked me up, we drove two hours and 15 minutes back to our home, and I explained everything that had happened. He was amazed by it all too. He listened intently.

Then he said, "I want to remind you that Cody's home."

DNA GOES DEEPER

Cody is my son who, at that time, was 23. Caden, the son I had been talking about with my ex-husband the previous day, was 20 at this time. We had had a very rough time with Cody starting when he was around 18. He went into some sort of existential depression and his behaviors weren't ideal. I had told him then, "I'll be holding space for you. Come back around in a way that's respectful." He had spent the night only once or twice at the lake house in the past two years.

But now, he was coming home to live with me for the summer.

I told myself, "This is all about timing. This is going to happen in the way it needs to." But I couldn't help but feel that shit was about to hit the fan. I was tired, I had been up early and had just traveled a long way after a significant surgery. I really could have used some sleep.

When I got home, Cody was downstairs in his room. I went in and said hello and hugged him. Then he went outside and he was just hanging out by the hot tub while I got resettled. I wasn't sure what he was doing. Up in the kitchen, my daughter Ariel, Sean, Willow and I were hanging out, telling funny stories and having a good time.

Remember that I had created healing portals around my house, and that when people come to my house, things often happen to make them heal—such as what happened with Sean's mother.

Well, Cody came upstairs, and I could tell he had been smoking marijuana. I asked him point blank, "Have you been smoking marijuana?" He said, "Yeah." He came into the kitchen, opened the refrigerator door, and some yogurt just flew out. The container fell on the floor and went *everywhere*.

Cody looked at my husband and said, "What did you do that for?" Which was pretty bizarre, because Sean was nowhere near the fridge. Sean said, "What? I wasn't even touching the refrigerator." I looked at Cody, and that martyr energy started to come up again, and I wanted to avert disaster. I said, "Cody, just go downstairs. I'll clean it up." But Sean protested, "No, he needs to clean it up." Then Cody said, "I'll clean it up. Don't be mad."

Then Cody started to get really dramatic. "If you want you can kick me out of the house, I know everything's my fault." He started to get really loud and intense, and with Willow right there, he said, "I'll just go by the side of the road and suck dick for a living!"

I got really angry at that. I said, " Okay, you have to leave. When you were five, you never were exposed to environments like this. No one would have dreamed about saying something like that in front of you. You can't live here and act like this. You need to go get your stuff, pack it, and leave."

Then Willow tried to come over to us, slipped right in the yogurt, fell on her butt, and started crying. Sean picked up and hugged Willow, and told Cody, "You should apologize to her." Cody blustered back, "Apologize? What did I do?" The he started yelling at Sean, saying "She's going to hate you so much when she's older, she's going to hate you!" Sean, too, then, joined me in saying, "You know what, you need to leave."

He had been home less than five hours.

So things were just going crazy. Cody stomped downstairs and started to get his stuff together. I saw my daughter Ariel, who was now 17, follow him down. I called my ex-husband, and I said, "Look, it didn't last. I'm sending Cody down your way. He can't live here." He asked, "Wow, what happened?" I told him, and he said, "Okay, I'll start to clean a room out. He'll either live with me or my mom." I didn't like the idea of Cody living with my ex's mom, but I knew he had to leave.

Then, all of a sudden, Ariel came back up, and she begged, "Mom, please come downstairs." I said, "No, Ariel, he's just manipulating. I'm used to his manipulation." She said, "No, trust me on this. This is different. Just come downstairs." So I went downstairs, though I had my guard up.

Cody was crying. He cried and cried and cried. He said, "Mom, there's something wrong with me. I haven't cried like this in four years. What's happening?" I understood then what was happening. He was literally having an ayahuasca purge, just like Sean's mom had. He was purging from his entire body. He said, "I feel sick." And he started telling me, "I just feel like a failure. I shouldn't be here, living off my mom…" A massive eruption of self-judgment.

Mind you, he had just graduated a month earlier from college. He was coming to live with me to wait tables over the summer and have some fun before going to Europe with his friends in the fall. Then find a career-oriented job. It was perfectly reasonable. He was only 23. But he kept calling himself a loser, saying how he shouldn't be waiting tables for a living, and "I don't deserve all of this, this beautiful house…"

Suddenly what I realized was that he sounded like *me*. He was saying things that I would have said at his age. I was hyper-motivated at his age. I graduated with honors, went straight into the Army, had my first professional job at the age of 24, was training foster care parents and putting children in foster care homes at the age of 24, then went to graduate school, had my first large business when I was 29, and so on.

So he had those imprints. Realizing that this was what was coming up for healing, I began pulling my imprints out of him. I said, "This isn't you. This isn't necessary. Let's get rid of this." I was doing self-love exercises with him, healing myself at the same time, shedding this sludge. These were imprints that I in turn had gotten from my father. He was a workaholic, and carried that energy of shame and not being worthy and needing to work really hard to be okay and loved.

Cody said, "Mom, I don't know what's happening, I'm so embarrassed that I'm crying this much." My five-year-old, Willow, came downstairs right then, and she walked up and said, "Cody, when I fell on my bum upstairs, I started crying. But I let the cry flow, and I released it, and now I feel better. You have to do the same thing."

That made him laugh. Then Sean came down, and he realized what was going on, like a full-blown ceremony. Cody looked at my husband and said, "I can tell you don't like me, you don't want me here." That had some truth to it, because Sean wasn't used to having my older kids around. So Sean stepped up too. He said, "Okay, I'm listening. I'll change."

It was one big family healing. We were really doing some deep, deep work for all of us.

Sean was working, I was working, Cody was working, Willow was helping, Ariel was watching. It was incredible.

Then Cody said, "Mom, I want you to love me. I want you to be proud of me. Everything I do is to make you proud of me." I said, "I *am* proud of you, Cody. I just want you to be happy. I don't care what your career is, I just want you to be in joy." He kept saying "Mom, I just want you…" And I interrupted him. I said, "No, look in the mirror; look at yourself. Talk to yourself as though you're talking to me. You just *think* you're talking to me. This is about you loving yourself."

He said, "I just want you to love me. I just want you to be proud of me. I just want you to accept me." He realized he was saying it to himself, and he kept releasing and releasing.

This went on for the whole night. After a few hours I was too tired to keep going, and I told him "Okay, you do this for the rest of the night, and I'm going to go to bed, and then we'll speak in the morning." I gave him a couple of capsules of psilocybin that I knew would support him in opening his heart more fully and seeing the divinity of things as he purged himself of everything that wasn't love.

Before I went to bed, though, I called my ex-husband again to fill him in on what was going on now. My daughter had already called him, but I explained more about how Cody was releasing. Once again, my ex was very supportive. I reminded him, "Remember, you and I *just* talked the other night about working on ourselves to clear the DNA?" I explained, "We are the hard drives. If we clear our DNA, our children are going to shift miraculously around us."

Darrell told me that one of his best friends was dying of liver cancer, which started with cirrhosis of the liver. He said he was now questioning his own drinking, and how it might catch up with him. I said, "Yes, this is all connecting together. It's all about self-love. That's what Cody is working on now, and you can too. When you connect with yourself, when you love yourself enough, you'll no longer desire substances that you once used to escape."

He asked me, "Rebecca, do you still drink?" I said, "No." He was floored. He wanted to know, "How can you be happy when you're not on anything?" I said, "It's this work that I'm telling you about. It teaches you to be in the frequency of joy. It got to the point where alcohol would just bring me down. When you're in the frequency of joy and truth and authenticity, you don't need to escape anymore. You don't want to. You want to be present."

I added, "Just do the work that we discussed the other night on the phone. Just keep working on yourself, keep up with the self-love, and remember that you can have freedom and be in love at the same time. And I hope you do stop drinking, because we don't want you to take yourself out of the world."

He promised, "Okay, Rebecca, I'm going to do this. I'm going to stop drinking. And you and I are going to work on our DNA, and we're going to watch everybody heal."

This was all profound ancestral healing for the family. My father had been an alcoholic, my ex-husband's father at one point was an alcoholic, and my ex-husband definitely had a drinking problem. Cody had just been saying during this episode that he was felt like he was abusing alcohol, and it was one of the things he wanted to stop, along with smoking marijuana. He felt like he was using them to escape.

He noted that whenever he would do something like psilocybin, it was different—he used plant medicines to connect within himself, and he could tell that those medicines were about inner work. He wanted to do more of that, and less escaping.

Finally I went up to bed, and after I got up there, suddenly I smelled smoke. It was all over the room and it smelled familiar. I asked Sean, "Do you smell that?" He said, "No, I don't smell anything." I wondered if I was going crazy at this point. It was so strong, how could he not smell it? Sean said sympathetically, "Just relax, Rebecca, you've been through a lot. You haven't gotten a lot of sleep."

But I could smell it, and suddenly I realized what it was. My father had smoked a pipe. Not cigarettes, but a pipe. He had used a certain tobacco, and the exact aroma I was smelling now was that of the tobacco smoke that I remembered from my father's pipe. It was coming out as Cody and I were continuing to release toxic patterns from our DNA, as we were healing that alcoholic pattern.

This would heal the past, present, and future within our family. This is a testament to how peace can be created, one person and family at a time, rippling out.

LESSON

I invite you to treat the world as your mirror. Life will reflect to you the work you need to do. Sometimes it may feel like things are flipping upside-down, but at the end it will make sense, if you surrender and trust.

Chapter Twenty-Three

IN MARCH OF 2023 WHEN I GOT BACK FROM COSTA Rica for my surgery, I was healing and preparing for the ceremony that was upcoming in Mount Shasta. I wasn't sure if Ryan was going to come yet. I had told him that if he showed up for himself and got himself there, it was open for him to come and facilitate.

As it turns out, he did end up stepping up, showing up, and getting to Mount Shasta. He had decided that he was definitely going to do it, and he was paying for himself to get there. Sean and I had to go to Michigan to visit his father earlier that month, so Ryan had agreed to come and watch the dogs for us while we were on that trip. Then he was going to fly from our house to Mount Shasta. He was going to go to Mount Shasta a little ahead of us. Sean was going to drive to Mount Shasta, like he always does, so that he could bring all the sound equipment and visual gear.

When we got home from Michigan, we overlapped with Ryan still being there for a couple of days. Once I was home, Ryan kept telling me that something was stuck in my heart chakra, that it needed clearing. He was really persistent about it, and I started to get aggravated. At first, I started to let him do it, but then I was just getting too frustrated. (That often indicates energy that doesn't want to leave, so it makes the person angry.) So he was drumming and trying to work on my back, and finally I said, "Please just leave me alone, I'm fine!"

That night, I was sleeping in my bedroom with Sean, and Ryan was sleeping across the hall. Sean had told him that maybe he should sleep downstairs, just because my daughter Ariel was sleeping in the room right next to us, and he thought she might not want to share a bathroom with Ryan. For some reason, Ryan said, "I'm absolutely not going downstairs." He was afraid to leave me. He felt like I needed him up there. I was a little freaked out by that, because it was a little strange.

Then, all of a sudden in the middle of the night, my right breast just kind of…exploded open. At this point, I was six weeks into healing from my Costa Rica surgery, and the breast was almost healed. There were little scars, but for it to do what it did was crazy. I felt a sense of warmth, which was a burst of warm fluid, and I got up and went to the bathroom to look. It was blood mixed with pus, oozing from an inch-long slit that had opened up in the breast. I was shocked, but I just lay back down and told Sean, "Um, my breast just exploded. I'm going to deal with this in the morning."

I somehow did go back to sleep, but when I woke up it was really scary. Not just because there was a hole in my breast. A part of me knew what I was about to go through. But I knew I needed to get it taken care of. I think I was still in a little bit of shock.

Ryan and I were supposed to go on a hike. I went to Ryan and I said, "I can't go on a hike." I told him what had happened. He looked spooked. He said, "That's really weird. Last night I got up in the middle of the night and started drumming and doing energy work, just because …I knew I had to." We compared timelines, and it was right when he began doing that drumming and energy work that my breast exploded. He said he had been working on my heart chakra. He kept saying that he felt it was infected or clogged or something.

I knew I had to do something with the breast, because it was still bleeding and oozing. So first I went to urgent care. Sean was taking Willow to school, so Ryan went with me. The urgent care staff basically said, "We're absolutely not touching this." They wouldn't get involved because it had been a surgical site and they didn't want to touch anything related to cosmetic surgery.

It was really red at that point, really swollen. It looked very scary, and the doctor thought this could be a really deep infection. She said, "We don't know how deep this infection goes." She suggested I go to a hospital.

YET ANOTHER JOURNEY

So I went to West Virginia University Hospital at Morgantown. It was disorienting and felt so bizarre, because that was where Gabe had worked. The last time I had been there, he had been a psychiatrist at that hospital. I used to do rounds with him there. So we parked and got out and I immediately threw up. Maybe it was memories, or maybe I was just really sick at that point.

I went and checked in at the emergency room, and sat in the waiting room. It was so crowded. I was starting to actually feel a little bit feverish at this point. I could feel that there was definitely an infection. At that point, Ryan in his fearless way said, "Stand up. We're going to do some Kundalini work on you." I was kind of embarrassed. We were right in the middle of a waiting room. But he was like "Who cares?" It's just how he is.

He sat with me the whole time. He was doing energy work on me. And then, this was totally crazy: an ambulance drove up that said *Cairo* on it. Cairo, in Egypt, is where Gabe was from. There is no town in Morgantown called Cairo. I pointed it out to Ryan. I said, "Why is this happening? Why does it say Cairo?" He said, "I don't know, Rebecca. But we're doing all this work on you. So who knows."

We were out there in the waiting room for a good hour before they finally called us back and we were put into a small room with just a curtain. Then a girl nearby, probably behind another curtain, started screaming in agony. I felt like we were in hell. It was like a madhouse. My fever was going up, and all I could hear was screaming. I was starting to lose it. I started feeling very angry and I said, "I'm going to kill that girl. I can't handle it. I can't."

Ryan was so calm and wise. He said, "This is what you're going through inside." He's that well-versed in energy work. He started playing ayahuasca music from his phone right there to help me work through it. And eventually I did. Really, this whole infection scenario was like a purge.

Finally I was seen by a doctor. He examined me and said, "You have to have emergency surgery. We're going to get an OR ready for you." I was like "What?" They said, "Yes, this infection needs to be removed and cleaned up." And they wanted to look at both breasts, for some reason.

So I was admitted, and I would be going into surgery in the morning. Ryan stayed with me the whole night. Believe it or not, at this point, Sean did not come to the hospital. I think now he would, but at that point, that was still kind of how things were. I called and explained everything, he asked if I was okay, and we agreed he would stay with Willow. A little odd, but I also felt like I was in good hands.

Ryan slept on a chair beside me all night. He listened to me talk in my sleep, and told me I had been talking about my sister Wendy in my dreams. It was very sweet.

In the morning before my surgery, he left. He had to catch a plane to Mount Shasta. He gave me a hug and told me he loved me. And off he went to Mount Shasta. He had planned meet me there. I was supposed to be leaving in three days. I said, "Well, this is kind of a big situation. We'll see what happens."

Soon after, I was prepped for surgery and wheeled into the OR. The surgery took about an hour, and then I was in recovery. When I was lucid again, the infectious disease doctor told me that I had an *unidentifiable purple virus* growing in me rapidly. They said it would take weeks to get the actual name of the virus because it was very rare. (Ryan equated the "purple" virus aspect to Purple Rain, the song, which had been a part of our journey. We believe that Prince was referring to being with the one you love and letting your faith guide you. So Ryan felt that the virus being "purple" actually was significant.)

What's more, I was told that I would need to receive intravenous antibiotics for weeks and then be on oral antibiotics for a *year*. This was a team of doctors, an infectious disease team and a surgical team. There were eight doctors involved in this case.

Well, I hate pharmaceutical medication. Absolutely hate it. It makes me sick. And there was no way I was going to be stuck at home with IVs for weeks. I said to the infectious disease doctor, "There's absolutely no way. I have get on a plane and go to Mount Shasta." And I actually told them about the natural plant medicine ceremony and energy work and what I was doing there.

There were five docs on the infectious disease team and one of them actually listened to what I had to say. I didn't expect that, but the team went away and conferred about my case, and then the whole team came back in and the main doc said, "Okay, we're going to work with you. We're going to let you go." They gave me oral antibiotics in a bottle, instead of the IV antibiotics they wanted to do, and I was discharged with two drain tubes coming out of my breasts, one on each side. I had blood work that had all these high inflammation markers, white blood cell count high, everything just not good. They said, "Just make sure you go to the hospital in Mt. Shasta if anything happens." I promised that I would.

But I said to myself, "I'm going to heal this in ceremony." I went to Mount Shasta with the intention that I was going to heal.

I ended up taking only two days' worth of the antibiotics. That was all that I could stomach. And I only took that much because Sean was very insistent about it.

HEALER, HEAL THYSELF

I flew to Mount Shasta. Ryan was there, and Sean arrived later in the evening after me. This was Paulina's new house that she had purchased as a retreat center, and she was facilitating as well. We had two ceremonies back to back. For the first ceremony, I would be working with the students but at the same time, I would be working with myself.

The ceremony itself went very, very well. When we began, I told the students what I was facing because I like them to see transformations. I knew I was going to be a guinea pig. I told the participants about the infection, the surgery, the tubes, everything. I said, "We're going to work together. I'm going to try to heal this, and you'll all be a part of it. Just as I'll be helping you heal, you'll be helping me."

Everyone was very understanding. They were pretty shocked that I was there, that I had showed up to work in that condition, but they were also eager to support, and it ended up going very well.

There were two women there who were sisters. I like to see family at ceremonies because when one person begins to heal, the family member who shares their DNA also begins to heal. I had been obviously seeing this in my own life, and I was always glad to see it happening for other families.

There was also a guy among the participants named Tristan. He walked in with a guitar and said, "I have no idea why I brought this, but I knew I had to."

At one point, one of the two sisters was down on the floor in a fetal position rocking back and forth in agony. She couldn't get out of the fetal position. The other sister, who was in another room, started to feel sick too. This is really common between family members in ceremony because of the shared DNA—when one starts shifting, the others feel it.

So Paulina and I helped this curled-up woman stand up and half-carried her, and we got her on a bed near her sister, so they were right next to each other, and three or four people were called to come in and work with them. Ryan was one of those people. So Ryan and I and a couple of other people were doing energy work on them.

One sister said she felt like she was giving birth to aliens. She said she could feel her DNA shifting, but it was hard. She said it was like breaking through snake skins, and it was very painful. Then she suddenly said, "I'm stuck because my husband's an asshole." She started naming all of the abusive things her husband had done to her. Ryan was trying to work with her, but every time he touched her, she pushed him away. She kept saying "I tell you I want you to do this and you don't listen to me!"

I told Ryan, "Listen to what she's saying." She was talking about her husband, but he was taking it personally, having a reaction and working through his own stuff. (Ayahuasca doesn't discriminate, or recognize that some people are "facilitators" and others are "participants" or "students." We're all doing the work, all healing.)

Intuitively, I knew what she needed was divine masculine. But Ryan was struggling at that moment. I turned to Sean and said, "She needs divine masculine. Please, go get that guitar and play for her." So he went and got the guitar that Tristan had brought, and started to play it.

And it was absolutely, insanely magical.

Mind you, I had *never* heard him play the guitar in all the time I had known him. It was crazy, really. He would never play guitar for me. He thinks of himself as a bass player. But he started out on guitar, and we have guitars all over our house. Yet he had never played for me, even though I used to beg him to play and sing for me. He can sing and has a beautiful British accent, but he wouldn't sing for me either.

Now, suddenly, he was playing and singing for these students at the ceremony. It was breathtaking. It shifted the whole room, everyone, me included. Ryan was dumbstruck, like he could see Sean in a whole new way. I needed to hear it, too, and I couldn't believe he was finally doing it. I actually stopped working on the women, and I walked over to him and said, "I don't know whether to smack you right now or to be happy." He just kind of blushed and kept playing.

And after working on the two sisters for an hour, they were sitting up on the bed laughing with each other. So we were done there.

Then we went outside, and there was another woman there who she was very much playing the victim. She kept talking about everything that was wrong with her, everything bad that was going on in her life. I said to everybody around the fire, "Why don't we celebrate life right now? Put your hands up and say, "Hey, thank you stars. Thank you for allowing us to have this life, this beautiful time together, this moment, everything we have."

Well, she didn't like that at all. She's said, "I can't do this" and she stalked inside the house. I waited for a bit to go after her, not wanting to feed into martyring energy, until Spirit told me, "Okay, go work on her." So I went to Ryan and said, "Let's go work on her. Let's just give her love."

So we went in and started to give her pure unconditional love. This woman had had severe trauma in her life. And as we worked on her, she started to "give birth." That's something that women do a lot in ceremony, energetically. Not birthing an actual baby, but birthing something they need to release or let go of or create. It's amazing, because their bodies actually gear up as if it's a real birth. Their hips widen, their legs spread out, their stomach starts to get bigger and whatever it is they're releasing, you can feel it. Afterward, the stomach shrinks back down. It's really remarkable.

In this case, she was actually rebirthing all of her children because she'd had traumatic, abusive births. So Ryan was getting tissues, and we were really like doulas, like birthing assistants. There had been five births, so it was a rather drawn-out ordeal. She was really tired afterwards, and went to sleep, sleeping it off.

After that, I was tired too. I went and checked on everybody. Everybody was quieting down for the night. But Tristan was still up and around.

I started to work on Tristan. Intuitively, I asked him where his star was, and he was startled. He said, "How did you know that I had this little star?" He had a star pendant lying next to his bed. I said, "I don't know. I was just told to ask you about your star." He had just gotten it from a local shop and had been told it was supposed to have healing properties. I got the message that he had to have that star, and I put it on his chest, and did bodywork, and he had some healing from that around intimacy and women.

He started talking to me about relationships, because that was his issue. He was 45 years old, had been married, was divorced, had been single for quite a long time, and was contemplating getting into a relationship again, but he was really scared.

Right then, St. Germaine "came in." When this happens for me, it's just a channeling. I can feel him, and I get messages through my own thought forms. Mount Shasta is known for St. Germaine's energy. He just comes into the space whenever he feels like it. He appeared to me and said, "Something's going to happen in the next 24 hours and it's going to be a radical change. And you will have a choice to make."

I was kind of blown away. I said, "What choice?" He just said, "It's going to be huge."

Ryan and Sean came and joined Tristan and me as we were talking. Ryan was looking at me in that way he does, where I could tell he was thinking he was in love with me, in spite of everything that we had said about not being the ones for each other.

Then Tristan looked at Sean and said, "When did you really get used to being married?" Sean replied, "Well, I'm not used to it yet. It's hard. It means giving up your friends. It means leaving your home, moving away. I still have difficulty with it." Once again, he just said all the wrong things.

I was upset. I didn't care who was there because I'm very authentic. My students see me go through things, and I'm fine with it. I said, "If you're in love with somebody and you've been married for three years, you should be happy about being around them at this point and not missing your old life."

Ryan was staring right at me, and I knew what he was thinking. He was thinking that Sean was not in love with me, but he is.

Tristan felt terrible, like "Oh my God, I can't believe I just started this." I said, "No, it needed to go here. This needed to come out." But I went upstairs by myself, pretty angry and hurt. We had been doing so incredibly well, had felt so happy and connected, and yet here this kind of thing was still arising. It was disconcerting.

Ryan came upstairs after me and sat down on the bed. He said, "That is not love. That's not someone who's in love with you." And he pulled me to him and kissed me, a real kiss, deep.

But I pulled away. I didn't surrender to the kiss. I said, "No. We agreed that we're not going to be together. And Sean and I were doing well. You saw it at the last ceremony in Sedona. I have to talk to Sean." And I left Ryan there and went downstairs to find Sean.

Sean and I went back upstairs to our bedroom and Ryan was gone. I told Sean about Ryan kissing me. He was extremely upset. I lay down with him and we talked. I said, "Obviously I have work to do too, clearly I have some kind of clogged heart space, but you say crazy things that don't make sense to me if you love me. I feel like we go two steps forward and one step back. I keep thinking we're having breakthroughs and I feel like 'this is what I wanted, I have the husband and partner I always wanted' and we're working together, flowing…and then there's this step backwards."

Once again, he appealed to me for my understanding of his clumsiness. As before, he said, "Rebecca, I don't talk the way I should. I don't say things right. What I said is not what I meant to say." He told me again how much he loves me. And once again, I relented because I could see it. I could tell by how upset he was that he loved me. I could tell by the way he was looking at me. Yes, he says the stupidest stuff sometimes. But he loves me.

So we were processing through all this. We talked about how much we do love each other. He clarified and explained what he was trying to say when he so ineptly answered Tristan. As we talked, my breast started to drain *rapidly*. I actually pulled up my shirt it show him. It was gushing out like crazy. I said, "You can't make this up." He was amazed as well. We kept talking and working, and by the morning, he and I were good.

He was not the happiest when he had to cook breakfast with Ryan. But I reminded him, "Ryan is still a catalyst here." Sean had recognized that before, and it was still true.

I went out to the tent to talk to Ryan after breakfast. I knew that he was thinking that he still had a chance with me, for us to be together, and I needed to make things very clear and set them straight.

I said, "So you think you're in love with me? And he said, "Yes. I shouldn't have said that in Sedona about you not being the one for me. I do think I'm in love with you."

But I was still feeling like the place we had come to in Sedona was real. That clarity—that we were not for each other and that I was going to be with Sean—held true. I was a little bit attracted to Ryan, maybe I always would be, but I knew that he was not my twin flame or my true love.

I didn't say this about loud to him, but I think he knew. I just looked at him. We sat there in silence for a little bit, I rubbed his back lightly for a moment, and then I walked out to say my goodbyes to the first group.

RYAN'S TIME

Then the first group of people left, and the second group of people came in. Included in this group was a woman named Hannah. She came in with this very beautiful light around her. She was extremely vibrant, bright, a beautiful soul. The very first night I started working with her, she just knew energy work, naturally, even though she didn't have a lot of previous experience with it. We were working well together. I had a very good vibe with her and we were getting along really well. She was only 27, but had a lovely maturity. (Ryan was about 40 at this point.)

Hannah started to notice Ryan, and I noticed her noticing. I knew immediately what that look that she was giving him was about. She was drawn to him. But he was totally oblivious. Even when she told him, "When I look at you, I see a real shaman." And it's true—when you see Ryan in ceremony, he *is* that way. He's a different person in ceremony. He knows what he's doing in energy work and his heart's so into it, and you can tell this is the soul of who and what he is.

So she was looking at him all wowed and starry-eyed. I was picking that up—and he wasn't. Then at some point, she actually told me that she felt like he was her twin flame. And this woman was beautiful, smart, pure, astute energetically—a real catch.

So when St. Germaine said, "you have a big decision to make in 24 hours" I knew that this was it. Ryan was still looking at me. He didn't even notice this woman. I could have him if I wanted. But was that what

I wanted? Here I had this incredible husband with whom I had worked so hard to create a great life and partnership, who I felt was my match—and here was this beautiful amazing woman who was obviously taken with Ryan. Was I going to hold on to Ryan, or let him go?

I knew it was time to really let him go.

Then Ryan came up to me asked me to work on his back. I said no. I knew I was going to try to get them together, so I wasn't going to work on him in front of her. I said, "No. We'll do it later." He was hurt. He said, "I work on your back whenever you need it. I'm really needing you to work on my back right now. And you're not going to do it?" I said, "I promise you, I'll tell you why later. I have a good reason. It'll be worth it. Trust me."

The ceremony continued. As always, we had really cool healings. One woman had been sexually molested as a child and at some point passed out, falling over from a sitting position as this memory overcame her. We carried her into the living room and all began working on her energetically and giving her unconditional love. I knew that the whole group had to be together giving her unconditional love. It worked—she woke up, came out of it, and said that the unconditional love had completely healed her.

In a lull when things were flowing smoothly and I wasn't needed, I went upstairs and called Ryan up there. I said, "I have something to tell you." I told him what Hannah said. It dawned on him slowly, and then he got a smile on his face that was amazing. I had literally never seen him interested in any woman besides his ex and me. There could be beautiful girls dancing naked in front of him, and he didn't care. But now he actually had a look on his face that told me he was very intrigued. He said, "Really?" "I said, "Yes, and she's a really decent person; she lives on the beach in California; and she does really good, pure energy work. Her spirit is beautiful." He looked thunderstruck, but we went back downstairs and I could see that this news had really touched him.

We continued to work on the students, and then Hannah and Ryan began working on each other. I could tell they were connecting. They were getting closer. I sat in a chair and watched, and tried to figure out how I really felt about this. I felt happy, and I knew Saint Germaine had been right. This was it for me and Ryan. Ryan had found his person.

Just then Willow came out to where I was sitting and exclaimed, "Mommy, you have to draw Chuck E. Cheese!" I said, "What? Just have your dad do it. You know I can't draw." Sean was the artist in the family. I've always said that one thing I can't do is draw—even though Sean very kindly helped me try to learn. But she was adamant and persistent, shouting at me, "You have to draw Chuck E. Cheese!"

Another thing that Spirit has always told me is that I will heal others by being with my family. I've always been told that. So even though it seemed like a crazy moment and a random thing, I trusted that everything that happens in ceremony is for a reason, and I also know how uncanny Willow is with her intuitions and timing. So I knew that for whatever reason, I had to draw Chuck E. Cheese with Willow.

So I pulled up on my cell phone a photo of Chuck E. Cheese, and it was a photo of Chuck E. Cheese holding a little girl and looking at her. So I had to draw him paying attention to a kid, which exactly what Willow was asking me to do with her right then—pay attention to her. I knew that this was important. I know that sometimes I get too busy and I want to say, "Willow, go do have your dad do it."

But I didn't do that this time, even though I really wanted to. I really tried to draw Chuck E. Cheese. I was trying my best. Of course, she was watching me and saying "Mommy, that doesn't look like Chuck E. Cheese!" So I called Sean over and asked, "Can you please help me draw this Chuck E. Cheese?" And it turned out to be really cute and profound. He said, "Sure. You can just fix what you did here and make the eyes like this." He was showing me how to do it.

All of a sudden as we worked on the drawing, a commotion broke out in the living room with four people who were going through some intense purging and healing. One woman was crying. And I heard my guidance say "Just finish drawing Chuck E. Cheese." Now, that is not me. My natural inclination would a hundred percent be to go to the clients. But I said, "I have to sit here and finish this Chuck E. Cheese drawing." Sean said, "Okay."

We just spent a few more minutes doing the drawing, but by the time we were done drawing Chuck E. Cheese, the whole living room was singing in harmony. They had gotten through it without me, and I had this beautiful family moment. It was an important lesson on several levels. It was important that I be with my family and be present, so that was one lesson. But it was also that as I was bringing the picture to harmony—bringing my family to harmony—I was harmonizing my students.

This whole time, my breasts had continued draining and healing. By the end of the trip, it all was completely drained. There had been small round cylinders into which the fluid was draining, but at some point I couldn't stand having those anymore, so I looked up on YouTube how to take drains out, and Sean helped me. Then I just put the tubes in my bra with tissues. Again, by now I had stopped the antibiotics too.

At the end of the ceremony we had integration. Everyone was hugging and took pictures, we had a final breakfast, and said our goodbyes.

Ryan actually ended up going back to California with Hannah. He had come to Mount Shasta with all of his bags packed. He had left Missouri. He had said, "I'm never going back to Missouri. I don't know where I'm going after this, but something big's going to happen." It was like somehow he knew. So he ended up going back with Hannah to San Luis Obispo.

Ryan is still in the relationship with Hannah to this day. It's had its ups and downs, but he's very happy. We'd actually planned to work together again in September 2023, but while he was developing the relationship with Hannah, I had this sense that we should do our own things and just let our own relationships develop. I had always wanted Sean to be that one I worked with anyway. Ryan reached out to me soon after Shasta and said, "I kind of want to do my own thing right now." So we were on the same page. It was perfect.

So we flew back, and after we had been home for a few days, I went back to the doctor to get checked. I got blood work and the breast was examined. I was completely healed and my bloodwork was totally normal. A couple of the doctors were really happy, but one of the doctors said sourly, "It's going to come back." Whatever!

Then everything was pretty smooth throughout the summer, just kind of just living life, which was really so good, so full. I had healed this intense breast infection/heart clearing, and Ryan had moved on in a healthy way, and our family was thriving.

But Sean and I still weren't done with catalysts to our relationship.

⋘⋙ **LESSON** ⋙⋘

I've been very open about the back-and-forth movements that occurred during my twin flame journey. This is really common in a twin flame journey, and when you read others' twin flame experiences you'll see this reflected. However, sometimes as you're living it you can feel like you're losing your mind.

On this journey, one of the many healings that can occur is our deprogramming from the collective belief that relationships should be "perfect" or somehow perfectly clear-cut. The twin flame experience isn't just about a partner—it's about you and life. It's about developing an intimate relationship with yourself. Unless you honestly follow your heart, you will never truly know yourself.

The kind of monogamy I believe in is what I would call natural monogamy. This means that when you're faithful to just one person, it's because your heart only desires that one person. Not because you made a vow, oath, or commitment. Many people will disagree with this. I believe, though, that you're not being true to yourself if you're doing something because of a "rule" or expectation that society or anyone else imposes on you. As soon as you put a rule into your relationship, you've instituted a precedent for conditional love.

I wouldn't want to discount that a "back and forth" or moving from relationship to relationship can also be a form of addiction. It's important to be discerning. Earnestly exploring and following your heart to understand the highest truth for your destiny is one thing. But to move from relationship to relationship for "instant" gratification is not a healthy or high-vibration energy and will only lead to a life of loneliness and disappointment.

This is why we need to work on our own internal wounds 24/7 to make sure our decisions are coming from our true being and grounded through the heart space. This is a lifelong journey in which it's important to stay true to yourself and the life you want to create.

My guides told me once that humans' hearts are only open at the most 50%. This is why we live lives that bring not only love but also experiences of grief and sorrow. These experiences all aid in opening the heart. The more we learn to open our hearts, the less we have to experience pain to open the heart space.

Tantra means "to weave in and out." When you're on this journey, people—mirrors—will weave in and out to show you what you need to see and feel in order to open your heart. This took me a while to accept. But it was clearly a part of my journey.

Chapter Twenty-Four

BEFORE I DESCRIBE WHAT HAPPENED NEXT, it's very important to emphasize, again, that no matter what I might be experiencing in my relationships, and however much I can point to the behavior of someone else, I always know that ultimately I'm the one who needs to do the clearing. Everything I'm experiencing is a reflection of my external reality.

For example, when I'm struggling with something about Sean's behavior or our relationship, I almost always find out later that it was my own clearing that I had to do—and then he shifts.

With that in mind, and to set the stage for what happened next, I need to explain a few dynamics that Sean and I still struggled with at this time, in spite of all our healing and clearing and growth. These were areas of tension or inflammation that we still tended to argue about.

One was that Sean never called me pretty—ever. He literally told me that I'm like the "99%" of the world. The really pretty women are the 1%. He'd actually said that to me. I could go out and other men would notice me, call me beautiful, but Sean just didn't. He would admire a photo on his phone and note that a woman was beautiful, and then he would tell me I was "cute."

Another inflamed area was that Sean just didn't stand up for me. If someone was yelling at me, he'd let them yell at me. He would let me take the heat in situations. He wasn't protective. When as a couple or family we were getting "screwed over" by something in some way, I was the one who had to stand up for us and deal with it—let's say, with contractors, or banks. That was something that if I would've changed if I could.

As you'll recall, I had told my guides that I want divine masculine *everywhere*. That was my request. And as I said earlier, I believe it can come from everywhere and everybody, at any time, in any situation. We have to be discerning, but divine masculine is not isolated to one person. And I'd been experiencing divine masculine showing up a lot in my life, in large and small ways, from ceremonies to healings to small encounters on planes and in cafes. There was a lot to be amazed by in all that had shown up for me already.

But I had a very full, complete, and unabashed vision for what I want in my life and relationship, and part of that vision was for my partner to look at me and think I'm beautiful. I think even if your wife is not necessarily beautiful to other people, she should be beautiful to you. And we'd had this particular conversation many times; I would tell him, "If you don't find me attractive, you should not be with me."

Of course, he would answer, "But I do think you're beautiful. I call you beautiful all the time." And I'd say, "You've *never* called me beautiful, ever. That has *never* come out of your mouth unless I'm yelling at you about how you don't do it!"

And now, into this picture, comes Sean's best friend Liam.

LIAM'S VISIT

Liam's wife had fairly recently died of cancer, as you'll recall, and we had attended her funeral on our trip to England.

I knew from that trip that Liam was a bright light. He was full of energy. He's extremely good-looking, successful, well-dressed, well-spoken, well-mannered, and fun. He was scheduled to visit on August 7, for about ten days, planning to stay with us for seven days and the rest in Washington, D.C.

I can't explain what I knew, but I was nervous about his visit, and I didn't really know why.

Liam kept to himself the first night of the visit, just getting settled in. We had planned to do an ayahuasca ceremony with him during this visit, because he wanted to try it. We thought that there might be some healing regarding his wife in that process.

But first, we had a whitewater rafting day planned with two of my girlfriends. They were coming down to spend the night for a couple nights as well. Our lake house in a resort area where there's whitewater rafting and skiing very nearby, so there are lots of fun things to do.

So my friends arrived the first day, and we were getting ready to go rafting. And this is where things started to get interesting. Liam was really noticing and appreciating me.

For instance, I have this funny quirk where pretty much the only time I drink any more is when I'm going to be in cold water. So I was making a drink, and Liam said, "Why are you drinking at 11:00 AM?" I replied, "So I can get in the cold water." He just burst out laughing and said, "Wow, a girl after my own heart." Jokingly, Sean said, "Hey, I'm going to have you stay in a hotel." But Liam wasn't really hitting on me. He just seemed to think I was really funny.

Then we got to the rafting site. I was excited. I love a good whitewater rafting trip. This was a manmade course, so you can go wild on it and know you're not going to get hurt, as you might on a totally natural course. The group was my daughter Ariel, her friend, and Liam and Sean. The guide arrived and said, "Okay, guys. I can go mild, or I can go severe, but you all have to agree." I said, "Well, that's good. We already had this meeting right before you came. We decided we want crazy." Liam started laughing even harder, and again just seemed really taken with how funny I was.

We got in the raft and we had the most fun, crazy whitewater ride that you can imagine. We were going over waterfalls, jumping out…the guide kind of fixed the ride so that we would fall out. I was stuck under the raft at one point, but I wasn't scared. It was just an incredibly fun time. Everyone was laughing and spirits were high. Liam was really having a great time.

After the rafting, we went out to eat. We took Liam to the bar where Sean and I had met and gotten married. We wanted him to see that. We told him the whole story. And then we went back to the house and everything was pretty normal.

ILLUMINATING ISSUES

The next day, we went on our boat. For some reason, I was kind of nervous that day. Just a nervous energy. I was the one driving the boat, and Liam was kind of surprised. He observed, "Wow, you do everything around here."

He was pretty observant, because as I said, that's kind of true. Before we went out boating, he had been sitting on the porch as I was draining the hot tub. I had wanted to refill it and heat it up for when my friends got there. He asked, "Do you need help?" I said no, I'm good. This was unusual to him. Liam was more accustomed to a typical male/female relationship where women don't do much, where the man takes care of a lot, if not everything. But the truth is, I can do just about anything.

So I had filled up the hot tub, and we all went out to the boat. I got behind the wheel, and again he was surprised. I told him I had been driving a boat since I was 16. He nodded, but he was watching me closely.

I think his keen eyes on me were making me nervous, because in spite of all my boating experience, I did something dumb. We'd had a nice time anchored for a while, just laying around on the boat in the sun. But when we went to go back, I started to drive the boat with the anchor in, and the boat got caught. So we were stuck, and someone needed to swim out and go under the boat and cut the rope.

It was so interesting how this happened, and it felt like the universe was again bringing this issue forward where I had to do everything—even all the "guy stuff." Because Liam had just had eye surgery, he technically wasn't supposed to swim under the water. He had already gone under the water once for whitewater rafting. So, he said, he could not swim and get his eyes wet again, especially not in that dirty lake water.

He looked at Sean, expecting him to be the one to do it. Sean said, "No, I can't do that." So there I was again, the fixer! I dove in, and I tried to cut the rope. But I couldn't do it—it was just way too stuck. I couldn't stay under long enough and the pocket knife I was using wasn't enough. We had to call a scuba diver who eventually came out and cut the rope.

After we paid the scuba diver, we went and had dinner at a restaurant on the lake. When we got home, I was really tired so I took a shower and went to bed. Sean and Liam sat downstairs and talked.

The next day, my friends came out for the ayahuasca ceremony. We spent the day getting ready, and as we began, we were all sitting out by the fire. I gave Liam and my friends Sherry and Patricia the ayahuasca, and Sean and I had some as well.

Liam started to talk about his wife, who had died of bladder cancer. It had been a year and a half since she had passed, and he still had his wedding ring on. He had mentioned that he wanted to get into another relationship, but that he felt like there was an appropriate time limit. He had an idea what that time limit was, but he wouldn't really say.

Once he had taken the brew, all this stuff really started coming out. He began talking about how people say she can see him, is looking down at him, and that it makes him nervous to think about taking his ring off while she's looking at him. He felt quite guilty. We talked for a while about when he could move on. He said it would have to be acceptable to his family, especially his daughter. He said he would think about it.

We also processed some issues with his daughter who had just had a miscarriage. He talked about how his wife was the one who would have come up with the special ideas for his daughter's birthday, and he didn't know if he could. Then he came up with his own conclusions about what to do. He wanted to be there for his daughter in the best way possible, since she had lost her mother and now lost a baby.

It was fairly normal, mild processing for ayahuasca. I didn't give him much at all—I just let him share and process. It was the first time he had done it, and he didn't throw up. But he did process a good bit. I did some energy work on him.

We got into the hot tub afterward to relax and wind down. At this point, I was still very much into Sean, touching him, kissing him. At the end of the night, we all went to bed, planning to do another night of ayahuasca the next night.

The next day, Liam, Sean, Willow, my friends Sherry and Patricia and I went back out on the boat with plans to surf. We had a special boat that creates surfing waves behind it so that you can surf behind the boat. I hadn't actually tried that much yet to surf with the boat, and now I was determined to learn. It's a learning process, where you get up behind the boat like you do when water skiing, then let go of the rope and surf the waves.

It was in this process that I could start to see how alike Liam and I were, how we had similar personalities. We went at many things the same way. We're both entrepreneurs, both leaders. We don't give up till we've mastered something. With the surf boat, we were both very intent on learning and not giving up. I would have been on that boat forever. So we just kind of bonded and connected through that process, through the rafting and then surfing and tubing. Again, everybody had a really good time.

After a morning of playing hard on the water, we decided to get off the lake to eat lunch. I was driving the boat to our lunch spot. (There are a few major restaurants right on the lake, with docks, and in the summer they have bands and dancing.) I was apparently going too fast through a no-wake zone. A guy on a pontoon boat with a bunch of kids started yelling at us, "I can't believe you're going that fast." I wasn't really going *that* fast, but I did create a wake, I suppose, in that no-wake zone. The guy was just really angry, and he just kept yelling at us as we went by.

And Sean yelled back at him, "Why are you yelling at me? It's my wife that's driving."

Well, that just blew Liam's mind. He was like, *"What?"* I joked, "Oh yes—my hero." I was used to it. But really, it was kind of insane. It was like the universe was bringing all this out for me to see, for Liam to see, and for me to see it through someone else's eyes—to see that it wasn't right. It was highlighting boldly this way that Sean doesn't stand up for me, and lets me do everything.

We parked the boat at a restaurant and went to eat. At lunch I reminded everyone, "Hey, we're going to do the brew again tonight!" But Liam said he didn't really want to do it again. He said, "Do we have to? I think I've got the feel of it now. I don't really feel the need to do it again." I told him that of course we didn't have to—we would never force anyone to do ayahuasca. So I suggested we go out dancing instead—there are tons of dancing places where we live.

Before we went out that night, we decided to take the jet skis out to get ice cream. There are also ice cream places along the water, and you can jet ski to them instead of drive. The jet skis are supposed to have life jackets under the seats, but my daughter Ariel always misplaces the life jacket when she's putting away the jet ski instead of putting it away. So Willow, Liam, Sean, and I got all the way out to the lake with the jet skis and we were one life jacket short. We didn't want to go all the way back to the house. Sean looked at me and said, "I need your life jacket," and put his hand out for it. And I gave it to him.

Liam was now completely agape, stunned. He looked at Sean like "What the fuck is going on? I can't even believe what I'm seeing." Liam and Sean had been friends for a long time, and he did sort of know that Sean was that way, but he had never really seen it in action in a relationship like this. He was absolutely dumbstruck. And Sean didn't even notice Liam looking at him that way.

After the jet ski/ice cream incident, we all went on a walk together to take the dogs out before we went dancing that night. Liam was asking questions about the dogs, like about their schedule and how often they need to go. I answered, and Sean—who does walk the dog a lot— said something like "How would you know? You *never* walk the dogs." In other words, he alluded to me kind of slacking.

Liam was disturbed by this and jumped to my defense. He said, "Dude, I've only been here for a couple of days, but she does everything. Like *everything*. I've never seen anything like it." He was like, "Dude, why are you treating your woman like this? I never knew you." Sean just said, "What would you know?" Liam said, "Well, from what I've seen…" I was quiet, but I felt affirmed in something I now knew was not just my own perception.

BIZARRE BLACKOUT

That night we all went out dancing as planned. It was beyond fun. The band was fantastic. And it was the kind of place where you can bring kids and the kids play outside. I was dancing with my friends and we were having a blast. We even got invited to dance up front near the band, which is amazing when you can get a place up front.

Now I have to give credit where it's due, since I'm spending so much time on these "lapses" of Sean's, or gaps in his attention or awareness. Sean is an absolute sweetheart when it comes to knowing when I'm having fun, and letting me do my thing. On this night, as he often will do, he said, "Hey, I'll take Willow. You love dancing. Go dance." He's so thoughtful when it comes to Willow and helping me.

So I was having a blast with my friends, and Sean and Liam were outside talking while Sean hung out with Willow in the children's area.

But then after a while, I turned around on the dance floor and I saw Liam, and he was waving at me. My friends were still dancing near the band, and he was about 20 feet away. He had a big smile on his face, watching me. And then it hit me, this wave of attraction. I can't even really explain it.

I started to walk towards the bar, which was behind him. He followed me.

Now, I should mention that I *was* drinking that night. As I've mentioned, I don't usually like to drink, other than that cold-water quirk. I had told my ex-husband about why I didn't drink any more, about why I would rather be present. Liam had kept offering to buy me a drink, though, and after asking for club soda a few times and him wheedling me to have a real drink, I finally gave in and said, "I like Bloody Marys." But I didn't drink that much on this night, and definitely not enough to explain what happened next.

All I remember is him catching up to me and pulling me towards him at the bar. Our faces were close. He looked right in my eyes. I was looking at him and I could feel the energy and I didn't know what to say. I wanted to break the silence, and I'm so authentic that I just can't seem to keep my mouth shut sometimes. So I said, "You know, I'm having....feelings." He said, "I am, too."

And then for some reason, I had a strong instinct to ask this question: "When did you start to feel this way?" I just had an intuition, and I wanted to know if I was crazy. And he said, "At the funeral."

I wasn't shocked. Even at the funeral I had the feeling he was having some feelings for me. Sean actually did notice it then, even though he seemed dazedly oblivious to it now. Sean and I were fighting so much on that trip that we had our rings off. That may be why Liam's wife, at the time, entered my field and took over in this way. It made sense of the way I felt like I knew him. That's why there was a strong sense of comfort and magnetic pull. But at that time, it made no sense to my brain, and I certainly didn't think of him romantically in that kind of setting.

But even back then Liam had been pulling me aside and wanting to talk to me. Now that I understand what happened, I think she wanted time with him alone. And now, she was taking over again.

Sean noticed it back then. During this visit, he was just kind of in a daze, to the point that my friends couldn't even believe how clueless he was. But in England, I remembered that he felt so sick all the time that all he could do was go to bathroom. He's more in tune now, yet at the time he just knew something felt really off.

Meanwhile, Sean was still out at the swing set, and Liam was holding me close at the bar, locking eyes with mine.

And before I say what happened next, I have to bring in one more thing that had happened at lunch earlier that day. I'd had my head down looking at something, and Willow was sitting next to me and Sean was sitting on the other side of the table. Sean started saying, "Hey, beautiful. Hey, beautiful. Hey, beautiful. Hey, beautiful." I didn't even look up, because, of course, he never calls me beautiful. I thought he was talking to Willow the whole time.

After about the tenth time he said it, I looked up and was like, "What the hell? Are you talking to me?" I don't know if he was testing me or doing it because I had yelled at him recently for not saying I was pretty. But I said, "Well, this should prove to you that you never say that to me, because it wasn't even a thought in my head that you might be talking to me."

So that had just happened at lunch. Now Liam was looking right at me after pulling me close and telling me he had feelings for me. Then he looked me right in the eyes and said, "You are drop-dead gorgeous."

The thing is, although he had seen Sean not stick up for me, and let me do everything, and take my life jacket...he *didn't* know Sean and I were having *this* issue. He didn't know that Sean never called me pretty or beautiful, and that it hurt, and that he and I argued about it.

So the universe was turning up the light on this too. But I was stunned and my head was in a whirl. At the time, I thought to my myself, "I can't believe this is happening. I don't understand why this is happening. This is crazy." I remember telling him, "I don't get this. I'm around a lot of men. I don't go around doing this."

And then...I sort of blacked out. The whole rest of the conversation was blotted out. I don't remember much else. The only other thing I remember is my two friends coming up to us and it was quite awkward; they were actually trying to pull me away, and I wasn't having it. I was saying, "I'm finishing this conversation." But I didn't remember anything else we said.

I don't remember getting from the bar to the car. It was like being drugged. Not just drinking or blacking out. It was like nothing I'd experienced other than being drugged one time in college. Apparently I sat way back in the SUV, where you'd put luggage or gear, and I said to Liam "Come sit with me, I want to finish this conversation." (He refused.) I don't remember anything else about getting home and going to bed. Sean said that he had to help me up to bed, and assumed I was drunk. Liam and Sean afterward went out in the hot tub.

UNEXPLAINABLE

The next morning, Liam and Sean went jet skiing by themselves. I woke up in a huge amount of grief. I couldn't explain it, I didn't understand it, and it felt awful.

We had already planned to go out and listen to a band that afternoon. In the summer, there are bands everywhere at the lake. We were going to hear a Rolling Stones tribute band, and we had already planned that for Saturday. Some of us were going to go over late morning and get seats before the afternoon concert, since it gets crowded fast. So my two friends and I had planned to go save us a table, while they were jet skiing. We would meet them there later.

Sherry and Patricia were not happy with me after the scene they'd witnessed at the bar the night before with me and Liam. They were both good friends, so I would have expected their understanding. Also, both work for AWAKE, so they were scared to upset me, which is silly because they should be able to say anything to me. But they were definitely judging me. They were shocked by my behavior with Liam.

As I found out later, besides judging my behavior in general—a married woman seemingly going after her husband's best friend—each of them had ulterior motives. Both of them were interested in Liam. Which was understandable; any eligible single woman would be. Gorgeous blue eyes, English accent, kind, mannered, wealthy—he was an amazing catch. The funny thing was that neither of them knew the other had designs on him.

I didn't know all that till later, though, and the fact was that Liam wasn't interested in either of them. He was drawn to me, and I knew it was crazy, but that was why I wanted help. I kept telling them I didn't remember anything, that I felt like I had been drugged and I was so sad and couldn't explain it, and wanted their support processing. Normally they would have engaged me and helped me sort it out, but now they just stared at me like I was an alien.

So we sat there holding the seats, waiting for the guys, and then I texted Sean to ask what drinks everyone wanted, because it was really busy. I went to the bar to get the drinks, so I wasn't at the table when they showed up. But I saw them walk in, and Liam hurried over to the bar to help me with the drinks. Everything he was doing was like we were together; anyone looking at us who didn't know us would have thought we were the couple.

He grabbed the drinks from me and put them down the table. Then he looked at me and said quietly, "Are we okay?"

I said, "Look, I was going to bring it up when it felt appropriate. I really need to know some of the things I said to you last night. I remember some of them, but I don't remember all of them. Let's talk about it later." He nodded.

So we sat down. We were at a table with three benches around it, and two people can fit on a bench. Somehow, Liam ended up sitting next to me with Sean sitting across from us. I sat first, so that was what the guys did. My friends were looking at each other wide-eyed, like "what is going on?" And yet Sean still didn't seem to think anything of it.

We got back home from the band around 5. When we got off the boat, parked, and put the cover on, he and I were walking together toward the house. And that's when Liam said to me, "So, you told me that you love me." I was like, *What?* I said, "I'm sorry. That was so crazy. I do crazy stuff sometimes when I'm drinking."

He was really hurt that I said that. He said, "Oh, that's why you did it." We got into the house, and he walked downstairs to the room he was staying in.

I felt terrible. I knew it really wasn't that. I had not been drunk. I remembered before and after the conversation. Only that conversation was blacked out.

I wondered if I had been channeling his wife. Sometimes when I channel, I don't remember things. And we'd just done a ceremony, and I'm a conduit, so that could have been it. I just didn't know what was going on. Later, I would understand, but at the time it felt overwhelming and inexplicable.

I followed him downstairs. The hot tub area is also off the bottom floor where his room was. His room door was open, so I followed him into his room. I said, "I'm sorry. I shouldn't have said that I said those things because I was drunk. I wasn't drunk and I do have feelings. I just didn't remember saying I loved you. I'm sorry. I don't know what to say."

He still seemed hurt and miffed. He said, "Well, you don't seem like the type of person who doesn't know what to say." I said, "Come out here with me so we can talk." We went out to the hot tub and I started doing hot tub maintenance chemicals. I said, "I don't remember saying it. I don't know why I don't remember. But I'm sure I felt it at the time if I said it."

He said, "Rebecca, if this wasn't my best friend, I would be all over this. You're the woman I've always wanted." He said that even said that after being married, he always wished for someone with my kind of energy. "We get along so well. We can play together. You'd be perfect for me. But you're my best friend's wife." And of course, I completely understood that, and also...I *was* the wife. I was married.

We talked a little more, but then we were joined at the hot tub by Sean and my friends. Still, Liam and I were pretty close talking in the hot tub that night. My friends still thought it was very strange. Sean was still just kind of in a daze. It *was* really strange. I couldn't explain it, but I think with the slightest bit of encouragement from Liam I would've left with him. I had never felt like that. Even with Ryan. Ryan had asked me to leave so many times, and even though I wondered a lot and questioned a lot (and that one time I had told Sean about how I felt and asked him not to make me choose because I felt like I would go with Ryan), I *never* left Sean for Ryan.

A STRANGE TRIP

The next day, we drove out to Chesapeake, Maryland, to go sailing. I had known that Liam sailed, and I had booked this trip for him in advance. I had really just booked everything that he loved. He was floored that I had guessed all his wishes for the trip. He said, "How did you know everything?" I shrugged, "I don't know, I guess I just tapped in."

So we had gotten an Airbnb in Chesapeake and rented a sailboat. Liam, Sean, Ariel, Ariel's friend Ella, Willow and I all went. We even brought the dogs. Liam would be leaving the next day for the Washington, DC, part of his trip.

All I could think about was that he was leaving. It was on my mind the entire time. The sadness was so deep. I tried to act happy, though, and we had fun on the sailboat. We had a sailing instructor. Liam had been a sailor in the Navy, but hadn't sailed for a while.

Besides being sad, the other thing that was gnawing at me all day was that I was receiving downloads of messages I was supposed to give him. It was overwhelming and I didn't know what to do with it. There was all this info and I had to remember it. Later I would understand where it was coming from, but at the time I had no idea. I just tried to take in and hold on to the messages, while grappling with this overpowering grief and trying to keep it together for this day of sailing.

We sailed the boat all day. Everyone was hungry after that, so we planned to go out for a big dinner. But as soon as we got off the boat, I said quietly, "I absolutely need to talk to you tonight." He said, "When is that going to happen? I said, "We have to walk the dogs when we get back to the Airbnb, so you come with me."

So we did that while everyone else got ready for dinner. I knew we wouldn't have much time. I had a lot of messages. There were messages about a particular picture that needed to be rehung on the wall, blown up and put in a gold frame. His eyes got big; he said, "I know what you're talking about, I put that picture up. It's a photo of Carrie that the family and I decided on." I said, "No, not that one, that's the wrong one. This is a photo where her hair is all messed up, a special moment." He was flabbergasted. He knew just what I was talking about.

I continued, "And another thing is, you can't be walking around with grief imprints thinking you're helping Louie, your grandson. You need to resolve your own grief so he's not carrying all this sadness."

When I was done with the messages he said, "We need to get back, it's going to look weird." And he was back to saying, "I can't do this to Sean."

So we went back and went to dinner with everyone. Dinner was really bad for me. My daughter Ariel, who knows me so well and is really sensitive, said she had never seen me this sad. She said, "Come and walk with me to the bathroom, Mom," and then tried to tell me, "You're going to be okay. Sometimes when people leave you get sad." She was really sweet. But she was worried. The insane thing was that Sean still didn't seem to notice.

After dinner, back at the Airbnb, somehow Liam and I ended up outside alone again, talking. Everyone else went inside. He just looked at me and repeated, "Nothing can ever come of this. "If you were anybody else's wife…but I can't do this to my best friend's wife."

By this time, I wasn't having it. I argued, "Never say never. We don't know what's going to happen." I told him some of the things about Sean at that point that I was frustrated with, and he'd already seen some of it.

He said, "That's just his personality. That's the way he is. He's always been like that. When the rest of us guys were dating, he was doing marijuana and recreational drugs and he didn't have girlfriends. He doesn't have that social couth, he wasn't trained on how to do that. I had to teach him that you don't order before the woman at a restaurant. But he's a very amazing person inside, you know that."

I heard what he was saying, and I knew it was true, but I still said, "I might leave him. It's not because of you, so don't feel responsible. But maybe you're a catalyst. I don't know. But right now I am not happy with the way things are. And besides, I think he's still in love with his ex-girlfriend." I'd always wondered if the reason he never called me beautiful was because he was still in love with the woman he'd dated right after he met me.

Liam said, "Don't do anything. Just let me talk to him tonight." He was really trying to defend Sean and protect our marriage, help us out, even though he was so drawn to me. It was really noble.

In so many ways, Sean and I had obviously been doing so well. We had done so much work. He was doing better with the ceremonies. The tantra was amazing. We had been connecting more deeply. We were working through stuff with his mother. I had gone through all these phases where I kept letting go, and then he would show up how I wanted and I would feel like "Now I have my husband. This is the man I've always wanted." We had come so far and gotten so close and created so much. There had been moments of great clarity and certainty and deep contentment, even quite recently. But right now I was confused again.

So where was all this coming from now? I knew it seemed crazy and impulsive. But this is what a twin flame relationship is like. You just keep going deeper and deeper. I wanted pure divine masculine. I knew I already had so much, and it may sound selfish, but I also wanted the guy who calls me beautiful. I wanted the guy who stands up for me. I wanted more, and I felt I deserved more. I know that many women would settle for "enough." My sisters thought I was insane.

Another thing that's unique about me is that I invite people to show up in each moment without attachment to how it was before. And if there is some kind of new energy, I don't talk myself out of it. I'll go into it, feel it. A lot of people talk themselves out of those awarenesses and instincts and changes. I can have radical changes because I'm allowing new things to emerge in each moment, and I can process that.

A lot of the time, of course, that processing and awareness leads to a deepening of the relationships I already have. It doesn't always mean changing the circumstances—often it leads to growth and evolution in the current situation, as it had for so long with Sean. But I'm also open to change. So it wasn't out of the realm for me that maybe Liam was my true twin flame—that yes, I have someone really good, but maybe this is even better.

Liam did talk to Sean that night and was kind of feeling him out about all these things I had mentioned to him. It was so interesting, because Sean was already in bed with me, everyone but Liam had gone to bed, Liam was still sitting outside, and suddenly Sean said, "You know, I'm going to go out and talk with him. He's leaving tomorrow, so let me go hang out with him a bit." He went out and they talked for about two hours.

The next morning, my daughter Ariel (who absolutely loved Liam, by the way) wanted to take him to breakfast. She wanted to him to try Chick-Fil-A because he'd never eaten there before—they don't have them in England. It was kind of an odd breakfast choice, but they do serve breakfast and Liam was leaving later than morning. So we all went out to Chick-fil-A—except for Sean, who hates fast food and stayed behind.

At the table at Chick-Fil-A, I tried to pay for our breakfast and Liam wouldn't let me. This is another aspect of what was bewitching me. I was used to paying for a hundred percent of everything with men. But Liam was whipping out his credit card, giving it to me left and right for everything we did. He couldn't understand the way I was paying for everything. At the bar the other day he had told me, "Just stop. Stop paying for things." I had *never* experienced a man constantly handing me his credit card. And it felt so good. Liam had had a very successful business and had sold it. He was set up well.

It's not so much that I'm after big money in a man. It's the sense of being taken care of, being feminine and not always in charge of everything, that I was missing. It was another aspect of the divine masculine coming out.

Sean is amazing and is the kindest heart. And it was because of me that he quit his job. He had been making $80,000 a year, and I had said no, we're going to work together, and we did. He took that leap. And he does his share of the work. He does so much around the house, too, and I'm not unhappy with that at all. When he sold his house, he gave all of the money to help us buy the lake house. But if I didn't have my work, we'd be done. The $80,000 a year he had been making would not be enough for the type of life we live.

Anyway, we had breakfast. Liam was very standoffish during breakfast, sitting far from me. I don't know if he was sad or just not wanting Ariel to think anything bad. After we were done, Ariel suggested we stop at Dunkin' Donuts to get Sean some avocado toast and coffee. Ariel and her friend Ella went in to get it and left Liam and I in the car.

That was when Liam told me, "I talked to him about all this stuff last night, about you and how he feels. And Sean loves you. He's not in love with his ex-girlfriend. He's in love with you." I was silent.

We got back to the Airbnb. I had planned to drive with Sean to drop Liam off in DC for his last three days, but I just couldn't do it. I couldn't handle being with both of them, or saying goodbye to him in front of Sean. Ariel had planned to head back home separately, earlier than we were going to head on to DC. I decided to go back with Ariel instead of going with Sean and Liam.

So I went and told Liam I had decided to go back with Ariel. We hugged goodbye, and he kissed me lightly on the cheek. I murmured quietly, "I'm not ever going to see you again." He said, "No, you will. I'm going to come down again next summer, and whenever you come to England, we can visit." And we'd already exchanged phone numbers, because I'd sent him photos from the visit. I left with Ariel, and he was just standing on the porch, watching me leave.

So Sean went alone to drop Liam off in DC, and I was overcome with sadness. I was so sad that Ariel was concerned. She said, "Mom, you're out of it." I hadn't been that sad in a very long time. I was heartbroken. I *know* it was somehow beyond my control, whatever it was, because it was so completely weird and so powerful.

Once back home, I waited a couple of day and then I texted Liam and asked him how things were going, how he was, how his DC trip was. He replied, but then he said, "We cannot do this. We absolutely cannot do this. This is my closest friend. You're his wife. And he loves you very much."

So I texted back "Okay, I won't contact you anymore." And I didn't. That was it.

But I was a nightmare when he left.

WHAT NOW?

I was a mess. It was crazy. Sean didn't know it had anything to do with Liam. My friends said it was so obvious, but he didn't see it.

I don't even remember half of that time, but I know that I can't pretend. I've never been able to pretend. So I was yelling at Sean and complaining about everything and just going back over the things he didn't do and throwing up the life vest thing and how I don't understand it. It was bad. I hadn't felt that bad since Gabe. I actually hated Sean.

Finally, at one point he said in defeat and exasperation, "I'm just not what you want. I'll just leave." And I agreed. He had been planning to visit his father. This was in September. I said, "Why don't you ask your dad if you can stay there for a while so we can have a trial separation and see how it goes. Just so I can clear my head."

At the same time, I asked myself, "Rebecca, why are you doing this?" I didn't contact Liam. I wasn't planning to contact him. I wasn't going to try to get together with him or anything. I was just feeling like I needed space. I knew at some level I was just unraveling everything I had built and cultivated and worked for over so many years, and it didn't make sense. I couldn't explain it, but I couldn't stop it.

After Sean left, I contacted Nathan, the psychic I had worked with before who was so uncannily accurate and had predicted Sean, the lake house, and everything else. He picked up on Liam's wife. He said, "He has his wife in his field—he's trying to figure that out." I said, "She's dead." And he said, "Well, she's not seeming dead—it seems like she's here." Nathan picked up her presence and her energy as being present in this earthly realm.

This would later explain a lot. But meantime, I was still very confused…and alone.

 LESSON

When you feel something so overpoweringly that you just don't seem to have any say in it, and it doesn't make any logical sense, it's very challenging to trust that something is unfolding that does make sense on some level of reality. It's important to cultivate enough self-trust and discernment that you know when your overwhelming feelings really may just be irrational (of course, emotionally, this can happen)—and when there is something deep moving that is beyond you. If you do your work, are "clean" in your energy and then something that feels crazy hits you out of left field, don't judge yourself or dismiss it. It's important to give yourself space and time to find out what might actually be emerging. Being willing to sit in that discomfort takes a lot of courage and patience, but you will usually learn something powerful if you can do it. This is just another way of trusting life and source energy.

Chapter Twenty-Five

AFTER SENDING SEAN AWAY SO THAT I COULD have some kind of break to clear my head, I set about trying to do just that. But I didn't have any real insight yet, just confusion. I found it very strange that some other guy could make me want to leave Sean so quickly, especially when we had come such a long way and were doing so very well. This is what I had to figure out. My feelings had changed so rapidly and so drastically. If I was truly in love with Sean, as I had really come to feel, why would this have happened? How could I feel so devastated over a guy I barely know—like he's a lifelong love who had just left me? It made no sense.

Though Sean did go to Michigan to visit his dad, he said that when he got there, he just felt more than ever how much he really wanted to be in Maryland with me. He said he really wanted our family to stay together. And although I was still very confused, and had been a nightmare of criticism and resistance after Liam left, I knew deep down that I loved him dearly.

But he would be staying in Michigan to visit his family for a while longer (and he had Willow with him) because I was getting ready to go to a trip to Costa Rica for business (to meet with the architect about our new property) and a surfing retreat. This Costa Rica trip had already been planned long before all this happened. So it was a good time to take some space and let things unfold.

When he told me how he was feeling, I told him was missing him too. I said, "Okay, but let's take this time and see what happens. We'll work on it."

AN IMPORTANT TEST

Once I got to Costa Rica, Sean informed me that he would be meeting with his ex-girlfriend to say goodbye to her dying dog, who he was close to when they were dating. This was the woman he had dated right after he met me. She'd always been a sore subject for us because he talked about her quite a bit after they broke up. She was the one he talked about so much when I was pregnant with Willow, which you may recall had confused me and made me question whether Sean really wanted to be with me.

I often wondered and questioned whether he had unresolved feelings for her. Part of this thinking came from the fact that he had posted pictures of her quite often on his social media when they were dating—yet he never freely posted any pictures of me or both of us together on his social media, or really anywhere.

I remember us getting into a fight in the year 2019 because it had been eight years since they'd broken up and he was still bringing her up in conversation. At that point, I suggested, "Why don't you go and see if there's something unresolved with her? Because I'm really tired of you talking about her." Of course he denied still having feelings for her, and after that he stopped talking about her—but I felt that it was only because I threatened him.

So I actually felt relieved that he was going to go see her. I just felt like it was important to test that out. At the same time, of course, I was nervous about him seeing her—in spite of the fact that I had just developed rapid and intense feelings for his own best friend, so I knew that my apprehension was really a double standard. Clearly, I still felt very bonded to Sean because there was definitely a big part of me that felt threatened by her and did not want to find out that he still had feelings for her, or wanted to be with her. But I also did feel that it was time to finally test that theory.

I wondered, "What if he sees her after 10 years and realizes that he's still in love with her?" But I had done so much work by this time and grown so much that I quickly surrendered. I knew that if he actually was still in love with her, then that would be what was true and real, and I would have to let it go.

PALM SPRINGS

I was sitting in my hotel room in Costa Rica thinking about all this when the phone rang and I picked it up. I usually don't pick up the phone if I don't recognize the number, but for some reason I just felt compelled to this time.

I said, "Hello?" and a man at the other end started acting like I was on a radio show or something. He said, "Rebecca, I know that you love to be sung to, so just relax while I sing you a song on the guitar."

Then he started singing and playing "Desperado." I was half wondering if I was really on a radio show or if he was just pretending. But it was so odd because, as I've mentioned, I would always complain to Sean that he never sang to me and played the guitar for me. And here was this stranger singing to me who says he knows I like to be sung to. I didn't even know who this guy was.

Then he said, "I know you don't like to be called Becky, but I'm going to call you Becky for my purposes." I was totally confused. What was going on here?

It turns out that this man had been a Hollywood actor at one point. Now he was retired, but he was working with a hotel in Desert Hot Springs. They were looking to turn that resort into a healing center. He had heard about me from an AWAKE student (I found out later), especially regarding the plant medicine ceremonies that I had facilitated, and wanted to know if I would fly out and meet with him to see about creating some retreats at the hotel.

Later, I found out that he had been paralyzed in a ski accident and had healed himself through his own quantum work. Even though at the time I didn't know exactly what it was about, I knew that I had been drawn to pick up the phone for some reason. I had learned to trust the way these things came to me. I also knew that he was channeling, because of the way he knew that I couldn't stand to be called Becky, and that I loved to be sung to.

So I took a deep breath and told him sure, I could potentially do this. I told him to let me talk to my husband and we would come up with a date that perhaps I could come out and explore the possibilities there. He suggested that if possible, it would be nice to do right before Christmas.

I told him that I would get back with him later. We hung up, and I just sat there thinking, "Wow, you really can't make this stuff up."

The next day I called Sean to see what had happened with him and his ex-girlfriend, and he said that everything went smoothly.

He had decided to bring Willow with him. He said goodbye to her dog. It was very sad, he said, but the dog didn't know him any more. And he said there were no feelings there for the woman. It was just like she was an old friend.

He said that he felt really good to have seen her, for closure, because he had left her abruptly after she had given him an ultimatum about moving in with her. They had never really communicated again after that abrupt parting. So this felt like healthy completion, and he said it actually felt like he was retrieving a soul fragment back.

I felt this when I was talking to him. He just felt more…completed. So I was actually really happy that he had gone to see her. Then told him about Desert Hot Springs and the whole strange interlude with this man, Don. Sean was very supportive and said, "Okay, you have to follow the signs and see where this leads."

LIAM IS NOT GONE

Throughout the surfing trip to Costa Rica, Liam would pop in and out of my mind. Once again, this was very strange because now finally Sean and I were getting along again, quite nicely. And that's what I wanted—I didn't want that to change. I wasn't purposely thinking about Liam. Honestly, I didn't even know that much about Liam. From the start there was so little premise for this intense feeling of attraction and of loss. It absolutely felt like a force beyond my rational control.

The surfing trip went really well overall, though. We were surfing right after a full moon, during an eclipse, so the waves were just absolutely gigantic. And I met two women who I hit it off with a lot. One was from Peru and one was from China. We all kind of hung out together while we were learning how to surf. There were times on the beach we were crying to each other and working through fear and discouragement because of how big the waves were, and sometimes we were bleeding from cuts. We ended up working through a lot of stuff together. We also went salsa dancing. So I made some new friends out of it.

Something else interesting and really affirming happened on this trip. One part of the surfing trip included analyzing ourselves surfing. The coaches took videos of us surfing, and when we went back the next day the coaches would show us the videos and point out to us what we were doing well and where we could improve. I noticed that every single time I was analyzed, the surfing coach would always choose videos of me doing really well, my best surfing, and say "Good job, Rebecca." Even the other women noticed and commented on this.

On the last day, we were watching our final surfing videos, and the surfing coach came up to me and he said, "I see the medicine in you." I looked around at everybody, and my new friends from Peru and China were looking at me. I said, "You mean the surfing medicine?" He said, "You know what medicine I'm talking about. Mother Ayahuasca. I can see her in you." I was stunned. He didn't know anything about me! He didn't know what I did for work. But he looked in my body, somehow, and he could see the ayahuasca in me.

He said, "She's no longer outside of you, Rebecca. She's in you. She's a part of you. So remember, stay in your heart space, work on opening up your heart. That's what this is all about. You're doing a wonderful job." And then he kind of bowed to me.

Wow! I hugged him. It was such a privilege, and so magically affirming. I left there knowing that I was on the absolutely right track in my life and work, and blessed by this kind of magic showing up in my life all the time.

AFTER THE SURF

Then it was time for me to go back home and see Sean and Willow. It was November 15 when I got home, and everything was going well. But Liam was still flitting in and out of my mind. I was thinking about him more than I wanted to admit. I just tried to push it away. A big part of me wanted to tell Sean what was going on because part of being authentic in relationships is completely being truthful, and that's what I want and expect and demand in my relationship. So I was trying to watch for the right moment, the right space to tell him everything that had happened.

Meanwhile, I was planning this trip to Desert Hot Springs, which would be around December 15. After that, I planned to meet Sean, Willow, and my other three children in Mount Shasta for Christmas. And right after Christmas, we were planning to take Willow to Disneyland, and then from Disneyland driving to Sedona to do a plant medicine ceremony with the AWAKE students.

I was still kind of wondering what my purpose was in even going to Desert Hot Springs, just based on this one stranger's phone call and invitation. But I started doing research, and it turned out that the area's aquifer called Miracle Springs was believed to be fed by "miracle water" that came from the San Andreas fault. The place that I was going to be staying the first night, before I met Don at the resort, actually had a hot tub in the room fed by the springs. They came right up into the hotel room and into a big tub. Reportedly, this water had produced miraculous healings on people. So I was pretty excited to experience that, and if it turned out that was the purpose of the trip, I was happy with that.

I had invited one of my AWAKE co-teachers, Paulina, to join me for this resort visit. Part of it was for fun, and partly I wanted to have company in case there was something shady about this guy—you never know, and I didn't really know much about him! So we flew into Palm Springs, and took an Uber to our hotel. I had planned to spend one night in this cool hotel with the spring water tub, just to have my own space and get oriented, and then we would go to the resort the next day and meet Don.

When we got to the hotel, the first thing I did was take a bath in that miracle water, and it actually was amazing. It felt so rejuvenating I stayed in for hours, feeling aches and pains melt away. I was so impressed that I actually went out and bought gallon jugs, filled them with the water, went to the post office, and shipped them to Mount Shasta to use in making the ayahuasca brew there. I was very excited about what would come from that, and felt that if nothing else, that was indeed my purpose in discovering this place.

The next day, we got picked up at the hotel to be brought to the resort. In that little transaction was kind of a funny anecdote that illustrates the power of beliefs and thoughts and the law of attraction. Don had told me that we would be picked up by a limousine to be brought to the resort. Paulina and I were joking that it probably wouldn't be a limousine, it would probably turn out to be an old clunker.

When our driver showed up, sure enough, it was an old beat-up car! We exchanged glances and smirked. We had called that one!

Except…as we got near the resort, the driver looked over his shoulder at us and said, "You know, if I had known there would be two of you, I would have taken the limousine today. Not sure what made me think of taking the old car today." And he pulled up into the resort…right next to an actual shiny black limousine. Paulina and I looked at each other, floored. Now the joke was on us!

Our rooms were complimentary, so that was really nice. But they wouldn't be ready until 4 p.m., so we settled in at the bar to wait. While we waited, Don said, "I need you to meet all these people." There were a handful of producers—men and women—and a scriptwriter, all gathered there to work on a huge movie project. They were friends of his and of the hotel owner. They were considering bringing in crew for the movie and renting a large part of the resort for that project. Don was there to explore the healing center and retreat idea with me, not the movie, but he knew all these folks. It was very uncanny that it was all happening at once.

So he introduced me around.

One of the gentlemen he introduced me to was a key player in this major movie production—a major producer. Right away he asked me if I would have dinner with him. I said, "Sure—my friend and I will have dinner with you."

This man—I'll call him Jones—seemed very interested in me and my work. He was fascinated by all of my healing work and all that I had experienced and that I taught. He told me that I spoke very well and that he could see how he could help me to grow my platform and influence, get my voice out there.

Then a really interesting and powerful test happened for me. He told me that in order for him to help me—and he described a lot of exciting things that he could potentially do for me in my career, to help bring my work to a wider audience—that I would have to talk the way he wanted me to talk, which was more Christian-based and less "woo woo."

Right away I felt, and said, "There is no amount of money in the world that could take my voice away." I said, "Absolutely not. I'll say what I want, when I want, and how I want. And there's nothing that would change my mind."

He was shocked and incredulous. He said, "So you're willing to give up this big opportunity just because I want you to say things differently? Do you realize what you'd be giving up?" And I said, "I don't care."

I felt like that was huge for me. I realized there is nothing that could ever take away who I am. With that put to the test, I believe I passed it.

Something else really cool happened that night as well. A man who walked over say hello while I was out trying the resort's outdoor hot springs. He was a physicist. He was telling me that he had seen a spaceship just the day before, right where we were in the tub, and that the spaceship was completely made up of geometrical shapes and symbols. He said it looked like kind of like a hexagon in the sky. He saw the symbols and then it flashed, and then it disappeared.

This man, Tim, was telling me about how his dad, also a physicist, had worked for Area 51, which is a highly classified U.S. Air Force facility within the Nevada Test and Training Range. The USAF and CIA own the site, and because there's been intense secrecy surrounding the base, many believe that the government uses it to conceal and test alien technologies, such as those recovered from UFO crashes. All research and occurrences in Area 51 are classified Top Secret/Sensitive Compartmented Information. So Tim definitely believed in the paranormal.

This physicist said that after he saw this ship, a little boy who had been standing outside saw it too, and the boy screamed and ran inside. Resort staff stationed outside by the hot tubs also gasped, "Did you see that?" Then Tim said, "I'm always meeting psychic people," and I started laughing.

Right then, I knew that I was in a very special place, the right place. Absorbing the frequency and energy of an otherworldly visitation that had occurred right above where I sat, getting the healing water—that was my purpose. I had once again been led to just the right place at the right time. And of course, meeting these interesting characters from Hollywood—and getting that test and lesson that affirmed (to me and to the universe) there was no stopping me and no silencing me.

Before I left, as well, I met with the owner of the resort, and he told me that anytime I wanted to have a gathering there, anytime I wanted to invite my students there, anytime I wanted to talk on the stage, teach a class—whatever—he was willing to give me a good rate and also help me with cameramen and the sound and everything. So that made the trip fruitful as well. I left there in a really good space.

I got on a plane, met everybody in Mount Shasta, and we had an amazing, beautiful Christmas. It was the first time that all of my kids and I had been under one roof for Christmas in about five years, because of my children being in college. We all got along great, we put up a huge Christmas tree, ate Christmas dinner—it couldn't have gone better.

Willow got her Disneyland tickets as a Christmas present. She was so excited. My older children took off and flew back to their colleges and home. Sean and I went to the headwaters in Mount Shasta and got some glacier water, which is also miraculous and healing, and mixed it with the Desert Hot Springs miracle water, and made the brew for the Sedona ceremony. We worked really hard making that brew. We blessed it and mixed in some unique energies.

When making ayahuasca brew, as I've mentioned, the intention and energy is everything. Every brew is unique, but it's very important that it be positive and spiritually potent. This time, I was inspired to bring in the Fibonacci sequence, which is a series of numbers where each number is the sum of the previous two. The sequence is named after Leonardo Fibonacci, a 13th-century Italian mathematician who introduced it to Western mathematics.

Many patterns in nature reflect the Fibonacci sequence. It often shows up like a spiral. The sequence is considered spiritually powerful. It has multiple spiritual meanings. Many natural structures, like pinecones, sunflowers, and seashells, have spiral patterns that follow the Fibonacci sequence. Some believe this suggests a potential underlying mathematical principle in nature.

A fascinating aspect of the Fibonacci sequence is that the ratio between consecutive numbers approaches the "Golden Ratio" (approximately 1.618) as the sequence progresses. The Golden Ratio is a ratio between two numbers that equals approximately 1.618. This number also shows up in many places in nature.

I "downloaded" the sequence into the brew by thinking of it and intentionally focusing on it the way one focuses on Reiki symbols when giving Reiki. Later, when people drank the brew, so many asked, "Why do I keep seeing spirals?" It was magical and powerful, and very gratifying to see that what we bless and infuse the brew with really does come out in the healing.

Then we packed up the car and drove about 10 hours to Disneyland and spent a few days in Disneyland there with Willow. She absolutely loved it.

I was really in a good flow at this point. The energy from Desert Hot Springs and the energy from Mount Shasta had me buzzing. This led to another great example of a small but interesting synchronicity—the kind that can happen when you're really aligned and in flow.

On a stop on the way to Sedona, I went into a gas station because I was just really in the mood for a black raspberry ice drink. They didn't have any at this gas station, so I just grabbed a Gatorade and left. When we got to our Airbnb in Sedona, we loaded out and went inside and one of the first things I did was open the refrigerator. I was putting in some water bottles that we had…and inside were two black raspberry ice drinks.

It may seem small, but moments like that are really a confirmation of what it's possible to create. When you're in alignment, grounded, and vibrating at a high frequency, the universe delivers what it knows you want. I knew I wanted the black ice drinks and the universe brought the black ice drinks to me. So I knew that good energy was flowing and that I was aligned.

NEW YEAR'S EVE AGAIN…IN SEDONA AGAIN

Now we were at New Year's Eve once again. For some strange reason I was *still* thinking about Liam. I just couldn't get him out of my mind. It was like an external force was saying "text him Happy New Year." I knew he had gone to Thailand for the holidays. I remembered him telling us that.

So I texted him Happy New Year. And I did not hear back from him, which bothered me. But I let it go.

That night for New Year's Eve, my husband and I had something special planned. We had decided to do MDMA, a psychedelic drug (also known as ecstasy or Molly) which is a heart-opener often used in psychedelic-assisted couples therapy (as well as other applications such as for

PTSD). Although it's technically illegal, it's been used in many studies on depression, trauma, and relationships, and it's very powerful. Therapists do administer it in controlled settings. If it's used correctly, I'm a huge advocate for this medicine.

We were doing this with the intention of more deeply connecting to one another. So we put Willow to bed that night and then we took the MDMA, in capsules, which I had sourced very carefully. And boy, did my heart open. It opened so much! I looked at my husband and I knew without a shadow of a doubt how much this man loved me. And I realized it wasn't that he loved me more on the MDMA. It was because I could *see* it. Because I had my guard and barriers down, and my heart was open. I just completely saw how much he loved me.

Then Sean started telling me things about the night we met that I didn't even know he remembered. He remembered what my breath felt like up against his ear, how our lips almost touched when I was asking him a question and he was bent down trying to hear me over the crowd. He remembers us looking at each other. He remembered little important details about that night that I had never thought he really cared about.

Then I decided that this was the right moment to tell him everything about what had happened with Liam. I told him the reason I was telling him was because I still didn't know why it had happened. I didn't know what was going on, it was really bizarre, and I had yet to figure it out. And I didn't want there to be any secrets between us, anything held back. I don't want *anything* to be in the way of our relationship.

He took it very, very well, though he was a little bit shocked. I explained how it seemed as though every time something came up that wasn't working between us, the universe sent some kind of catalyst that forced the issue to the surface. If we were struggling with how he never called me pretty, the universe sent somebody who looked at me and said, "Hey, you're drop-dead gorgeous." And when I didn't feel protected by him, the universe sent someone who was protective. At first, I assumed that I was just attracted to those traits—to being seen, to receiving the specific attention or recognition I was craving.

But I told him that I had started to think that this was different, and something else might be going on. It was more like I had known Liam all my life—and I had felt like that the first time I'd ever seen him, at his wife's funeral. I told Sean everything about how we had connected, what was said, and how we had left it.

I reminded him of what a nightmare I had been after Liam left over the summer and that this was why—that I had been totally confused, and had never really understood it. But I was so grateful that Sean and I had reconnected and that things were good between us now.

And it turned out beautifully. The whole night was beautiful. And interestingly, by the time we were done, the whole room—which didn't have heat and had been really cold when we started—was so hot that we opened up the door to the 30-degree night. Willow walked in at one point because she just wanted to see what we were doing and she said, "Wow, this room is hot, Mom and Dad!" I know that was definitely Kundalini rising.

The next day was New Year's Day, and we were getting ready to do the ceremony the following day. Once again, everything just worked out great. We had two ceremonies back to back. There was some really powerful people in these ceremonies and some fabulous healings.

As I mentioned earlier, one of the things I had downloaded into the brew was an intention to include the Fibonacci sequence. I didn't tell anybody that, yet people were seeing spirals suggesting the Fibonacci sequence all over the place. It was quite remarkable.

Sedona is one of the most incredible places to see the stars. The sky there is so clear and vast. All of us at some point went outside to honor the stars. In Sedona, you can actually see the stargates—portals through the stars into other dimensions and realities, which give us access to information we can assimilate into our own consciousness. We can receive codes and symbols that activate our DNA. There is something very paranormal that goes on in Sedona with stargates. A lot of the healing we see happening in Sedona is not only through the medicine but via the stars and their activations.

People left that first ceremony having had miraculous healings once again, thanking me and hugging me.

Sean and I were doing very well, very well. I remember at one point in the first ceremony, I really didn't have too much to do because everybody was doing so well, and Sean took my hand as we stood outside under the stars and I said, "No, I have to go check on people." He said, "No, you don't. Everybody's fine. You have to come out here and dance with me." And he pulled me to him, underneath the stars—and then I purged! I felt myself start to throw up and I thought, wow. That's my intimacy stuff. Fortunately, Sean really understands ayahuasca and how this works.

There was a Chinese woman in the second ceremony who was in her sixties and had spent a lot of her life meditating and traveling. She found out about AWAKE from a Buddhist monk while she was in Budapest. I don't advertise in Budapest, so that really struck me. I noticed that whenever I touched this woman's crown chakra, the energy blew me away. She was so evolved and awakened. I could have touched her head for three hours, it felt so good. I could feel surges of energy go through my body and out through my crown chakra. So that night I knew to pay attention to her. I did a lot of work on her and helped her ground, which was important for her because she had so much power going through her.

At one point, I touched her third eye and crown once again, and I was zapped into a portal. Suddenly I was flying fast down a portal, and all of a sudden I stopped and right in front of me was Liam's face. This shocked me because he hadn't been on my mind at all at that point—Sean and I were doing fantastic, I was feeling really into him, and I was also deeply immersed in the ceremony and participants.

And yet here was Liam's face intruding into my awareness. Once again I thought, what is going on? I pulled my hand from the woman's head, and immediately I was back in the present reality. I was puzzled and a bit disoriented, but I just shook it off and continued to do my work.

I was very proud of Sean during this ceremony. He had come such a long way from those days when he would sit apart from us scrolling his phone. He was doing sound healing, playing the drums, playing crystal bowls, helping with the ceremony in so many different ways.

For example, we had put three Chinese women in the same room. I was told by my guides that one of the things that had brought them here was a common sort of self-resentment towards Chinese women and how Chinese women let men treat them. They projected this resentment onto other women, but really it was a self-loathing. This was a big part of what they needed to clear.

So we had two younger Chinese women and the older Chinese woman in there. They were all so triggered by each other. So much resentment was being purged just by them being in the same room. Sean went in, played ayahuasca music and did energy healing on them, and got some powerful purges from each one of them.

In that ceremony, I felt like he and I were really equaling out. He wasn't just doing the cleaning and the cooking while I walked around and did all the energy healing. We were balancing, and he was doing the energy work too. I would say to myself, okay, he's working on people. So I would start to clean up. I would start to get the food ready for breakfast the next morning. I was very happy about how that was going.

So we had an extremely successful two ceremonies, and then it was time to go home. Sean was driving home, because he had all the sound equipment, and my daughter and I were flying home. Willow and I flew to Pittsburgh and decided to stay the night at a hotel. Then we flew from Pittsburgh to Morgantown and drove home. Sean actually ended up getting home before us.

BIG, BIG TRAVELS

We were looking forward to getting settled at home for a bit, because we had a new huge round of traveling that we were about ready to do. It was January when we got home, and starting in March we had a series of trips planned.

First, for my husband's Christmas present, I had bought him a trip to Cuba. Two of the things that had been on his bucket list, since he and I had first met, were that he really wanted to go to Cuba and he really wanted to go to a percussion camp. Before Christmas I had been looking at old Facebook messages from back then and was reminded of how he'd talked about that. Both wishes didn't necessarily need to be fulfilled in one trip, but as it happened, I had actually found a percussion camp in Cuba March 4-12, and I booked him those tickets as his Christmas present.

So he was going to Cuba. Then on March 23, we were leaving for England. We were going to visit his mother because his mother was not doing too well. We planned to be in England for about 10 days and then go to Italy, and after Italy to Costa Rica to check on the house and the retreat center, and then come back home.

So we had a lot of traveling up ahead, and between Sedona and then, time flew. Sean went to Cuba. He really enjoyed it. I took care of Willow during that time and she and I bonded and took care of the dogs and had fun. He came back, we got ready for England, and then off we went.

We were staying at a beautiful place called Luton Hoo Hotel. It was during Easter, so we took Willow to the zoo and participated in an Easter egg hunt and did her Easter basket while we were there. And she got to spend some quality time with Sean's mother.

Also during the stay, we planned go out and meet with Sean's friends, which meant that I would be seeing Liam. I was very nervous about this. I knew I still had some work to do. Sean and his friends went out to meet at a bar, as they often do, and I was to join them later.

As I've mentioned, the only time I drink is if I'm with Sean and his friends and everybody else is drinking, or before a cold-water exposure adventure like rafting (remember the visit with Liam). Other than that, I stopped drinking a long time ago. As I had told my ex-husband when he asked about it, during that conversation where he committed to not drinking any more, I don't even crave it because I prefer to be present, grounded, and in a high frequency. Drinking generally isn't aligned with that state, so it doesn't appeal to me.

But I went and met up with Sean and his friends at the bar. Once again I had a couple of drinks, but not nearly enough to black out. When I walked in, Liam came up and hugged me immediately. There was no tension, no nervousness. He looked right at me, very genuine. He said, with obvious care and concern, "How are you doing, Rebecca?" I told him I was good, and he said, "Good. I'm so glad that you're doing well." We chatted some more, and he was very attentive talking to me.

As Liam and I talked, I saw Sean walk away to the bathroom and then I didn't really see him much. It was strange. Once again, my memory almost completely left me. I don't remember most of that night at all.

One of the few things I did remember was my husband going over to say hello to his friend Terry, and he did not introduce me to Terry. I remembered feeling hurt about that. But I was talking to Liam at the time.

The other thing I remembered was that at one point Liam said, "You're giving me those eyes." And I said something like, "Well, you would be the only one who knows," or something like that. Something I would *never* have said! I don't even know what it meant. Worse, Sean later told me he had heard us have that exchange and was just shocked—even though I had explained the strangeness with Liam during our MDMA ceremony.

Once again, I was stunned and confused about this absolutely bizarre response to Liam. I thought, "That wasn't me who said that"—yet it was me. What was going on?

The last thing I recall was telling him I'd been hurt by the fact that he never responded to my "Happy New Year" text, He said something nonchalant like "Well, you know, texts can get lost," and I said, "No, I don't think so."

When it came time for us all to leave that night, Liam said, "I really wish you could go to this gig my band is playing next week." I told him that we would be going to Italy, so I couldn't. The next thing I remember, he had grabbed me by the shoulders and gently brushed his lips up against mine and then hugged me.

I left in kind of a daze, wondering what was going on. I pulled my phone out of my pocket when we got into the Uber and he had texted me "Happy New Year" with a whole bunch of exclamation points.

We got back to the hotel and I told Sean, "This is so weird, but I don't remember most of the night." He said, "Yeah, that's odd because that's what happened to you before with him. Are you drinking a lot when you're around him or something?" And I said, "No. I'm just blanking out."

That's when we started to suspect the possibility that his wife was influencing me. I've been known to take on spirits and allow them to influence me without me being aware of it—though never to this degree. I didn't like it at all. But it would explain Liam's response to me and mine to him. Sean was believing me about this, which was good, and genuinely seemed concerned.

Something else my husband said kind of bothered me too. When I asked why he didn't introduce me to his friend Terry, he said, "Oh, I didn't introduce him to you because he didn't know you were my wife. He looked over and saw you, and he said, 'who is that woman?' as though he wanted to hit on you." Sean added, "I didn't want to stand in his way." I said, "*What?* You didn't want to stand in the way of him hitting on me?" Sean said, "Right. I didn't want to be all territorial like 'Hey, she's my wife.'"

Again there was that old feeling that Sean could kind of "take me or leave me." It was all very unsettling. It seemed like every time we got really strong and connected and went deeper, there was some "turn around the spiral" and we would bump into this issue again. But we had been deeply connected lately, and he was being very solicitous about the Liam craziness, so I let it go. Later, I would understand it better.

Anyway, Liam took us to the airport when it was time to fly to Italy, and when he dropped us off—me, Sean, and Willow—he hugged all of us. And he said, "I'm coming to Costa Rica when your house is done." I tried to just put it all out of my mind for the moment.

We went on to Italy, where we stayed at the cutest little Airbnb. It reminded me of a castle straight out of Harry Potter. I liked how everybody was riding bikes, even women in their 80s and 90s, which was so impressive. The food was amazing. We got fresh bread every morning. It was so lovely.

However, the second day that we were there, once again I started thinking about Liam a lot, and I went to sleep thinking about him. Here we go again! I was starting to feel distressed about the strangeness and lack of control. Once asleep, I started to have a dream—except it really wasn't a dream. It was very lucid. I was yelling at Liam about women he had been with. In "real life," of course, I didn't know if he had been with any women. I said to him something like, "They aren't serious to you, are they?" He said, "No." I said, "Then why did you do it?" He was putting his hands out in front of him saying, "I don't know. I don't know."

Suddenly, Sean kind of slammed into me and I woke up. I looked at him confused, but he went back to sleep. I was still thinking about Liam. It felt unbearable. I was yearning to download WhatsApp so I could talk to him, not just text. I kept hearing, "You need to actually talk to him. He needs to physically hear your voice. That's the way he is. If you do a text message, he can separate himself." It was like someone was talking outside of me. And this voice wanted me to say things like, "I'm thinking about you. We're supposed to be together."

What was happening? What was I supposed to do? I left the room and went out to sit on the steps of the terrace, rocking back and forth, trying to deal with my compulsions. I was scared and very confused. Was I losing my mind?

Then Sean came out and said, "I have to talk to you." And thankfully, finally, this gave me the insight that changed everything. He said, "I was sleeping, and Rebecca, I never hear your guides speak. But I heard your guides—which are probably mine too—say 'wake her up.' At first I didn't. I just ignored them. But they insisted, and then they pushed my arm into your back, and that's how you woke up."

I told Sean about the dream and he said, "That makes so much sense." It turns out Liam had told Sean that he had sought out some women to get "satisfied" when he was in Thailand, two different women. I said, "Oh my God, that helps me out so much. It was *her* in my dream." His wife.

That's when I knew she was definitely influencing me, or working through me, trying to stay connected to him and reach him. I remembered all the messages I had received when we were on the sailing trip, and the things I had known that had shocked him, and how Nathan the psychic had said, "She doesn't seem dead." It all made sense. Sean and I reflected more about it together and it was pretty clear that this was what was going on.

I suspected that it was my empathy for the whole situation that had created an opening for Liam's wife, her spirit, to enter and "use" me to connect with her beloved husband. When I had been at the funeral, I felt very connected to Liam, but not in a romantic way. I just wanted to help him. I felt very, very sad for both of them. Then, when he came for the ayahuasca ceremony, there was that portal that I had opened in the backyard, the portal of unconditional love. And he was missing her, and I was intending to help him. It was the perfect opening.

One of the few other things I had remembered that Liam said when we were talking at the bar in England just a few weeks earlier was, "Wow, Rebecca, that portal was powerful." And this is a man who likes football and drinks beer. He wouldn't be someone who would normally talk about portals (which is yet another reason he really wouldn't be my twin flame). But he knew that something had happened with that portal.

So finally, I was able to really get a grip on what was going on and not feel completely insane. Sean and I talked about how one way to tackle this was that we had to stay super solid in our relationship, so nothing could infiltrate us. The more present you are, the safer you are from entities and energies of any kind attaching to you.

BACK TO COSTA RICA, BETTER THAN EVER

After all that travel, we went back to Costa Rica, where we fell even more deeply in love with it. It was April at this point. We had decided to just go look at the schools. We were not planning on living in Costa Rica full-time. We were just thinking about sending Willow to school there half the time. We were planning to be there January through June.

However, when we went to look at the schools, we were so captivated and delighted by how they worked with the children. We visited one school in particular called Playhouse. That really struck a chord with me because a modality that I teach in AWAKE is called PLAE (play!)—psychedelic languaging, activation and encoding. This is basically the style of the retreats I do. When you play and have fun, you stay in the flow, and the universe shows up for you. And that was kind of the methodology of this school, too. The owner of the school said, yes, we teach things and the kids learn. But we also play and dance and sing, and we bring our creativity out. We got introduced to a pig, who the owner/teacher joked was the school principal. The school was outside, but there was a lot of shade. There was incense and music. The children played in their bare feet. They were running and splashing in mud puddles. It was perfect.

So we fell in love with the school, and we decided we couldn't have Willow go half a school year in one place and half a school year in the other. We wouldn't do that to her. So we decided on that trip that we were going to move to Costa Rica for the full school year.

This was a monumental decision. The Costa Rica house was not going to be done until February. The retreat center was going to be a retreat center for us and for other people to rent out as well. So we needed to find someplace else to live until all that was ready (and a place to stay when renters were using the house for retreats).

To manifest that, Sean and I did a whole night of ceremony with one another, connecting our hearts, kissing, going into our deepest desires, our deepest fears, sharing how we felt about one another. It was a lot like the manifestation we had done at the cabin back in 2020, using our intimacy and tantra to "birth" our dreams. We also did MDMA that night again, and once again it was really beautiful and powerful.

Our dreams had already come true over and over again. We'd had a five-year manifestation cycle that started right after our wedding. That manifestation included building a house at the lake, having an amazing family, and getting a house and land in Costa Rica. It was all there. We were doing it all. And now, we just wanted to stay in Costa Rica longer. Of course, once again, I would leave it up to the universe. I said to the universe, "Guide me!"

And it worked—again. I found condominiums called, of all things, *Become*. They were beautiful! But I felt a little daunted, in spite of my manifestation abilities and confidence. It was a pretty big ask, at this point. We were building a new home—again. We had a lot of bills with the retreat center. Could we really swing buying this condominium too? We were expats in Costa Rica. We didn't have any established credit.

But we went to a bank, and there we were helped by an amazing Costa Rican gentleman named Brian. I knew when he looked deeply into my eyes that he was connecting with me on a soul level. We were talking to him about the financing, and he said, "I'm going to get this done for you." And he did!

And that started our journey with getting the condo at *Become*.

We left Costa Rica half in shock and half in awe because of the decision we had made. We were sad to fly home.

LESSON

The experience with Liam's wife was confusing and frightening at times, but invaluable. Sean was my savior and hero in the way that he allowed me to process this with him, to help me figure it out, and to work it out with Liam despite the confusion it caused him too.

When we waver from our truth and self-love, we leave openings for waywards, attachments, and discarnate energies to take us over. This can be very subtle or it can be extreme. It was so strangely difficult to discern Carrie's feelings from mine at times. I had done so much work to ground and center myself, to love myself, and to be energetically clear and powerful—but sadness and fear that began at the funeral left me open to this "infiltration."

Also, when we're invested in helping someone, it's important to have solid boundaries and not to martyr. The second you give yourself up to help someone, foreign energies can get in because you just subtly invited them in. It's beautiful to help others, but always stay in your power—never give up who you are, and love yourself first and foremost! Make it a practice to command these energies from your field and stay grounded in love and the truth of who you really are.

Chapter Twenty-Six

WE GOT BACK TO THE STATES, AND WE HAD a lot to face in order to make this massive move happen. We were following our hearts, and it felt right, but there were a lot of people and things involved. We had to tell everyone what we had decided. We had to figure out what we were going to do with our belongings. It was April, and Willow was starting school on September 2, 2024.

It seemed to me that my guardian parents and universal energy were very much flowing with our decision to move to Costa Rica. The Costa Rica home, the retreat house, the Costa Rica condo, the Costa Rica School, everything that we tried to do in Nosara just worked out beautifully. But it seemed as though whenever we were trying to do something related to our home in Maryland, we got pushback.

When we were in Costa Rica in April and we were deciding about whether or not to actually make the move, after we found the schools, we talked about everything that we would be giving up in Maryland. We had created this beautiful lake house. We had an awesome surf boat, jet skis, kayaks, paddleboards. Our home was like a vacation home—but it had turned out that the frequency of the area and of the locals was not that high. And we were both sensitive to that. Ultimately, it mattered. But we were still torn because our lake house dream had been a big one too, and we had a lot invested in it.

At that time, back when we were still in Costa Rica, our boat was about to be put on the lake for the summer. We were on the beach in Nosara, and the phone rang. It was Joey, the gentleman who takes care of our boat for the winter. He said, "I hate to inform you of this, but muskrats have chewed through some of the wires in your boat. Sometimes they do this when your boat is docked. I've only seen it a handful of times since I've worked here, but it's happened to your boat, so you'll want to put in an insurance claim immediately."

I looked over at Sean and I said, "Okay, this is pretty much our answer from the universe." The muskrat as a power animal empowers individuals to embrace change and adapt to new circumstances with grace and resilience. So the universe—through the muskrats—was basically saying, "It's time to make this change." I knew that right now it was time to let go of all attachments, whether with humans, situations, or things. This was our journey.

As soon as you become attached to something or you define it. You've put conditions on it. I had already long noticed and believed that the best and most healthy way to live life is to detach from everything, in a certain sense. Even from the people you love, strange as that may sound. Let them show up how they need to show up every single day. When you become attached to them in a certain way, you're going to know them only the way they used to be, not as they may be now or they may be becoming. You'll be putting conditions on them. I had learned this to a degree, and I already tried to live that way. The universe was now asking us to step up to this value in a much deeper way.

But it wasn't easy. My older daughter had just turned 18. I was in the process of getting her an apartment as she went off to college. My children all lived in the United States. My sisters lived in the United States. My mom lived in the United States. And here I was moving to Costa Rica.

In addition to people, we also had to let go of *things*. We decided that we were going to sell the house, the boat, the jet skis, everything we could. One of the things about moving to Costa Rica is you almost literally can't take anything. You can only take what you can put on the airplane. And especially where we were living, in Nosara, people dress minimally. They're driving cars that can make it during the rainy season—not fancy cars. It's definitely not a society that runs on social status. I liked this, because you had no idea of anyone's socioeconomic status and couldn't judge or distinguish based on wealth. Everyone was kind of equal. Everybody was riding dirt bikes and quads, muddy from the rainwater. People live a life that's very simple, yet absolutely amazing and free.

I was excited to jump into this. I was ready to let go of defining myself by any sort of attachment, and that was going to be new and different for me. In the past, if I purchased a car, it had to have the bells and whistles. The boat had to have the bells and whistles. The jet skis had to have the bells and whistles. Everything surrounding me had bells and whistles. But now I had realized that to have heaven on earth, *things* definitely don't matter.

Yes, if I'm sitting on a couch, I like that couch to be comfortable. If I'm lying on a bed, I want the bed to be comfortable. I love to fly on a flight where I'm comfortable. But beyond comfort and utility, heaven on earth wasn't about things. It was about love, family, work, play, contribution. The beauty of those things, and of nature. Not the beauty of material stuff.

So we were preparing to move and let go of basically everything. Even Willow's toys, which was quite a big deal for her. Even she had to participate in this letting-go process, this divesting of *stuff*.

And everything was going pretty well with that…until I started to contemplate keeping the house that we were currently living in as well.

It was such a beautiful house. It's on the lake. It's around my sisters. We had put so much into it, so much work and so much love. Ryan had worked on it. So I said to Sean, "You know what? We should just keep this house too."

But when I look back on it, I know that keeping that house would've been something for me to run back to in case it didn't work out. The condo that my husband and I were moving into in Costa Rica was a two-bedroom condo. Each bedroom has a bathroom, and then there's a main living area that's connected to the kitchen. There's no hiding.

Every single home I've lived in as a married person was a very large home. My husband could easily go and have his own domain downstairs while I stayed upstairs. But now, at our condo in Nosara, at least until the house was done, we would be living in very close quarters.

It's fascinating what happened next after I started thinking about keeping the lake house.

Almost the second I spoke that idea, things changed dramatically in my business. My business took a turn for the worst. I had changed nothing except for one video. But enrollments fell off the cliff. Imagine going to the mall and all of the stores are open and thriving, and the next day you go back and all the stores have closed. That's how dramatic this was.

And I was in dire straits, because we needed a large sum of cash to be able to close on that condo in Nosara. I was spooked. I told Sean, "I don't know what's going on." And this went on for two or three months.

In the end, the only thing that we could point to was the fact that I had suddenly decided I wanted to keep the lake house. I also started to hear from my higher guidance that where we were living was not healthy. Even though it was beautiful, it was getting stagnant. And it's very important that we stay in flow in life. That just was not happening in Maryland, at that house.

Finally I realized what was going on. So, I said, "Okay, we're not going to do that. We're definitely not going to keep the house." And Sean agreed. He said, "No, we're not keeping the house, Rebecca. We're moving to Nosara. When we come back to the States to visit, we'll get an Airbnb."

BIG INSIGHTS ABOUT SEAN

Sean was such a trooper during this process. We had been flying all year long, and now he had to take a flight to go back to Nosara just for the closing. We were still busy getting the house ready, selling things and packing.

What I was starting to really admire about my husband were the very differences that I used to think were an issue. Many of the qualities (or supposed deficits) that chafed at me and made me resist him and want to change him, or question whether he was really *the one*, turned out to be some of the qualities I most needed. Finally, with all we had been through, and all the work, I was starting to see how much Sean grounds and centers me because of those very differences, and how much strength and dimension he brings it our relationship and family.

I looked back and thought to myself, why was I ever attracted to anybody else? In some cases, it seemed like I was attracted to men who were in certain ways a lot like me. It was familiar. That was really me being stuck in my ways and not opening up to something different, getting out of my comfort zone. A true twin flame shows you your uncomfortable zones. Not in a way that's unhealthy (because of course Gabe was certainly uncomfortable, but in an extreme and toxic way!) but in a way that stretches you and demands that you grow and open wider. You have to be able to discern the difference, and that took me a while.

I also had to learn not to be attracted to men who needed me to take care of them, like Ryan. Sean was really self-sufficient.

Differences that complement you can be really helpful. When we were going through all that stuff with finances, when my business flagged, I got into a space of fear, even though I knew better. But the truth is, we were okay even when that happened, because Sean had saved up a lot money over the previous few years. When that dry spell hit, we used that savings to get by. If not for Sean, I hate to say it, but that money wouldn't have been saved.

Another way he helped us financially was with his credit. Although with AWAKE I was the high earner, and I had earned extremely well before that in my mental health practice—while he had quit his modestly well-paying engineering job to work with me in AWAKE—my credit was destroyed when I got out of prison. As you'll recall, after prison I didn't want anything to do with my previous practice. And I didn't want anything to do with my old house, my huge home that went into foreclosure. So I let everything kind of collapse, which meant my credit was terrible for some time, even though I still was making income. So with all the big financial stuff we were doing, buying homes and property and so forth, we used his amazing credit score—which was 850—to do everything.

So I started to see how some of the things I had complained about with Sean were things that actually saved us. And my complaint that he wasn't getting mad because someone was picking on me or hitting on me or taking from me—that was old programming. That was wanting him to act like some swaggering man. It was really like complaining because he's not in his ego! Yes, I wanted to feel protected, but the truth is he *was* protecting me—in all the important ways that mattered, without getting his ego all up in it.

And that same non-egoic quality was what allowed him to take a deep breath and step back and let me do my thing in life. He protected my creativity, my ability to be who I am in the world without apology, and he protected us by being practical with money—to name just a few.

I realized that in spite of all my unusual, out-there, paranormal and nonconformist ways of doing many things, I'd held this kind of cookie-cutter picture-perfect view of relationships. Like you should have the perfect wedding and the perfect Valentine's Day and the perfect proposal. But really, when I looked into my husband's soul, I saw someone who simply knew what he wanted, and didn't follow those rules. He doesn't think like that. He shows me he loves me by being there all of the time through everything.

One night around this time, we were sleeping and I had just had laser eye surgery done to correct my nearsightedness, and I woke up and felt like something was stabbing my eye. I was screaming in pain, and he just took me in his arms. He whispered in my ear. He told me to breathe, and then he eased me into doing energy work. He walked me into surrendering to the pain. I fell asleep, and when I woke up again, I was fine. I looked over at him and thought, wow, you were really there for me.

This man is my partner in life. We wouldn't have been able to do anything that we had done unless we had worked together.

THE APPRAISAL

We were getting ready to move and sell the house, but we soon learned that the house would not sell for a few more months because everyone knew interest rates were going to drop. People were waiting to buy homes until that happened. The real estate agent said we might as well wait until three or four months, because the house wasn't going to move when everybody was waiting for interest rates to drop.

But we needed money out of the house to finish the retreat project in Costa Rica. We weren't going to be able to sell right away, so we decided to refinance instead. And for the refinance, in order to get the money we needed, we had to have our appraisal come out at a specific price.

You can't choose your appraiser. We had put our house up for sale for a week, and then taken it off the market quickly when we realized it would not sell right now. We were working with a mortgage company, and the young man helping us was an amazing wizard starseed, but the underwriters told him we could not refinance this house because of the fact that we'd had it on the market. Now, they said, we'd have to wait six months before we could refinance it.

But the one exception to that was if an appraisal came back a certain amount higher than our asking price, *then* they could still refinance it.

I was thinking to myself that there was no way that this house would come back at that magic number.

But we got an appraiser out there, and his name was John. The cool thing about this is that my dad's name was John, and about two weeks prior to this, Sean and I were really working on some residual stuff with my dad. Sean and I were always working on intimacy stuff. And something had come up about my dad, and we went deep into it. This work shed light on my mom and I realized that both my mom and dad played a part in everything that happened to me as a child.

I had an amazing childhood in many ways. As I've said, my mom was a wonderful mother and I felt very loved and supported. But my dad was an alcoholic and abusive, and that made me question men in general. That takes a long time to get over. It had been reflected in many of my twin flame challenges in relationships thus far. But in doing this work now I realized that it was not just my dad who should have protected me. My mom should have too. This wasn't about blaming, it just really helped me to look at it all holistically at this point. I now looked at my mom and dad as more equal, and felt a surge of forgiveness for my dad.

And then here comes this appraiser whose name was John. He looked at me, and—I'll never forget this—he said, "What do you need this to come back at?" I was shocked. I just stammered, "What?" He repeated, "No, really. What do you need this to come back at?" Stunned, I told him the insanely high number we need in order to make it work. He looked at me and said, "Okay, I think we can do this. And he did!

The guy at the mortgage company was very happy we had gotten this appraisal, but then he found out that at this price, you actually need *two* appraisals, and they go with the lower amount. I had thought we were done, but now we had another hurdle.

I thought, who *else* is going to appraise it for that high? By a miracle I had gotten one person to do it, but a second time?

But we tried—we sought a second appraisal. The next appraiser who came in was a guy named Peter. I started thinking about it— John, Peter—I haven't been to church a lot, but this was ringing a bell. The apostles. This was getting almost funny, but I felt divinely protected.

Sure enough, Peter came in and basically did the same thing John had. He actually asked, "Can I have that first appraisal you just got? That way it'll be easier for me to work off of." He actually appraised it for $50,000 *higher* than John did.

So it all worked out. We were able to get the rest of the money that we needed, exactly the right amount to give to the architect so that he could finish the Costa Rica retreat house. To sell it, we can wait until the interest rates go down.

Everything seemed to be falling into place. It was now around the beginning of August 2024. One thing we really needed to figure out at this point was how to get our dogs to Costa Rica. I have a husky malamute wolf, and he could not fly in cargo in the heat, and every flight stopped in Texas or Miami. It was way too hot. You couldn't fly any dog, actually, when it was that hot. We actually had to look up shared private flights where people pool their money together to fly their dogs from Fort Lauderdale to Liberia. The only date that we could get was September 19.

We decided that I would go to Nosara with Willow on August 28 and get her settled, get her in school, and Sean would come September 19 with the dogs.

LETTING GO OF FEAR

Something else came out through this process at this time. When I was doing that work about my mom and dad, I did a lot of clearing of imprints they had overlaid into me, that I now held in my own DNA.

Our families, our ancestors, can imprint their beliefs, programs, worries, fears and stories into your DNA. It can be almost like a photo print in your energy field. You can end up attracting more of whatever that is, even if it isn't yours. For many of us, part of our job is to clear those imprints for ourselves and for the line.

I had come to realize I held everything for my mom. I was the only one of four sisters she did this with—I had asked my sisters, and all said she had never told them a lot of the things she told me. So I had a lot of energy, stories, imprints to clear.

Something that emerged for healing during this work was my extreme fear of losing a child. All my life, when watching my children, I'd had a fear of them dying or literally just disappearing. I remember with Willow, if she walked behind a tree, I was actually scared that she wouldn't come from out behind the tree. If she went into a different aisle in the supermarket. I was scared she'd just vanish. I was always very, very fearful of a child dying.

Also, I can't really remember a time when I was responsible for my children's care alone. I lived near four sisters and a mother. My ex in-laws were very big in my older three children's care. There was always a huge extended family that helped with the kids before and after school. The cousins were always there. There was never a time when any of us was really alone with a child.

Now, I was realizing where this came from. My mom's first child, my brother, died of leukemia when he was four months old. That was the imprint that I was holding onto. After I released that imprint, I was ready to go to Costa Rica with Willow by myself. This happened just in time.

This would be a first for me to have a young child by myself—in a different country, no less. I'm such an independent person usually, but I had been nervous at first thinking that Willow was going to be a hundred percent in my care. I had been with her by myself when Sean still lived in Michigan, but I'd still had my kids and mom around. Thankfully, I started to feel a lot better as these imprints were releasing. I was returning that energy back to my mom and quietly helping her to alchemize it.

Sean and I made sure to have a lot of heart to hearts during the process of moving because everything needed to fall in place. There needed to be flow and clarity, and that meant keeping the field clear for source energy to move through. Any stagnant and stuck energy had to be processed—any guilt, doubt, shame, fear, or resentment.

We continued to work on that old longstanding issue of Sean not standing up for me. As I said earlier, I was really getting it now, and I was seeing and understanding more deeply all the ways that Sean really protected me, did his part for us, and made our lives better by being who he truly is as an individual.

It was powerful when we revisited that time in England when his friend Terry expressed interest in me. As we continued to work though this, he explained better what he had meant when he said, "I wanted him to hit on you, Rebecca." It wasn't that he didn't feel bonded with me or "could take me or leave me." It wasn't that he didn't care. It was that he trusted me that much. He explained, "I was going to let you deal with it. I don't want to be that possessive, territorial guy who says, 'Hey man, that's my wife. Leave her alone.'" He said, "I trust our relationship and I have no fear about confronting anybody, but I wasn't threatened and I also knew you could handle it."

I realized how much Sean helped me balance my own divine feminine and masculine by trusting me in this way and not dominating the masculine. I needed to be able to step into my power and stick up for myself when I needed to, which Sean's stepping back so often allowed me to do—yet be in my feminine side like that time my eye hurt, or when I was in prison, or when I thought we were going to lose all the money. Everything I have ever been through, he is there by my side. He will look at me and say, "I will do whatever you want." He tells me that all the time. And that is incredible, to have that. It's the perfect balance of feminine and masculine.

And in light of all that, I finally realized, no big deal if he wanted the life jacket. Maybe he did need my life jacket because he can't swim well. I'm a really good swimmer. The ways we each took charge of things and took care of each other made sense, even if they didn't fit the stereotypes, which I was now allowing to fall away.

I'd had a lot of stereotypical, mainstream programming about men—for all of my spirituality—that needed to be stripped away on this journey. As I said, I had been programmed to think that a man carried you across the threshold after you're married, that Valentine's Day and a wedding proposal should look a certain romantic way. But the truth is, there are plenty of men who can give you the best Valentine's Days, give you the best proposal, even give you the best wedding day—who just don't know how to be there and be your best friend through the deepest stuff of life. It took me this whole journey to realize that the best thing to do is to connect on a soul level. Don't worry about all the programming. Figure out if this person is your best friend.

I look back on everything with Sean now and think, "That's a great guy." He's done some things that weren't perfect, but he's a truly good guy. He's a keeper.

Plus, I'll never forget how I felt the first second I saw him. I knew the first second I saw this man that I was going to marry him. That had never happened with any other man before, and based on that, I could have listened to my soul all along. My soul knew that he was the one for me, even though I had to go through so many layers of work to really expose that diamond at the core of it all. It's a great lesson in the power of trusting ourselves, even when it might look really crazy at times—to ourselves or to other people.

So everything was really falling into balance, and we were appreciating how much we could speak to one another about this.

COMMANDING CARRIE AWAY

As Sean and I were becoming closer, appreciating each other more than ever, understanding our journey, and standing in our truth, guess who couldn't influence me anymore? Carrie! Liam's wife. Every time Liam's wife tried to come to me, now I knew it wasn't me because I was standing in my truth so fully at that point. I knew the difference.

Liam was about ready to welcome a grandchild on August 23. At this point, therefore, Carrie was talking really loud in my ear, and there were things that she wanted me to do and say. Some of what she wanted me to say to him would have been really inappropriate. For example, she wanted me to text him things like "I miss you" and other things it was simply not right for me to be saying to him—and besides which, wasn't what *I* wanted to be saying to him.

One day, when I was driving to my eye appointment—a two-hour drive—she wouldn't stop trying to influence me to text him about the baby. Finally, I had to pull over to the side of the road, sit under a tree, ground my energy, and command her away. I did agree to text him something, but it wasn't what she wanted. I said, "I wish you the best. This is a really good addition to your family. This is going to be precious." I did it in my own words.

That night after my husband had held me because I had the eye pain, we decided that it was time to go back to the portal around the fire, start a fire just like we did the first night of ayahuasca with Liam, and send her back through the portal where she came from. We commanded her back through the portal, and we went to bed.

We were about ready to go to sleep, and suddenly we heard something running downstairs. I could hear the footsteps. It was very clear. Things were crashing. Willow was in bed. It was just us and the dogs. Sean he looked at me and I looked at him because we both one hundred percent thought there was someone downstairs. It was so scary.

I'd never called 911 the whole time we'd lived there. But I got the phone, I called 911 and when the operator came on I said, "Someone's broken into our house and they're downstairs and they're throwing things."

But as I was doing this, Sean bravely walked right downstairs. He brought the dog down with him. And there was no one there.

I said to the operator, "I'm sorry, I guess there isn't anyone down there after all, I'm so sorry." But…there was. It was *her*. She was angry because she had to leave. She couldn't reside in me anymore because I was standing so deeply in my truth.

Ever since then, she's been gone. I haven't felt or heard from her. Liam's grandchild was born. The baby is really healthy, and the baby's middle name is her name.

The only times I think about Liam right now are just regarding how he's going to perceive all of this, because he was affected too. He could feel her energy.

My husband saw Liam brush his lips against mine when we were at the bar. He couldn't believe his best friend had just done that to his wife. But then, he said, he *knew*. He absolutely knew that something strange was up. And it was. Liam was being influenced because he felt her energy in me, and I was being influenced by her energy to the point where I didn't even have a memory of some of the times with him. It was so overpowering. Even after we figured out what was going on, there were times she had taken me over so much that I had to keep reciting my name and my sisters' names to keep hold of myself and know that I was me. The thing that was also interesting was that not only were Liam and I profoundly affected, but so was Sean. Sean later told me that when I was around Liam, he too was in a kind of dream state. And he constantly felt driven to go to the bathroom, which was why he kind of disappeared so much when Liam and I were together. When he did see us doing strange and inappropriate things, he was in such a daze he could hardly respond.

So I often wonder when I see him now, how's it going to be? My husband thinks I should tell him everything that happened, because if he's aware enough to know that the portal was there, he's aware enough to know that something like this could happen. And he's planning on visiting Costa Rica. When we get the house done, all of Sean's friends are going to visit, and I'm going to find the right time to sit down and talk to Liam about this.

ARIEL'S STARSEED

Something else happened right before the move to Costa Rica that helped to affirm the sense that it was time, smooth the way for a comfortable transition, and reinforce the value of all the work I had done on myself and my children.

My daughter Ariel had just turned 18 at this time. As mentioned, she and I are very close. One of the hardest aspects of leaving the U.S. at this time was leaving Ariel, knowing she was just going off the college. I knew she'd be fine, but I did feel wistful about not being close by for her first year.

And then something happened that was just perfect.

One of the things that I have always loved about Ariel is her confidence in holding out for the right man. She was never one to date just anyone, or to have a boyfriend simply in order to not be alone. She only had one major boyfriend from the ages of 14 to 17. Once they broke up, she didn't date again until she found the right person, even though a lot of men asked her out.

The way she found the right person was amazing.

There was a boy who went to her high school, who was part of her friend group, who had come from Ukraine during the war, only a few years earlier. The very first time I saw him, I just felt like I knew him.

It was at graduation in May 2024. At the graduation breakfast, Andriy came up to her, and I felt this kind of activation I feel when I meet other starseeds or people who are in my soul tribe. It's hard to explain but I can just feel this connection. I just...knew him. After we chatted, I hugged him. And I just knew he was interested in my daughter.

Ariel told me later that he told her, "Your mom is not from here. She's an alien. She has a really special, bright light around her." She laughed and said, "My mom says that all the time, that she's not from here. She's gonna love you." He also told her, "I really want to talk to your mother."

You could tell that he and Ariel liked each other. But they were hanging out as friends. Then one evening not long after graduation, a bunch of the kids came over to the lake house to be in the hot tub. By the time I went out to say goodnight, it was just Ariel and Andriy, and two other kids who were a couple. I was joking with them, "When I'm gone, you guys better watch over Ariel!" But I was looking right at him.

Then Andriy actually asked if he could talk to me. I said, "Sure!" We went upstairs to an empty bedroom. He started asking me all of these questions about spirituality. He had intense blue eyes, and was so sweet and earnest. He asked "Why does your third eye have all these lights coming out of it?" I started laughing, and he said, "No, really. And symbols. What is that?" I said, "Well, I do a lot of energy work. I'm definitely connected, I do feel like I'm really not completely human." And I added, "And I think neither are you." He said, "I know."

So I explained some basic things I think about who we are and why we're here (including some things I've explained in this book). I kind of mentored him with a quick crash course. I told him about balancing the masculine and feminine—which he was already doing so naturally. I told him he was likely a starseed and what that meant. I could see he was he kind of person to do for everyone else and put himself last, and he acknowledged that was true. I explained to him that I had dealt with that—that I understood the martyring issue. I shared some things about preserving his energy and protecting himself, about boundaries.

I told him to stand in his truth, that those he loves are less likely to get hurt if he does that. I told him to find a partner who was his best friend and tell them everything, because if you can't then something is wrong.

I looked at him and I thought, this boy is a man already at the age of 18. And he had such a good heart.

Eventually, I wasn't surprised to learned that before I left, Andriy and Ariel started dating. And I have to say, his "will you be my girlfriend" was better than a lot of men's "will you marry me." He did a whole elaborate runup to it with letters and gifts, and he even called us and asked our permission as parents. And my daughter has never been treated so well by a man in her life.

This all unfolded in such an amazing way, and I think all because of the work I had done on myself. I got to talk to the boy before he asked my daughter out and basically coach him. He already knew a lot intuitively, but I got to put my two cents in and support him. Now she's super happy. I was too—because for me, leaving her was the hardest part of leaving the U.S., and now I know she's taken care of.

As I've mentioned, any time we do our work to shift our consciousness and clear our DNA, you'll see a parallel transformation in your own children. My daughter at 18 was now healthier than I had ever been at a much later age. By doing my work, I had spared her decades of heartache and clearing. She could start a healthy relationship with a clean slate and the whole family benefited from it.

WE DID IT!

I'm finishing this book while living our early days in Costa Rica. I'm picking up my husband from Liberia Airport with the dogs on September 19, 2024. It's been amazing. Willow and I have been bonding. I've been taking her to school, baking for the school, taking her surfing. We've done aero yoga together. We've spent so much time together. She seems extremely happy, and I'm just so grateful for everything that I've learned through this entire process.

We're waiting for the healing retreat house to get done. We'll be hosting many healing retreats here, natural plant medicine ceremonies and other types of retreats.

We're still doing well with living without attachments. We came here with less than a closet full of clothes, and we're doing absolutely fine. It's remarkable to realize how much stuff you don't need when you're in a place where Mother Nature just embraces you and gives you her love. I'm grateful every day for Gaia and what she has to offer. I'm remembering to live every single day in gratitude, knowing that I need nothing. I just go into my heart space and know that I have everything I need.

Knowing I'm taken care of no matter what helps me stay in the flow. When life stops flowing, we figure out where the stagnant energy is and face into it. It's usually uncomfortable, but freeing that energy frees your greatest power.

LIFE IS A TWIN FLAME JOURNEY

As I've said many times, a twin flame is a mirror. The things I needed to work on most were reflected back to me through Sean. I had to get out of my comfort zone for this whole entire journey—over and over and over again. Being willing to do that will reap you dividends beyond your wildest dreams.

What a long, winding twisting road it has been to go as deep as we have and to be as clear as we are. Remember that when you're on your long path. It won't be fast, it won't be easy. But it will be worth it. Never forget as you reflect on this story how much of it has been about growth, self-love, self-knowledge, trust, awareness, and the relentless pursuit of the true and the beautiful. Notice also that at every turn this has been a LIFE journey, not just a love story. All twin flame stories are life stories, soul journeys, and ultimately about living our true divine purpose. It's just that when you have a true twin flame at your side, your power is enhanced and expanded. I believe we become our true selves and express our divine purpose most fully by working everything out in partnership with another. I hope you have that blessing and opportunity. Stay open to the workings of the divine, the song of the universe, and your higher guidance—and I believe it will happen for you too.

Thank you for taking this journey with me! I hope you're inspired about the possibilities for your own life, health, prosperity, and love. As you probably gleaned from this story, it's an amazing path, but also takes work! To support you on your own journey, please take advantage of this complementary library of meditations and healings. These will support you in the many practices discussed throughout this book. This library is curated especially for readers of this book. Enjoy!

www.rebeccasullivan.love/upsidedownmirror

www.ingramcontent.com/pod-product-compliance
Lightning Source LLC
Chambersburg PA
CBHW032059090426
42743CB00007B/173